CHURCH AND THEOLOGY IN ENLIGHTENMENT SCOTLAND

THE POPULAR PARTY, 1740–1800

SCOTTISH HISTORICAL REVIEW

MONOGRAPHS SERIES

No. 5

CHURCH AND THEOLOGY IN ENLIGHTENMENT SCOTLAND

The Popular Party, 1740–1800

JOHN R. McINTOSH

TUCKWELL PRESS

First published in Great Britain in 1998 by
Tuckwell Press Ltd
The Mill House, Phantassie, East Linton, East Lothian, EH40 3DG
Scotland

ISBN 1 86232 098 5

British Library Cataloguing-in-Publication Data. A catalogue
record for this book is available on request from the British Library

Typeset in 10/12 Baskerville by
Aligra Lancaster
Printed and bound in Great Britain by
The Cromwell Press Ltd, Trowbridge, Wiltshire

for
ANNE, JAMES, and DONALD

Contents

Acknowledgements

There are several debts which I would here wish to acknowledge. The present work first saw the light of day as a doctoral dissertation at the University of Glasgow, and my indebtedness to my supervisor, Professor Roy Campbell, has a claim to recognition beyond that of others. To attempt to quantify his help would be to devalue his patience, encouragement, and scholarship to which the dissertation owed much of its final form. I would also place on record my gratitude to the Provost and Fellows of The Queen's College, Oxford, who elected me to a Visiting Schoolteacher Fellowship for Trinity Term, 1987. This enabled the completion of a substantial part of the research on the theological sections of the work in a most stimulating and congenial environment.

I would also thank Dr David Bebbington of the University of Stirling who read part of the work and discussed with me considerably more; Dr John Walsh of Jesus College, Oxford, who gave me several valuable suggestions relating to the secular thought of the Popular party; Dr Ian D. L. Clark who most graciously allowed me an extended loan of his notes for his seminal thesis on the Moderates; and Professor Stewart J. Brown and Mr David F. Wright of New College, Edinburgh, both of whom encouraged and advised me regarding publication of the work in revised form. Professor John L. Mackay of the Free Church College, Edinburgh, helpfully discussed some aspects of the theology. I am also much indebted to Alison and Sandy Grant, who prepared the text for the printers and in the course of that suggested more than a few insightful improvements. I am also grateful to the Trustees of the *Scottish Historical Review* and to Dr John Tuckwell of the Tuckwell Press for their assistance in the publication of the work. Mr William S. Anderson made a number of suggestions which pointed me in the right direction in this connection. I am in debt to them all, although, of course, they bear no responsibility for the views to be found herein.

I would also acknowledge the courtesy and help of the staff of the libraries of New College and of the Free Church College, Edinburgh; of the Bodleian Library, Oxford; of the British Library, London; and of Glasgow University Library.

Lastly, I must record the forbearance and support of my wife, Anne, and my two sons, James and Donald, for whom the expression 'Upstairs, working' will no doubt always carry a range of connotations not immediately obvious.

Lochgilphead, Argyll   J. R. McI.

Glossary of Theological Terms
as used in this work

* denotes cross-reference to other entries

Antinomianism: A complex heresy which has had many manifestations since apostolic times. In general terms it concerns the place of the moral law in the lives of Christians. In eighteenth-century Scotland those who were held to have espoused Antinomianism were believed to reduce the significance of feelings of guilt for sin before conversion*, and to hold that the moral law was not binding on a Christian after conversion. James Hog's famous novel, *The Private Memoirs and Confessions of a Justified Sinner* (London, 1824) deals with the subject.

Arianism: A major heresy regarding the doctrine of the Trinity*. In various ways it denies the (full) divinity of Christ.

Arminianism: see *Calvinism*.

Atonement: The general term used to denote the way in which Christ substituted himself for his people and reconciled them to God by dying for their sins* on the cross.

Calvinism: The system of Christian doctrine, dominant in Scotland after the Reformation, which is often summarised under five points: the total depravity of man (see sin*); unconditional election of sinners by God to salvation*; limited atonement* by Christ (that is, Christ did not die for everyone without exception but only for those predestined* by God for salvation and who therefore come to faith* in Christ); irresistible grace* (that is, those predestined for salvation will not be able to resist it); and the perseverance of the saints (that is, once saved, the believer cannot become unsaved). In eighteenth-century Scotland, Arminianism was a doctrine generally held to deny the five points of Calvinism; Pelagianism was a doctrine generally held to deny the doctrine of total depravity of man and the full sufficiency of Christ's death for the salvation of man.

Conversion: In evangelical terminology, this denotes the once-and-for-all act of becoming a Christian. It involves repentance for sin*, regeneration (or new birth), and a conscious awareness of the grace* and love of God as revealed in Christ.

Deism: In eighteenth-century Scotland this term was commonly applied to any religious or philosophical system which denied the regular intervention of God in the day-to-day world, or which was held to replace divine revelation in religion by reliance on natural revelation.

Erastianism: Technically, a theory of church government which accords to the state varying degrees of control or influence in matters relating to the government of the Church. In Scotland, the term has tended to be applied more loosely to any perceived encroachment by the civil powers on the (spiritual) independence of the Church.

Evangelicalism: Detailed definitions abound. The hallmarks of eighteenth-century Scottish evangelicalism, however, were acceptance of Scripture as the inspired word of God, and a conviction that the Christian Gospel was to be preached with a view to securing a personal commitment of faith* in Christ, known as conversion*.

Faith: An individual's trust in Christ as his personal Saviour.

Grace: The undeserved favour of God to mankind, especially as revealed in the salvation* made available through Christ.

Incarnation: Literally, 'enfleshment'. The second person of the Trinity* (the Son) also becoming man.

Justification: The act of God's grace* in which he pardons sin* and accepts the believer as free from the guilt of sin, by virtue of the efficacy of Christ's work as Saviour.

Legalism: The tendency to see obedience to God's law as a part of justifying faith*, rather than as a fruit or evidence of faith.

Mediation/Mediator: Christ's role as the one who reconciles people to God by his atoning* sacrifice of himself on the cross, and his continual intercession for them in heaven.

Pelagianism: see *Calvinism*.

Predestination: In its essence, the doctrine that in his sovereign purposes, God has determined to rescue some from their sin* and to pass over others. It extends to God's foreknowledge and control of everything that happens in the created world.

Providence: God's government of the world by which he brings about the purposes for which he created it, especially his purposes of good for his people.

Rationalism: In eighteenth-century Scotland, the term commonly used to denote a position holding that reason was the chief or only guide in matters of religious truth.

Redeemer/Redemption: In general, these are terms denoting Christ's role in salvation* and deliverance from sin*. More precisely, Christ gave his life as a ransom for sinners, to save them from punishment for sin.

Regeneration: New birth or spiritual renewal of people at the start of their Christian lives. In eighteenth-century Scotland, the term tended to be used interchangeably with conversion*.

Remission: Forgiveness or pardon of sins* against God. Literally, the term refers to sins being banished from God's sight.

Repentance: In evangelical theology, not just sorrow for sin* but the moral act of turning of the whole person in mind and will to agree with and obey the will of God.

Revival: A spiritual movement of unusual power which leads to awakened or renewed interest in religion. Usually accompanied by strong convictions of sinfulness which lead to significant numbers of conversions*.

Salvation: Deliverance of the sinner from the power of sin* and God's wrath. In Protestant theology it is dependent on the grace* of God.

Satisfaction: Christ's enduring of the penalty for sin* by his dying on the cross to satisfy God's justice.

Schism: A division or split in the Church.

Sin: Any lack of conformity to, or transgression of, any law of God. In Calvinist* theology, this includes the natural disposition of mankind towards evil and away from God and what is spiritually good, which is known as Original Sin.

Socinianism: In eighteenth-century Scotland, Socinianism was a term used by orthodox theologians to denote criticism of the doctrines of the Trinity*, predestination*, and human depravity. The heresy had its origins in sixteenth-century Europe and was condemned as error by the General Assembly of 1704.

Trinity: The Christian doctrine of God which holds that he is three persons – Father, Son, and Holy Spirit – of equal power and glory, in one substance or essence.

Introduction

The eighteenth-century Church of Scotland has received little attention from historians, and there has never been a comprehensive analysis of its nature and theology. It has therefore been necessary to study it through the usually unsatisfactory general surveys of ecclesiastical history, or through nineteenth-century biographies of some of its leaders. As has been asserted in this connection, however, 'the large literature on Scottish ecclesiastical history is often parochial, partisan, outdated, or unscholarly, if not all four'.[1] In particular, the Popular party in the eighteenth-century Church has been substantially neglected.

This state of neglect can be ascribed to two main factors. In the nineteenth century much, if not almost all, historical writing on Scottish ecclesiastical history was produced in the aftermath of the Disruption of the Church in 1843, or was heavily influenced by subsequent ecclesiastical or theological wrangling later in the century. Secondly, most twentieth-century interest has centred around the relationship between the Popular party's opponents, the Moderates, and the Scottish Enlightenment.

The twentieth-century historiography of the Scottish Church, in fact, shares the same type of defects which characterised it in the nineteenth century. Although there was no reawakening of interest in eighteenth-century Scottish ecclesiastical history until the 1960s and '70s, the flurry of activity since then has not been the result of direct interest in the Church as a whole, far less of interest in the Popular party, and there has in fact been a move away from traditional ecclesiastical history. Some of the works which discuss the subject, indeed, are the result of interests which are not necessarily ecclesiastical in a fundamental sense at all. This is the case, for example, with those works which have their origins in the study of the Scottish Enlightenment. Also, in the twentieth century the influence of the social sciences has brought new approaches in old fields, but it has not directed any more attention to the Church in its own right; the result has perhaps been even less. Certainly attention has not been paid to the thought of the opponents of the Moderates, the Popular party which arguably contained the majority of the Church's ministers. This explains the present study's extended attempt to come to terms with the theology of the Popular party, since theology is a major part of the ideology of any ecclesiastical grouping. It is important to appreciate, furthermore, the importance of an examination of the Popular party even for the secular historians of the period.

---

[1] R. B. Sher, *Church and University in the Scottish Enlightenment: The Moderate Literati of Edinburgh* (Edinburgh, 1985), p. 351.

After an initial chapter which briefly describes the history and ecclesi-astical life of eighteenth-century Scotland, the present study is based on a survey of the extant theological, political, social, and cultural writings of the ministers and laymen who were identified with the so-called Popular party in the Church of Scotland from 1740 to 1800, and of their activity at the General Assembly. Particular attention is paid to their theological writings, since they are a prerequisite for understanding the nature of the party. Areas covered include the doctrinal premises, the nature of sin and salvation, and the practical implications of the theology. The picture which emerges is one of considerable theological complexity, which calls into question the assumption of doctrinal unity within the party that has enabled previous writers to propagate a picture of the opponents of Moderatism which is in many ways little more than a caricature.

Popular thought on secular issues is analysed with respect to the areas of the nature of society, government, poverty and wealth, and culture. The interplay of liberal and conservative political impetuses is examined, and the theological bases of the party's secular thought elicited. This provides an explanation of such factors as why the Church was divided over the American War of Independence and Roman Catholic emancipation, but united over the French Revolution and radicalism in general.

The patronage dispute is analysed and an interpretation is offered, based on both the published works of the party and proceedings at the General Assembly, which argues that the fundamental religious or spiritual motivation of Popular opposition to the patronage system has not been appreciated, and that therefore the evolution of the Popular response to patronage as revealed at the General Assembly has been misconstrued. Far from the key issue in the Church of Scotland in the latter half of the eighteenth century being the dispute between the Popular and Moderate parties over patronage, of much greater importance was the evolving theological alignment.

The way forward for the study of the Scottish Church in the period, therefore, involves a supplementing of the history of ideas, and a moving away from preoccupations both with the debates and actions of the General Assembly, and with the significance of a small group of possibly unrepresentative Moderate literati. The need is for a re-examination of the evidence for hitherto-accepted assumptions, and for a wider-ranging investigation of the available sources than has yet been attempted. This is what the present study tries to achieve.

CHAPTER ONE

Church and Society, 1740–1800

In the years between 1740 and 1800 Scotland was a society in transition. Living conditions, the economy, intellectual life, and religion were all characterised by change. Perhaps the area of national life least affected was that of politics and government. Partly for that reason eighteenth-century Scottish history has been perceived in the popular imagination as centring around the Jacobite Rebellion of 1745–6, with little else of note apart from a ripple of Radical unrest in the 1790s. In recent years, however, general historical misconceptions are being revised as research into Scotland's history during the century progresses, and as the significance of the various developments becomes more widely appreciated. Eighteenth-century Scottish history can no longer be comprehended within the twin romanticisms of Bonnie Prince Charlie and Robert Burns.

I

Fundamental to the life of the Scottish people was the process of agricultural improvement, a process which culminated in the widespread commercialisation of rural society. This development, which was most marked from the 1760s, contributed to the lowering of death rates which was to ensure the rising population behind urbanisation, and also improved the food supply which the urban development required. The transformation was achieved through increases in both production and productivity brought about by the reorganisation in farm structure, by more efficient labour organisation, and by higher yields derived from improved fallowing, adoption of root crops and new crop rotations.[1] Throughout the century agricultural improvement was carried out to varying degrees and in varying ways from locality to locality, and even from estate to estate. It sometimes involved the dispossession of tenant farmers as a result of the ending of the runrig system of cultivation. The process of improvement accelerated after the 1760s and was an

---

[1] Further detail on the aspects covered here of the social and economic history of Scotland, 1740–1800, may be conveniently found in the relevant chapters of R. H. Campbell, *Scotland since 1707: The Rise of an Industrial Society* (Edinburgh, 1985); T. M. Devine and R. Mitchison (eds.), *People and Society in Scotland*, vol. I (Edinburgh, 1988); and W. Ferguson, *Scotland: 1689 to the Present* (Edinburgh, 1968). The present survey of these areas is largely based on material to be found in these volumes.

extended one. But the *Statistical Account of Scotland*, published in the 1790s, reveals that even then it was incomplete; dramatic differences from one parish to the next were common. There were several reasons for both the delay and the variation: the granting of long leases on land was not really possible until new legislation was passed in 1770; large-scale development had to await the rise of new banking and credit systems, and that in turn required the growth of capital reserves from commercial and professional sources; and the large markets provided by urban growth were required to provide the stimulus for investment in improvement.

Agricultural improvement was much more marked in the south than in the north. With the exception of Aberdeenshire and the Laigh of Moray, heavy soils in the north required drainage techniques which were not developed until the nineteenth century. In the Highlands, thorough-going implementation of improvements initially foundered on the commitment of Highland society to the concept of *duthchas*, which postulated an obligation on the chief to provide security for his clansmen. The aura of this concept lingered on after the collapse of the traditional Highland social patterns and authority structures. Not until the nineteenth century was large-scale enforced clearance widespread, and by that time the economic advantages of a sheep-based estate economy were less marked.

The living conditions of the rural working classes, however, remained hard, although there were advances. In the Lowlands, agricultural housing improved, and the real wages of agricultural labourers increased during the century in spite of the rise in prices. At the beginning of the period, though, food scarcity, while by no means endemic, was not quite yet a thing of the past, and local conditions could cause significant problems especially in the more remote areas, notably the Highlands. Not until the end of the century did serious short-term scarcity completely disappear, not to reappear until the potato famines of the mid-nineteenth century which were mainly confined to the Western Highlands. This was the long-term result of improved poor relief, more sensitive response to emergencies, developments in transport and marketing, the possession of surplus income to purchase food abroad, and, from the 1770s, rapid agricultural improvements and the introduction of the potato in the Highlands. Only in the more prosperous areas of the Lothians, the North-East, and the Laigh of Moray did farm labourers achieve reasonably secure living and working standards without needing to leave their home localities. In general, however, real wages rose in many areas of employment, especially after the 1760s, since the labour supply does not seem to have matched the demands for labour power. This certainly contributes to explaining the relative absence of agrarian unrest in Scotland in the latter part of the century.

There were also demographic changes. Throughout the whole of the period population moved from rural areas to the towns. In particular there was a marked three-way population shift: from the Highlands to the Lowlands, especially to the towns of the west-central belt; from the Highlands, though not exclusively from there, to the colonies; and, as yet largely on a seasonal basis, but especially significant after about 1780, from Ireland to the Lowlands.

In the case of the Highlands, emigration to both Lowland and colonial destinations arose ultimately from lack of land, but after about 1730 more immediately from the higher rents which were being universally levied by the clan chiefs on tenants and through them on sub-tenants, as the chiefs became ever more aware of the correlation between status and wealth. This desire to maximise revenue led to the introduction of sheep-raising, which was widespread by around 1760 and which changed the patterns of landholding. The aftermath of the Jacobite Rebellion of 1745–6, of course, accelerated this process by destroying finally any remaining 'patriarchal' authority of the clan chiefs and great magnates by transforming it into more conventional systems of land tenure. The people of the Highlands became tenants and cottars rather than clansmen and retainers. As yet, however, there were few enforced clearances of crofters from their lands. Large-scale colonial emigration did not arise in the eighteenth century as a result of pressure on land or from clearance. The first cause of significant emigration from the Highlands occurred after the disbanding of the Highland regiments at the close of the Seven Years' War in 1763 and the subsequent favourable reports home of colonial life from veterans who had settled in North America; and this was increased as the tacksmen or main tenants were squeezed out of the traditional Highland landholding pattern by the landlords' demand for economic rents. But throughout the century, in fact, both the governments of the day and the great Highland landlords strove actively to prevent emigration. In the case of the former, their opposition increased as a result of the manpower shortages which affected the armed forces during the war with Revolutionary and Napoleonic France.

The other side of this process of migration and emigration was that of urbanisation. Between 1755 and 1801, the population of Scotland rose from 1.25 million to 1.6 million. In 1750 it is estimated that 9% of the population lived in towns with a population of 10,000 or more; by 1800 the figure had risen to 17%. It has been suggested that between 1760 and 1830 the pace of Scottish urbanisation was probably the fastest in Europe. Care should, however, be taken not to overestimate either the extent or the speed of the process of urbanisation: even at the end of the century, Scotland was still overwhelmingly a rural society. The process of urbanisation, however, as well as that of emigration, explains why some areas of the Highlands experienced a net population loss by the 1790s.[2]

In the same way that Scotland was a country in a state of social and demographic transition, so too was it in a state of industrial transition. The Union of 1707 had depressed the economy, as a result of Scottish inability to compete with England in the absence of protection, and in areas of economic activity which required government aid or legislation the picture was often one of half-hearted or delayed attention. Nevertheless, there were areas of progress. As a result of the 1742 Bounty Act and the founding in 1746 of the British Linen Bank, the middle of the century saw the struggling linen industry, which produced the only significant Scottish export, start to play an increasingly important role in the trade between the Clyde and the American colonies. By 1803, linen accounted for 64% of Scotland's exports. After 1730 until 1800 linen production roughly doubled every twenty-five years. The middle of the century also saw the rise of a more varied commerce with North America, epitomised at its most successful in the Glasgow tobacco trade which peaked in the 1770s. The trade with North America, and the tobacco trade in particular, stimulated the entire economy and was especially important in that, for the first time since the Union of 1707, it made possible the accumulation of useful amounts of capital. These contributed to the emergence of a factory-based industrial system towards the end of the century.[3]

Starting to occur to a certain extent in the mid-century, furthermore, was the process of industrialisation. Spinning mills, iron works, and relatively small-scale chemical works were appearing in various parts of the country. Although there had been earlier small ventures at various sites from Inverness to Argyll, the most important of these, especially in view of its future significance for the Scottish economy, was the iron industry. The foundation of the Carron Company near Falkirk in 1759 is often seen as the watershed for such developments. It was to be followed within the next twenty years by several other ironworks in the west of Scotland. It should not be assumed, however, that this process was either widespread or large-scale. By 1796 there were only sixteen blast furnaces in the whole of the country. At the end of the century, there were only around a dozen ironworks and large segments of Scottish manufactures were owned by a relatively few families. Although there had been a start made to canal building, the Forth–Clyde–Monkland canal complex was not completed until 1792, and the full emergence of the industrial economy of Scotland had to await the transport and communications improvements of the next century. Until the 1780s, Scotland was still a rural society, but one in which

[2] Ferguson, *1689 to the Present*, p. 175; Devine and Mitchison, *People and Society in Scotland*, i, p. 74.

[3] Campbell, *Scotland since 1707*, p. 46; Ferguson, *1689 to the Present*, p. 184.

transformation was imminent. It has been suggested that eighteenth-century Scottish economic development was in a 'take-off' phase, which made possible the emergence of an industrialised society, and this view has much to commend it.[4]

The urbanisation of the country, and its concomitant industrialisation, soon placed not only the structures of the Church, but also those of society and government, under enormous pressures. Politically, the embryonic modern parliamentary state which existed before the Treaty of Union with England in 1707 had been replaced with a conglomerate structure of somewhat incongruous institutions by means of which successive governments sought to implement centralised control from Westminster, while retaining the courts and administrative structures of the previous system. Increasingly, however, English forms and procedures hampered efficiency. In particular, the Court of Session, although its prerogatives were guaranteed by the union Treaty itself, experienced a process of anglicisation largely as a result of the appellate jurisdiction of the House of Lords, which overturned Court of Session decisions with little knowledge or concern.

The middle of the eighteenth century saw the government of Scotland evolve from a system in which power was maintained in the hands of the great noble families, most notably those of the duke of Argyll between 1715 and 1742, and his brother the earl of Islay until 1761, to one in which power was wielded by the ministers of the Crown through an intricate and all-pervasive system of interest and patronage. As the century progressed, the factional nature of English politics and govern-ment rendered the efficient marshalling of the Scottish parliamentary vote essential to the stability and survival of any ministry. Consequently, management of the Scottish electoral system became a crucial priority. The system which emerged was epitomised in the career of the 'manager' Henry Dundas who was the *de facto* ruler of Scotland from 1774 until 1801. Despite the change in the seat of power, however, the nature of Scottish government and political activity changed scarcely at all for practical purposes, and certainly not in so far as it impinged on the people as a whole. Legislation continued to have limited efficacy, and would not do so until transport and communications improved.

II

One of the most notable features of the political history of Scotland in the period between 1740 and 1800 was the extent to which few of the events in these years actually had a general impact on the life of the Church. At most they had limited effects. Even the Jacobite rebellion of 1745 caused scarcely a ripple in the Church nationally, though the

[4] Campbell, *Scotland since 1707*, p. 14; Ferguson, *1689 to the Present*, p. 197.

Church's opposition was a crucial factor in its defeat and numerous ministers in the north suffered personal hardship or difficulties. The Seven Years' War of 1756–63 provoked little more than a few sermons on the duty of loyalty and expressions of thankfulness for victory. It did, however, give point to the agitation for a Scots militia in the 1750s and '60s, which came to a head in 1757 with the passage of the Militia Bill excluding Scotland from its provisions. The establishment of a Scots militia became a *cause célèbre* of some of the leaders of the Moderate party, but it remained a matter of almost complete uninterest to the rest of the Church. Of much greater impact was the American War of Independence which broke out in 1776. Although it was the Seceders who were the first to become involved by passing a resolution in favour of conciliation, before long opposition to or support for the war against the colonists became a party issue between the Popular and Moderate parties in the Church.[5] Because the American Revolution was linked in Popular eyes with what was seen as the Moderate-dominated General Assembly's denial of religious liberty, the war years saw substantial publication concerning the issues of civil and religious liberty and church discipline.

Of more influence in the life of the Church, as in the life of the nation, was the outbreak of the French Revolution in 1789. Initially, the Revolution was welcomed by most sections of British public opinion, but after the publication of Edmund Burke's *Reflections on the Revolution in France*, the excesses of the September Massacres in 1792 and the execution of Louis XVI, support waned, and it evaporated with the declaration of war on Britain by France in 1793. This pattern was reflected in the Church of Scotland. After initial support for the Revolution as a harbinger of liberty on the part of the Popular party, before long there was little opposition from any quarter to the suppression of any indication of support for the Revolution or of the promotion of reform in Britain. Public opinion in the Church, as in the country as a whole, became increasingly preoccupied with the pursuit of the war against France.

The years after 1740 saw the flowering of the great intellectual movement now known as the 'Scottish Enlightenment'. In 1739, David Hume's *Treatise on Human Nature* was published. This was rewritten as the *Inquiry Concerning Human Understanding* in 1748, and was followed in the 1750s by the *Inquiry Concerning the Principles of Morals*, the *Natural History of Religion*, and finally his *Dialogues Concerning Natural Religion*. The late 1760s and '70s saw the appearance of several works of intellectual significance: to name but a few, Sir James Steuart's *Inquiry into the Principles of Political Economy* of 1767, Adam Ferguson's *Essay on the History of Civil Society* of 1767, William Robertson's *History of the Reign*

---

[5] See below, pp. 155–60. See also E. Vincent, 'The responses of Scottish Churchmen to the French Revolution, 1789–1802', *Scot. Hist. Rev.*, lxxiii (1994), pp. 191–215.

of Charles V of 1769 and *History of America* of 1777; and Adam Smith's *Wealth of Nations* of 1776. The *Encyclopaedia Britannica* was also first published in Edinburgh between 1768 and 1771, and included among its contributors a considerable number of ministers.

The concept of the 'Scottish Enlightenment', however, is one which has aroused considerable controversy as to what it actually was. Definitions offered are sometimes general and sometimes restricted.[6] Possibly the most workable is one which, among other features largely relating to social and political conservatism and concern for certain aspects of literary style, stresses the love of learning and virtue, faith in reason and science, and a dedication to humanism and humanitarianism, together with a distrust of religious 'enthusiasm'.[7] The Scottish Enlightenment, of course, was part of the wider European Enlightenment of the late seventeenth and eighteenth centuries which affected religion by stressing the significance of Reason in the pursuit of knowledge, by embodying belief in a law-governed universe, and by producing an essentially optimistic state of mind about the prospects of mankind. The particular emphases of the Scottish Enlightenment, however, lay in its interest in the social behaviour of man, and in political economy and moral philosophy.

Probably the seminal influence in the Scottish Enlightenment was Francis Hutcheson, who was Professor of Moral Philosophy at Glasgow University from 1729 to 1746. Influenced by the liberal or even latitudinarian views of Professor John Simson and of the English rationalist Samuel Clarke, he had come to hold that philosophy and theology could only be pursued by means of rational enquiry. In particular, he espoused the ideas of the English deist writer Shaftesbury from whom he acquired the notion that benevolence is the criterion of morality. This concept was to have a profound impact on Scottish theological endeavour. As important as Hutcheson, however, was the work of David Hume. Postulating that all knowledge was based on experience, and thence arguing that at bottom all knowledge was nothing more than mental impressions, Hume rejected the possibility of religious knowledge and adopted a position of scepticism. While his philosophy has remained vastly influential until the present, however at the time, Hume's line of reasoning, although arousing much antagonism amongst orthodox theologians, made few inroads into the perceptions of the faithful. That this was so was the result of the development of the Scottish 'Common Sense' philosophy propounded initially by Thomas Reid of Aberdeen. His work was readily accepted by all sections of the Scottish Church, irrespective of their theological inclinations, as embodying the negation of Hume's principles.

---

[6] For a recent discussion of this debate and the associated bibliography, see Sher, *Church and University in the Scottish Enlightenment*, pp. 3–19.

[7] Ibid., p. 8.

III

The position of the established Church of Scotland, and in particular its presbyterian constitution explicitly guaranteed in the Treaty of Union, has now to be considered. The system of Presbyterianism involved a complex relationship of ecclesiastical and civil bodies. At the parish level the basic institution of the Church was the kirk session. This body, consisting of several 'ruling elders', met regularly under the chairmanship of the minister who, when acting in that capacity, assumed the title of 'moderator', the term applied also to ministers when they act as chairmen of presbyteries, synods, or General Assemblies of the Scottish Presbyterian Churches.[8] The kirk session had within its remit all matters relating to the faith and practice of the members of the congregation. It controlled admission to membership and thus to the sacraments, it oversaw the morals of the parish, it arranged the times of public worship and the dates of communion seasons, and it distributed relief to the needy from the collections taken at public worship. Technically, it had the right to decide whether an infant should be baptised, but generally speaking this was left in the hands of the minister unless the child was illegitimate. In that case the mother and father were brought before the session to confess their fornication or adultery, and thereafter to accept public rebuke on six successive occasions before the child would be baptised. By the latter third of the century, however, public confession and admonition became less often required by sessions and presbyteries, and first offences at least were dealt with in private and often by the minister alone.

The fabric of the church and manse buildings, and the payment of the minister's stipend, as also the school and schoolmaster's salary, were not the responsibility of the kirk session, however, but of the heritors, who were the landholders of the parish. If the church door collections were inadequate for poor relief, the heritors were more or less obliged to raise a voluntary or even a compulsory assessment for an additional sum. Failure to honour their obligations, which was by no means uncommon, could be taken up by the presbytery and referred, if necessary, to the Court of Teinds, a branch of the civil jurisdiction. Problems were often caused by heritors who were non-resident in the parish, or who were members of another communion, most commonly Episcopalian.

The central body in the Presbyterian system, of course, was the presbytery, from which the whole system derives its name. While in part a court of reference and appeal from the kirk sessions of the congregations within its boundaries, the presbytery had a range of matters in which it was the court of first instance, such as the oversight of ministers, and the provision for congregations during vacancies by means of the appointment

---

[8] Except in the case of the kirk session, the office of moderator is held for one year only.

of one of its ministers as interim-moderators. It admitted and examined divinity students and probationers for the ministry, it conducted or 'moderated' calls and admissions to vacant charges, and it decided on overtures which were referred by it to the synods and to the General Assembly and vice versa. It also had a general oversight over the adequacy of ministerial stipends and church property within its bounds. The minister and one ruling elder from each of its congregations attended its monthly meetings; all its members were expected to attend meetings of the provincial synod to which it belonged; and each of the eighty-two presbyteries which existed from 1740 to 1800 sent commissioners to the General Assembly in proportion to their numerical strength (in most cases a minister and a ruling elder).

Next, there were the sixteen provincial synods. These have always had a somewhat unclear status in the practice of the Church of Scotland, but in general terms they were courts of reference and appeal from the presbyteries, and they were obviously responsible for dealing with matters which were of a more than local concern to one presbytery, but which were not necessarily of national importance. They met twice a year, and in practice they functioned as a filter between the presbyteries and the General Assembly, although it could be argued that in the course of the eighteenth century they filtered out very little, since most cases went on appeal to the General Assembly in any case.

At the apex of the presbyterian system, and in the course of the eighteenth century accruing more status and power than constitutionally it was entitled to, was the General Assembly. This body met once a year in Edinburgh, usually for a fortnight in May, and, strictly speaking was the court of final reference and appeal in the Church of Scotland. Each presbytery sent at least a minister and a ruling elder as commissioners, and to this number each royal burgh was entitled to send another elder to represent it. Ruling elders made up approximately 40% of the official membership of the Assembly. The universities were also entitled to send one representative each, who was invariably a minister. In judicial matters, the decision of the General Assembly was final, although a formal dissent was permitted. In other affairs, such as changes in the constitution of the Church, or any matters of legislation, the General Assembly had no executive or prescriptive power. Action had to be taken by means of overtures from the Assembly to the presbyteries requesting their approval of the proposed legislation, and the majority of them had to concur before the proposed legislation became the law of the Church at the General Assembly of the following year.

One of the most significant phenomena of the eighteenth-century General Assembly was the predominance of Edinburgh lawyers among the ruling elders who were commissioners at the Assembly. One of the problems facing many commissioners was the difficulty of getting to Edinburgh owing to bad weather or transport problems. This was especially true of those from remote presbyteries. For example, for most of the eighteenth century, the membership of the General Assembly nominally should have numbered around 360. In practice, it never exceeded 300, it rarely exceeded 200, and it was often less than 150. At the vote on the important Schism Overture of 1766, for example, only 184 individual votes were cast.[9] Partly to offset such problems, many presbyteries regularly nominated, as their ruling elders, Edinburgh lawyers who frequently had no real connections with the presbyteries they represented. This had profound consequences in the dispute over patronage.

Another object of increasing concern to many was the operation of the Commission of Assembly. This body, in effect a committee of the General Assembly, was set up each year to complete unfinished Assembly business and to implement the detail of Assembly decisions. In the period around 1750 and after, however, it became increasingly involved in the enforced settlement of vacant congregations. It was almost universally believed to be 'packed' with nominees favourable to patronage, and to be arrogating to itself executive powers which even the General Assembly itself did not possess. It certainly had a marked disproportion of Edinburgh lawyers. Judges of the Court of Session were often appointed to it as a courtesy, although it is not clear whether they were accustomed to avail themselves of the privilege. Much of the hostility of the opponents of ecclesiastical patronage came to be aimed at the Commission of Assembly as much as at the Moderate-dominated Assembly itself.

Although nominally free from any intervention by the State in its affairs, for most of the century the Church was wracked, or so it has seemed to subsequent historians, by the problem of patronage. This was the system, restored by the Patronage Act of 1712, whereby the 'patron' had the right to nominate a 'presentee' to a vacant parish, who was then to be accepted or rejected by the congregation. The patron was most commonly the largest landowner in the parish, but in between a quarter and a third of the parishes it was the Crown in the person of the government minister responsible for Scottish affairs. The right of patronage was a civil possession, and was therefore under the jurisdiction of the civil courts. At the same time, however, the presbytery had the ecclesiastical obligation to ensure that the person inducted to the parish was acceptable to the kirk session and to the heads of families of the congregation. There was thus great potential for clashes, so much so that the life of the eighteenth-century Church of Scotland, and indeed much of the life of the nation as a whole in the period, was frequently dominated by the bitter struggles over patronage.

Questions of patronage and of political influence on the Church have often been seen as the predominant issues in the life of the eighteenth-

9 See below, pp. 130–4.

century Church of Scotland. Ecclesiastical patronage came to be regarded as an extension of the system of political patronage, in that politicians saw the presentation to vacant parishes of families or friends of political allies as a means of preserving or extending their own power. Governments of the day were also aware of the advantage to be derived from having a Church which refrained from criticism of their policies. In the eighteenth century, acquisition of political power in London inevitably led to changes in the 'management' of the Church. The minister of the government responsible for Scottish affairs tended to seek the advice of an influential minister of the Church regarding who should be nominated to those vacant parishes where the right of presentation belonged to the Crown. For example, from 1736 to the fall of Walpole in 1742, Argyll and Islay entrusted the management of Church business in the government's interest to Rev. Patrick Cuming; from then until the resignation of Lord Tweeddale in 1746, Rev. Robert Wallace was the government manager; and he was replaced by a reappointed Cuming. Later in the century, Principal William Robertson was the central figure in the relationship between Church and State.

IV

Much of what has been mentioned thus far concerns the life of the Church in its official manifestations and has little to do with the life of the ordinary members. The piety of the ordinary men and women in the pews, far less of those who, in the cities especially, were not to be found regularly among the ranks of the faithful at public worship, is as yet little known. What is known is that during the eighteenth century there was clearly a voracious demand for printed sermons. Not only were the great devotional writers, such as Thomas Boston of Ettrick and John Willison of Dundee, in demand for most of the century and until well into the next, but also the sermons of even unknown parish ministers were regularly published in what were usually small local editions. Sometimes, no doubt, they were intended to bring the preacher to the notice of a wider audience; while at other times they were published in response to local demand. The subject matter was sometimes devotional, sometimes practical, sometimes evangelistic, though rarely exegetical in the modern sense of the term. If systematic exegesis of Scripture was the practice in the pulpit, there is little sign of that in what found its way into print.[10] There is some evidence, too, that some works of the leading seventeenth-century English Puritans were read in the homes of ordinary members of the Church of Scotland.

Apart from regular attendance at public worship, which was enforced to varying degrees throughout the country, the main occasions of

---

[10] Cf. F. Voges, 'Moderate and Evangelical thinking in the later eighteenth century: differences and shared attitudes', *Recs. Scot. Church Hist. Soc.*, xxii (pt. 2) (1985), pp. 151–2.

religious observance were the great communion seasons. Although one should probably hesitate to assume that Robert Burns's satirical picture of one such occasion in his *Holy Fair* was a typical example of all such observances in all parishes across the country, there can be no doubt that there was at least a modicum of truth in it. Probably, too, the estimates of attendances for such gatherings should be treated with considerable reserve, such is the difficulty of accurate assessment of crowd size. Nevertheless, the celebration of a communion season probably attracted several hundreds from neighbouring parishes as well as from the parish in which it was being held, and this was certainly increased substantially when a famous preacher was to be heard. This, of course, was entirely within the intentions of the fathers of Scottish Presbyterianism. The sacrament of the Lord's Supper was not the preserve of one parish, but was on the contrary a means of strengthening the unity of the whole Church through the united observance of it by representatives of the different sections of the Church.

The relationship between Church and people in eighteenth-century Scotland is also to be seen in the holding of 'Fast Days' at times of local or national crisis. These days of 'humiliation and prayer' were not infrequent additional observances at times other than the regular fast day before a communion season, and were held in situations of drought, famine, or war. Often the proclamations of these fast days, issued usually by presbyteries, displayed the wide-ranging concerns which provoked them. For example, in 1742 the Presbytery of Stirling argued in support of its decision to call a fast:

> The Presbytery of Stirling ... deeply affected with our present circumstances in that we are engaged in a dangerous and expensive war abroad, and that we are pinched with scarcity at home so that the number of the poor are increasing, hunger and famine appearing in many faces ... our manifold abounding sins among us, particularly Infidelity, contempt of Christ and his ordinances, profanation of the Lord's Day, neglect of public and family worship, profanation of the Sacred Name of God, and perjury abounding ... excessive prodigality and profuseness abounds with some, while their fellow brethren are groaning under want and poverty.[11]

The role of the Church in the lives of the people, however, transcended the forms and patterns of piety. The Church of Scotland played a vital social role in the day-to-day events of the community as a whole. There were three basic assumptions which marked the relationship of the Church to the people of Scotland in the eighteenth century. First, it was assumed that Scotland was a Christian country, and that the established Church was to be seen as the embodiment of that

---

11 *Minutes of the Presbytery of Stirling*, 3 Jun. 1742.

reality. This perception did not imply that the social and ecclesiastical divisions caused by the secessions from the established Church were disregarded. In fact, in a way they were institutionalised because for most of the century the Secession Churches maintained the principle of establishment by holding to the duty of secession from a false establishment in order to preserve a true one. In theory, at least, the possibility of return to a purged establishment was always open. It was this point which Thomas Chalmers was to assert so unequivocally at the Disruption of 1843, when a third of the ministers and around half of the membership of the Church of Scotland left it to form the Free Church of Scotland. The second assumption was that within the Christian community that was Scotland, there were some who had fallen into sins such as atheism and 'infidelity', as well as immorality. Such sinners were the responsibility of the Church unless they could credibly claim to be the adherents of the Secession Church or of another denomination. And, thirdly, there was the assumption, especially in evangelical sections of the Church, that the answer to such problems lay in renewed personal and collective devotion.

It has been commonly accepted that there was little real relationship between the Church and the ordinary people of Scotland other than through the regular immorality cases which were dealt with by kirk sessions and presbyteries. In actual fact, the picture is less one-sided than is the common perception. In addition to the Church's conviction, enshrined in its constitution, that it had the right and obligation to exercise discipline over its members, immorality cases came before the Church courts for three main reasons. In the first place, public confession and reprimand was the way to expiation of moral short-comings and reinstatement in the eyes of the community. This was the prerequisite for the baptism of illegitimate children, desire for which was especially strong in rural communities. Secondly, the naming of an illegitimate child's father before a Church court and the gaining of an admission of paternity was often the only means of ensuring provision for the child's support. Thirdly, there is some evidence that the Church courts were the only means of redress for and prevention of 'anti-social behaviour' in rural areas.

In other words, with the qualifications that the Church's writ did not run even remotely to the same extent in the cities, and that it was not accepted by those with connections with other denominations, the people of Scotland accepted the assumption that they were legitimately the responsibility of the Church and subject to its discipline. They valued the accolade of Church membership and baptism for their children. To retain these privileges they were prepared to submit to public censure when they strayed from the prescriptions of the Christian moral law. On the other hand, the Church was prepared to exclude from its discipline those who by secession placed themselves outside its jurisdiction, and those who by their open rejection of its moral standards denied the basis of society as it was conceived at the time. These latter were to be regarded as social outcasts and to be dealt with by the civil authorities if and when they broke the law. Until they did, and probably even when they did, they were still the objects of Christian charity and were to receive poor relief when necessary.

Apart from the negative functions of the Church in dealing with immorality, it also fulfilled a positive social function. It would seem to have been the case that in rural Scotland in the eighteenth century the civil law was not always regularly involved in exercising jurisdiction, except in cases of murder, rioting, and theft. Conversely, perhaps, this may be an indication that there was little minor law-breaking or social violence. More significantly, however, the fact remains that for offences such as wife-beating, minor assault, drunkenness, and general anti-social behaviour there was possibly no redress other than recourse to the kirk session and presbytery. Judging by the number of men who apparently promised to contribute to the upbringing of their illegitimate children, who then reneged, but who eventually confessed before a session or presbytery, there would seem to be a strong case for arguing that in this area, too, the Church was fulfilling a vital social role. The eighteenth-century Church of Scotland, then, enjoyed the support, or at the very least the acquiescence, of the people in its role as moral guardian, and also as a guarantor of social stability.[12]

V

The period from 1740 to 1800 saw several profound developments in the nature and interests of the Church. Two of the most important were the drift from a mainly theological preoccupation to a more ecclesiastical one, and the acquisition of ecclesiastical power by the party who were to become known as the Moderates and the consequent struggle with their 'Popular' opponents.

In the early part of the century the question of the nature of grace, that is, the nature of how God deals with man in bringing about salvation, had preoccupied many of the more theologically minded ministers of the Church. The Simson case of 1716–17 raised the question of the extent of the redemption: had Christ died for the salvation of all, or only for that of the elect? Professor John Simson of Glasgow University was investigated, but at the 1717 General Assembly was acquitted of heresy and instead found guilty of using dubious expressions which 'attribute too much to natural reason and the power of corrupt nature to the disparagement of revelation and efficacious free

---

[12] An analysis of these matters is to be found in J. R. McIntosh, 'Evangelicals in Eighteenth-Century Scotland: The Presbytery of Stirling, 1740–1805' (Stirling University M.Litt. thesis, 1981), pp. 19–29.

grace'.[13] As a response to the sort of trend which Simson seemed to epitomise, the Presbytery of Auchterarder introduced a series of propositions to be affirmed by candidates for licence to preach as ministers and at ordinations. The central one was concerned with denying 'that we must forsake sin in order to our coming to Christ and instating us in covenant with God'.[14] The 1717 Assembly condemned the so-called Auchterarder Creed as in effect antinomian, that is, as reducing the significance before conversion of feelings of guilt for sin, and as holding that the moral law is not binding on the Christian after conversion. The revered Thomas Boston had thought much about the problems of redemption and justification before deciding that the seventeenth-century English Puritan work *The Marrow of Modern Divinity* had the answers. On the one hand he had reacted against seventeenth-century antinomianism, but on the other he was responding to the legalism of those who may perhaps be regarded as 'proto-Moderates'. The complex nature of the debate is perhaps best demonstrated by the fact that the General Assembly condemned *The Marrow* as antinomian in spite of the fact that it had been aimed specifically against that heresy.[15]

Professor Simson had again been prominent in 1726, when he was charged before the Presbytery of Glasgow with Arianism, that is with denial of the divinity of Christ. Although the case brought together both the Marrowmen and their opponents such as Principal Hadow of St Andrews, the Assembly of 1729 only suspended Simson. Perhaps his real importance is, as has been suggested, that he prepared the way for the rise of a secular philosophy under Francis Hutcheson.[16] Hutcheson, too, was charged with heresy on the grounds that he taught that 'the standard of moral goodness was the promotion of the happiness of others', and that 'we could have a knowledge of good and evil without a knowledge of God'.[17] The case got no further than the Presbytery of Glasgow, but Hutcheson remained the inspiration of most Moderate theology and thought.

Heresy continued as an issue throughout the century, but there was evidently a reluctance to take decisive action. For example, in 1736 Professor Campbell of St Andrews was charged with Rationalism over his book *The Apostles no Enthusiasts*, though the case was not pursued. Professor Leechman of Glasgow was charged in 1743 on the same grounds and again the charge was dismissed, though this time on less

13 *Annals of the General Assembly of the Church of Scotland*, 1717, p. 518, quoted in J. H. S. Burleigh, *A Church History of Scotland* (Edinburgh, 1983), p. 288.

14 N. M. de S. Cameron (organ. ed.), *Dictionary of Scottish Church History and Theology* (Edinburgh, 1993), p. 45.

15 For brief analyses of the *Marrow* controversy, see Burleigh, *Church History of Scotland*, pp. 288–91; and Ferguson, *1689 to the Present*, pp. 117–18. The most authoritative work on the subject is D. C. Lachman, *The Marrow Controversy* (Edinburgh, 1988).

16 Ferguson, *1689 to the Present*, p. 116. See above, p. 9.

17 Quoted in Burleigh, *Church History of Scotland*, p. 295.

secure grounds.[18] In 1767, Rev. Alexander Ferguson of Kilwinning, in an article in the *Scots Magazine*, denied or at least omitted to assert the doctrines of the Fall of Man, human depravity, and the vicarious sacrifice of Christ on the cross; once again the case against him was dismissed.[19] In 1786, Dr William McGill of Ayr published *A Practical Essay on the Death of Christ*, in which he attempted to restate the doctrines of the purpose of God, and the person and work of Christ. Although he clearly differed from the positions of the Westminster Confession of Faith, a compromise was reached and his alleged Socinianism, in his case stress on the humanity and example of Christ rather than on Christ's divinity and Atonement, went unpunished.[20]

Not unconnected with the question of heresy or heterodoxy was the rise of what its opponents called 'infidelity'. This term, while something of a 'catch-all' expression, was employed to denote the espousal of doctrines or practices which were seen as undermining Christianity or as leading to godlessness. In some respects, the rise of 'infidelity' as a target for the orthodox was a response to the Enlightenment. The response of the mainstream Scottish evangelicals, however, was a much more constructive and complex one than has usually been suggested.[21]

From 1739 the publication of the works of Hume produced a flood of attacks from orthodox theologians, and even from some of the less orthodox, for most felt that Hume was propounding dangerous and misleading doctrines. Lord Kames of the Court of Session, who had no mean repute as an amateur philosopher, was caught up in the attack in 1755 when he strayed into theological areas. There were a number of attempts to answer Hume, which were generally regarded as successful at the time; the most important were by Professor George Campbell of Aberdeen in *A Dissertation on Miracles*, by Thomas Reid, Professor of Philosophy at Aberdeen and then at Glasgow, in his *Inquiry into the Human Mind on Principles of Common Sense*, and by James Beattie in his *Essay on the Nature and Immutability of Truth*. On the other hand, although the Moderate leadership had accepted a rationalistic theology, they rallied to Hume's support, failing to realise that he was an exceedingly effective critic of their type of theology. The friendship with Hume of the Moderate Edinburgh literati, together with the cavalier approach of some of them to some aspects of conventional morality which was later to culminate in the dispute over Rev. John Home's play *The Tragedy of Douglas* in 1756,[22] led to the publication in 1753 of the trenchant and

---

18 See the relevant issues of the *Scots Magazine* of 1743; N. Morren, *Annals of the General Assembly of the Church of Scotland, 1739–1766* (Edinburgh, 1838–40), i; and A. L. Drummond and J. Bulloch, *The Scottish Church, 1688–1843: The Age of the Moderates* (Edinburgh, 1973).

19 *Scots Magazine*, xxix (Apr. 1767) – xxxi (Apr. 1769). See below, p. 152.

20 Ibid., li (Jul. 1789), liii (Dec. 1791). See below, p. 153.

21 See below, pp. 45–54, 58–61, 151–3, 210, 219–28.

22 See below, pp. 84–91.

immensely successful *Ecclesiastical Characteristics* of John Witherspoon of Paisley.[23] Witherspoon was arguably the most able ecclesiastical leader of the opponents of Moderatism until his departure to become President of the College of New Jersey (which was yet to become Princeton). In the longer term, appreciation of the significance of Hume's work steered Scottish evangelical theologians away from a system of apologetics based on arguments derived from the evidences of Christianity, and towards a more biblical approach to the defence of the faith. This trend reached its climax with Thomas Chalmers in the nineteenth century, and in some respects as interestingly with the career of Dr Andrew Thomson of Edinburgh, who preceded Chalmers as the leader of the Evangelical party in the Church, and who preached theological conservatism but social and cultural liberalism both in the pulpit and through the pages of his influential *Edinburgh Christian Instructor*.

VI

All this, however, raises the question of the definition of the terms 'Moderate' and 'Popular'. The term 'Moderate' is now rightly used in the contemporary partisan sense. That is, it refers to the party which emerged after 1750 under the leadership of William Robertson, who in 1762 became Principal of Edinburgh University. As such, it excludes a number of older ministers whose theology was not dissimilar to that of the Moderates, on the grounds that they rarely voted for the specific policies of the Moderate party. Such men included Robert Wallace, Principal William Wishart (*secundus*), Patrick Cuming, and even their philosophical mentor, Francis Hutcheson.[24] The term 'Moderate', then, has a precise reference, and the term 'Moderatism' similarly relates to the ideology of the same group which was heavily influenced by Christian Stoic ethics as purveyed by Hutcheson in particular. The problem, however, is that this usage assumes a degree of homogeneity among the supporters of Moderate policies regarding patronage which has never yet been demonstrated.[25]

The term 'Popular party' was the name given to the ecclesiastical party in the eighteenth-century Church of Scotland which opposed the

23 John Witherspoon, *Ecclesiastical Characteristics: or the Arcana of Church Policy being an humble attempt to open up the Mystery of Moderation, wherein is shown a plain and easy way of attaining to the Character of a Moderate Man, as at present in Repute in the Church of Scotland*, in *The Works of John Witherspoon, D. D.* (Edinburgh, 1804–5), vi.

24 Sher, *Church and University in the Scottish Enlightenment*, pp. 16–17.

25 The seminal work on Moderatism and the Moderates is I. D. L. Clark, 'Moderatism and the Moderate Party in the Church of Scotland, 1752–1805' (Cambridge University Ph.D. thesis, 1963); but it is based on the works of less than 20 identifiable Moderates. See also W. Ferguson's review of Sher's *Church and University in the Scottish Enlightenment*, in *History*, lxxii (1987), pp. 530–1, in which Sher is criticised for exaggerating the importance he attaches to the five Edinburgh literati he selects and for neglecting luminaries of the Scottish Enlightenment not connected with Edinburgh.

implementation of the law of patronage. The name was given on the grounds that it represented the views of the ordinary members who were generally regarded as being in favour of the election of ministers by popular vote. The term 'Popular party', though, must be used with a high degree of qualification. The party did not maintain any of the appurtenances of a party: it was rarely organised in any coherent manner; it had no discernible preferred publishers; its members do not seem to have subscribed to any particular journals to the exclusion of others; there were no regular meeting places so far as is known; and so on. As an ecclesiastical grouping, in fact, the Popular party stands in almost direct contrast to the Moderate party. Its members were clearly uncomfortable with the whole concept of ecclesiastical organisation or discipline in order to secure the implementation of their policies at the General Assembly, holding such to be a manifestation of an unscriptural spirit of faction which they saw as characterising their opponents, the Moderates. To a large extent because of this, although the party almost certainly represented the views of the majority of both ministers and members of the Church, it rarely controlled the General Assembly. Although it is generally assumed that it was an evangelical party, it is important to appreciate that it was a theologically complex grouping, and contained men whose theology had much in common with Moderatism. The whole concept of the 'Popular party', therefore, has limited use beyond the patronage dispute proper, and even there one must bear in mind the rather tenuous nature of its resemblance to a cohesive and organised ecclesiastical grouping.

This, however, does not much advance us in further defining the theological characteristics of the eighteenth-century Church of Scotland. As long ago as 1967, however, it was suggested that four theological attitudes were present in the Church during the first half of the eighteenth century, though the divisions were not absolute and shaded into one another. The first group were those 'scholastic Calvinists' who were suspicious of any seeming deviation from the Westminster Confession of Faith and held the Calvinism of the Westminster Standards in a rigid and mechanical fashion. They made the doctrine of predestination of central importance. Secondly, there was a large grouping of 'Evangelical Calvinists' which included men like Thomas Boston, Ralph and Ebenezer Erskine, John Willison and John Maclaurin, who were popular preachers, zealous for free grace, and who, while rejecting the notion of any deviation from the Westminster Confession, in contrast to the first group made a warm personal appeal to their hearers to repent of their sins and to respond to the offer of salvation by placing their faith in Christ. They tried at the same time to do justice to the broad statements of an offer of salvation to all.[26] It could be argued,

[26] S. Mechie, 'The theological climate in early eighteenth-century Scotland', in D. Shaw (ed.), *Reformation and Revolution: Essays presented to the Very Reverend Principal Emeritus*

indeed it is probably generally assumed, that the majority of the Popular party subscribed to the general theological position of such men, and for that reason it is worthwhile quoting a description of them from a nineteenth-century source:

> their main object was to establish the warrant of every sinner to whom the Gospel comes to receive and rest upon Christ as his Saviour. This warrant they found, not in the unrevealed, but in the revealed will of God – not in His eternal decree, but in His inspired Word – not in His secret purpose, but in His public proclamation of grace. They knew that the unrevealed will of God forms no part of the rule either of faith or duty; that His eternal purpose, whatever it may be and however it may regulate His own dispensations towards His creatures, can in no way affect their duty to believe the Gospel.[27]

The third group were 'liberal Calvinists'. These men, of whom examples were William Leechman, Robert Wallace, George and William Wishart, Patrick Cuming, James Oswald and William Hamilton, are to be distinguished from the younger Moderates such as William Robertson, John Home, and Alexander Carlyle. The 'liberal Calvinists' adopted a pragmatic position: they did not defend the full Christian faith in the traditional sense but argued that the divine origin and authority of Christianity could be inferred from its intrinsic excellence and the great benefits it had conferred on mankind. They conceded considerable grounds to the deists in their apologetic and could be regarded as accommodating the rationalistic spirit of the age, as showing reserve on various areas of confessional orthodoxy, and as trying to show their contemporaries that Christianity was intellectually respectable. Through all this, they maintained an earnest and devout piety. Finally, there was a fourth group, Professor Simson and his students at Glasgow, who may be rather generally regarded as 'Arians'. This group, which is much less well defined and documented, adopted a speculative approach to theology and were influenced by Samuel Clarke's *Scripture Doctrine of the Trinity*, published in London in 1712, and by the deists. Simson's students showed little regard for the Westminster Confession and saw their subscription to it as no more than a formal act of adherence required by the State in return for the establishment of the Church. Their theology was probably of an Arian or Pelagian tendency, in that they seemed to disregard doctrines of the Fall, original sin, and the necessity of divine grace for salvation, and their general attitude was humanistic or moralistic.[28]

Hugh Watt, D.D., D.Litt. on the Sixtieth Anniversary of His Ordination (Edinburgh, 1967), p. 268.

[27] J. Buchanan, *The Doctrine of Justification* (Edinburgh, 1867), pp. 187ff, quoted in Mechie, 'Theological climate', p. 268.

[28] Mechie, 'Theological climate', pp. 271–2.

This analysis provides a sound, if brief, starting-point for an examination of later theological developments. Its significance lies in its recognition of the existence of divisions within the evangelical wing of the Church. If one bears in mind that such diverse men as Willison, Maclaurin, William Wishart and Cuming all voted solidly for the Popular position on patronage at the General Assembly from 1740 on, a picture of potential tension in the Popular party arising from theological differences immediately begins to emerge. Furthermore, although it does not bring the Robertsonian Moderates into account, such an analysis does provide hints of what Popular writers, especially in the earlier years of the period of this study, may well have seen themselves as combating in their apologetical works.

But while that analysis serves as an introduction, any attempt to re-appraise the diversity of the theology or any other aspect of the Church of Scotland in the latter half of the eighteenth century must also take into account the interpretation of Scottish theology in the period proposed by the Cambridge scholar who made the first modern analysis of Moderatism and the Moderate party in the eighteenth-century Church. Dr Ian Clark argued that the characteristics of Moderate theology are to be found at their clearest in three areas: the relationship between natural and revealed religion, the person and work of Christ, and the connection between faith and works. Here, he maintained, the teaching of the Moderates is most distinguishable from that of orthodoxy, which he defines as 'the dominant High Calvinist interpretation of the Westminster Confession'.[29] There are, of course, several important qualifications which Clark made concerning the extent to which the varying approaches and pre-occupations of the two schools can be differentiated. He suggested that the 'scaffolding of Moderate thought' affected even the Evangelicals, in that the Moderates' appeal to natural religion to establish the veracity and reasonableness of Scripture was reflected in Evangelical thought at the time, as was their pre-occupation with the ethical content of religion, the existence of an attenuated version of traditional Christology, and the development of a revised estimate of human nature and the effects of the Fall and Original Sin.[30] He went on to maintain that doctrines preached from Scottish pulpits cannot be rigidly classified as either 'Moderate' or 'Evangelical', and suggested that there was a feeling among eighteenth-century Scottish theologians that unity had to be preserved, if need be at the expense of rigid doctrinal orthodoxy. He believed that theological debate within the Calvinist framework was increasingly replaced by an apologetic directed against contemporary opposition or indifference to the basic doctrines of Christianity, and that in general theologians either agreed to differ about details or else concentrated exclusively on the

[29] Clark, 'Moderatism and the Moderate Party', p. vii.
[30] Ibid., p. 204.

things that still united them.[31] But how far these qualifications are in fact borne out by an examination of Popular theology is more difficult to determine than is the existence at presbytery level of less division between the Moderates and members of the Popular party than is often believed.[32]

In summary, Clark categorised Popular theology as reacting against a Moderate theology which gave too great a place to the role of Reason as the source of faith and which erected it into a standard of right and wrong through the role of the conscience.[33] As a result of this, there developed significant differences between the two schools on the Atonement, since the Popular view was that the Moderates rejected any element of 'propitiation' or 'substitution' in Christ's work. This led to the Moderates being charged with 'Socinianism'.[34] Clark saw the Popular criticism of the Moderate position as harping on significant omissions rather than on positive errors, and as reflecting a lack of balance in the Popular presentation of the concepts of 'Saviour' and 'Pattern' in the Incarnation. He concluded his analysis of Moderate theology by asserting that the real achievements of eighteenth-century Moderatism are to be seen in the nature of nineteenth-century Evangelicalism. The Moderate objectives of a balanced presentation of the Christian faith, belief linked with practice, doctrine linked with behaviour, and the correction of what he saw as the imbalance of seventeenth-century Scottish Calvinism were all incorporated in the nineteenth-century Evangelical Revival.[35]

Now, if it is true that both contemporary and current usage of the terms 'Moderate' and 'Moderatism' assume an undemonstrated homogeneity in both party and theology, it is even more the case with their opponents. As has been pointed out, there is no completely satisfactory term for the anti-Moderate or Popular party.[36] What is certain is that while they were united in their opposition to the policies of the Moderate party on patronage, until now there has been no attempt to examine either their theology or even their general ideology. The term has been used to indicate opponents of patronage in such a way that there is commonly assumed to have been a correlation between being against patronage and being an evangelical.[37] The history of the Church of Scotland in the second half of the eighteenth century has therefore been written on the basis of a set of unproven assumptions, and in particular the assumption that the touchstone is the patronage dispute which reflected not merely ecclesiastical divisions but also the central

---

31 Ibid., pp. 205, 207.
32 See, e.g., McIntosh, 'Evangelicals in Eighteenth-Century Scotland', pp. 54–64, 77.
33 Clark, 'Moderatism and the Moderate Party', pp. 200, 203, 229–30, 251–2, 281.
34 Ibid., pp. 236, 294–5.
35 Ibid., pp. 259–64, 270, 370.
36 Sher, *Church and University in the Scottish Enlightenment*, pp. 16–17.
37 See, e.g., ibid., p. 17.

theological divisions as well. While acceptance that the term 'Popular' is essentially related to opposition to patronage has the merit of providing a simple test to determine who belonged to the Popular party, detailed identification of adherents of the party by this means is possible only for relatively small numbers. Nevertheless, confident assertions about the relative strengths of Popular and Moderate numbers, about their geographical distribution and, perhaps most important of all, about their theological unity, have then been made without the supporting evidence they require.

VII

A detailed examination of the publications of those ministers of the Church of Scotland who can be identified as members of the Popular party, either by their published works or by their voting record at the General Assembly (that is, those who were firmly opposed to patronage), indicates that the party displayed a greater geographical diversity than has hitherto been supposed. It was clearly spread throughout the country; it was probably the dominant party in a majority of presbyteries; and it was more likely to be dominant in a presbytery where there was an urban centre of local significance.[38] Analysis of Popular publications also demonstrates several important and hitherto unrecognised features of their interests and concerns. Nine main subject areas were covered by members of the party: doctrine, spiritual experience and devotion, biblical exposition, ecclesiastical issues, political issues, the Christian life (which included questions of morality, manners, and the problem of religious 'infidelity'), civil and religious liberty, the relationship between the individual Christian and the State, and those volumes published merely as 'Sermons'. Apart from 'Sermons', the fourth of these areas, ecclesiastical issues, was the widest and included works published on a number of topics such as patronage, heresy, Popery, the nature of the ministry, missions, Moderatism, the nature of public worship, revivals, covenants, religious education, and stipend augmentation.[39]

Experiential or devotional and evangelical works, however, formed the largest group of Popular publications, and within it the two most common topics were exhortations to evangelism and preparation for death. A wide range of devotional topics was also covered. Doctrinal works and expository analysis of scripture passages or commentaries on books of the Bible amount to roughly the same total combined, as do

---

[38] See J. R. McIntosh, 'The Popular Party in the Church of Scotland, 1740–1800' (Glasgow University Ph.D. thesis, 1989), chap. 2.

[39] The question of patronage was the most common topic; then those of revival, missions, heresy, Popery, and religious education, and then topics such as stipend augmentation, Moderatism, and the three minor issues of public worship, the nature of the ministry, and covenants. See ibid., Appendices C, D, E, F.

those of a more devotional or evangelical nature. Apart from these theological publications, however, there was also a significant interest, or rather concern, about the issues of heresy or infidelity in the Church, and morality and manners in general, two problems which were held to be closely connected with defection from the faith.[40] There was also some publication in secular areas by Popular ministers. Here the emphasis was very much on political issues which provoked or were capable of a religious or spiritual interpretation. Such interpretation tended to emphasise the dealings of God with the nations, which reflected on their adherence or otherwise to the principles of Christianity, and on the acknowledgement of divine involvement in the affairs of men.[41] At the same time, there was no direct interest in social issues. Such matters were raised in the context of analysis of what may be regarded as the Christian life.[42]

Compared to Popular publication, Moderate activity in most areas was substantially less.[43] The exceptions were literary works where there were twelve times as many Moderate works as Popular ones, agriculture where there were ten times as many, and social issues where, however, the total number of publications of both parties was very small. Areas where roughly equal interest was aroused were morality and manners, and ecclesiastical history and biography. There was little Moderate interest in doctrine, apologetics, and relatively few publications in the area of devotional and evangelistic matters. 'Infidelity' does not appear as a Moderate topic. Very little Moderate publication existed in the areas of heresy, Popery, or church discipline, or on the questions of national religion or the nature of the ecclesiastical establishment. There was no Moderate publication at all in the areas of missions or revivals.

The first, inescapable conclusion to be drawn is that Moderate ministers were less likely to write on theological, religious, or ecclesiastical topics than were Popular ones. In ecclesiastical matters, only patronage and the defence of Moderatism produced more than isolated works. Secondly, it is clear that the picture, perhaps even the caricature, of the Moderate ministers as men of the literary world, or of that of the arts and sciences in general, has some foundation on a national basis. Neither the relative strengths of the parties in a presbytery nor its geographical location made much difference to Moderate interests. Whereas the Popular party enjoyed a relatively wide geographical origin for its publications, the Moderate party relied disproportionately on the East of Scotland. The Moderates, then, were overshadowed in religious and ecclesiastical works by their Popular opponents.

40 See below, pp. 45–54, 58–61, 151–3, 210, 219–28.
41 See below, pp. 74–84, 153–60, 219–32.
42 See below, pp. 54–7, 210–18.
43 See McIntosh, 'Popular Party in the Church of Scotland', Appendix E.

Several general conclusions may be drawn from these patterns of publication of the two parties. The clear Popular pre-eminence in the area of publication draws attention to the unrepresentative nature of the General Assembly, where Moderate control remained almost unshaken on key issues throughout the period. Some elucidation of the nature of this control has been carried out in recent years and there is a greater understanding of the mechanisms of Moderate manipulation of the Assembly,[44] but it has not yet been reflected in an appreciation of Popular activity in areas of doctrinal, ecclesiastical, ethical, or secular thought. Those who would allege, or imply, that the Moderates dominated the intellectual life of the eighteenth-century Church of Scotland have little *statistical* basis for their allegations.

The survey of Popular publications also leads to a clearer understanding of that party. In the first place, patronage was not necessarily an important issue even for those who, on the evidence of their actions at the General Assembly, were most opposed to it. It was the subject of only fifteen Popular works out of over 300 which can be ascribed to Popular authorship. It was, however, from evenly balanced presbyteries that the majority of works appeared dealing with patronage. It is possible, therefore, that patronage and the implementation of the authority of the General Assembly were matters of concern mainly in presbyteries where the problem was likely to have an impact on the balance of power. A clear majority, for one party or the other, seems to have defused the issue. A possible interpretation of this is the very interesting one that the issue of patronage was seen as pressing only if it had significance at local level. Such a possibility might well have contributed to the difficulties which the Popular party experienced in its attempt to mount an effective opposition to the Moderates at the Assembly.[45] A further probable implication is that the eighteenth-century Church was much more locally orientated than historians have consistently assumed, and that what happened at the Assembly was much less important than has been supposed to have been the case.

Secondly, there was little preoccupation with doctrine in the strict sense of the term, far less a particularly pronounced concern throughout the Popular party to campaign for doctrinal orthodoxy, although that was a matter of deep concern for some important Popular figures.[46] Only three works which can be firmly ascribed to a member of the Popular party dealt with Moderatism as such. Thirdly, there was a predominantly internal apologetic aimed at defections from within the Church rather than defence against attacks from without; there was

---

[44] Notably, this is due to the work of Richard Sher: see R. B. Sher, 'Church, University, Enlightenment: The Moderate Literati of Edinburgh, 1720–1793' (Chicago University Ph.D. thesis, 1979), pp. 29, 52–5, 154; and in Sher, *Church and University in the Scottish Enlightenment*, pp. 50–3, 72, 120–47.

[45] See below, pp. 120–4.

[46] E.g., John Willison of Dundee and John Russel of Stirling.

indeed no systematic attempt to carry the attack to those outside. Of course, for much of the century the Popular party, like the Moderates, deemed Scotland to be a practising Christian society. And finally, the pattern of publication establishes that for the Popular party the matters of paramount concern were not ecclesiastical issues, but spiritual matters. If one bears in mind that much of the content of the works entitled simply 'Sermons' was of a devotional nature, that concern becomes even more obvious. The weight of Popular publication emphasises the strong devotional and, increasingly, the evangelical preoccupations of the party as a whole.

VIII

Partly as a consequence of the alleged tendency of Moderate elements in the Church to gloss over divergence from unequivocal adherence to the doctrinal standards of the Church, the period under discussion saw the growth of secession from the established Church. This had commenced with the departure of Ebenezer and Ralph Erskine and their supporters in 1733 over the issue of patronage. Secession was made a permanent feature of the Scottish ecclesiastical scene with their eventual deposition from the ministry in 1740. The number of Christians outside the established Church was increased with the deposition of Thomas Gillespie in 1752 and the subsequent formation of the Presbytery of Relief when Thomas Boston of Oxnam resigned his charge at Jedburgh and joined Gillespie's followers. In general, the Seceders were vehement in their criticism of the 'fudging' of theological issues in the established Church (though noticeably less so in the case of the Relief Presbytery), and in the case of McGill of Ayr it was largely Seceder attacks which brought the case to the Church courts.[47] In 1754, the Seceders in fact produced a document on the Atonement which stated that Christ died for the elect only, a clear sign of their adherence to traditional orthodoxy.

The strength of secession in its various forms continued to grow, partly as a result of these disputes and divisions. Even more important as a cause of secession, however, was the operation of the patronage system in the Church of Scotland. Disputed calls occurred constantly through-out the period, notably at Torphichen in 1751, Inverkeithing from 1749 to 1752 (where it led to the deposition of Gillespie), and St Ninian's near Stirling from 1766 to 1773. Until 1750, in the event of a disputed settlement in which the relevant presbytery was unable or unwilling to enforce the induction of the presentee, the General Assembly or its Commission was accustomed to appoint a 'riding committee', usually from outside the presbytery, to conduct the induction. Thereafter,

---

[47] *Scots Magazine*, li (Jul. 1789), p. 359; liii (Dec. 1791), pp. 592–3.

largely at the instigation of an influential group of up-and-coming young Moderates such as William Robertson, Alexander Carlyle, John Home, and Hugh Blair, the Moderate-dominated General Assembly and Commission turned more and more to a policy of forcing presbyteries to induct the patron's nominee irrespective of the congregation's wishes or their own scruples. The continued imposition of patronage provoked constant departures from parish churches all over Scotland to the ranks of the Secession, and in 1765–6 led to the Secession Overture in which the Popular party attempted unsuccessfully to use concern at the losses to inflict a strategic defeat on the Moderates. The debate continued, however, until something of a truce emerged around 1784 when the Assembly decided by a majority to discontinue the annual instruction to its Commission 'to make application to the King and Parliament for redress of the grievance of patronage'.[48] In so far as there was a truce, however, it was not to last long into the next century, when the debate broke out again with renewed vigour over non-intrusion as it had come to be known.

These issues of secession and patronage dominated the way that the history of the Church of Scotland in the period between the Secession of 1733 and the Disruption of 1843 was traditionally written. The interpretation was purely in terms of the conflict between the Moderate party with their policy of support for the patronage system, and their Popular party opponents who became the 'Non-Intrusionists' of the nineteenth century. This can be ascribed to two main factors: in the nineteenth century virtually all writing on Scottish ecclesiastical history was produced in the aftermath of the Disruption of the Church in 1843, or was heavily influenced by subsequent ecclesiastical or theological wrangling later in the century; and secondly, most twentieth-century interest has centred around the relationship between the Popular party's opponents, the Moderates, and the Scottish Enlightenment.

In the Disruption years, and in those following, there emerged an attempt on the part of Free Church historians and of seceders who subsequently joined the Free Church in the various unions which followed in the 1840s and '50s, to establish continuity for their cause with that of the eighteenth-century evangelicals and the Popular party. This also involved the denigration of their nineteenth-century opponents by showing them to be the heirs of the eighteenth-century Moderates. What was taken to be Moderate theology was implicitly rejected by that of the evangelical revival of the early nineteenth century, and Moderate ecclesiastical polity was held to be the origin of the troubles of the mid-nineteenth century.[49] The patronage controversy of

---

[48] Quoted in Burleigh, *Church History of Scotland*, p. 285.

[49] E.g., W. M. Hetherington, *The History of the Church of Scotland* (Edinburgh, 1841); G. Struthers, *The History of the Rise, Progress, and Principles of the Relief Church* (Glasgow, 1843); D. Scott, *Annals and Statistics of the Original Secession Church: till its Disruption and*

the eighteenth century was interpreted as being the same issue as that of 'non-intrusion' in the nineteenth. Such concerns, however, did not on the whole serve to direct scholarly attention to the eighteenth-century Popular party since most of what was written was anti-Moderate rather than consideredly pro-Popular in its objectives.

Interpretation was further complicated by the histories of denominations which derived from eighteenth-century secessions from the Church of Scotland. These usually included a range of partisan statements about the ideology and activities of the Popular party which ranged from expression of the belief that the eighteenth-century Church was so Moderate-dominated as to justify the assertion that 'True religion was at a low ebb in the Church of Scotland',[50] to the sustained denigration of the Popular party, both implicit and explicit, indulged in by the historian of the Relief Church. The latter blamed the Popular party for deserting the people in their time of need over the Secession, implied that all who stayed in the Establishment 'preferred a royal commissioner to Christ as head of the Church', asserted that in the 1752 Inverkeithing case the leaders of the party failed to refer to the law of Christ and to the practice of the Apostolic Church in their arguments with the Moderates, and maintained that the party 'laid the rights and privileges of the people at the feet of royalty', and so ruined the free constitution of the Church of Scotland.[51]

The second factor which coloured the historiography of the eighteenth-century Church in the following century was the impact of 'Higher Criticism' on the Free Church and on the Church of Scotland, together with moves away from traditional forms of worship notably through the introduction of hymns and instrumental music. Such changes were opposed by those who deemed themselves to be the heirs of the opponents of the eighteenth-century Moderates.[52] These factors coincided with the emergence of a party within the Free Church seeking union with the doctrinally more liberal United Presbyterian Church, and encouraged the appearance of works which were less partisan but also less interested in the evangelical or 'Popular' tradition within the Scottish Church.

The defects suggested as being typical of the nineteenth-century works of ecclesiastical history affect their value for today's historian. In the first place, almost all agree on what amounts to a common factual

Union with the Free Church of Scotland in 1852 (Edinburgh, 1886); J. Walker, *Theology and Theologians of Scotland, 1560–1750* (Edinburgh, 1872); and G. B. Ryley and J. M. McCandlish, *Scotland's Free Church* (Edinburgh, 1893).

50 Scott, *Annals and Statistics of the Original Secession Church*, p. 13.

51 Struthers, *History of the Rise, Progress, and Principles of the Relief Church*, pp. 18, 66, 79–80, 121, 226.

52 These matters have received recent analysis in R. A. Reisen, '"Higher Criticism" in the Free Church Fathers', *Recs. Scot. Church Hist. Soc.*, xx (pt. 2) (1979), pp. 119–42; and A. C. Cheyne, *The Transforming of the Kirk: Victorian Scotland's Religious Revolution* (Edinburgh, 1983).

account from the beginnings of the Secession to the end of the century and it is impossible to find any significant divergence. The differences tend to appear in the extent of the coverage, for example, of debate at the General Assembly, or of the amount of anecdote and its sources. This agreement is no doubt due to the ready availability of Assembly reports in the pages of the *Scots Magazine* or, later in the century, in Nathaniel Morren's *Annals*.[53] Subsequent research has produced little in the way of new factual information about the basic events, though it has modified the understanding of them. Secondly, even in the nineteenth century there was a pronounced tendency to concentrate on the Moderate party and its policies. In some of the secondary sources there was a near dearth of attention given to the Popular party.[54] Thirdly, nineteenth-century preoccupations led to a wide range of partisan statements about the activity and ideology of the Popular party in the eighteenth century. These nineteenth-century preoccupations, purposes, and prejudices intrude to varying extents on the twentieth-century historian's search for information and understanding, though he too must be careful not to intrude the prejudices of his own generation. Fourthly, all post-eighteenth-century works allowed themselves to slip unconsciously into the assumption that the terms 'Popular' and 'Evangelical' were synonymous. Until now, this assumption has precluded any systematic analysis of the theological views of members of the Popular party. It is important to note that the main effect of the defects is to lead to a lack of independent attention to the Popular party on its own terms. Distortion of truth is not evident; lack of interest all too often is. The problem is one of failure to probe beneath the surface of a commonly agreed factual account. The value of these works is for the historian of the nineteenth century, not for the one of the eighteenth.

Twentieth-century historiography of the eighteenth-century Scottish Church shares similar defects to those which characterised it in the nineteenth century. In fact, much of what has been written recently in the area of ecclesiastical history has not been inspired by a direct interest in the Scottish Church at all. The history of the Scottish Enlightenment, of the growth of Radicalism, and of social trends, and indeed the sociological history of religion have all produced works which tend towards a secular approach to ecclesiastical history which diverts attention from more narrowly ecclesiastical areas, and certainly from the theological and spiritual dimensions in the life of the Church.[55]

53 N. Morren, *Annals of the General Assembly*.
54 Notable examples of this are A. P. Stanley, *Lectures on the History of the Church of Scotland* (London, 1872); J. Rankin, *A Handbook of the Church of Scotland* (Edinburgh, 1888); and J. Macpherson, *A History of the Church in Scotland from the Earliest Times to the Present Day* (Paisley and London, 1901).
55 E.g. C. G. Brown, *The Social History of Religion in Scotland since 1730* (London, 1987); A. C. Chitnis, *The Scottish Enlightenment: A Social History* (London, 1976); K. J. Logue, *Popular Disturbances in Scotland, 1780–1815* (Edinburgh, 1979); A. Murdoch, *'The*

Certainly, the reawakening of interest in eighteenth-century Scottish ecclesiastical history which began in the 1960s and 1970s has not led to a more comprehensive analysis of the Popular party. Its preoccupations, indeed, have tended to militate against it. This has been, it might be said, to the detriment of the work and conclusions of the secular historians of the period.

People Above': Politics and Administration in Mid-Eighteenth-Century Scotland (Edinburgh, 1980); and J. S. Shaw, *The Management of Scottish Society, 1707–1764: Power, Nobles, Lawyers, Edinburgh Agents and English Influences* (Edinburgh, 1983).

CHAPTER TWO

The Challenge of Enlightenment and Moderatism

In 1744 there appeared one of the most important publications by an eighteenth-century minister of the Church of Scotland: John Willison's *A Fair and Impartial Testimony, essayed in Name of a Number of Ministers, Elders, and Christian People of the Church of Scotland, unto the Laudable Principles, Wrestlings, and Attainments of that Church, and prevailing evils, both of former and present Times, And namely, the Defections of the Established Church, of the Nobility, Gentry, Commons, Seceders, Episcopalians, etc.* Willison, the minister of the South Church of Dundee from 1716 to 1750, was probably the most commonly read religious writer in eighteenth-century Scotland. The earliest and possibly the most fundamental opponent of Moderatism, he was a notable evangelical and supporter of the Cambuslang and Kilsyth revivals of the 1740s; indeed the latter started after his sermon on the way back from Cambuslang. His earlier ministry had been preoccupied with struggles against Episcopalians and Jacobites, he had actively countered the Glassites, and he fought unsuccessfully for the rehabilitation of the Seceders with whom he sympathised. As can be gathered from its full title, *A Fair and Impartial Testimony* was much more than just an analysis of patronage and its effects. Amongst the reasons for its publication, Willison identified the following: the prevalence of infidelity and error; the toleration of heretical doctrines; 'looseness', immorality and doctrinal laxness among ministers, some of whom were allowed to hold divinity posts in the universities; the decline of evangelical preaching and the spread of 'legal doctrine'; the encouragement given to patronage by some in the ministry when there was no legal necessity to do so; the practice of intrusions which denied congregations their scriptural and constitutional right to call their pastors; the divisions and separations which existed amongst Presbyterians contrary to scriptural injunctions; reproaches cast on spiritual awakenings; and the taking up of Popish doctrines and practices by the Episcopal clergy.[1]

In the broad sweep of his objectives, Willison was launching a comprehensive onslaught on the state of the Church from an orthodox evangelical position, and it is in the context of this that his analysis of

---

[1] John Willison, *Fair and Impartial Testimony ...* (Edinburgh, 1744), pp. vi–vii.

patronage must be seen. Patronage concerned Willison fundamentally as being incompatible with the entire purpose of the Church and with its rights. In the words of an act of the Synod of Fife of 2 April 1735, which he quoted with approval, patronage 'with power of presenting men to take the oversight of souls, is a manifest encroachment upon the rights and liberties of the Church of Christ'; and those who accepted presentations showed 'little regard to the weighty ends of a Gospel-ministry, the glory of the great and chief Shepherd, and the edification of his flock'.[2] These objectives were largely to be ensured, Willison argued, by careful observation of the 7th Act of Assembly 1736, which stressed 'the preaching of Christ and regeneration' to the people, and 'pressing morality in a Gospel-strain'.[3] This function of preaching was described by other writers as 'taking charge of the souls' of the people,[4] or as the 'edification of the Body of Christ',[5] or, at perhaps its most evangelical, as 'the very means of salvation to yourselves, your friends, your countrymen, and even to posterity'.[6] The most important function of the ministry, therefore, was the preaching of the Gospel in an evangelical manner.[7] This perception was common to all sections of the Popular party almost without exception, though there were some different emphases as to what preaching the Gospel involved. The significance of Willison's *A Fair and Impartial Testimony*, then, is that it may be seen as setting the agenda of the Popular party for the rest of the century.

I

Fundamental to an understanding of the position of the members of the Popular party, not only on the problem of patronage but also indeed on all ecclesiastical and theological matters, is an appreciation of the significance of four central themes which are applicable to virtually the whole life of the Christian Church. The first two are the doctrines of the primacy of Christian liberty and the unity of the Church, the first being stressed particularly within the Protestant tradition. The third and

---

[2] Ibid., p. ix.

[3] Ibid., pp. 122–3.

[4] James Gordon, *The State and Duty of the Church of Scotland, especially with respect to the Settlement of Ministers set in a just light* (Edinburgh, 1732), pp. 25–6.

[5] John Lawson, *A Speech concerning the Settling of Parishes in general, and more especially relating to the Settlement of the Parish of Terreagles* (Glasgow, 1752), p. 18.

[6] John Snodgrass, *An Effectual Method of Recovering our Religious Liberties, addressed to the Elders of the Church of Scotland, Showing, That they may easily bring about a total Change of Administration in this Church, and thereby remove the principal Grievances arising from the Law of Patronage; with particular Directions for attaining this desirable End* (Glasgow, 1770), p. 42.

[7] John Erskine linked this idea with an exhortation to patrons to consider carefully the qualifications of their presentees when they exercised their legal right lest the souls 'that may be lost by a bad nomination, will be required at their hands': John Erskine, 'The Qualifications necessary for Teachers of Christianity' (1750), in *Discourses preached on Several Occasions* (Edinburgh, 1798), i, pp. 38–40.

fourth themes, while not actually doctrines, are found within most branches of the Christian Church: they are the democratic impulse, and the need for consistent and coherent church government and discipline. In the case of the Popular party, the last came to be a demand for 'constitutionalism'. All four point towards the fundamental doctrine of the nature of the Church. Arguments against patronage returned constantly to the conception of the Church as a body whose paramount purpose was the salvation and edification of souls. Nothing could be allowed to hinder that role. If that were the definition of 'evangelical', then the Popular party was predominantly an evangelical party. In the context of the history of the Church of Scotland, however, what is meant by the 'Doctrine of the Church'?

It is agreed that this doctrine was one which received considerable attention in Scotland from the Reformation on.[8] Traditionally in post-Reformation Scotland, it was held that the Church of Christ consisted of all who had been elected to salvation by the grace of God; it was for these that Christ had died and that he had purchased salvation. Those who were effectually called by God's Spirit became the Christian Church. The Church, therefore, was historically made up of those who had been saved, some of whom had died and were with God in heaven, and some of whom were alive on earth and were striving towards the goal of being with the Lord in heaven. The Church was a unity which was God's instrument for carrying out his purpose of grace in the salvation of men. As well as a past and a present, the Church also had a responsibility for the future, namely, to take the Word to those who were yet to hear God's call and who were needed to complete the Body of Christ.

From the idea of the Church as the Body of Christ came the identification of Christ as the source of blessing and the seat of authority. The Church was his means of giving what he died to purchase to those who were his. But it was for him to say what those for whom he died ought to be and ought to do. He had full control over natural forces and rational beings as individuals and as organised bodies. Whether men resented this authority, or rebelled against it, his will was destined to be implemented.

The implications of this doctrine, however, were in many ways as important as the doctrine itself. In general terms it is probably true to say, along with Macleod, that 'it came to hold such a place of control as that it is largely in connection with the application and working out of this doctrine that the most remarkable struggles and discussions of national Church life have taken place'.[9]

---

[8] The following analysis of the Doctrine of the Church is based on the accounts given in Walker, *Theology and Theologians of Scotland*, pp. 95–156; J. Macpherson, *The Doctrine of the Church in Scottish Theology* (Edinburgh, 1903), *passim*; and J. Macleod, *Scottish Theology in Relation to Church History since the Reformation* (Edinburgh, 1946), pp. 31–40. Macleod's work draws heavily from that of Walker.

[9] Macleod, *Scottish Theology in Relation to Church History*, p. 33.

The central issue in the doctrine, especially in so far as it affected the patronage dispute, was the regulative authority of Scripture. This came to be interpreted in such a way that the headship of Christ and the subjection of the Church to his authority meant that the Church was a society under the obligation to obey his Word. As a result, his revealed will in the Scriptures was the ultimate source of authority both in the Church and in the world in general, and the freedom of the Church could only be attained when it was subject to no other authority. In the same way, too, as Christ's revealed will was regulative for the Church, it was regulative also for the individual. Hence was derived the doctrine of Christian liberty. Only when the Christian had freedom to conform his life to Christ's injunctions did he have real freedom or liberty. This explains the Scottish Church's concern, and indeed that of the Reformed Churches in general, for the rights of the individual and for civil liberty.

The history of the Popular party in the Church of Scotland in the second half of the eighteenth century can be fully understood only with an appreciation of this fundamental doctrine. While the Popular response to the problem of patronage, as it developed from around 1740, was along the lines of traditional Scottish theology, it was nonetheless a flexible and constructive response. It was also more consistent than were the policies of the Moderates to which it was responding. It was, furthermore, an eminently respectable response intellectually, even if the Popular leaders were on occasion less than impressive as ecclesiastical managers or theological polemicists.

II

In the last analysis, all religious knowledge must derive from one of two sources: from some form of revelation, or from religious truths which can be ascertained by observation or by the process of reasoning. The latter forms of religious knowledge were known in the eighteenth century as natural religion. It could be maintained that, starting from Aquinas, one of the greatest debates in the history of Christian doctrine has been over the relative importance and compatibility of these two forms of knowledge. In the wake of the Enlightenment this was especially true of the eighteenth century, and a discussion of the nature and origins of religious knowledge plays a large part in several significant works of Popular theology. The mid-eighteenth-century Church of Scotland, then, found itself operating in an Enlightenment-based secular environment which was raising substantial questions concerning such aspects of the foundations of the Christian faith as the nature of religious knowledge, the attributes of God, and the nature of man.

The fundamental problem in discussing the eighteenth-century Scottish debate on the origin and nature of religious knowledge is that of deciding exactly what contemporaries understood by natural and revealed religion. There is no clear-cut answer. William Crawford of Wilton, for example, defined natural religion as that which arose from the relationship between God the Creator and his creatures, 'considered as innocent creatures', and defined revealed religion as arising from the relationship between God 'as reconcilable in Christ' and men 'as recoverable sinners'. There was, though, no 'Law of Nature' which forbade God's requiring and accepting our repentance.[10] This position, however, was not necessarily accepted by all Popular writers. George Anderson, who was to achieve fame as the accuser of Hume and Kames in the 1750s, for example, quoted Bolingbroke with approval for asserting that 'the Christian Law is nothing else than the Law of Nature enforced by a new revelation'.[11] There was, therefore, some blurring of the distinction between the two forms of religious truth, the natural and the revealed.

There was disagreement, however, as to whether natural religion should be attacked or defended, since from 1740 until the end of the century there was a constant strand of criticism.[12] In general, however, Popular writers of all shades of theological opinion saw natural religion as having a role to play in the communication of religious truth and in the defence of true religion. Principal William Wishart of Edinburgh University, at one extreme of theological opinion and regarded as heterodox by some, saw God's requirements and the recommendations of the love of Jesus as being 'in their own nature good', even without Scriptural injunctions. Sceptics, as well as attacking the principles of revealed religion, opposed those of natural religion too, in attempting to overturn the difference between moral good and evil, and to confuse vice and virtue.[13] At the other extreme of the party, George Anderson attacked Bolingbroke for his direct endeavours 'to root out of the minds

---

[10] William Crawford, 'A Discourse – wherein such Principles are established as sap the Foundations of Mr. Tindal's Book, entitled Christianity as old as the Creation [London, 1730]; and also of a Letter in his Defence', in *Works* (Edinburgh, 1748), i, p. 118. This particular essay is usually entitled 'A Discourse against Infidelity'.

[11] George Anderson, *A Remonstrance against Lord Viscount Bolingbroke's Philosophical Religion* (Edinburgh, 1756), pp. 10–11. See also John Erskine, 'The Nature of the Sinai Covenant, and the Character and Privileges of the Jewish Church', in *Theological Dissertations* (London, 1765), p. 45: 'The unchangeable law of nature requires a perfect obedience both in heart and life, which no son of Adam can say with truth he has yielded.'

[12] Alexander Webster, *Supernatural Revelation the only sure Hope of Sinners* (Edinburgh, 1741), p. 5; John Russel, *The Nature of the Gospel Delineated, and its Universal Spread founded upon the Declaration of Jesus Christ: A Sermon* (Ayr, 1796), p. 8.

[13] William Wishart, *The Certain and Unchangeable Difference betwixt Moral Good and Evil. A Sermon preached before the Societies for the Reformation of Manners, at Salters' Hall on Monday, 3rd of July, 1732* (London, 1732), p. 4. See also, William Wishart, 'An Essay on the Indispensible Necessity of a Holy and Good Life to the Happiness of Heaven, shewing That this Necessity according to the plain tenor of the Gospel, is without any Reserve or exception, with a Practical Improvement of the Argument', in *Discourses on Several Subjects* (London, 1753), p. 11.

of men, a belief of the capital articles of natural religion'. These he defined as including 'God's moral attributes, the immateriality and immortality of the soul, a particular providence, and a future state of rewards and punishments'. Natural religion, furthermore, he argued, could be defended without reference to revelation.[14] Earlier, Dr John Erskine of Edinburgh Greyfriars, probably the ablest theologian produced by the Popular party, had maintained that natural religion taught the existence of a God, and the immortality of the soul.[15] A range of Popular writers, then, would have agreed with John Maclaurin of Glasgow when he saw natural religion as having the function of leading men to 'honour God's perfections manifested in the works of creation and providence, as contrasted with the Scriptural revelation which leads us to honour his perfections revealed in the work of salvation and redemption';[16] and most would have accepted John Witherspoon's suggestion that it contributed along with revealed religion to give such a view of divine Providence as would lead men to adore, thank, trust, and submit to God.[17] A common assertion, in fact, was that natural religion provided ample justification for accepting the existence of a future life which involved rewards and punishments, and as revealing insights into the nature and attributes of God.[18]

Though many in the Popular party were prepared to accept natural religion as conveying important religious truths, Robert Dick of Edinburgh wrote for many when he distinguished the chief characteristics of the Christian religion, marking it off from natural religion and from the Jewish faith, as being the assurances of mercy to the penitent for the sake of the atonement made by Christ, the promises of divine aid in this life, and the abridgement of the ritual ordinances instituted for the early world. Christianity, which had the sole end of promoting piety towards God, charity towards man, and sober, righteous and godly living, was to be contrasted with religions which proposed to expound the 'original principles of natural, moral, and

---

14 George Anderson, *Remonstrance*, pp. 8, 12. It must be admitted, however, that Anderson confused the picture by arguing that one of Bolingbroke's crimes was to reduce the authority of Christ by arguing that a particular providence and the existence of future rewards and punishments are merely articles of natural religion: ibid., p. 11. See also, [John Bonar], *An Analysis of the Moral and Religious Sentiments contained in the Writings of Sopho, and David Hume, Esq., addressed to the consideration of the Reverend and Honourable Members of the General Assembly of the Church of Scotland* (Edinburgh, 1755), pp. 48–9.

15 John Erskine, 'The Law of Nature sufficiently propagated to Heathens' (1741), in *Theological Dissertations*, pp. 213–14.

16 John Maclaurin, *An Essay on Christian Piety* (1755), in *The Works of the Rev. John Maclaurin*, ed. W. H. Goold (Edinburgh, 1860), ii, p. 64.

17 John Witherspoon, *A Serious Enquiry into the Nature and Effects of the Stage. Being an Attempt to show, That contributing to the Support of a Public Theatre, is inconsistent with the Character of a Christian* (Glasgow, 1757), p. 64, note.

18 E.g., John Dun, *Sermons.* (Kilmarnock, 1790), ii, pp. 10–11, 38–9.

political knowledge'.[19] Such a position was either explicit or implicit in the writings of most Popular authors.[20]

Though some Scottish evangelicals at least appealed to natural religion to support the veracity and reasonableness of revelation,[21] there is no evidence that they were directly influenced to do so by the Moderates. It would not seem to be true, either, that natural religion preoccupied Popular writers. By the same token, Popular thinkers had little to say about revelation.[22] Perhaps the most that can be said is that, like the Moderates, they did not believe that natural religion could provide a saving knowledge of God. There could be little doubt as to the essential truths which natural religion taught: God has provided men, in the principles of natural religion, with adequate proof of his existence, of his perfections, and of the immortality of the soul, so that if they refuse to believe them, as John Erskine put it, they have only themselves to blame when 'they expose themselves to ruin'.[23] Beyond this baseline, the Popular party displayed a diversity of response to the question of the origins of religious knowledge.

Ideas about the attributes of God, which arise to some extent from conclusions about the nature of religious knowledge, are of fundamental importance in determining the shape of anyone's theology, especially those aspects relating to the Fall of Man and its consequences, and the person and work of Christ. The latter doctrine, of course, is central to Christianity. Throughout the century, diversity of opinion also appeared in Popular writings on the attributes of God. Three interpretations are to be found, though individual writers frequently incorporated more than one. The first had an intellectual, as contrasted to a theological or devotional, emphasis in which analysis of the divine attributes originated in a discussion of God as Creator with its implications for human happiness, and for God's involvement in the world. The second was rooted in perceptions of God as benevolent and loving, giving a devotional emphasis centred around the divine perfections. The third approach had a theological emphasis, which stressed God's justice, holiness and hatred of sin as well as his love. The devotional element incorporated in this third was more Christocentric than in the second. Both the second and the third, however, led to a discussion of the Atonement.

As in other ways, the ideas of Principal William Wishart, who was unsuccessfully prosecuted for alleged heresy or heterodoxy in 1738,

---

[19] Robert Dick, *The Simplicity and Popularity of the Divine Revelations, and their Suitableness to the Circumstances of Mankind* (Edinburgh, 1758), pp. 9–10, 14–15.

[20] See, e.g., Webster, *Supernatural Revelation*, pp. iv, 204.

[21] See, e.g., Daniel Macqueen, *Letters on Mr. Hume's History of Great Britain* (Edinburgh, 1756).

[22] Dick, *Simplicity and Popularity of the Divine Revelations*, p. 247; cf. p. 249.

[23] Erskine, 'Law of Nature sufficiently propagated to Heathens', p. 213; see also pp. 206, 214, 217.

percolated to many otherwise orthodox quarters of the Popular party. He was apparently the first to introduce to the Popular mind in the period the stress on the character of God as 'the supreme Mind, the Head and Father of the Rational System', or as the 'Universal Governor'.[24] This terminology was taken up first by Daniel Macqueen in his *Letters on Mr. Hume's History of Great Britain* in 1756, but by way of qualification: thoughts of God as 'the great legislator and governor of the world' may create fear in the minds of the ungodly; it is the sentiments of Christian faith and of genuine repentance which lead to an understanding of mercy and acceptance in Christ.[25] This in turn leads to seeing acceptance in Christ as the way to both present and everlasting peace. This truth must be assented to by all who believe in God 'as the supreme ruler of the intellectual world', who bears relations to us as 'creator, preserver, benefactor, our redeemer, lawgiver and judge'. God is self-existent, the almighty maker of heaven and earth, and his works proclaim his power, intelligence and goodness; he is 'glorious in holiness, justice and truth', the 'parent of nature', all-powerful; his providence is universal, his goodness diffusive.[26] We are absolutely dependent on God for supplying all our needs, for his protection and guidance. The doctrine of divine assistance is rational and derives from the goodness of God. It is shown at its clearest in the Christian scheme with its promises of abundant grace. God is ever-present with us and all this is 'perfectly agreeable to the dictates of our purest reason'.[27]

The second emphasis in the analysis of the attributes of God once again appears in the works of William Wishart. The truth that the end of the Christian institution is Love, he maintained, gives us key insights into the nature and character of God. Love animates 'the whole conduct of the Governor of the world', who is 'perfect Goodness and Love reigning above'. It shows us 'the pure Goodness and disinterested Benevolence of the Deity'.[28] Wishart went on to link divine love, infinite goodness, and infinite wisdom and power with man's recovery to purity and happiness through the Father's sending his Son and '*giving Him to be a propitiation for our Sins*'. This shows the divine love and goodness in its greatest lustre and glory.[29] God is a Being, he put it elsewhere, 'in whom perfect and unalterable goodness is joined with almighty Power and unbounded Wisdom, Eternity and Omnipresence; who is the fair and unspotted Original and Pattern of Goodness; and the foundation of all good'. The highest love of God is the exercise of the principle of the

---

24 William Wishart, *Charity the End of the Commandment: or, Universal Love the Design of Christianity. A Sermon* (London, 1731), pp. 7, 14; Wishart, *Difference betwixt Moral Good and Evil*, p. 18.

25 Macqueen, *Letters on Mr. Hume's History of Great Britain*, pp. 311–12.

26 Ibid., p. 312.

27 Ibid., p. 313.

28 Wishart, *Charity the End of the Commandment*, pp. 14–15.

29 Ibid., p. 20. See also, Wishart, 'Indispensible Necessity of a Holy and Good Life', pp. 16–18.

'Love of Goodness'. God's love of goodness is such that the wicked should live in fear of the displeasure of Heaven.[30] The other attributes of God, which attracted the attention of many Popular writers, remained of secondary importance for Wishart.

The second interpretation of the attributes of God was very much a minority viewpoint in Popular thought, and did not reappear until towards the end of the century. More representative of the views of the rank and file of the party, and less selective in their emphasis on the divine attributes, was a range of Popular writers who propounded the third approach with its theological emphasis. In the mid-century, these included Alexander Webster, Robert Dick, John Witherspoon and others. Their analysis emerged in response to the concentration on the attribute of divine love. Webster, who was the minister of Edinburgh Tolbooth Church from 1737 to 1784 and one of the main leaders of the Popular party in the mid-eighteenth century, was also an eminent statistician who compiled the 1765 *Census of the Population of Scotland* and performed the actuarial calculations for the Ministers' Widows and Orphans Fund set up in 1742. He stressed the need to view the attributes of God in relation to each other and not in isolation. God is just as well as merciful. His goodness, explicitly, is not automatically to be taken as evidence of 'Pardoning-Mercy' to all:

> we have already shown the Absurdity of pretending, that God will act in this or that Manner, because one or other of his Perfections render it naturally possible, as in the present Instance, his Power and his Knowledge, the whole of his Attributes must be taken into Account, and their mutual Relations considered, otherwise, as before hinted, it would be no difficult Matter to prove, from the Nature of infinite Power and infinite Goodness, that Sin, and its fatal Consequences, Pain, Misery, and Distress, are Things which never had any Existence, nor can possibly happen.[31]

In general, however, the origins of this third strand of analysis of the attributes of God are less clear. In his *Letters* on Hume's *History*, Macqueen described the devout character as including in it awareness of God's power, wisdom, and goodness, of his government and supreme

[30] Wishart, *Difference betwixt Moral Good and Evil*, pp. 13–14, 23.

[31] Webster, *Supernatural Revelation*, pp. 9–10, 16–17; David Blair, *The Fear that's due unto God and the King, consider'd and recommended; in two Sermons preached at Brechin, April 11th, 1744* (Edinburgh, 1744), p. 9; John Witherspoon, *The Trial of Religious Truth by its Moral Influence. A Sermon, preached at the opening of the Synod of Glasgow and Air* [sic], *October 9th, 1759* (Glasgow, 1759), p. 14; [James Paton], *An Attempt to Show that the Knowledge of God, has, in all ages, been derived from Revelation or Tradition, not from Nature* (Glasgow, 1773) p. 114; John Love, *The Majesty of the King of Kings: A Sermon, preached on the subject of the Revolution, Nov. 9, 1788* (n.p., n.d.), pp. 3, 14; John Love, *The Radical Cause of National Calamity. A Sermon, Preached at the Scotch Church, Crown Court, Russell St., Covent Garden, October 27, 1794* (n.p., n.d.), pp. 24–5; John Love, *Memorials of the Rev. John Love* (Glasgow, 1857), i, p. 110.

authority, of our entire dependence on him, of his inspection of our conduct, and of his innumerable benefits and mercy towards us. He is 'the most high God in all his glory and grace', and he is 'our creator, benefactor, our redeemer, lawgiver and judge'.[32] But Macqueen, whose main drift of thought places him in the first group of thinkers, did not see fit to explain the derivation of these ideas and did not go beyond them. Robert Dick of the Old Kirk of Edinburgh, on the other hand, approached the subject from the necessity of Christ's death being seen as a sacrifice. Divine justice was central to the Atonement. God is offended by sin but he is 'placable', and the mediation of Christ conduces to that end. The ultimate reasons why this is so are not revealed in God's Word and no discovery of them can be expected, nor should it be sought.[33]

The three explanations of the attributes of God discernible in the writings of the Popular party had potential seeds of theological controversy which did not develop. Those who defined the attributes of God essentially in terms of a Creator who was the head of a rational system were prone to use arguments from natural religion to elucidate their perceptions. They stressed the rationality of their concept of God, but they generally had little to say about sin, the need for repentance, or about the Atonement. The second group, who tended to see the essential characteristics of God as love and goodness, usually described him in terms of his role as Creator in preserving and governing his world. Within this group, those who arrived from Scripture at the conclusion that love and goodness were the essential qualities of God should be distinguished from the few in number who, after the manner of Wishart, arrived at that conclusion through their perceptions of the prevalence of benevolence in man, which had the profound theological consequence of leading them to see the Atonement as proceeding from the love and goodness of God. It is only the third approach which is usually regarded as being typical of the Popular party as a whole. It defined the attributes of God in terms of his power, wisdom, holiness, and especially his justice. The starting-point for these writers was usually the Atonement: if God so hated sin that he was prepared to cause his Son to suffer his divine wrath to remove its consequences, then it followed that justice was crucial to the character of God. He was fundamentally holy. His love was to be seen rather as mercy than as benevolence. This emphasis produced a devotional emphasis centred on Christ as enduring divine wrath for men. It also merged with a much older devotional tradition exemplified in John Maclaurin's famous sermon, *Glorying in the Cross of Christ*.[34] Overall, then, there is clear evidence that there were significant

---

[32] Macqueen, *Letters on Mr. Hume's History of Great Britain*, pp. 298, 313. See above, pp. 18, 39; and also John Snodgrass, *Prospects of Providence respecting the Conversion of the World to Christ* (Paisley, 1796), p. 4, where he stresses the 'absolute sovereignty' of God.

[33] Dick, *Simplicity and Popularity of the Divine Revelations*, pp. 28–9.

[34] John Maclaurin, *Glorying in the Cross of Christ*, in *Works*, i, pp. 61–102.

differences within the early Popular party in the way its members perceived the God they served. These perceptions varied from positions of Calvinist orthodoxy to those which shared the presuppositions of contemporary Moderate thought, especially as they were purveyed by Wishart who, through his part in the education of divinity students, played a key role in the spread of Enlightenment-influenced theological ideas amongst the ministry of the Church of Scotland.

The variety, indeed the confusion, in the theology of members of the Popular party continued to be evident in their writings on the nature of man. Whereas three fairly coherent and consistent trends can be distinguished in their thought on the attributes of God, no such clarity emerged when the nature of man was considered. The divergence of ideas came from differing interpretations about the extent of the consequences of the Fall. Were the human conscience and affections totally depraved and therefore unreliable and to be suspected? Was Reason to be relied upon as valid or was it, too, affected by the Fall? Could man be disposed to benevolence or not? The proliferation of such questions would appear to have been the Popular party's response to the secular intellectual climate at the time.

In general, the Popular position was probably the result of belief in the validity of conscience as a testimony to truth, to good and evil, and, in some cases, to the existence of God and to the future punishment of sin; but there was also a prevalent doubt about the extent of the value or reliability of conscience. On this latter question there was no real consensus. Furthermore, members of the Popular party, like all mainstream Christians of the time, clearly saw themselves as under pressure from those who sought to deny the rationality of the Christian religion. Partly this was the result of acceptance of the identification of natural religion with Reason. More importantly, it arose from an impression that Christianity was under attack by those who espoused Enlightenment ideas about the primacy of Reason in relation to knowledge and truth. As such, their position on the nature of man was perhaps one of the more fundamental responses made to the Enlightenment by members of the Popular party.

Once again, William Wishart gives a convenient starting-point. He was the representative of a small group of theologians who took a sanguine view of the impact of the Fall on human nature. As a result of the goodness of God, there was, he maintained,

> such a disposition of Benevolence, or social affection in Human
> Nature independent of all deliberate views of self-interest; and
> exerting itself oft-times without any other prospect of advantage,
> but the pleasure arising from the view of happiness around us, and

seeing others well ... every plain man is sensible of such a benevolent principle in himself.[35]

This principle rises to its greatest heights when it is exercised towards 'a
Being of unalterable Goodness, the Head and Father of the rational
creation'. Our other affections must be brought into subjection to this
love of goodness, and 'those unnatural passions, and excesses of our self-
affections, that are contrary to it, must be uprooted'.[36] He went on to
argue elsewhere that 'doing good to others' is a natural inclination of
our hearts. Self-love and benevolence are not necessarily inconsistent or
in competition.[37] Since man is able to pursue and embody benevolence,
it follows that he must be able to appraise the moral worth of his actions.
This is the function of conscience, which informs us of the difference
between beauty and deformity, good and evil, and of what and what not
to do. When we act contrary to the dictates of universal benevolence, or
of 'Love and resignation to the Deity', we act 'contrary to our own Sense
of things, and render ourselves deform'd and odious to ourselves'.[38]

Wishart went on, however, to a more narrowly theological matter
when he attempted to define the relationship between benevolence and
the passions. Initially he had maintained that 'through the prevalency of
men's selfish passions and factious humours, rebelling against Love and
against the Light, it [benevolence] has not the happy effect of promoting
Love as universally as might be expected from the genuine tendency of
it ...'[39] Here, though, he faced a problem: if, as he admitted, 'no natural
passion was formed in vain, they are all to be gratified, as far as they can
consistently', how, then, can we have the greatest satisfaction possible in
life, which is the object of God's benevolence, when not all human
affections are compatible with that benevolence? His answer was that
since passion and appetite are in themselves blind guides, they will often
be deceived and lead to the growth of unnatural passions.[40]

The rejection of Wishart's analysis of human nature emerged initially
in writings on the passions. John Witherspoon, arguing against the
theatre, maintained that though passions were not necessarily evil in
themselves, the Fall of Man had so perverted them that they distracted
from the prime duty of glorifying God. Furthermore, conscience was
capable of being deceived by the passions, and therefore the Christian
should try to moderate their influence.[41] This analysis of the
consequences of the Fall, however, was not extended with the same

---

[35] Wishart, *Charity the End of the Commandment*, p. 7.
[36] Ibid., pp. 10–11.
[37] Wishart, *Difference betwixt Moral Good and Evil*, p. 11; Wishart, 'Indispensible Necessity of a Holy and Good Life', pp. 16–17.
[38] Wishart, *Difference betwixt Moral Good and Evil*, pp. 14–15.
[39] Wishart, *Charity the End of the Commandment*, pp. 28–9.
[40] Ibid., pp. 16–22.
[41] Witherspoon, *Serious Enquiry into the Nature and Effects of the Stage*, pp. 18–19, 43. See also pp. 14–16.

degree of unanimity to the status of the conscience or of reason. Popular writers were not prepared to dismiss the contribution of conscience as a witness to truth or to right and wrong, but they varied on the question of its reliability. Some were prepared to assert that conscience tells us that we have sinned, or that the power of conscience remains in fallen man to remind him of sin and future judgement.[42] Most Popular authors, however, were not prepared to go as far, and maintained that conscience was capable of being deceived, or that the enticements of a particular pleasure could overcome conscience. The majority lay somewhere between the extremes. Daniel Macqueen, for example, accepted that the reflections of conscience could be turned aside, and its judgement and condemnation evaded or suppressed, but nevertheless argued that its operation directed our thoughts to God and to our future, and gave proof of the subjection of man to God's righteous government.[43] While accepting that conscience was a flawed instrument as a result of the Fall, Popular thought thus retained a belief in its potential efficacy as a testimony to such truths of Christianity as the existence of God, the nature of sin, and the need for forgiveness. Opinion diverged more significantly on its reliability, depending on the assessment of the consequences of the Fall of Man.

Popular analysis of the nature and role of reason faced the same dilemma. In this case, Wishart was almost a solitary figure when he argued that conscience was a more reliable guide than reason in our progress to 'Love and resignation to the Deity'.[44] Witherspoon, however, followed Wishart part of the way when he contrasted the 'often immediate and clear' dictates of conscience with the 'long and involved' deductions of Reason needed to understand a doctrine, though he still regarded Reason as 'the best guide and director of human life'.[45] Yet, in spite of all these doubts, Popular thought was concerned to stress the rationality of the Christian religion. This preoccupation came to the fore in Macqueen's response to Hume's *History of Great Britain*. Protestantism, he argued in contradiction to Hume, was 'rationally grounded', and was unafraid of free enquiry, which was in accordance with 'the principles of

---

[42] John Gillies, *An Exhortation to the Inhabitants of the South Parish of Glasgow, and the Hearers in the College Church* (Glasgow, 1750–1), p. 36; David Savile, *Dissertations on the Existence, Attributes, Providence, and Moral Government of God: and on the Duty, Character, Security, and Final Happiness of His Righteous Subjects* (Edinburgh, 1807), p. 171.

[43] Macqueen, *Letters on Mr. Hume's History of Great Britain*, p. 309. See also Witherspoon, *Serious Enquiry into the Nature and Effects of the Stage*, p. 43; Robert Walker, *Sermons on Practical Subjects* (London, 1796), iv, p. 356. It is interesting to note that Walker elsewhere drew a distinction between the regenerate and unregenerate conscience which does not seem to have been made by any other Popular writer. In the true Christian, he says, 'Conscience, long dethroned by imperious passions, hath resumed his authority; and all the faculties of his mind purified and exalted, unite in the pursuit of spiritual enjoyments': ibid., iii, pp. 359–60.

[44] Wishart, *Difference betwixt Moral Good and Evil*, pp. 14–15.

[45] John Witherspoon, *The Works of John Witherspoon, D.D.* (Edinburgh, 1804–5), i, p. 279.

the clearest reason'.[46] Reason and religion combined to produce assent to religious truth.[47] Regard to God was 'perfectly agreeable to the dictates of our purest reason'. True piety, that is the worship of God with mind and heart, was strictly rational, and as such it denied the validity of the work of Hume.[48]

III

Consideration of the Fall of Man leads naturally to the problems of sin and salvation. To a large extent, beliefs about the doctrine of Christ are the touchstone for the placing of any theologian in the theological spectrum. Such was the case in the latter half of the eighteenth century,[49] when views on the Atonement both influence and are influenced by views on the nature of sin. It is almost customary to think members of the eighteenth-century Popular party were preoccupied with the guilt and punishment of sin, and Burns's 'Holy Fair' is the prototype for many interpretations. Yet, if this was true of the sermons preached in the parish kirks of the country (which is almost impossible to determine), it was certainly not true of the published works of members of the party. Perhaps because it was taken as self-evident, they give little indication that the Westminster Confession's definition of sin was thought to be in need of elaboration or indeed of comment.

Sin, of course, came with the Fall and arose more immediately from the corruption of the heart.[50] Christians, too, were subject to it for, as Witherspoon put it, 'there are latent remaining dispositions to sinning in every heart that is but imperfectly sanctified'.[51] Generally speaking, however, sin tended to be interpreted in one of three ways. First, though only occasionally, discussion did not go further than the Westminster standards' definition. Either sin was taken to be the breaking of the Ten Commandments, or specific types of sin were examined. John Gillies of Glasgow Blackfriars', for example, gave a list of varieties of sin, each one of which he defined in terms of a broken commandment.[52] Second and more common was reflection on the nature of the evil of sin, though in somewhat generalised terms. It was grieving, provoking, and vexing to God, and it defiled and polluted the soul;[53] it led to feelings of guilt

---

[46] Macqueen, *Letters on Mr. Hume's History of Great Britain*, pp. 55, 67.
[47] Ibid., p. 312; Webster, *Supernatural Revelation*, p. 18; John Erskine, *Prayer for those in Civil and Military Offices recommended, from a view of the influence of Providence on their characters, conduct, and success. A Sermon. Preached before the Election of the Magistrates of Edinburgh, Oct. 5 1779* (London, 1779), p. 28.
[48] Macqueen, *Letters on Mr. Hume's History of Great Britain*, pp. 324–7.
[49] Clark, 'Moderatism and the Moderate Party', pp. 236, 294–5.
[50] John Maclaurin, *On Prejudices against the Gospel*, in *Works*, ii, p. 1.
[51] Witherspoon, *Serious Enquiry into the Nature and Effects of the Stage*, p. 45.
[52] Gillies, *Exhortation*, p. 38; J. Somerville, *Practical Sermons* (Edinburgh, 1827), p. 290; Love, *Memorials*, i, p. 370.
[53] Gillies, *Exhortation*, pp. 37–8.

which involved dejection and anguish of mind and involvement in folly and vice; it was hateful and the object of God's highest displeasure.[54] The third interpretation at this stage appeared only in the writings of John Gillies of Glasgow: we should be exceedingly sorrowful when we considered how our sin led to the suffering of Christ on the cross.[55] This approach to the nature of sin arose in the course of the consideration of the nature of the Atonement and it was to become significant later on in the century. The conclusions which can be drawn from writings on sin, however, are limited and tentative through lack of evidence.

The varied nature of Popular theological thought is also to be seen in writings on the nature of the Atonement. A general comment, however, is called for first of all. The rigour of thought on the subject displayed by Popular ministers should not be overstressed. Throughout the century, there was often a looseness in terminology which raises the question of how aware some writers were of the theological minefield in which they were operating. For example, Christ's atoning work was described as a 'sacrifice',[56] as 'propitiation',[57] and as 'mediation'[58] by a range of writers comprehending the spectrum of Popular theological thought. The variety continues with 'expiation',[59] 'reconciliation',[60] 'intercession',[61] 'substitution',[62] and 'redemption'.[63] Two things are clear: that there was considerable flexibility in the use of the classic terms to discuss the Atonement, which seemed to transcend apparent differences of sympathy in theological approach; and that the terms most commonly used by the Popular party to describe the work of Christ were 'sacrifice' and 'propitiation'. This usage is not without theological significance.

The main preoccupations of Popular theological writers in the period, however, concerned the origin of the Atonement, its essential nature,

---

54 Macqueen, *Letters on Mr. Hume's History of Great Britain of Great Britain*, p. 309.

55 Gillies, *Exhortation*, p. 38.

56 Dick, *Simplicity and Popularity of the Divine Revelations*, p. 27; Maclaurin *On Prejudices against the Gospel*, in *Works*, ii, p. 99; Russel, *Nature of the Gospel Delineated*, p. 28; John Snodgrass, *The Leading Doctrines of the Gospel Stated and Defended* (1794), in J. Brown (ed.), *Theological Tracts, Selected and Original* (Edinburgh, 1854), iii, p. 304; Walker, *Sermons on Practical Subjects*, i, p. 142; ii, p.173; John Muckersy, 'The Excellence of the Gospel', Sermon XII in R. Gillan (ed.), *The Scottish Pulpit: A Collection of Sermons by Eminent Clergymen of the Church of Scotland* (Edinburgh, 1823), p. 294.

57 Wishart, *Charity the End of the Commandment*, p. 20; Maclaurin, *On Prejudices against the Gospel*, in *Works*, ii, p. 80; Russel, *Nature of the Gospel Delineated*, pp. 35, 45; Savile, *Dissertations*, p. 76; Somerville, *Practical Sermons*, pp. 426–8.

58 Gillies, *Exhortation*, p. 35; Walker, *Sermons on Practical Subjects*, i, p. 142; Somerville, *Practical Sermons*, pp. 147–8, 151, 155–8, 160–1.

59 Russel, *Nature of the Gospel Delineated*, p. 14.

60 Macqueen, *Letters on Mr. Hume's History of Great Britain*, p. 311; Walker, *Sermons on Practical Subjects*, ii, p. 141; John Love, *Benevolence inspired and exalted by the Presence of Jesus Christ. A Sermon* (London, 1794), p. 13.

61 Maclaurin, *On Prejudices against the Gospel*, in *Works*, ii, pp. 98–9.

62 Ibid., p. 21; Russel, *Nature of the Gospel Delineated*, p. 28.

63 Dun, *Sermons*, i, p. 25.

and its consequences for piety. It is in terms of these three issues that light can be thrown on the areas of tension in Popular theology in the field.

All writers saw the origin of the Atonement as embodied in the attributes of God which engendered his response to the existence of sin. As William Wishart wrote in a sermon in 1731:

> In the discovery of this great mystery of Divine Love; we behold Infinite Goodness employing Infinite Wisdom and Infinite Power in a way of Compassion to wretched men, and for bringing about their recovery to purity and happiness: we behold the Father sending his only-begotten Son to save us; and *giving him to be the propitiation for our Sins*: we behold the Son of God veiling his Glory, and appearing in the World *in the likeness of sinful flesh, and, being found in fashion as a man, humbling himself to death, even the death of the Cross*, for our Salvation and Happiness. In this glorious Work the Divine Love and Goodness shines forth in its greatest lustre and glory: and the other Perfections of the Divine nature are exhibited to us, as acting in concurrence, for promoting the designs of the most wonderful Love and tender Mercy.[64]

John Maclaurin wrote in almost identical terms in his *Essay on Christian Piety* concerning the glory of redemption displaying, 'with peculiar lustre', God's justice, power, and wisdom, but especially his mercy and love.[65] He underlined this point most effectively of all when, in contradistinction to the mainstream of Moderate authors, he argued that Christ's intercession was not the cause of God's love or goodwill to sinners, but rather the effect of it. Christ's intercession and sacrifice were intermediate and subordinate causes by which the love of God produces its effects on transgressors. Both Christ's sacrifice and his intercession are manifestations of God's perfections.[66]

Of much greater significance than perceptions of the Atonement as originating in and embodying the love of God towards sinners, however, was that strand of Popular thought which, following the line enunciated in its analysis of the divine attributes, interpreted the essence of the Atonement as the satisfaction of divine justice. John Maclaurin, for example, asserted: 'By the propitiation of Christ's blood God declares his righteousness in the remission of sins, so that he may be just, and the justifier of the sinner who believeth in Jesus.'[67] Or, as John Gillies put it slightly earlier, Christ 'satisfied Justice and obeyed the Law'.[68] This was a strand of thought that was to be developed subsequently.[69]

[64] Wishart, *Charity the End of the Commandment*, p. 20.
[65] Maclaurin, *Essay on Christian Piety*, in *Works*, ii, p. 80.
[66] Ibid., p. 99; Russel, *Nature of the Gospel Delineated*, p. 28.
[67] Maclaurin, *Essay on Christian Piety*, in *Works*, ii, pp. 80–1.
[68] Gillies, *Exhortation*, p. 39.
[69] See below, pp. 176–9, 184–5.

Consideration of the nature of the Atonement raises the question of the nature of faith. Surprisingly, relatively few Popular writers had much to say on the subject, though there was a degree of uniformity in what they did say, which continued throughout the rest of the century. Only John Willison, John Gillies, John Maclaurin, and John Erskine made more than a passing reference to it in the mid-century years. Conversion to Christ was seen essentially as repentance and belief in the redemptive office of Christ; faith was seen as knowledge of the nature of God which led to repentance, and belief in the gospel which in turn resulted in surrender to God and union with him. Such concepts, however, were rarely developed.

From an evangelical viewpoint, it can be argued that the starting-point for any discussion of the nature of faith is an examination of the process of conversion, or even, prior to that, the work of conviction of sin, but there is surprisingly little to be found in the works of members of the Popular party on conversion as such, and even less on the process of conviction. John Gillies of Glasgow provided a rare attempt at a systematic analysis of the steps to conviction, and in doing so he followed the five steps given in Thomas Boston's *Human Nature in its Fourfold State*: the Lord's blow of conviction of sin leads to the sinner's refraining from gross sins and fleeing to the performance of neglected duties; this is followed by another blow which shows the soul the pollution of its duties and its inward vileness of heart which leads in turn to endeavours to purify the heart and watch over its thoughts; the failure of this attempt leads to the borrowing of Christ's righteousness to make up the defects of its own; the failure of this endeavour is succeeded by belief, but with a non-scriptural belief of the sinner's own making; and finally, God cuts off the sinner from any reliance on his own works and gives a faith of his own working which ingrafts the sinner into Christ.[70] This detailed analysis of conviction of sin seems to have found no imitator, and, instead, Popular discussion of the process of conviction concentrated on the essential sense of guilt in much the same way as it concentrated on discussion of the nature of sin. Only Gillies, too, had much to say about the process of repentance for sin.[71]

Greater attention in the process of conversion was devoted to belief in Christ as the means of salvation. 'Belief' in the process of conversion was to be contrasted with 'knowledge' or 'understanding' in the exercise of faith. John Willison of Dundee, one of the most devotionally orientated of the Popular leadership, for example, demonstrated clearly the powerful influence of the intellectual description of faith. He believed that his faith could be defended on rational grounds. He was satisfied 'of the necessity and excellency of the gospel-revelation, and of its divine original'. His reasoning, based mainly on the inadequacy of natural

[70] Gillies, *Exhortation*, pp. 196–7.
[71] Ibid., p. 35.

religion, was as follows. Natural reason, though corrupted, tells man that there is a God and that he ought to be believed and obeyed; the Christian religion confirms and perfects natural religion since it corresponds with the dictates of natural reason and religion, and supplies their defects. Natural reason, while it enjoins a just and virtuous life, and the worship and glorification of God, leaves man ignorant of how these things should be done, whereas the Christian religion informs us how to worship and serve God and enforces the purpose of natural religion, namely, the abandoning of sin and vice, and the practice of virtue and piety. Reliance on reason alone leads to vagueness in divine things, to unworthy notions of God and even to gross idolatry and perverse practices. Natural religion, furthermore, can give no satisfactory account of the creation of the world, the original state of man, or of his fall into guilt and impurity, nor can it account for the conduct of divine providence in the government of the world: Christian revelation can account for all. Natural religion, based solely on reason, cannot ease the conscience of a convicted sinner, nor assure us that there is forgiveness with God. Natural religion gives no certainty of the immortality of the soul and of a future life. Biblical revelation supplies the defects of natural religion by setting forth Christ as the mediator who satisfies God's offended justice, removes the guilt and power of sin, and brings sinners into the favour of and communion with God. The miracles testify to Christ's heavenly kingdom. Historically, the success of the gospel leads to the conclusion that it was brought about by God himself, the author of the Christian religion. All these things, being certain facts, says Willison, clearly demonstrate not just the truth of Christianity, but the unreasonableness of infidelity. And, lastly, there is the inward evidence and 'experimental demonstration of the truth and excellency of the gospel-revelation' from the effects of it in the souls of the thousands who have been touched by the Holy Spirit.[72] It is important to note that, even for Willison, the 'experimental demonstration' of the truth of the gospel does not come from any inward experience on the part of the individual, but from the united testimony of Christians to the operation of the Holy Spirit.

Possibly the only significant place given to a 'non-rational' factor in the conception of the nature of faith most commonly found in the late eighteenth-century Popular party was the ultimate dependence of the sinner and the believer on the operations of the Spirit of God.[73] The importance of this point should not be overlooked. Stress on the role of the Holy Spirit as a complement to stress on faith as knowledge of, and

---

[72] John Willison, *An Example of Plain Catechising* (Edinburgh, 1731), in *The Practical Works of the Rev. John Willison*, ed. W. M. Hetherington (Glasgow, 1844), pp. 594–8.

[73] See also, e.g., Russel, *Nature of the Gospel Delineated*, p. 73; Snodgrass, *Leading Doctrines of the Gospel*, pp. 304, 317; Maclaurin, *Essay on Christian Piety*, in *Works*, ii, pp. 52–3, 67–8, 72–3, 82; and Walker, *Sermons on Practical Subjects*, ii, p. 74.

belief in, the mediation of the Son of God provided the balanced portrayal of the nature of the Christian faith which was fundamental to the concerns of most members of the party.

The main features of Popular thought on the nature of faith, then, were general agreement that faith was concerned with the nature of the Christian's relationship with God, and that it was a matter of knowledge of or belief in God and the mediatorial role of Christ. There is little indication that many members of the party defined it in devotional or experiential terms. Although on the whole the process aroused relatively little interest, there was some disagreement about how faith was attained and especially about the nature of conviction of sin. For most writers, however, the crucial thing was repentance for sin. There was no desire to dwell on the guiltiness of sin, or indeed on the nature of belief in Christ as Saviour. Such matters were marked by vagueness and imprecision and by the use of conventional terminology.

The middle of the century cannot be left, however, without referring to the contribution of John Maclaurin to the development of Popular thought on the nature of faith. Maclaurin, the minister of the Glasgow (Ramshorn) parish, was one of the ablest preachers and theologians of the eighteenth-century Church of Scotland, and his sermon *Glorying in the Cross of Christ* is widely regarded as the epitome of Scottish evangelical preaching of the century. The precise significance of his work on faith, however, is somewhat difficult to assess. In some ways he is best seen as a transitional figure connecting an earlier evangelical tradition, embodied in the works of Thomas Boston, and finding its latest exponent in John Willison, with what can be regarded as the main tradition of the late eighteenth century which was to see its classic formulation in the work of John Erskine.[74] There remains also the problem of assessing the influence of a thinker and preacher whose works were published posthumously and which in any case only antedated Erskine's by a decade or so.

The fullest account of the doctrine of faith in the writings of Maclaurin is in his *Essay on Christian Piety*. Faith in Christ, he says, includes acknowledgement of the meritorious cause of salvation, that is the blood of Christ; our applying to God's mercy through redemption; and the building of our hope and pleading upon it. It must include the acknowledgement of those things concerning Christ that are of greatest importance, namely, his role in redemption and his atonement for sin, and of the redemption as the highest manifestation of divine love and mercy. This last is an especial function of the operations of the Holy Spirit. Maclaurin summed up:

---

[74] For this line of analysis, I am indebted to a conversation with Dr David W. Bebbington of the University of Stirling. A fuller analysis of the issues has appeared in D. W. Bebbington, *Evangelicalism in Modern Britain: A History from the 1730s to the 1980s* (London, 1989).

Seeing therefore that due acknowledgement of redemption is a main design of the work of the Spirit of God, of the doctrine of his law, of all the instructions of his word, and of all the ordinances of his worship; it is evident that such an acknowledgement not only is included in that faith in Christ which the gospel requires but even that it is the very main and principal thing included in it.[75]

Faith, he continued, is the means of securing privileges such as access to God in worship, and fullness of peace and joy in God. It has for its object that redemption in Christ's blood which is the meritorious cause of the privileges. The doctrine of redemption explains God's bestowing all these blessings on us, and his acceptance of all our sincere services, for Christ's sake. Acknowledgement of the redemption, therefore, may be considered as the life and soul of practical Christianity.[76]

He proceeded to stress that the chief end of faith in Christ is the glory of God. The end of belief in the truths of natural religion is the honour of God's perfections as displayed in the works of creation and providence; in a like manner, the end of knowing and believing the gospel is the honour of God's perfections in the works of redemption and salvation.[77] It is a further 'chief end' of faith, that by it we are justified before God, and given a *right* to eternal life and to all the blessings of the covenant of grace. The influence of faith in Christ on our justification does not reduce the necessity of repentance since it includes as well as a sincere sorrow for sin, a returning from sin to God and universal holiness. These things, argued Maclaurin, are inseparable from true faith and of equal necessity with it, although not of the same influence on our interest in Christ's mediation. Acknowledgement of that mediation is the 'immediate effectual means' of salvation.[78]

A further 'principal end' of faith is sanctification or universal holiness. True holiness, held Maclaurin, is the end of our redemption by the Son of God. It is the end of faith in Christ not only to direct us in seeking all the parts of salvation in prayer and other duties of worship, but also to direct us in all other endeavours in the work of our salvation, and especially of our sanctification. By faith, too, we are to seek assurance of our salvation.[79] This led Maclaurin to an examination of the role of the Holy Spirit in faith.

---

[75] Maclaurin, *Essay on Christian Piety*, in *Works*, ii, pp. 50–3.

[76] Ibid., pp. 53–5.

[77] Ibid., pp. 63–4; cf. Willison, *Example of Plain Catechising*, as discussed above, pp. 48–9; and John Erskine, *Dissertation on the Nature of Christian Faith*, in *Theological Dissertations*, pp. 182–3.

[78] Maclaurin, *Essay on Christian Piety*, in *Works*, ii, pp. 64–5. Erskine, however, seems to dispute the idea of faith giving the believer a 'right' to eternal life when he asserts that faith has 'no moral efficacy' in procuring pardon and acceptance: Erskine, *Nature of Christian Faith*, p. 141.

[79] Maclaurin, *Essay on Christian Piety*, in *Works*, ii, pp. 65–6.

Scriptural descriptions of the object of faith, and of the nature and ends of it, show that interest in Christ as Mediator is given by means of a free and gratuitous donation. The sanctifying grace of God's Spirit which is the 'efficient cause' of holiness, and faith itself which is 'a principal cause' of it, are both the fruits of Christ's redemption, and both are to be regarded as the gift of God. The gospel, in other words, promises salvation through sincere acceptance of Christ with the whole heart, and it also contains promises of God's Spirit to enable sinners to gain such acceptance.[80] Maclaurin held closely to Calvinist orthodoxy.

Acceptance of Christ with the whole heart in turn implies, first, 'sincere persuasion of the divine offers and promises' and dependence on them; and, secondly, a 'cordial esteem' of them. This last is sometimes, held Maclaurin, called acceptance of the offers of the gospel. Without believing and relying on the offers and promises of the gospel, its doctrines cannot give that relief and consolation needed by an awakened conscience, nor by a sinner sensible of sin and concerned about salvation.[81] This is, in effect, almost a psychological argument for the validity of a definition of faith in terms of knowledge and belief. Above all, however, it is important to all the attainments appertaining to faith in Christ, 'to have just apprehensions of the object of it', and of its end, namely, the glory of God's perfections. The end of our acknowledging redemption is our glorying of God's perfections manifested in it. This is the main feature of a life of faith in Christ, and as such is the main purpose of the work of the Holy Spirit.[82]

This line of thought brought Maclaurin to consider the means by which the heart is brought to accept the offer of salvation. It is, he suggested, the result of appreciation of the necessity, worth, and excellence of what is offered. The principal means by which this is produced is a 'just impression of the hatefulness and danger of sin'. But faith in Christ is a faith which is characterised by love, and this fixes men's hearts not just on deliverance from the punishment of sin, but on deliverance from sin itself. Faith produces not just desire for the favour of God as a means of happiness, but for the enjoyment of God himself, and our active glorifying of God, as the principal effects of God's favour, and as the most valuable objects of desire. The benefits of the covenant of grace are the principal objects of the desires central to the nature of holiness. The favour, image, and enjoyment of God are the object of the chief desires included in divine love; whereas deliverance from sin is the object of the chief desires belonging to the nature of repentance. All

---

[80] Ibid., pp. 66–8.
[81] Ibid., p. 70.
[82] Ibid., pp. 70–2, 81–2.

these desires meet with full satisfaction in the promises of the covenant of grace.[83]

It has been suggested that Popular thought on the nature of faith dwelt on repentance from sin and belief in Christ's redemptive office as being embodied in conversion, and on faith as involving knowledge of the nature of God which led to repentance from sin and belief in the gospel, which in turn led to union with God.[84] While John Maclaurin reflected some of these emphases, inasmuch as he depicted faith as involving acknowledgement of Christ's redemptive role as its main ingredient, stressed the dependence of man on the Holy Spirit as the 'efficient cause' of faith, and perceived its results to be the securing of access to God, the enjoyment of him, and conformity to his image, on the other hand his approach to the subject was much more analytical, and there are significant differences between his analysis and those offered by other Popular writers. First, while he made common cause with other Popular theologians in seeing faith as a matter of intellectual assent in so far as the words most commonly used by him in its connection were 'acknowledgement', 'persuasion', 'esteem', and 'appreciation', he differentiated between acknowledgement of the 'meritorious cause of salvation', which was Christ's sacrifice on the Cross, the acknowledgement of his redemptive role which he saw as the principal ingredient of faith, and acknowledgement of Christ's mediatorial role, which he described as the 'immediate effectual means' of faith. Secondly, while he defined human sanctification as being a chief end of faith, he gave much more prominence to the idea of the ultimate end of faith as being the glorification of the divine perfections. And, lastly, he appeared to see the whole question of the nature of faith more in terms of the classic doctrine of the covenant of grace than did any of the other Popular writers on the subject. The conclusion to which this would appear to lead is that while Maclaurin stood head and shoulders above other Popular theologians in the earlier years of the period, his influence was relatively small. As was suggested earlier, however, this is not altogether surprising, in view of the late appearance of his works in printed form.

A survey of Popular works which deal with the nature of faith leads to several conclusions. First, there was present within the party a number of ministers who were content to remain vague, imprecise, and generally uninterested in defining the nature of faith. They were content to write in terms of belief in Christ as being the means of salvation, of faith as being concerned with the Christian's relationship with God, and of faith as being knowledge of or belief in God and the mediatorial role of Christ.

[83] Ibid., pp. 73, 78. On the use of the terminology of covenant theology, see above, pp. 51–2; and below, pp. 191–2.

[84] See above, p. 48.

Secondly, this approach to the nature of faith came to be regarded as unsatisfactory by some elements within the party, not because they saw it as unscriptural or inconsistent with the doctrinal standards of the Church, but because it was perceived as opening the way to two defective tendencies. The first was its dissociation of the work of sanctification from the act of faith, which could lead to the Moderate treatment of sanctification as arising from the contemplation of the example of Christ, and more generally to a reduction in the levels of holiness and spirituality in the community. This response is clearest in the thought of John Maclaurin, but there is insufficient evidence to indicate that his devotional emphasis was adopted or shared by significant numbers of the party.

In the third place, the attempts of Maclaurin, Erskine, and the later writers who were influenced by them, to define more clearly the nature of faith, saw a preparedness to be influenced by contemporary secular thought. Maclaurin in particular was willing to use and to adapt Enlightenment perceptions concerning the human mind, and the nature of knowledge and of the will in explaining basically orthodox theological positions.

IV

The complexities of the theological scene are evident in the response of Popular thinkers to the problem of the nature of piety, or, to put it another way, in the answers they gave to the question of how to define godliness. To some extent, the complexities of the subject are revealed in the terms they used, often interchangeably, in connection with it: holiness, piety, godliness, devotion, and practical religion were all used without precise definition. Not only that, Popular theologians at opposite ends of the theological spectrum are often to be found sharing the same emphases.[85]

Popular thought about the nature of Christian piety or holiness followed three directions. Some regarded holiness as contained in those religious 'affections' or dispositions which manifest themselves in the leading of holy lives. The second group saw holiness lying in the balance between holy dispositions and pious actions. The third group stressed the essential nature of the example of Christ and the obligations on the Christian to follow it.

An admirable summary of those Popular writers in the first group, who found the essence of piety and devotion in the religious affections, and one of the earliest definitions of the devout character or of 'true piety', appeared in the course of a rebuttal of Bolingbroke's philosophy in Daniel Macqueen's *Letters on Mr. Hume's History of Great Britain*. 'The devout character', asserted Macqueen,

---

[85] Thomas Somerville, *Sermons* (Edinburgh, 1813), pp. 426–8; Dun, *Sermons*, i, p. 26.

includes in it such a sense of the power, goodness, and wisdom of God, of his government and supreme authority, of our entire dependence upon him, of his inspection of our conduct, of his numberless benefits and overflowing mercy, as effectually sways the soul to the fear and love of its creator and benefactor, to a willing subjection to his authority, to an ardent desire of his favour, and a full resignation to his disposal, mingled with humble trust, and with the animating prospects of a future state. This in general is true piety; and these are its natural effects. External worship and obedience flowing from such sentiments and dispositions – this is the service, the reasonable service which God requires.[86]

Furthermore, true piety essentially concerns the dispositions of the heart, and does not consist in 'abstract speculations' or even in 'a full assent of the understanding to the fundamental articles of religion', though it does suppose a knowledge of and belief in 'the prime articles of religion'. It includes 'every becoming affection of the soul' towards God in his grace and glory and in all the relationships he bears to us as creator, preserver, benefactor, redeemer, lawgiver, and judge. Piety, it is to be noted, is Christocentric in that in all pious acts we are to be encouraged by those doctrines which lead us to consider Jesus the Saviour as our mediator and intercessor. True piety, that is the worship of the heart and mind, consists of sentiments and dispositions which are strictly rational and excellent, and are founded in right apprehensions of ourselves and of God. External acts of worship 'are the proper expression of devout dispositions'. The spirit of diffusive benevolence is the true Christian spirit and will enter into our private and social worship, and, while we will thank God for his benefits towards us, we will also pray for the good of all mankind, for their greatest good in the advancement of God's kingdom on earth.[87] In summary, said Macqueen,

> true piety in all its parts, in all its acts, has a manifest tendency to strengthen every virtuous principle, to cherish every noble aim, to purify and elevate the soul, to encourage and to animate us in the path of our duty, and to lead us onward through every stage of life, to its concluding period, with serenity and hope.[88]

In other words, true piety is an act of worship. It does not of itself involve the performance of acts as such, though it contributes to the improvement and strengthening of the Christian's disposition to virtuous actions. It concerns the relationship of the Christian to God, and only indirectly the Christian's relationship to his fellow men.

---

[86] Macqueen, *Letters on Mr. Hume's History of Great Britain*, p. 298.
[87] Ibid., pp. 307, 312–13, 321, 325–6.
[88] Ibid., pp. 326–7.

While this definition of the nature of holiness found its most detailed expression in the works of Macqueen and later of John Russel of Stirling, it was the dominant line taken by members of the Popular party. An early manifestation was in the work of David Blair of Brechin, who is believed to have opened the first Sunday evening school in Scotland. He spoke of holiness as embodying the knowledge and love of the Lord, an abiding sense of the divine excellencies and perfections on the mind, and a dread of the divine majesty; and asserted that religious fear led to a holy life and a well-ordered conversation.[89] Later, John Bonar of Perth, who as well as publishing one of the main apologetical works against Hume and Kames was also the author of one of the major studies of ecclesiastical polity, limited himself to asserting the perpetual obligation of the moral law, the necessity of holiness (which he did not define) for salvation, and the inefficacy of a faith which did not purify the heart.[90]

The second line of interpretation of Christian piety or holiness may be illustrated by John Witherspoon's assertion in 1757: 'Now we glorify God by cultivating holy dispositions, and doing pious and useful actions.'[91] This blend of devotion and practice was the hallmark of the second group. For Witherspoon, an action was 'truly holy' when it was done from a sense not just of our obligation to God, but of the perfect excellence of God's law, with a renunciation of all pretence of merit on our part, with a dependence on divine assistance, and with the purpose of glorifying God. Witherspoon, however, defined pious actions in language similar to that used by Macqueen to define the devout character.[92]

This interpretation, in fact, had appeared as early as 1741, when Alexander Webster urged Christians to help to convert others by 'an *exemplary Walk and Conversation*, copying out in their Lives the *amiable Precepts* of our holy Religion, and the lovely Pattern of its *Divine Author*'. If all Christians gave non-believers such a tangible proof of the worth of Christianity, its influence would grow beyond belief. He urged private Christians to be useful in the conversion of others by 'warm Addresses' to the throne of grace on their behalf, by 'instruction and advice', and by good example.[93] Ten years later, he bemoaned not just the absence of the power and life of godliness in its professors, but of the sympathy, love, and mutual forbearance, which is 'the distinguishing badge' of Christ's disciples.[94] At around the same time Patrick Bannerman made

---

[89] Blair, *Fear that's due unto God and the King*, pp. 8–21.

[90] John Bonar, 'The Nature and Tendency of the Ecclesiastic Constitution in Scotland' (preached before the Synod of Perth and Stirling, 16 April 1760), in *The Scotch Preacher* (Edinburgh, 1775), i, p. 15.

[91] Witherspoon, *Serious Enquiry into the Nature and Effects of the Stage*, p. 14.

[92] See above, pp. 54–5.

[93] Webster, *Supernatural Revelation*, p. 44.

[94] Alexander Webster, *Zeal for the Civil and Religious Interests of Mankind recommended* (1754), Sermon XVI in *Scotch Preacher*, i, p. 347.

the same point and, more influentially, so too did John Erskine.[95] Throughout the period from 1740 to the end of the century, then, there existed a second approach to the nature of piety: the life of the Christian was to be marked by his relationship to God being demonstrated in the operation of the Christian virtues in practice.

The hallmark of the third stream of interpretation, however, was stress on the example of Christ, as embodied in Wishart's assertion that the Creator did not form us to be idle and merely contemplative, but to be active and useful, which virtues could only be fulfilled by following the example of Christ.[96] He later maintained that contemplation of the divine perfections led the devout mind 'to form his own mind and conduct more and more after the Model of that exalted pattern of moral excellence'.[97] In fact, Wishart was the only Popular author to write extensively in this period about the obligations of the Christian and he did so in terms which tended to be dangerously close to justification by works. Repentance, he argued, did not make a man immediately fit for heaven, but should mark the beginning of a course of good works by which the sinner would be trained up for a state of perfection. The Christian's state in this life was a state of trial and exercise, discipline and improvement, in which he could only advance towards perfect bliss, in so far as he improved in this present state. A disposition toward goodness and integrity belonged to a truly worthy and amiable character. The true happiness of rational creatures was to be found in such rational and virtuous enjoyments for which a sensual man had no desire. As far as the Christian was improved in true goodness and divine love, so far had he subdued the flesh to the spirit, and brought his inferior appetites into subjection to the nobler dispositions.[98]

In general, then, the Popular party would seem to have displayed a good measure of that tension between faith and works which could be regarded as having been a feature of the Christian Church since apostolic times. The dominant strand was one which stressed the primacy of a personal relationship with God, but there were also significant numbers of Popular authors who were concerned to emphasise the essential nature of the balance between personal faith and its demonstration in the performance of good works.[99]

---

[95] Patrick Bannerman, *A Sermon upon Reformation and Revolution Principles. Preached in the Church of Stirling, April 10, 1751: By Appointment of the Very Reverend Synod of Perth and Stirling* (Edinburgh, 1751), p. 33; Erskine, 'Qualifications necessary for Teachers of Christianity', pp. 13–22, 25–7.

[96] Wishart, 'Indispensible Necessity of a Holy and Good Life', pp. 16–17.

[97] Wishart, *Difference betwixt Moral Good and Evil*, p. 19.

[98] Wishart, 'Indispensible Necessity of a Holy and Good Life', pp. 17–18, 31.

[99] Clark, 'Moderatism and the Moderate Party', pp. 204, 370–1.

V

Analysis of the writings of members of the Popular party on the nature of faith and its manifestation in the lives of Christians leads naturally to analysis of their views on the reasons and remedies for the perceived rise of nominalism amongst the people of Scotland, and the decline of personal commitment to Christian principles. In the terminology of the time, such developments were combined under the general term of 'infidelity'. It is striking that during the whole of the century fewer than twenty works specifically directed against 'infidelity', can be identified as having been written by those who can be regarded as being members of the Popular 'leadership'.[100] But this apparent lack of concern, while initially surprising, is less so when Popular perceptions of the problem are examined more closely. It is also striking, yet again, that an analysis of the problem led to different alignments of members of the party.

Three approaches to the problem of the identification of the causes of infidelity may be distinguished, prior to examining each in more detail. First, there were some who believed that infidelity was not a fundamental danger to Christianity, since infidelity and atheism were ultimately irrational. The appropriate response was to emphasise this and to stress the rationality of the Christian faith. By the late 1750s, confidence in this analysis had been seriously eroded and, although there were manifestations of it as late as the early years of the nineteenth century, such a complacent response was felt by most Popular writers to be inadequate. Increasingly, that intellectual response came to be replaced by an essentially theological or even spiritual one. This second approach was that infidelity was the result of man's depravity arising from the Fall. It was to be fought by the encouragement of godliness and piety. The third approach had its origins in the second, and derived from an analysis of the reasons for the ineffectiveness of the Church's attempts to counter declining spirituality. The growth of infidelity was the result of the Church's lack of faithfulness in its preaching of the gospel and its failure to promote sound doctrine.

In the first place, then, a significant number of members of the Popular party believed that, while infidelity had to be guarded against, it was not a fundamental danger to Christianity. The justification for their complacency derived from a conviction of the ultimate irrationality of

---

[100] John Bonar, *Observations on the Character and Conduct of Judas Iscariot, in a Letter to the Rev. Mr. J. P.* (Edinburgh, 1750); [Bonar], *Analysis of the Moral and Religious Sentiments*; George Anderson, *An Estimate of the Profit and Loss of Religion, Personally and publicly stated: Illustrated with References to Essays on Morality and Natural Religion* (Edinburgh, 1753); Anderson, *Remonstrance*; Macqueen, *Letters on Mr. Hume's History of Great Britain*; John Russel, *The Reasons of our Lord's Agony in the Garden, and the Influence of Just Views of them on Universal Holiness* (Kilmarnock, 1787); James Somerville, *The Fatal Consequences of Irreligion and Negligence in the Heads of Families. A Sermon preached in the Tron Church of Edinburgh on the Twenty-third of May 1790* (Edinburgh, 1790); Snodgrass, *Leading Doctrines of the Gospel*; Savile, *Dissertations*. See also above, pp. 24–5.

infidelity and atheism and of the rationality of Christianity. Wishart, for example, asserted that the belief of sinners in the heavy and tyrannical nature of divine government and the arbitrary form of divine law is groundless, since God requires only those things which are in their own nature good. Scoffers who revive the 'schemes and cavils of the ancient Scepticks, and worst sort of Epicureans', attack not only revealed religion and Christianity, but also the common principles of natural religion itself.[101] The implication is that no rational mind is going to reject the latter. At the other end of the theological spectrum, John Willison expressed his conviction that his faith could be defended on rational grounds. He maintained that the inability of natural religion to provide adequate answers to questions about the nature of God, the creation of the world, the Fall, and the possibility of forgiveness for sin all clearly demonstrated not just the truth of Christianity but also the unreasonableness of infidelity.[102] John Bonar, although he qualified the assertion, noted that advocates for infidelity had been unable for a hundred years to weaken the smallest support for the Christian religion.[103] Virtually no prominent Popular author seems to have felt confident enough, however, to dismiss infidelity in quite such a cavalier fashion after the 1750s.[104] In this the influence of Hume may well have been decisive.

Instead, the 'complacent' line on infidelity was supported more often by stress on the converse of the irrationality of atheism, that is, on the rationality of Christianity. George Anderson, for example, castigated authors opposed to religion as prone to despise the science on which abstract reasoning is based when the latter does not favour them, and quoted Hume as an example of this for his disparaging of the Thirty-nine Articles as 'the metaphysics of the church of England'.[105] Subsequently, he dealt with the connection between Christianity and the continuance of established society, and contrasted it with the social implications of atheism.[106] This approach to the problem was common in the 1750s. Daniel Macqueen, for instance, adhered to it by describing irreligion as 'manifestly subversive' to the interests and love of virtue, and to the peace and happiness of mankind. The vicious and debased may be strongly inclined to adopt irreligion, he asserted, but there is nothing attractive in it to virtuous minds. Hume and others were criticised for speaking of the imagination instead of the understanding and will, and of contemplation and abstract speculation instead of the

---

101 Wishart, *Difference betwixt Moral Good and Evil*, pp. 3–4.
102 See above, pp. 48–9. On Willison, see above, pp. 48–9, 94–5; and Willison, *Example of Plain Catechising*, pp. 594–8.
103 Bonar, *Observations*, pp. 38–9.
104 Dun, *Sermons*, i, p. 69; cf. Macqueen, *Letters on Mr. Hume's History of Great Britain*, pp. 187–8.
105 Anderson, *Remonstrance*, pp. 18–19. The reference given is to Hume's *History*, p. 389.
106 Ibid., pp. 448–50.

rational aims, desires, and affections of the soul.[107] Such conviction of the essential rationality of the Christian position remained secure until the end of the century, though increasingly it became more of an assumption than the basis of the argument against 'infidelity'.

The essence of the second approach to infidelity was expressed succinctly by John Bonar in 1756: 'a heart-love to wickedness' was at the root cause of the opposition to the gospel of the advocates of infidelity. So long as men were vicious they wanted to throw off the restraints laid on their passions by Christianity and free themselves from the dread which it inspired.[108] Even earlier, John Willison linked this interpretation with attempts by deists and other heretics to advance the belief in reason as an adequate guide in matters of religion.[109] Macqueen quoted Plato in support, and argued that irreligion could be attributed to pride and an 'affectation of superior parts'.[110] This analysis of the origin of irreligion and infidelity was almost standard in Popular works on the subject.

Popular apologists were not necessarily content to leave their analysis at this general level, but sought to offer specific examples of the consequences of natural depravity. Witherspoon ascribed at least part of the cause of the irreligion of the day to those who considered Christianity as answerable for all the hypocrisies and wickednesses of those nominal Christians who had not renounced their faith, and to the difficulty of engaging in controversy with them because they had formed no fixed principles at all since they had never really thought on the subject.[111] More common still was the argument concerning the deleterious effects of luxury on the lives of the upper ranks in society. Alexander Webster, as early as 1742, spoke of the ridicule of the fashionable world for the preaching of Christ crucified, and its esteem for the dilution of the doctrines of the gospel and their substitution with secular philosophy.[112] John Warden of the Edinburgh Canongate blamed the abounding of infidelity and profanity and the fashionableness of vice on the example of the great. Luxury and sensuality, as well as being the origins of sloth and poverty, led also to weakness of mind and spirit.[113] Infidelity was thus essentially a spiritual as opposed to an apologetical problem. It was to be fought not by attacks on the various writers who were assaulting the faith, but by encouraging godliness, piety, and spirituality.

---

107 Macqueen, *Letters on Mr. Hume's History of Great Britain*, pp. 297, 308.
108 Bonar, *Observations*, pp. 38–40.
109 Willison, *Example of Plain Catechising*, p. 594.
110 Macqueen, *Letters on Mr. Hume's History of Great Britain*, pp. 185, 297. The reference is to Plato's *De leg*. lib. 10.
111 Witherspoon, *Trial of Religious Truth*, pp. 18, 29.
112 Alexander Webster, *Divine Influence the True Spring of the Extraordinary Work at Cambuslang and Other Places in the West of Scotland* (Edinburgh, 1742), p. 45.
113 John Warden, *The Happiness of Britain illustrated; in a Sermon* (Edinburgh, 1749), p. 56.

The third approach in Popular analysis of the causes of infidelity held that if infidelity arose from human depravity, it was the role of the Church to counter it by effective preaching and teaching. It followed that if infidelity was increasing, it could well be the fault of the Church in failing to remain faithful to its God-given commission. This approach first appeared in the writings of John Willison. In his *A Fair and Impartial Testimony* of 1744, Willison delineated the theological and ecclesiastical positions which provide the starting-point for any attempt to understand the theological and spiritual preoccupations of 'evangelical' thought in the later eighteenth-century Scottish Church. Willison saw the defence of Christianity from infidelity as integrally involved with purity of doctrine and worship. Earlier, in 1733, in *The Church's Danger and Ministers' Duty*, he prayed for their continuance, so that God would preserve the Church from deism and similar tendencies, and from all Popish, Socinian, Arian, Pelagian, and Arminian principles which prevented men from seeing the hand of God in all things.[114] Laxity of doctrine and failure to move against heretical opinions were sinful and were being punished by God in his refusal to bless the Church's endeavours in both spiritual and ecclesiastical matters:

> the Lord's hand is visibly lifted up against us at this day, and hath been for some years past, in shutting up the church's womb, blasting gospel-ordinances, and withdrawing his spirit from the assemblies of his people and from our judicatories.
>
> The flood-gate is opened to error, infidelity, and looseness, to overspread the land; so that the gospel of Christ, the holy scriptures, and all revealed religion, are condemned and ridiculed by many ... There is a way opened for a carnal, self-seeking minister to get into the vineyard, when faithful labourers are thrust out, and godly preachers and students are discouraged from entering in ...
>
> By all which proceedings it appears that God hath a peculiar controversy with Scotland, and threatens to punish her remarkably for her heinous sins and provocations ... Infidelity, immorality, and contempt for the gospel, are come to a prodigious height: our hearts are become cold and frozen to Christ and his interest, to his people and holy laws ... And yet so great is our impenitence and perverseness, that we will not see the Lord's hand, nor be reformed by all these judgements.[115]

The situation was made even worse because of the wrangling of those who professed Christianity, which was taking place while infidelity was steadily growing.[116]

---

114 John Willison, *The Church's Danger and Ministers' Duty* (1733), in *Practical Works*, p. 833.
115 John Willison, *The Afflicted Man's Companion* (1737), in *Practical Works*, pp. 730–1.
116 Willison, *Example of Plain Catechising*, p. 884.

Increasingly, however, Willison's priorities became more polemical. In *The Balm of Gilead*, a series of sermons published in 1742, his list of diseases for which, as he put it, the blood of Christ was needed consisted of the following: atheism; ignorance of God; hardness of heart; aversion to spiritual duties; indwelling corruption; hypocrisy and formality in God's service; discouragement and downcasting of soul; ingratitude to God for his mercies; trusting to our own righteousness; heresy and error (including Deism, Socinianism, and Arianism); schism and division; 'giddiness and unsettledness in religion' (by which he meant patronage, denial of national covenants, and Erastianism); and spiritual barrenness and unfruitfulness.[117] Thereafter, he was quick to identify these trends with the Moderates in the Church. He came to be more and more concerned that increasing numbers of the clergy were guilty of looseness and immorality in their lives as well as of laxness and unsoundness in their principles, and that some of these were allowed to teach divinity to students for the ministry at the universities. Furthermore, many such men neglected evangelical preaching, and espoused 'legal doctrine, and a sort of heathenish morality', instead of preaching Christ to sinners. Many of these, too, were giving unnecessary encouragement to patronage, which led to schism.[118]

Willison also criticised the Church's attitude to heresy, which he defined as 'errors in the fundamentals of religion, maintained with obstinacy',[119] and identified heresy as present in the cases of Simson, Campbell, and Principal Wishart. The latter he regarded as suspect in the areas of Erastianism, Christian liberty, subscription to the Confessions, the final state of non-Christians, and original sin. Leechman's sermon on prayer was likewise attacked as saying little of Christ's mediatorial role, and for generally omitting mention of Christ. He criticised the General Assembly for its failure to act unequivocally in its dealings with these cases.[120] A Popular minister like Willison arrived at his ecclesiastical position of opposition to the Moderates, therefore, not solely or indeed mainly because of opposition to what he conceived to be their doctrinal position, but because he came increasingly to see them as unwilling to challenge the defections of the Church and of the nation from evangelical religion, and as countenancing the holding and teaching of heretical opinions. This, above all, was dishonouring to God and could only lead to the withdrawal of his blessing on both the land and the Church.[121] Ultimately, therefore, opposition to Moderatism was

---

117 John Willison, *The Balm of Gilead* (1742), in *Practical Works*, pp. 401–5. A further exhaustive list is given in Willison, *Fair and Impartial Testimony*, pp. 937–40.
118 Ibid., p. 881. See also Willison, *Church's Danger*, pp. 824, 881; and Willison, *Balm of Gilead*, pp. 910, 930.
119 John Willison, *Sacramental Meditations and Advices* (1747), in *Practical Works*, p. 291.
120 Willison, *Fair and Impartial Testimony*, pp. 882, 905, 914, 926–8, 945.
121 For a more detailed account of Willison's response to Moderatism and the role of the Moderates in the patronage issue, see below, pp. 65–8.

not a doctrinal matter, it was a practical one, and in some ways even a devotional one.

The link between Moderatism and infidelity found in the writings of Willison was taken up by other Popular writers, but never so explicitly. Alexander Webster, in the 1740s, argued that attempts to satisfy or accommodate objections to Christianity had resulted in departures from its doctrines. He implied the existence of a link between the growth of Deism and Principal Wishart's analysis of the attributes of God which, he alleged, led to the denial of the reality of sin and of its fatal consequences. Religious liberty, he asserted elsewhere, had been turned into an occasion for propagating atheism and infidelity.[122]

In the same way as there was a variety of analyses of the reasons for the growth of infidelity, there was a corresponding variety in the prescription of detailed remedies. The first group, those who were convinced that the rationality of the Christian faith would overcome the problem, argued that an 'educative' response was called for. While few members of the party would have gone as far as William Wishart when he asserted that the general corruption of youth was in a great measure due to 'the gross and general neglect of a rational and virtuous Education',[123] most of those who saw infidelity as irrational thought the appropriate response was one of conventional apologetical writing. It could range from the relatively quiescent approach of John Gillies, who set about the printing of a collection 'from some of the Authors of greatest genius, who are friends of the Gospel ... as an antidote' to the poison spread by 'fashionable Deistical writers',[124] to the detailed defences of traditional doctrines relating to the Being and existence of God, causation, and of proofs of the Christian religion by leading Popular authors such as George Anderson, Robert Dick, and others.[125] In short, the analysis of infidelity as irrational and therefore as not embodying a fundamental threat to either Christianity or the Church led to a relatively muted and conventional response. It involved the defence of revelation and natural religion as being rational, and defence of the truth of Christian doctrine especially that regarding the nature and existence of God. It was fundamentally educative and above all confident.

The second analysis of the cause of infidelity, the identification of it as a spiritual problem, led to the formulation of a cohesive programme for recovery. Willison in particular offered a spiritual answer to deal with the encouragement given by human depravity to infidelity. He came to the issue through his complaint against the Moderates but his basic

---

[122] Webster, *Supernatural Revelation*, p. iii; Webster, *Zeal for the Civil and Religious Interests of Mankind*, pp. 347–8; [Paton], *Knowledge of God* (Glasgow, 1773), pp. 121–2.
[123] Wishart, *Difference betwixt Moral Good and Evil*, p. 33.
[124] Gillies, *Exhortation*, pp. 277ff.
[125] See above, note 100.

approach was determined by his view of the role of gospel preaching in the function of the Church. In *The Balm of Gilead* he regretted the deposition of the Seceders in 1740 because they were 'upright and zealous in preaching a crucified Jesus to fallen men, especially at a time when Deism and dry moral discourses are like to thrust out true Christianity', and spoke against 'the preaching up of a sort of heathen morality, and the neglect of the preaching of Christ and gospel holiness'. Any reform of these defects, though, depended on the operation of the Holy Spirit.[126] He identified, furthermore, two areas as holding the key to a crucial shift in the direction of the Church in response to the problem: ministerial piety combined with the conscientious performance of pastoral duties, and evangelical preaching. The evidence seems to suggest that Willison and his friends discharged their pastoral duties with increased zeal since they regarded the public sins of the Church as a matter of deep guilt, and that they strove with renewed vigour against spiritual lethargy in their congregations and to convince them of the necessity of regeneration, faith, and new obedience.[127] Certainly, in *The Church's Danger and Ministers' Duty*, Willison argued in favour of frequent visitation and catechising as a means of ascertaining the spiritual state of congregations and the results of sermons, and supported the more frequent celebration of the Lord's Supper as a means of encouraging spiritual growth.[128]

The significance of evangelical preaching in Willison's perceptions came to take a more prominent place in the 1740s when, for a time, he became interested in millenarian speculation, in the course of which he predicted a revolution in France around 1792. More importantly, it led him to identify encouraging signs of a revival of true religion throughout the world,[129] in which Evangelical preaching was of critical importance. The first signs of the fall of Antichrist were to be the great defection among the Churches of Christ, deadness and formality among the Lord's people, and abounding errors and false doctrines. The latter were identified in particular as involving corrupt principles concerning justification, the operations of the Holy Spirit, revelation, and the salvation of sinners by the imputed righteousness of Christ. There were indications that God was beginning to counteract these tendencies. In particular, religious awakenings in various parts of the world (presumably the Great Awakening in New England and the Cambuslang 'Wark'), were evidences of God's blessing. Ministers and preachers should concur in promoting the Lord's work 'by proclaiming the saving doctrine and offers of free grace to the world', and by exerting

---

126 Willison, *Balm of Gilead*, pp. 833, 929–30.
127 W. M. Hetherington, 'Essay on the life and times of the Rev. John Willison', in *Practical Works of the Rev. John Willison*, ed. Hetherington, p. xvi.
128 Willison, *Church's Danger*, pp. 837–8.
129 Hetherington, 'Essay on the life and times of the Rev. John Willison', p. xvii.

themselves 'for removing out of the way all lets and hindrances of the kingdom of Christ'.[130] If, therefore, evangelical revival was to be linked to the approaching millennium, it becomes easier to see why Willison was not especially interested in specific proposals to counteract Moderate influence in the General Assembly. Evangelicals were on the winning side, and they should contribute to its near approach by their preaching of salvation through Christ. It is not clear, however, whether millenarianism affected Popular strategies of opposition to the Moderates at the Assembly. There is virtually no sign of such speculation in Popular writings other than at the time of the Cambuslang revival.[131]

In view of the remarkable degree of support for a return to evangelical preaching as the most effectual means of counteracting the rise of infidelity, it is surprising that the third strand in the analysis of its causes, namely stress on the Church's failure to respond adequately to its rise, and in particular on its failure to insist on gospel preaching, should have received as little attention as it did. There was a clear reluctance to ascribe the blame for it to any particular section of the Church. There was an obscure reference in Bonar's *Observations on the Conduct and Character of Judas Iscariot* to friends of Christianity who 'have been more careful to preserve our principles, than to reform our lives', and he enjoined the Church to stand fast against impiety as well as against infidelity. This oblique attack stood virtually alone.[132] The only sustained and detailed attempt to ascribe blame for the Church's failure to combat infidelity successfully was that of John Willison, who laid the responsibility largely, though not exclusively, at the feet of the Moderates. If, as has been suggested,[133] Willison's opposition to them was as much a spiritual as a doctrinal one, the question arises as to why he saw them as unable or unwilling to respond firmly to the decline of true religion. The answer is twofold: first, he believed that for them religion had become a matter of mere morality; and, secondly, he regarded them as too much influenced by the views of the patrons and gentry on whom they depended for preferment. In *The Church's Danger* he bewailed the influence of 'many of the younger clergy and preachers, who seem to affect a new way of moral preaching and lax management, suited to the taste of many patrons and heritors'.[134] In 1742, he declared that

> it would help greatly if those consecrated to spiritual office would be more suitably and profitably employed in opening up and recommending the Balm of Gilead [that is the blood of Christ] and

---

[130] Willison, *Balm of Gilead*, pp. 391, 435.
[131] Snodgrass, *Prospects of Providence*, pp. 32–3; John Erskine, *The Signs of the Times Consider'd* (Edinburgh, 1742), *passim*.
[132] Bonar, *Observations*, p. 39.
[133] See above, pp. 62–3.
[134] Willison, *Church's Danger*, p. 824.

the glorious ministrations of the Spirit than in attending courts, and pursuing secular designs.[135]

He returned to the same theme in *A Fair and Impartial Testimony* of 1744, where he referred to 'legal sermons and moral harangues, to the neglect of the preaching of Christ, introduced by many of the young clergy'.[136] He identified the Treaty of Union of 1707 as marking the decline in spirituality of the nobility and gentry since it led to a neglect of family religion among them, and as leading to the multiplication of public oaths which he associated with the growth of infidelity.[137] In other words, the close links of the Moderates with the nobility and gentry explained, at least in part, the attraction to moral preaching and laxness in doctrine of the younger Moderates. What more could be expected 'while these are chosen by statesmen, magistrates, or regents, several of whom have no concern for Christianity, but may even be tinctured with error or infidelity?'[138]

In response to the alleged moral preaching of the Moderates, Willison provided an analysis of its defects as a supplement to the positive reasons for the promotion of evangelical preaching which have already been noted.[139] This analysis is to be found in *A Fair and Impartial Testimony*. Morality, or obedience to the moral law, maintained Willison, was absolutely essential to true Christianity since God required it, and without it and true holiness, 'no man can see the Lord'. But it must originate from the principles of the gospel, 'be performed in a gospel manner, and be pressed mainly by gospel motives and arguments'. If not, men were apt to think that they might win heaven by their own morality and without Christ or his righteousness. If allowed to replace the imputed righteousness of Christ, obedience to the moral law could prevent conversion and entry to heaven. Morality without Christ was a reversion to the covenant of works. While faith was required as the means or instrument by which Christ and his righteousness was received and applied, and true repentance and sincere obedience were required as evidence and fruits of faith, neither faith, repentance nor obedience were any part of justifying righteousness. None should think they were saved partly by their own obedience, and partly by Christ's; they were saved only by Christ's obedience.[140]

The problem remained of how morality and the duties of the moral law were to be preached. Willison's answer, which can be seen as a response to what was to become the Moderate stress on the example of Christ, had several aspects. First, duty was the natural and necessary

135 Willison, *Balm of Gilead*, p. 391.
136 Willison, *Fair and Impartial Testimony*, p. 910.
137 Ibid., p. 900.
138 Ibid., p. 882.
139 See above, pp. 64–5.
140 Willison, *Fair and Impartial Testimony*, pp. 923–4.

fruit of faith in a crucified Christ and love for him. Secondly, desire to keep the moral law could be encouraged by a devotional emphasis on the attractions of a crucified Christ which would make his laws acceptable and indeed compelling. Thirdly, duties should be enforced from a principle of love and gratitude to Christ in return for the love he has shown. Fourthly, the people should be directed to rely on the grace and strength of Christ himself to help them to perform their duties and not follow preaching which assumed the sufficiency of man's own natural powers, such preaching was typical of 'moral preachers'. Fifthly, men should be persuaded to leave sin and perform moral duties, by the terrors of the coming judgement and the 'wrath of the Lamb'. And finally, stress should always be placed on the fact that all our duties and good works had no worth or merit before God but were only accepted by him through the mediation and merits of Christ. While Christianity enforced morality strongly, morality without the renewal of the heart through conversion would never please God. Everything said about morality should point to Christ.[141]

Failure to preach morality along these lines, argued Willison, was failure to preach in the way God had appointed. Preaching should above all concentrate on the person and work of Christ. The preaching of Christ crucified was the God-appointed means of converting sinners to Christ; it was the method which the apostles used with such great success; it was the God-chosen way of reforming men from vice and encouraging virtue, godliness and good order in civil life; and those ministers who preached Christ most had the most success.[142]

Willison saw the Church of Scotland in the 1740s being led astray by the Moderates' exclusion of Christ in their preaching:

How can we expect assistance from Jesus Christ in our work, or the influences of his Spirit in preaching, upon which all our success depends, when we take no more notice of Christ in our sermons than the moral philosophers among the heathens? Woe will be to this national church, if such a way of preaching prevail in it, notwithstanding of the foresaid act of assembly [of 1736 concerning evangelical preaching], and a sound Confession of Faith, which all ministers subscribe to. God forbid that the church of Scotland ever become like the church of England in this respect, who subscribe to sound articles of doctrine, and never mind them more afterwards.[143]

For Willison, therefore, the touchstone of the truth of a Church depended on the orientation of its preaching. He found it difficult to

---

[141] Ibid., pp. 923–5.
[142] Ibid. It is tempting to speculate that this analysis, or derivatives of it, may well have been the origin of Clark's analysis of Popular theology. See above, pp. 22–3.
[143] Willison, *Fair and Impartial Testimony*, pp. 925–6.

condemn the Seceders, for they testified 'against the preaching up a sort of heathenish morality, and the neglect of the true preaching of Christ and gospel holiness, etc.'; he praised the English Methodists, 'although not altogether purged from the corruptions of that land', since

> they preached with great warmth, choosing subjects very much neglected in that church [the Church of England] such as the doctrine of grace, of justification by faith in the righteousness of Christ; of original sin and the corruption of our nature, of the nature and necessity of regeneration, and the new birth, etc.

The Cambuslang revival, which he saw as a justification of the correctness of his analysis of the state of the Church, could not but be accepted as a work of the Spirit because it had been produced by evangelical preaching, and its converts were marked by their testimony to the centrality of Christ's role in their religious experience.[144]

Analysis of moral preaching took Willison directly into the debate over patronage;[145] it emphasised the essentially spiritual nature of the opposition of the Popular party to its exercise, or at least of its more evangelically minded members. It is difficult to explain, however, the reason why Willison's anti-Moderate explanation of the rise of infidelity was not taken up by other Popular writers. The whole issue of infidelity became submerged in the struggle over patronage, and the symptoms of the malaise appear to have been neglected in the struggle to right its cause. If such were the case, it would embody a remarkable victory for Willison's position. More probable, though, is an interpretation which stresses the degree of equanimity about the whole problem of infidelity, Deism, and atheism, which was encouraged by the conviction of the essential rationality of the Christian faith. Mainstream Popular thought was sensitive to and influenced by the secular thought of the period. After the flurry of concern over the works of Bolingbroke, Hume, and Kames, infidelity was deemed to be a less important problem. In the longer term there are reasons to suggest that the 'lukewarmness' of the nobility and gentry, and its spread throughout the community, was beginning to be seen not so much as backsliding or as infidelity, but simply as non-Christianity. The problem was not one of reclamation, but one of conversion.

VI

There remains, however, the question of the extent to which these responses to the problem of infidelity were reflected in the life of the Church in the period under consideration. Examination of the accounts of the proceedings of the General Assembly verifies the lines of

---

144 Ibid., pp. 930, 933–7.
145 See below, pp. 94–5, 97.

interpretation which have been established from the survey of the published works of the Popular party.

It is not the intention here to examine the details of the proceedings in the various heresy trials or those of the charges connected with the issue of infidelity. The details may be found elsewhere.[146] The present issue concerns the Popular attitude to the questions of heresy and infidelity and how to proceed against them. It is clear, in the first place, that there was a considerable reluctance, among the Popular leadership at least, to initiate proceedings against heresy. In his closing address as Moderator of the 1744 Assembly which saw the accusation of heresy against Professor Leechman, John Adams of Falkirk asserted

> In that case of more than usual delicacy ... have we not seen the beauty of Christian charity, in condescension on the one hand to remove offence, and readiness on the other to embrace satisfaction. We have had the most agreeable evidence too of impartial regards to the merit of questions debated before us, in the honest declarations of many, that after hearing a case fairly stated, they came to judge of it in a quite different manner from what they had done upon some imperfect representations before the meeting.[147]

James Robe of Kilsyth, the Popular hagiographer, published an appendix to a pamphlet 'vindicating the Act passed by the Assembly in this affair'.[148] Such declarations set the tone for the response of the Popular leadership to heresy for the rest of the century.

Probably the most famous of the heresy trials at the Assembly was that involving David Hume and Henry Home, Lord Kames. The complaint against infidel writers, as it came to be known, was set in motion in 1755 by George Anderson, by this time almost eighty years of age and chaplain to Watson's Hospital in Edinburgh, who had published his *Estimate of the Profit and Loss of Religion* in 1753.[149] He was joined by the anonymous author, now thought to be John Bonar of Perth, of a pamphlet entitled *An Analysis of the Moral and Religious Sentiments contained in the Writings of Sopho and David Hume, Esq., addressed to the consideration of the Reverend and Honourable Members of the General Assembly of the Church of Scotland.*[150] Bonar summarised Kames's position in a series of propositions which held that Kames denied the possibility of knowledge of God and of divine providence over the material world; that he asserted the perfection of all classes of being; and that God had implanted a deceitful feeling of freedom of action in man, since all actions were in fact determined and subject to an irresistible necessity;

---

146 E.g., the relevant issues of the *Scots Magazine*; and Drummond and Bulloch, *Scottish Church*.
147 Morren, *Annals of the General Assembly*, i, p. 308.
148 Ibid., p. 61.
149 Anderson, *Estimate of the Profit and Loss of Religion*.
150 [Bonar], *Analysis of the Moral and Religious Sentiments*, published in Edinburgh in 1755.

and that therefore there could be no sin or moral evil in the world. Hume's position was summarised as denying all distinction between virtue and vice, and asserting that justice had no foundation beyond its contribution to public advantage; that religion and its ministers were prejudicial to mankind; that there was no evidence that Christianity was a divine revelation; and that Popery was the best form of Christianity, the Reformation being the work of 'madmen and enthusiasts'.[151] In other words, Kames was being alleged to hold heterodox if not heretical views, and Hume was attacked as denying the validity of Christianity and arguing the case for infidelity. To some extent, the case was a backlash after Gillespie's deposition in 1752, for the *Analysis* concluded by charging the Assembly that

> you deposed a minister who disowned your authority, but enrol as a member of your courts, an elder who has disowned the authority of Almighty God, and that some of you at least live in the greatest intimacy with one who represents the blessed Saviour as an imposter, and his religion as a cunningly devised fable.[152]

The 1755 Assembly contented itself with unanimously passing a general denunciation of 'those impious and infidel principles which are subversive of all religion, natural and revealed, and have such pernicious influence on life and morals'.[153]

The issue was not closed, for an overture was proposed in the Committee of Overtures the following year directed against certain infidel writers. The debate in this case hinged on whether or not Hume could be regarded as a Christian, and on whether opinion as opposed to action could be the object of censure. It was argued that what was happening was that 'the grossest immorality [was] taught and subscribed, and then defended as freedom of enquiry', and it was maintained that to censure writers was not to punish them in their bodies, or even hinder them from publishing their opinions, 'but only hindering them from injuriously possessing that to which they have no right, viz., the Christian name'.[154]

The question, therefore, hinged on two issues: who were liable to church censures, and whether Hume was one of them? It was argued in a pamphlet entitled *Infidelity a proper object of censure*,[155] that the Church was obliged to preserve the purity of the doctrines and sacraments of the Christian religion 'not by forcing any who are unwilling, to make a

---

151 Morren, *Annals of the General Assembly*, ii, pp. 56–7.
152 Ibid., p. 58. As Morren points out, Kames never sat in the Assembly although he was named a member of the Commission by the Assemblies of 1753 and 1754. He was not named as a member by the Assembly of 1755. See ibid., p. 58, note.
153 Ibid., p. 59.
154 Ibid., p. 89.
155 For this pamphlet, see the abstract published in the *Scots Magazine*, xviii (May 1756), pp. 223–37.

hypocritical profession in regard to them, but by separating themselves from those who openly and grossly impugn, abuse, and corrupt them'. Neither were Church censures of a temporal nature, nor should they be. They could not therefore infringe any right, for the highest form of censure, excommunication, was only declaring those not to be Christians who were not so in any case. It was pointed out, in addition, that the Confession of Faith required the Church to call to account and censure those who 'upon pretence of Christian liberty, do publish such opinions, or maintain such practices as are contrary to the light of nature, or to the known principles of Christianity'. Attention was also drawn to the annual instruction to the Commission of Assembly to investigate the publication of works promoting opinions inconsistent with the Confession, and that those who recommended such works should be called before it.[156]

The inference from these arguments is that those who were calling for the censure of Hume considered that the Church had a constitutional obligation to pursue the author of opinions deemed to be as objectionable as Hume's if he laid claim to the title of being a Christian. This was admitted by Hume's opponents after two days of debate in the Committee of Overtures. A person, however, who was not a member of the visible Church was not subject to its discipline. Hume, it was argued, was not in that category since he had been neither excluded from it by a sentence, nor had he excluded himself from it by a formal declaration or by renouncing his baptism. He frequently included himself in its ranks by referring to 'our holy religion', and this showed the necessity of a visible separation. But at this point, the argument of Hume's opponents broke down, for the Moderates pointed out that while Hume had not said in express words that he was not a Christian, he had said it as publicly and as strongly by other forms of expression. Furthermore, his antagonists' contention that formal exclusion would prevent professing Christians from associating with him was rejected on the grounds that Christians should frequent his company in order to attempt his reformation. The overture's supporters then retreated to seeking a judgement that Hume was no Christian and therefore not subject to discipline. They were outmanoeuvred by the argument that they were demanding a sentence without trial or proper defence, and that, since the overture represented Hume as no Christian, it ought not to be transmitted as proceeding on a supposition which made its own demand unnecessary. Against this, it could only be argued that any censure or exclusion by a sentence would be precluded since, as soon as anyone was guilty of anything worthy of censure, he would be declared, or declare to be, no Christian and so not a subject of censure. The overture was then dropped by the Committee because it would not, in their opinion, serve the purpose of edification. Their resolution was passed by 50 votes to 17.[157]

---

[156] Ibid., p. 226.
[157] Morren, *Annals of the General Assembly*, ii, p. 91; *Scots Magazine*, xix (Jun. 1756), pp. 283–4.

Several conclusions may be drawn from the debate over the alleged heresies of Hume and Kames. In the first place, it is often assumed that the attack was mounted by the Popular party as a whole. Mossner, for example, writes in his biography of Hume of 'the concerted effort of the persecuting cabal' and implies that the weight of the party was behind it.[158] There is no evidence that the attack on Hume and Kames was supported by the Popular party as a whole. Apart from Anderson and Bonar, no Popular minister of note is recorded as supporting the move for censure. Even Witherspoon did not attack Hume or Kames directly until the famous *Ecclesiastical Characteristics* of 1757, and that was provoked only by the *Douglas* affair.[159] The Assembly, furthermore, unanimously passed the 1755 Act which condemned infidelity and immorality in the most general terms only, and there was no attempt to move a more specific condemnation. In the Assembly of the following year, which had a large number of Popular commissioners and possibly even a majority, there was no attempt to move for the condemnation of Hume after it had been decided against in the Committee of Overtures.

After the unsuccessful attempt to persuade the Assembly to condemn Hume, Anderson raised a complaint before the Presbytery of Edinburgh against the publishers of Kames's *Essays on Morality and Natural Religion*. It was rejected by the relatively Popular presbytery with only two dissents. Furthermore, apart from the efforts of Anderson and Bonar and perhaps one or two of their firmest supporters, the debate over Kames was carried on at high philosophical levels and for a time involved Jonathan Edwards (the famous American philosopher and theologian in whose congregation the 'Great Awakening' began in 1734–5), through his correspondence with Kames between 1755 and 1757. It would seem from the debate at the Edinburgh Presbytery that Kames had modified his views by 1756, to the extent that some, if not the majority, of the Popular membership of the presbytery, were not prepared to pursue the matter. The stature of their criticism of Kames should not be lightly regarded, however, for in the Preface to the 1779 edition of his *Essays* he publicly retracted most of the doctrines on liberty and necessity which had been objected to by Edwards and which were the central point of the debate.[160]

The problem faced by the Popular party over church discipline in matters of heresy and infidelity was complex. Opinion differed on the

E. C. Mossner in *The Life of David Hume* (London, 1954), p. 348, asserts that many left the meeting to avoid voting one way or the other. He does not give any authority for this statement, however, and it seems somewhat dubious as neither the *Scots Magazine* nor Morren mention it. Furthermore, to judge by Morren's voting figures, a Committee of Overtures of 67 members was larger than usual in any case which must call Mossner's contention into question.

158 Mossner, *Life of David Hume*, p. 341.
159 See below, pp. 84–8.
160 Morren, *Annals of the General Assembly*, ii, pp. 98–100.

problem of infidelity and the means of combating it. The party was also compromised in its response by the arguments it used to counter patronage. From the Reformation until the middle of the eighteenth century, the Church of Scotland had been able and accustomed to assume that Scotland was a nation professing Christianity and accepting the writ of the Kirk, with the exception of small numbers of Episcopalians and Roman Catholics who were nevertheless forced to accept the authority of the Kirk in various ways such as its establishment, its control of education, and the reservation of the offices and emoluments of State. Doctrinal orthodoxy was to be enforced and, as late as 1697, Thomas Aitkenhead had been executed for heresy. These attitudes had been challenged in the area of church government by Ebenezer Erskine and the Seceders in the 1730s, and the Church had responded by deposing him. Those most hostile to the Seceders continued to advocate their exclusion, but most of the Popular leadership shared the principles for which the Seceders stood, and they continued to maintain friendly relations with them wherever possible. The policy of rigorous censure of those who denied the writ of the Kirk was clearly applied selectively.

The writings of Hume in the 1750s, however, seemed to be aimed at the very foundations of Christianity, and to be encouraging doubt and promoting 'infidelity' and 'immorality'. Members of the Popular party sought to combat the problem in their own writings. Partly, however, because of their assault on patronage and their defence of Thomas Gillespie in 1752 in terms of 'Christian liberty', and partly because they appreciated that they could not apply the strictures of the seventeenth century to those who denied the faith, they could not mount a confident move for censure, nor did they wish to. When a small group of Popular men moved to censure and in effect to excommunicate Hume, the Moderate defence of him was based on the same principle of liberty which the Popular party had been using in discussion on patronage. While it is going too far to claim, as has been done, that the Hume decision showed that the Church now saw itself as a voluntary body,[161] it would seem that the majority of the Popular party at the time was in favour of a tolerant approach to non-orthodox thought and to dissent, whether it was ecclesiastical or more general.[162] The mainstream Popular response to the writings of Hume and other 'infidel writers' remained one of counteracting the impact of their ideas by publication and sermons. More drastic attempts at suppression were eschewed. It is clear that the Popular party increasingly saw the problem of heresy and unorthodox belief as a phenomenon to be prevented before it occurred, rather than as something to be repressed after it had manifested itself.[163]

---

[161] Drummond and Bulloch, *Scottish Church*, p. 98.
[162] See above, pp. 24–5; and below, pp. 151–3.
[163] As early as 1744, in his closing speech as Moderator, the Popular leader, John Adams

VII

The case against Hume and Kames, however, concerned not merely ecclesiastical or theological matters. It raised issues concerning the relationship between Church and society, and it assumed certain perceptions about the nature of society and government. The most striking feature of Popular analysis of secular society was its postulation of a crucial link between religious faith and social stability. Infidelity was to be feared on social, as well as religious, grounds. Beyond that, however, Popular perceptions of the nature of society were not especially theological. Preoccupation with issues which had clear religious or theological implications meant that there was no distinctive Popular response to secular developments except for the questions of relief from civil disabilities of Roman Catholics and the American War of Independence. Moderate *causes célèbres* such as the Militia scheme and the Ossian controversy aroused no Popular interest at all.

Two main themes were the hallmark of Popular thought in its analysis of the relationship between the principles of Christianity and the nature of society. These were a stress on the essential role of religion as the basis of society, which stress derived from the relationship of all men to God; and an awareness of the link between society and morality which meant that all actions had consequences for others that were held to affect their morality. These preoccupations, in fact, appeared through-out the whole of the latter half of the eighteenth century.

The contrast with a secular analysis of the nature of society was most marked in Popular writing on the nature of government. Almost all Popular writers saw government as necessary and as instituted by God as a result of the Fall and the natural depravity of man. As a consequence, the emergence of a conservative view of government was a logical development. At the same time, though, Popular political thought embodied an espousal of more liberal ideas supported by parallel theories of religious liberty of conscience, and by ideas of the unity of men through all being the objects of God's love. As a result of these concepts, there developed a dichotomy in the ideology of the party. The liberal impetus led some of its members to oppose the Tory government of the period, and to adopt an intellectual alliance with the Foxite Whigs. The outbreak of the French Revolution, with its propagation of anti-Christian ideas together with its hostility to Britain, however, led to a thorough-going stress on the obligations of Christians to support the existing political establishment. That such support was often virtually without question emphasises the paramountcy in the Popular mind of

of Falkirk, alluded to the great care necessary in the licensing of probationers, so that none should be licensed 'to dispense the bread of life, but such as, on the best grounds that can be had, we have reason to judge have themselves tasted the good word of life, and felt the powers of the world to come': Morren, *Annals of the General Assembly*, i, p. 309.

religious principles and values in determining responses to secular developments.

The first identifiable adherent of the Popular party to contribute to analysis of the nature of society was Principal William Wishart. He is a key figure because in his writings are to be found the two main themes in Popular thought on the nature of society: the religious basis of society, and the link between society and morality. The influence of his thought on younger and subsequent members of the party was extensive. It also illustrates the diversity of opinion within it. Wishart, too, was one of the first to see the problems posed for the Christian and for the Church by such developments as population growth, the rise of crime, and the increase of entrepreneurial activity. He saw society as 'natural to men, and necessary to their Improvement and Perfection [as] both the natural Abilities, and the natural Weakness of Mankind concur to shew'.[164] It was required by 'the Defence of Men's Persons and Possessions against lawless Power, and the securing their Enjoyment of the Means of Prosperity'.[165] This description of society led Wishart to define the nation in a similar way:

> Our native country, then, is not so much that Spot of Earth on which we have our Birth; as that Society of Men in conjunction with whom we are born, under the same Government and Laws; Laws formed for the Welfare of every Person, as best suits the general Good of the whole Society; Laws by which we are protected and defended, in the Enjoyment of our just Liberties and Properties; and from which we derive various Advantages, long before we are capable of making any Return, or Acknowledgement for them.[166]

True love of country, then, was not 'a Fondness for any particular distinguishing Customs, good or bad; but a Concern for its real Welfare'. It was 'a special Branch of the Love of Mankind; never to be detached from, far less set in opposition to, that general Affection, of which it is a Branch'.[167] The problems of a society, therefore, were those actions which infringed the liberties, properties, and advantages which accrued from membership of the society.

Whatever the problems, Wishart saw the remedy as the application of Christian principles and, in particular, of what generally came to be called 'Universal Love'. He saw Universal Love as striking at the root of the mischiefs which disturbed and embittered human society. It promoted the benefit of those around as well as public prosperity in general. Furthermore, it was binding on the Christian: it was 'the End of

---

[164] William Wishart, *Public Virtue Recommended. A Sermon preached in the High Church of Edinburgh, on Thursday, May 8th, 1746, at the Opening of the General Assembly of the Church of Scotland* (Edinburgh, 1746), p. 3.

[165] Ibid., p. 5.

[166] Ibid.

[167] Ibid., p. 6.

all [God's] Laws and Institutions to us'. It was 'the Religion of Jesus'.[168]
It was of the greatest importance, therefore, that young people should
be educated in the principles of 'Universal Love and Goodness', since it
would lead them to become 'reasonable and social creatures'. Love of
goodness could be inculcated, and must therefore be studied since it was
owed

> to a Perfectly-Good God, and a compassionate Saviour; to their
> Native Country, our Happy Constitution, and the Auspicious
> Government of our Gracious Sovereign; to their Parents, Masters,
> Instructors, and Benefactors; and to all their Fellow-creatures.[169]

Here Wishart established the religious basis of the nature of society, a
perception which was to remain the essential feature of Popular social
thought. Universal love was seen as the cement which bound society
together in all its relationships. Twenty years later, he took this idea to
its ultimate conclusion, and argued that society was a concept to be interpreted in its widest sense, since God had not only formed human beings
'for the exercise of love and beneficence towards those of our own kind;
but for a more extensive exercise of kindness and goodwill towards the
whole body of reasonable beings'.[170] He had taken the idea a step beyond
what he thought in 1732, when he argued that 'the highest Love of God
is the proper and natural Exercise of this Principle, the Love of Goodness'.[171]

He went on to assess the application of universal love in society. It was,
he said, 'an active and operative Principle', and therefore its corollary
was the obligation on the Christian to do what he could to suppress vice.
This should be done by instruction, by persuasion, and by good example.
Suppression of vice, however, raised the question of the punishment of
offenders. The method of punishing offenders, he argued, should be
confined to such crimes as were hurtful to others around the criminal
and which 'disturb the peace of human society'. He justified this on two
grounds: because the rights of others to free enquiry, or to freedom of
conscience must not be infringed; and, more fundamentally, because virtue
and vice were to be defined in terms of social effect:

> Piety and Virtue is, in its own nature, always the Good; and Vice
> the Ill; of every man: that temper and conduct which is the best for
> others about us; is also best for ourselves: and so far as we are
> wanting to promote the good of our neighbours and of mankind;
> we are so far wanting to ourselves, and cease to promote our own
> good and happiness.[172]

---

168 Wishart, *Charity the End of the Commandment*, p. 27.
169 Ibid., pp. 32, 34.
170 Wishart, 'Indispensible Necessity of a Holy and Good Life', pp. 16–17; cf. Banner-
     man, *Sermon upon Reformation and Revolution Principles*, p. 23, quoted below, p. 78.
171 Wishart, *Difference betwixt Moral Good and Evil*, p. 14.
172 Ibid., pp. 13, 28–9.

This line of argument led to Wishart's blurring of the distinction between moral good and evil, in spite of the title of his work on the subject. He upheld 'the free exercise of ... [men's] natural and inalienable right of enquiring for themselves in affairs of religion; and acting agreeably to the light of their own minds'. Accordingly, he drew attention to the need not to limit this right in 'so far as it does not lead them to commit any matter of wrong or wicked lewdness, by which their neighbours are injured or their natural or civil rights invaded'.[173] Wishart's retreat from absolute standards of virtue and vice was a move which few in the Popular party were prepared to condone outright, though it proved a feature of Popular thought until the last two decades of the century.[174] His thinking on liberty of conscience was increasingly accepted in the 1740s and '50s.

The most serious moral problem facing society in Wishart's opinion, however, was what he saw as the 'general dissoluteness of Youth', which manifested itself in the espousal of 'the most loose and dissolute principles' combined with a desire to distinguish themselves from others. Wishart ascribed all this to the universal neglect of 'rational and virtuous Education'; parents took more care in training their dogs and horses than their children. Even more worrying was the fact that much of the 'looseness and debauchery' was found in those who had the benefit of a 'Religious Education'. This serious problem was to be ascribed to the preoccupation of parents and instructors with inculcating the 'Shibboleth of a Party', and with making children familiar with 'the particular doctrines or peculiar forms of their own Sect', instead of 'forming their minds to a rational sense of Good and Evil, a taste and relish for true Piety and Virtue'. Such instances of good behaviour as were taught were enforced by 'meer [sic] authority, or by the awe of future rewards and punishments' which were never explained. The devotion and piety of parents, furthermore, was not attractive but rather 'disgusting and forbidding'. All this encouraged 'every selfish passion and appetite'. No reformation of youth could be expected until the gross faults in their education were remedied, maintained Wishart.[175] In what he saw as the biggest problem facing society, there was little of the traditional preoccupations of orthodox Calvinists with original sin, the depravity of man, or the need for the intervention of the Holy Spirit to improve the situation. It may seem surprising that so many of his arguments were adopted by Popular thinkers who did not accept his theological positions. It should not be thought, however, that Wishart completely disregarded the spiritual or doctrinal aspects of the problem.

---

173 Ibid., p. 30. It was the commitment to the first of these propositions which was a major factor in the reluctance of the Popular leadership to participate in the prosecution of Hume and Kames at the General Assembly of 1756, in spite of the desire of some members of the party to do so. See above, pp. 72–3.

174 See Wishart, 'Indispensible Necessity of a Holy and Good Life', pp. 11, 16–24.

175 Wishart, *Difference betwixt Moral Good and Evil*, pp. 30–5.

The problem was that he was never precise about what he meant by such terms as 'pure and undefiled religion'. On the one hand he argued that behaviour could be improved by a general morality based on such concepts as 'goodness' and 'virtue', and on the other he implied that religion had a unique social role.[176] These two ideas, the latter of which was to become a dominant one in Popular thought, together with the definition of the morality of actions in terms of their effect on others, were first to be found in Wishart's work.

Not all supporters of the Popular party, however, shared Wishart's expansive view of the nature of society. This was especially true concerning their views on the necessity of religion for its very continuance. As early as 1751, Patrick Bannerman of Kinnoull had argued that 'To preserve a free state, without preserving its Virtue, is a mere Chimaera; and to preserve the public Virtue, without a sense of God and Religion, is no better'.[177] Another such was George Anderson. In his *Remonstrance against Lord Viscount Bolingbroke's Philosophical Religion* of 1756, Anderson argued for the incompatibility of atheism and society as the former led to 'an end of all trust, and an end of all society and government'.[178]

Such reasoning, possibly connected indirectly with Wishart's argument that social or public virtue arose from universal love, which in turn derived from the Christian religion, appeared in the thought of a number of other Popular writers. Bannerman talked of the 'Divine Principle of Love' being the 'true cement of society', and argued that it was the obligation of every member of society to cultivate it.[179] Daniel Macqueen of the Old Kirk of Edinburgh combated Hume on similar grounds.[180] As a result of this analysis, some Popular thinkers openly castigated the life style of the upper class. John Warden, of the Edinburgh Canongate, for example, argued that infidelity and profanity abounded, and that vice was fashionable and kept in countenance by the example of the great.[181]

The second identifiable interest among Popular writers in their evaluation of Christian influence on society is their stress on the social implications of morality. This was based on the belief that, as Alexander Webster asserted, 'private happiness is not to be enjoyed on any sure and lasting foundation, but in subordination to the public good'. Failure to appreciate this could only lead to the war of all men against each other. The giving up of personal ease and advantage, furthermore, was blessed by God in a similar way to that in which the spiritual interests of members of the Body of Christ necessarily depended on suffering or

176 Ibid., pp. 35–6.
177 Bannerman, *Sermon upon Reformation and Revolution Principles*, p. 16.
178 Anderson, *Remonstrance*, p. 449.
179 Bannerman, *Sermon upon Reformation and Revolution Principles*, p. 23.
180 Macqueen, *Letters on Mr. Hume's History of Great Britain*, p. 307.
181 Warden, *Happiness of Britain illustrated*, p. 56.

rejoicing with one another.[182] 'All visible actions have an effect upon others as well as themselves', wrote John Witherspoon. 'Everything we see or hear makes some impression on us, though for the most part unperceived, and we contribute, every moment, to form each other's character.'[183]

The social implications of virtuous behaviour led to the development of a critique of wealth.[184] In eighteenth-century Scotland, most Popular thinkers were more concerned with the social consequences of the possession of wealth than they were with those of poverty. John Gillies's views were representative. In his *Exhortation to the Inhabitants of the South Parish of Glasgow* he held that: 'If thy poverty is not the Effect of Idleness or Prodigality, it is not Flattery to tell thee, thou art probably an honester Man than many of the Rich.'[185] As such, poverty was a social problem if it was not brought upon oneself, and not a socio-religious or moral problem as was wealth.[186]

That poverty as such did not appear to require attention was the result of two factors. First, aid for the poor was taken for granted to be a Christian duty. Secondly, the latter half of the eighteenth century was a period of sustained, though slow, growth in prosperity, which affected many sections of the community.[187] In most areas, it was believed that poverty was being held in check by the traditional system of poor relief at the hands of the kirk sessions.[188] On occasions when the parochial system of poor relief was in difficulty, the response was to seek aid from special collections authorised by presbyteries. More widespread problems were met with the appointment of fast days and calls to communal repentance.[189] Since these problems were usually the result of poor

182 Webster, *Zeal for the Civil and Religious Interest of Mankind*, pp. 341–2.
183 Witherspoon, *Serious Enquiry into the Nature and Effects of the Stage*, p. 59.
184 See below, pp. 212–18, 223.
185 Gillies, *Exhortation*, p. 29. Whether the poor emerged particularly clearly as an identifiable group in the minds of Popular writers in the second half of the century is uncertain. Even the obligation to preach the gospel first to the poor was a subject to which reference was rarely made. John Snodgrass made one of the rare allusions to it when he pointed out that the Gospel was intended to be understood by the poor as well as 'the learned and speculative', and that, therefore, preaching should be suited to their level of comprehension: Snodgrass, *Leading Doctrines of the Gospel*, p. 291.
186 Ibid.
187 On this see, e.g., Campbell, *Scotland since 1707*; T. C. Smout, 'Where had the Scottish economy got to by the third quarter of the eighteenth century?' in I. Hont and M. Ignatieff (eds.), *Wealth and Virtue: The Shaping of Political Economy in the Scottish Enlightenment* (Cambridge, 1983), pp. 45–72; Devine and Mitchison, *People and Society in Scotland*, i; and the various other works on Scottish economic history.
188 On this subject see, R. Mitchison, 'The making of the Old Scottish Poor Law', *Past and Present*, lxiii (1974), pp. 58–93; R. A. Cage, 'Debate: the making of the Old Scottish Poor Law', *Past and Present*, lxix (1975); and R. Mitchison, 'A rejoinder', *Past and Present*, lxix (1975), pp. 113–21; R. Mitchison, 'The creation of the Disablement Rule in the Scottish Poor Law', in T. C. Smout (ed.), *The Search for Wealth and Stability: Essays in Economic and Social History presented to M. W. Flinn* (London, 1979), pp. 199–217; and R. A. Cage, *The Scottish Poor Law* (Edinburgh, 1981).
189 See, e.g., McIntosh, 'Evangelicals in Eighteenth-Century Scotland', pp. 16–19.

harvests, such difficulties tended to be of a transient nature. Preoccupation with the dangers and obligations of wealth reflected the increasing
prosperity in all sections of the community. Acceptance of the Christian
obligation to be charitable and relative complacency about the causes
and extent of poverty in Scotland was the first theme in Popular thought
on the subject.

John Witherspoon considered the problem of wealth in the context of
the debate over the nature and effects of the theatre. He divided the
possessors of wealth into two classes and, in so doing, established the
framework of the discussion of the uses of wealth which was the second
dominant theme in Popular thought on the subject during the rest of
the century. First, there were 'those who live in affluence, and know no
other use of riches but to feed their appetites, and make all the rest of
mankind subservient to the gratification of their violent and ungovern-
able passions'.[190] On the other hand, there were those who used their
wealth virtuously. The rich had 'the distinguished honour, if they please
to embrace it, of contributing to the happiness of multitudes under
them, and dispensing, under God, a great variety of the comforts of this
life'. In spite of the immoral attitude of the first category of the wealthy,
Witherspoon eschewed radical action against them or their wealth, since
'none in this world have any title to hinder them from disposing of their
wealth as they please, they must be called to consider that they have a
master in heaven' who would call them to account for their riches. The
seriousness of this final accountability should, in fact, cause those less
well off to be less envious of the rich and to moderate their appetite after
wealth, since the more that is committed to men, the more they have to
account for. Nevertheless, the greatest and richest have no licence in the
Word of God for unnecessary waste of their substance or its consumption
with unprofitable or hurtful pleasures.[191]

Those of the Popular party who wrote on the subject of wealth and
poverty were unanimous that there was a moral and religious obligation
on the wealthy to contribute part of their wealth to the relief of the poor,
and that they could be regarded as seriously accountable to God if they
did not. Equally unanimously, however, they held out little hope that the
wealthy would honour their obligations. The reason was that the wealthy
were less likely to be godly than the multitude of mankind. As
Witherspoon put it in connection with his argument against the stage:

> The far greatest number of the world are ungodly ... And as none
> can attend the stage, but those in higher life, and more affluent
> circumstances than the bulk of mankind, there is still a greater
> proportion of them who are enemies to pure and undefiled religion
> ... This does not at all suppose, that those in high life are originally

190 Witherspoon, *Serious Enquiry into the Nature and Effects of the Stage*, p. 22–3.
191 Ibid., p. 22. See also Bannerman, *Sermon upon Reformation and Revolution Principles*, p. 37.

more corrupt in their nature than others, but it arises from their being exposed to much greater and stronger temptations.[192]

This was because the rich were tempted to luxury and to irreligion because of it. Witherspoon's suspicion of wealth was reinforced by his pessimistic, cyclical interpretation of national development in which wealth led to luxury which was the precursor of a return to poverty.[193] His analysis of the future prospects of British society was singularly pessimistic, and indeed was possibly connected with his eventual departure for America. Societies, he believed, followed a cyclical pattern of growth and decline: poverty by virtue of industry became wealth and power, from which societies proceeded to luxury and vice, and thence to poverty and subjection again. It was probable, he felt, that Britain was now in the age of luxury.[194] The development of this type of critique of wealth was not to occur, however, until the later years of the century.

VIII

The Popular perception of a key link between religion and society led to theories on, among others, the nature of government and authority, the place of the magistrate, and the nature of civil and religious liberty. Popular analysis of the nature and purpose of government was much more theologically based than its analysis of society. Deriving some, but not all, of its aspects from William Wishart, the dominant Popular interpretation until after the middle of the century was that the origin of government lay in fallen human nature. Divine sanction was implied rather than explicit since the results of the Fall of Man meant that sin and evil in society had to be restrained. The purpose of government was to promote the security and welfare of the community. Society, for Wishart, was 'natural to Men, and necessary to their Improvement and Perfection [as] both the natural Abilities, and the natural Weaknesses of Mankind concur to shew'. These abilities and weaknesses led to the necessity of government for the 'Defence of Men's Persons and Possessions against lawless Power, and the securing their Enjoyment of the Means of Prosperity ...'[195]

Following from Wishart, several Popular writers accepted the possibility of secular explanations of the origin of government. Such a position, of course, ruled out any 'divine right' theory, as George Logan of the Canongate pointed out as early as 1746 in his debates with the Jacobite publisher Thomas Ruddiman.[196] More importantly, however, as

---

192 Witherspoon, *Serious Enquiry into the Nature and Effects of the Stage*, p. 35.
193 Ibid., p. 69. See also below, pp. 212–13, 216.
194 Witherspoon, *Serious Enquiry into the Nature and Effects of the Stage*, p. 69.
195 Wishart, *Public Virtue Recommended*, p. 5.
196 George Logan, *A Treatise on Government; shewing, That the Right of Kings of Scotland to the Crown was not Strictly and Absolutely Hereditary* (Edinburgh, 1746); George Logan,

subsequent Popular writers accepted, the exclusion of direct, divine approbation allowed alternative explanations of the basis of government and made possible the use of Enlightenment ideas about the origin of society. As Logan argued: 'whatever the Form of Government is, that Men have established, agreeable to the Dictates of right Reason, so as to answer to the valuable Ends of it; it draws after it the Divine Approbation, and is of God'.[197]

It was the assumption of the existence of fundamental natural rights, however, that led Popular thought in the direction of the political liberalism which was one of the main characteristics of the Popular party for much of the second half of the eighteenth century. In many cases the discussion of matters relating to government arose from issues such as the nature of vice, and religious toleration and liberty. Wishart, for example, did so in connection with how one should attempt to improve one's neighbour, and immediately assumed the existence of natural and civil rights which included 'the right of enquiring for themselves in affairs of religion; and acting agreeably to the light of their own minds' providing it did not lead to the injury of neighbours' natural or civil rights.[198] Furthermore, he assumed that it was 'the proper office of the Civil Magistrate to protect and defend all good subjects' in the possession and exercise of these rights. One of the hallmarks of the happiness of British society was that the existing government 'in the making of Laws and the administration of justice, acts with such a sacred regard to *these rights*'.[199] Although it must be admitted that Wishart was primarily concerned with such rights in their religious applications, it does seem that he felt no need to probe more deeply into their origins.[200] It is true, moreover, that if the case for religious toleration was accepted, given the primacy of religion in the Popular mind, then it was a relatively short step to acceptance of liberty of conscience in general.[201] Daniel Macqueen, for example, implied this step in his answers to Hume's strictures that Protestantism was inimical to rational enquiry, when he stressed Protestantism's commitment to 'freedom of enquiry and the rights of conscience'. This commitment accorded with 'the principles of the clearest reason, and with the natural rights of mankind'.[202] Certainly, Macqueen wanted to establish the existence of

   A Second Treatise on Government; Shewing, That the Right to the Crown of Scotland was not Hereditary, in the Sense of the Jacobites (Edinburgh, 1747).

197 Logan, *Treatise on Government*, p. vi.

198 Wishart, *Difference betwixt Moral Good and Evil*, p. 30.

199 Ibid., pp. 30–1.

200 See also Wishart, *Public Virtue Recommended*, p. 21.

201 Patrick Bannerman argued a curious case in which religious freedom was derived from civil liberty which 'admits no Infringements of the Rights of private Judgement ... No claims are allowed of Lordship over the Conscience, or Dominion over the Faith': Bannerman, *Sermon upon Reformation and Revolution Principles*, p. 9. See also p. 23.

202 Macqueen, *Letters on Mr. Hume's History of Great Britain*, pp. 55, 67.

the beneficial influence of Protestantism in this connection for advancing 'the interest of truth and learning in the world'.[203]

There was also a satisfaction with the capacity and willingness of the system of British government to act in accordance with the laws of God to produce an adequately moral society and to preserve religious freedom. It was 'the peculiar Blessing of Britons to enjoy Liberty and Government in Perfection', asserted Patrick Bannerman; and most would have agreed with John Warden when he claimed that the national liberty of Britons was 'greater than anywhere else in the known world'.[204] In view of this, it was the duty of Christians to accept the British government's legitimate authority, and to give it their consistent support and obedience.[205] As early as 1754, Alexander Webster stated unequivocally and comprehensively:

> whatever arguments, for promoting the welfare of mankind in general, arise from the laws of nature and of grace, from the practice and writings of the prophets and apostles, from the command and example of the great God and Saviour, and from our own best interests, they all plead strongly for the preservation and support of our constitution in particular, both in church and state, as the great means of our happiness in this world, and in the world to come.[206]

As with the Popular interpretation of the Christian view of society, which eventually led to stands on Roman Catholic emancipation and the French Revolution, so Popular ideas of government were also reflected in responses to more general political developments. Forays by members of the Popular party, in their ecclesiastical capacities, into other more specific political events were rare, especially in the twenty years or so after 1740. One exception was that, as a result of Queen Caroline's intervention in the Porteous affair of 1736, Alexander Webster identified himself with the faction of Frederick, Prince of Wales. He was joined by the Moderate, Robert Wallace, and both were rewarded with appointments as the Prince of Wales' chaplains for Scotland in 1739. Around the same time, Webster attacked Sir Robert Walpole in a

---

[203] Ibid., p. 187.

[204] Bannerman, *Sermon upon Reformation and Revolution Principles*, p. 38; see also pp. 17, 26, 39; and Warden, *Happiness of Britain illustrated*, p. 10.

[205] See, e.g., Bannerman, *Sermon upon Reformation and Revolution Principles*, p. 17. This type of appraisal of the government's qualities contributes, too, to an understanding of the Popular party's attempt to seek parliamentary action to remedy the grievance of the patronage system.

[206] Webster, *Zeal for the Civil and Religious Interests of Mankind*, p. 348. There is more than a little similarity in this line of reasoning to John Erskine's analysis of the sources of anarchy, in which he distinguished between licentiousness which permitted any to be false and malicious in their words, writings, and actions, and liberty which was only truly to be found under law which guaranteed both the rights of the citizen and gave him access to his superiors for his complaints: John Erskine, *The Fatal Consequences and General Sources of Anarchy. A Discourse on Isaiah, xxiv, 1–5* (Edinburgh, 1793), p. 12.

sermon in which he compared him to Haman in the Book of Esther.[207] In general, however, Popular ministers were not involved in day to day political activities. But the party as a whole, following the conviction that the Church of Scotland had a right, and indeed a duty, to represent the views of the people of Scotland on issues of moral or social importance, did become involved in the course of the second half of the century in political debate over three subjects: the American War of Independence, the abolition of the slave trade, and the operation of the religious Test Act.

IX

Since the Popular party was increasingly concerned with declining religious observance and growing 'infidelity', which it saw as connected with the growth of wealth and luxury, it would not be unexpected if Popular writers had shown an overall pattern of hostility to matters of culture. Certainly the Popular party united against the theatre in the *Douglas* affair during the 1750s. They were outraged that ministers should have attended its performance, and especially that a minister should have been the playwright. Most historians have therefore assumed that Popular sentiment was narrowly anti-cultural and obscurantist in general in such matters.[208] This view is based on a failure to analyse, or, in most cases, even to seek out, the relevant sources.[209] Even if the initial instincts of some members of the party were to repress, or at least eschew, cultural activity, they still produced reasoned defences of their position. More importantly, the consistency of their theological positions and their religious view of human activity led most of the influential members of the party to accept that general condemnation of cultural activities and amusements was untenable.

The debate, in fact, had been opened as early as 1733 by George Anderson in his *Use and Abuse of Diversions*, where he linked the pursuit of pleasures and diversions with Epicurean philosophy and contrasted it with the stress on pain, diligence, work, and labour which Scripture used to describe religion and the way to salvation. Those who were 'above the Wants and Necessities of this World' were already 'Lovers of Pleasure

---

207 Morren, *Annals of the General Assembly*, i, p. 302, note.
208 E.g., W. L. Mathieson, *The Awakening of Scotland: A History from 1747 to 1797* (Glasgow, 1910) pp. 197–9, 229–30; Burleigh, *Church History of Scotland*, pp. 304–5; Drummond and Bulloch, *Scottish Church*, pp. 76–8; and Chitnis, *Scottish Enlightenment*, pp. 54–5.
209 E.g., those works cited in note 208; and J. Cunningham, *The Church History of Scotland, from the Commencement of the Christian Era to the Present Century* (Edinburgh, 1859), ii, p. 511. Sher, *Church and University in the Scottish Enlightenment*, pp. 74–92, is a notable exception to this pattern, but even he misinterprets the context and the significance of the affair. See below, pp. 86–9.

more than Lovers of God'.[210] He described Edinburgh as the city most given over to 'a Spirit of Idleness and Levity', proportionate to its size, in all of Europe.[211] More importantly, he provided a definition of legitimate diversions which was subsequently to be rejected by several writers who were to determine Popular opinion in the years after 1750:

> there are few, yea very few of our ordinary Diversions but what exceed the Limits of Christianity. All Pleasures and Diversions are to be regulated and managed according to their End and Use. Now all the Use of Diversions is to ease the Body and Mind when wearied with Thought and Labour. Diversions, then, are only so far lawful as they unyoke the Mind from Study and Meditation, and the Body from Toil, in order to recruit and refit both for other and fresh Undertakings. This is their End, and this only is their Use. Whatever more enters into the Matter is beyond all Christian Measure, and consequently sinful and unlawful.[212]

Furthermore, diversions led to an unlawful waste of time, means, and wealth. 'They weaken the Mind for Piety and Devotion, and lead to many Temptations.' An idle life devoted to pleasure led to domestic quarrels, neglect of children, delay in the payment of debts, deception in order to gain further credit, and even to the possible ruin of families. The poor were deprived from benefiting from God's provision for them by works of charity, and diversion of potential funds away from charity was akin to sacrilege.[213] Analysis of this type paved the way for the attack on *Douglas* and its supporters. It was a pragmatic argument which, on its own terms, was difficult to counter. Its weakness was that it failed completely to consider that there were any legitimate activities other than spiritual improvement and the obtaining of physical sustenance. It certainly did not consider the implications of life in a society where increasing numbers were distancing themselves from traditional religious observance and spiritual activity. These were factors which led to the development of a more comprehensive attitude to the participation of Christians in secular culture.

It was John Witherspoon who was responsible for the transition to a more liberal interpretation of what was and was not legitimate in the area of culture and entertainment. On one level, he contrasted questions of taste with religious truths. 'There is a great difference', he wrote, 'between the shining thoughts which are applauded in the world by men of taste, and the solid and profitable truths of religion.'[214] He regarded

---

210 George Anderson, *The Use and Abuse of Diversions. A Sermon on Luke xix, 13, with an Appendix, shewing that the Stage in particular is an Unchristian Diversion* (Edinburgh, 1733), pp. 14, 19, 22.
211 Ibid., p. 12.
212 Ibid., p. 24.
213 Ibid., pp. 27–9.
214 Witherspoon, *Serious Enquiry into the Nature and Effects of the Stage*, p. 26.

the literary forms of 'romances and fabulous narrations' as doing the world little good and much harm, though he was far from specific about the nature of the alleged harm. He affirmed that such literature was only exceeded by stage plays in their capacity for mischief.[215] It was not merely because of his assessment of their moral impact that Witherspoon was suspicious of fashionable taste and judgement; it was also part of his assessment of the pattern of the development of societies.[216] His cyclical theory of national rise, decline, and fall viewed questions of cultural taste as potential benchmarks of the overall health of society:

> with respect to learning, men rise from ignorance to application, from application to knowledge, this ripens into taste and judgement, then, from a desire of distinguishing themselves, they superadd affected ornaments, become more fanciful than solid, their taste corrupts with their manners, and they fall back into the gulf of ignorance.[217]

It would be a mistake, however, to see Witherspoon's position as simply one of opposition to, or disinterest in, matters of culture. It was more complex. All human accomplishments without an immediate reference to spiritual improvement were not to be condemned; they should rather be kept in a subordinate position to the chief end of man. There were many useful and ornamental arts which had immediate effects other than making men holy, but since they were usually abused, they were often thought of as having no religious significance. This was mistaken, for a good man would choose and apply such arts in accordance with the main purpose of his life, which was more than just to make a name for himself in the fashionable world. That would be inconsistent with one's Christian profession.

> In short, these arts are among the number of indifferent things which should be supremely and ultimately directed to the glory of God. When they are not capable of this, either immediately or remotely, much more when they are contrary to it, they must be condemned.[218]

Witherspoon, therefore, produced a new touchstone to assess the acceptability of cultural pursuits or diversions: could it be either directly or indirectly capable of contributing to the glory of God? It was still a pragmatic approach, but it was more permissive than Anderson's.

Appreciation of the significance of the debate within the Popular party on these issues makes it possible to place the *Douglas* affair of 1757 in its proper perspective. *The Tragedy of Douglas* by John Home, minister of

---

215 Ibid., p. 49.
216 See above, p. 81; and below, pp. 212–13.
217 Witherspoon, *Serious Enquiry into the Nature and Effects of the Stage*, p. 69.
218 Ibid., pp. 66–7.

Athelstaneford, was first performed publicly in Edinburgh on 14 December 1756. The author and several other ministers were present. On 5 January 1757, the Presbytery of Edinburgh attacked the theatre and theatre-going in an 'Admonition and Exhortation to all within their bounds'. This document commenced:

> The Presbytery taking into their consideration the declining state of religion, the open profanation of the Lord's Day, the contempt of public worship, the growing luxury and levity of the present age – in which so many seem lovers of pleasure more than lovers of God – and being particularly affected with the *unprecedented countenance* given of late to the playhouse in this place, when the state of the nation, and the circumstances of the poor, make such hurtful entertainments still more pernicious, judged it their indispensable duty to express, in the most open and solemn manner, the deep concern they feel on this occasion.[219]

Some of this, admittedly, was of the nature of the conventional rhetoric of such occasions, but the social concern was a theme to which the document returned. Mention was made of the numbers of servants, apprentices, and students who had been diverted from their proper business by attending the theatre; attention was called to the unseemliness of mirth and jollity when the King had called for humiliation and prayer in view of the war then being fought; and the needs of the poor were proclaimed: 'When the wants and cries of the numerous poor require extraordinary supplies, how unaccountable is it to lavish away vast sums for such vain and idle purposes.'[220] The Presbytery of Glasgow endorsed this line of reasoning in a resolution of 2 February 1757 which covered much the same ground and talked of 'the wasteful expense of money and time' occasioned by stage entertainments.[221] To some extent, it is true that the Popular case against *Douglas* and its patrons was supported to a considerable extent by reiteration of earlier legislation and precedents hostile to the theatre and the traditional arguments against theatre-going and the theatre in general, but it does emerge that the campaign against *Douglas* was stimulated by social concerns as much as by religious ones. The affair was more complex and not just a re-emergence of traditional prejudices.

The *Douglas* affair is not only important for the light it throws on the Popular party's attitudes to culture. Its attitude on the issue indicates that the party was more in step with opinion within the Church as a whole than was the Moderate leadership. The 'great majority' of the Presbytery of Edinburgh were in favour of suspending rather than merely rebuking the minister of Liberton who had attended the

---

[219] Morren, *Annals of the General Assembly*, ii, p. 112.
[220] Ibid., p. 114.
[221] For the Presbytery of Glasgow's resolution, see ibid., pp. 130–1.

performance, though they limited the suspension to one month.[222] The Presbyteries of Haddington, Ayr, Earlston, Chirnside, Duns, and Dalkeith, which had been sent the names of ministers who had attended the theatre by the Edinburgh presbytery, all took action against their offending members.[223] It is notable that, in his defence before the Presbytery of Dalkeith and the Synod of Lothian and Tweeddale, Alexander Carlyle, the most celebrated of those charged, at no point attempted to argue in favour of the stage, although he did do so in his pamphlets *A Full and True History of the Bloody Tragedy of Douglas* and *An Argument to Prove that the Tragedy of Douglas ought to be Publickly Burnt by the Hands of the Hangman.*[224] Neither did the supporters of *Douglas* attempt to argue in favour of the stage in the Church courts; Carlyle's case, which was the only one to reach the Assembly, was a purely legal and procedural one which was accepted by an overwhelming number of Assembly members. The Assembly was equally overwhelming in condemning theatre-going by ministers. Carlyle may have avoided further censure in 1757, and may have avowed that the Act passed 'Forbidding the Clergy to Countenance the Theatre' was a deadletter, and John Witherspoon may have lamented in 1763 that it had served to encourage rather than to prevent the theatre, but it was passed overwhelmingly.[225]

The significance of the controversy over *Douglas*, therefore, is not that it represented another instance of the Popular-Moderate split in the Church, or that it indicated the reactionary nature of the Popular response to Enlightenment ideas, but that the majority of the Church felt that the theatre was a highly dubious place, if not in fact a sinful one, to be attended by a minister, since, for social as well as religious reasons, theatre-going raised inconsistencies with their professions of faith and with their duties both as ministers and as Christians. The former arose as a result of the immorality of much of what was depicted on stage, the latter because of the unacceptability of spending prodigal amounts on the theatre while the poor needed relief. It exaggerates the issue's importance to see it as a watershed which pointed the Church and Scottish society in the 'direction of cultural and intellectual freedom, religious moderation, and respect for serious endeavours in all branches of the arts and sciences'. No more did it signify 'the triumph of the Moderate ideal of a polite ministry leading Scotland down the path to

---

[222] Ibid., p. 115.

[223] Ibid., pp. 117–22. It is interesting to note that of the 6 presbyteries involved, Clark ascribes Moderate majorities at the time to all except Carlyle's Presbytery of Dalkeith, which he believes was evenly balanced. See Clark, 'Moderatism and the Moderate Party', pp. 182–3.

[224] Morren, *Annals of the General Assembly*, ii, pp. 122–30.

[225] Alexander Carlyle, *Anecdotes and Characters of the Times*, ed. J. Kinsley (London, 1973), pp. 159–63; Witherspoon, *A Serious Apology for the Ecclesiastical Characteristics*, in *Works*, iv, pp. 270–1.

enlightenment'.[226] Carlyle himself was closer to the truth when he asserted that the Assembly's decision to affirm the Synod's expression of its 'displeasure' with him and its requirement of him to refrain from theatre-going in the future, proved that 'the heat and animosity raised against the tragedy of *Douglas* and its supporters was artificial and local'.[227]

To some extent Popular sentiment, even in more 'liberal' quarters, saw taste and culture as connected to the growth of luxury. In view of the link of luxury with spiritual decline, it is probably true to say that culture remained an area of moral suspicion in the minds of Popular thinkers, even when it was regarded as a legitimate area of Christian involvement. It should be noted, however, that there are grounds for doubting whether the Popular party was monolithic in its delineations of what was or was not acceptable in these matters. Lay supporters may well have been much more flexible on the issues than their ministerial spokesmen. John Maclaurin the advocate, later to be elevated to the Court of Session as Lord Dreghorn, and a leading Popular lay figure (not to be confused with his relative, Rev. John Maclaurin), produced a substantial piece of literary criticism in his *Apology for the Writers against the Tragedy of Douglas*. It is evident from the work that Maclaurin was familiar with a wide range of literature and that he took an active interest in the literary life of Edinburgh. It is implied that he was accustomed to attend the theatre. He subjected *Douglas* to a sustained critical analysis but found no evidence to justify regarding it as other than 'a tolerable modern tragedy'.[228] He did not share the unqualified castigation of the stage as was demonstrated, for example, by Anderson or Witherspoon, though he deprecated the clerical status of its author:

> We would have rejoiced to see a countryman of ours excel in tragedy. We are indeed sorry that a *Scotch* clergyman has written a play; but we would have admired the tragedy, had it been good, though we thought it blameable in the author to write one.[229]

Apart from savaging 'the puffers of *Douglas*' for their gross overestimation of its qualities, Maclaurin's work was notable for an onslaught on the Edinburgh Moderate literati and their pretensions:

> Some years ago, a few gentlemen in this town assumed the charac-ter of being the only judges in all points of literature; they were and still are styled the geniuses, and lately erected what they called a

---

226 Sher, *Church and University in the Scottish Enlightenment*, p. 86.
227 Alexander Carlyle, *Autobiography*, ed. J. H. Burton (London, 1910), p. 338, quoted in Sher, *Church and University in the Scottish Enlightenment*, p. 85.
228 John Maclaurin, *Apology for the Writers against the Tragedy of Douglas, with some Remarks on that Play* (Edinburgh, 1757), p. 7.
229 Ibid., pp. 3–4.

select society, which usurps a kind of aristocratical government over all men and matters of learning.[230]

According to Maclaurin, the 'first and fundamental maxim of this dictatorial club is, That a punctilious correctness of style is the *summum bonum* of all compositions'. Preoccupation with grammar and syntax led these authorities to miss seeing genius in a work and led to bizarre estimations of the works of writers. Voltaire and Hume were to be preferred to Shakespeare and Addison, and *Douglas* was to be esteemed superior to anything written by Shakespeare and Otway.[231]

In a satirical work which he wrote around the same time in 1757, *The Philosopher's Opera*, Maclaurin made the same criticism even more pointedly, and in fact turned the Moderate boast of their contribution to Scotland's intellectual status on its head. If Shakespeare and Otway were to be replaced by the author of *Douglas*, 'the taste of the country is at an end'. The club of gentlemen was unable to direct it, but since some men of learning were among them, many were misled by their authority and, though detesting the innovations, were reluctant to contradict them. Consequently, *Douglas* was performed thirteen times in Edinburgh, but Othello (which had not been performed there for seven years) 'brought no house at all'. All this proved, held Maclaurin, 'that the run *Douglas* had here, was owing to the influence of a party'. And then came the conclusion which used the Moderate literati's claim against themselves:

> It is certainly the duty of every man who regards the honour of his country, to make a stand against that unhappy barbarism which the cabal I have already mentioned is endeavouring to establish ... a set of men who owe their title of geniuses to the country of Scotland alone.[232]

It is significant that an eminent lay member of the Popular party, related to the eminent Rev. John Maclaurin of the Glasgow Ramshorn parish, was to be found moving with such ease, expertise, and confidence in a field which the Moderate literati regarded as their own. And, so far as can be ascertained, there was no murmur of protest from other members of the party.

Overall, what is striking in the attitudes of Popular writers on the subjects of culture and entertainment was the flexibility of their position, and the extent to which they were prepared to go to accommodate participation in secular activities. Especially is this so when the evidence is contrasted with general perceptions hitherto. It is true that Popular writers were not greatly concerned with matters of taste, literature, or culture in general. Apart from the *Douglas* controversy, these were topics

---

230 Ibid., p. 4.
231 Ibid., pp. 4–5. Maclaurin took Hume especially to task for his denigration of Shakespeare.
232 John Maclaurin [later Lord Dreghorn], *The Philosopher's Opera* (Edinburgh, 1757), p. iv.

which impinged on their perceptions only when they were raised by the more fundamental questions of the nature and obligations of the Christian life. Their perspective was a religious one. If men ensured that they were in a right relationship with God, matters of taste and culture, as indeed their activities in the secular world in general, would not be causes for concern. While the religious state of the nation was unsatisfactory, culture could only be a potential preoccupation to take men further away from God. There was, however, no inherent reason why taste and culture could not be participated in and directed to the glory of God.

CHAPTER THREE

The Problem of Patronage

It is not uncommon to see it maintained that patronage became the dominant factor in the eighteenth-century Church of Scotland with the production of the so-called 'manifesto' of the Moderate party, the 'Reasons of Dissent from the Judgement and resolution of the Commission, March 11, 1752, resolving to inflict no censure on the Presbytery of Dunfermline for their disobedience in relation to the settlement of Inverkeithing'. Perusal of the published sources on the subject indicates an earlier appearance of concern with the abuse of patronage, but not as an object of concern in its own right. The leaders of what was to become the eighteenth-century Popular party were increasingly worried at its incompatibility with the doctrine of the Church and the legitimate purpose of the ministry. Their publications show that they had three main concerns: the nature of the Christian Church as a unique institution deriving its function and authority from Christ himself, which led amongst other things, to the doctrine of Christian liberty; the nature and operation of the constitution of the Church of Scotland; and the case for a secular or political initiative to counter the inability of the Popular party to produce effectual ecclesiastical strategies or policies to counter Moderate control of the General Assembly. It should not be assumed, however, that these three issues can be detected systematically in an analysis of Popular writings on the subject of patronage. In fact, the essential feature of the literature is that it was an evolving response whose emphases varied according to the pattern of events at the General Assembly, though it is noteworthy that there was not a close correlation from year to year. The Popular response to patronage, even in its literary manifestations, had a strikingly pragmatic character. For this reason, it would be wrong to attempt an analysis of the ideology of Popular opposition to patronage in terms of the three main concerns. That would be to accord to Popular thought a coherence which it did not consistently display.

Though events at the General Assembly were often the stimulus for the publications, contributions to Assembly debates were only generally informed by the published works and identifiable specific references are rare. The absence of a consistent, direct correlation between the ideology of the party as it evolved in the published works on patronage and its policies at the Assembly makes it likely that at the day-to-day level of proceedings in the Assembly the response of the Popular party was much more pragmatic than its ideology would suggest. The response, in fact, went through five distinct phases from 1740 to the beginning of the nineteenth century.

The first of the phases began in the late 1740s and reached its climax in the 'Answers to the Reasons of Dissent in the Case of Inverkeithing' of 1752. In it stress was placed on what was seen as the Reformation principle of liberty of conscience, or, as it was usually termed, 'Christian liberty'. The two most important Popular spokesmen in the Assembly at the time were John Adams of Falkirk and Dr Alexander Webster of the Tolbooth Church in Edinburgh. Their line of argument, derived from the nature of Christian liberty, was increasingly overshadowed by the growth of the Secession, and led to the second phase which lasted from 1752 until the Schism Debate of 1766. In this, the dominant emphases were an attempt to show that patronage negated the purpose of establishment, which was to provide a ministry that would look after the spiritual needs of the population, and was inconsistent with the constitution of the Church of Scotland.

I

The deposition of the Seceders in 1740 marked something of the end of an era in the history of the Church of Scotland. The Secession, of course, had occurred in 1733 when Ebenezer Erskine, one of the ministers of Stirling, who had previously figured in a famous disputed settlement case in Kinross between 1726 and 1731, was removed from his charge for failing to withdraw a protest against patronage he had made at the Synod of Perth and Stirling, and to express sorrow for having made it. He and the three ministers who supported him in the protest were then suspended, and by the end of 1733 they were removed from their charges. Despite the efforts of the 1734 and 1736 Assemblies to appease and accommodate them, they constituted themselves into a presbytery, and in 1737 were joined by four other ministers including Erskine's brother Ralph, the minister of Dunfermline. In 1740 the Assembly finally decided to depose them.[1] The Secession marked the first significant dissent from the established Church of Scotland. It marked, too, the first significant reservations about the principle of Establishment. It also signalled at the time the failure of the Seceders' theological and ecclesiastical sympathisers to persuade them to return to the fold of the established Church, for even their strongest sympathisers did not regard their action over patronage as justifiable. In fact, the enormity of their separation may well have discouraged both patrons and presbyteries from potentially divisive courses of action during the best

[1] See above, p. 27.

part of the following decade, for the first three important patronage cases of the years after 1740 were essentially legal disputes.[2]

As has been suggested already, the key publication which set the tone for the debate, which was to continue for the rest of the century, was John Willison's *Fair and Impartial Testimony*, published in Edinburgh in 1744. In this work, Willison's argument on the nature and purpose of the Christian ministry was that its most important function was the preaching of the Gospel in an evangelical manner.[3] This being the case, then, the next crucial issue was the way in which ministers should be appointed to parishes. Without exception, the position adopted by the Popular party was that a call was essential. If there was unanimity about the necessity of a call, however, the party was split over the exact nature of the call and over who was entitled to participate in it. It is important to appreciate the significance of this division, for in it lay the seeds of a change from a theological or spiritual strategy of opposition to patronage to a secular or political one. This change was provoked by the failure of the Popular party to modify the Moderate determination to enforce patronage. Ultimately, it explains the virtual disappearance of the issue of patronage from the ecclesiastical scene in Scotland until the nineteenth century.

The basis of the Popular position was undoubtedly that of Willison's *Fair and Impartial Testimony*. Intrusions spoiled the right of congregations to call their own pastors, 'contrary to the Word of God and our known principles'. These rights 'Christ hath purchased for them'.[4] Congregational choice of ministers was the practice of the 'primitive and purest Ages of the Church'. Any encroachment on such rights was

> a plain Incroachment on the natural Rights of Mankind, and upon the Laws of free Societies ... The Churches of Christ are as free Societies as anywhere in the World, having their liberties from Christ to chuse their own Pastors; and ought not to be brought in Bondage to any in this Matter.[5]

Yet, if this was the starting-point for the Popular position on the nature of the call, it is important to realise that it is difficult to find an eighteenth-century publication from an identifiable member of the Popular party in the Church of Scotland, after the secession of Ebenezer Erskine, who actually ascribed to the congregation, or heads of families,

[2] Morren, *Annals of the General Assembly*, i, pp. 133–53, 169–80. The cases were those of Culross (1749), Duns (1749), and Lanark (1750).

[3] John Erskine linked this idea with an exhortation to patrons to consider carefully the qualifications of their presentees when they exercised their legal right lest the souls 'that may be lost by a bad nomination, will be required at their hands': Erskine, 'Qualifications necessary for Teachers of Christianity', pp. 38–40.

[4] Willison, *Fair and Impartial Testimony*, pp. ix–xii.

[5] Ibid., p. 47.

the sole right of calling a minister.[6] Willison himself maintained that it was evident from the Word of God and apostolic practice that it was only the Church herself, *with her officers*, that exercised the power of nominating and electing ministers and officers to the Church, according to the authority derived by them from Christ their head and founder.[7] The basic Popular position, therefore, may be described as 'constitutional', in that it was based on doctrinal principles and their legal outworking, not on notions of ecclesiastical democracy or standards of piety.[8] The constitutional nature of the position was emphasised by James Gordon, minister of Alford, who was a leading opponent of patronage at the General Assembly in the 1730s and 1740s. In his *State and Duty of the Church of Scotland*, he felt it unnecessary to prove that God's people had the power of right by divine law to choose their own pastors, since this was a principle of the Church. Nor did he deem it necessary to discuss the question whether the people's power should be exercised directly by themselves or by their representatives, in other words by every individual voting personally or by the eldership only with freedom to the congregation to assent or dissent as they wished. This latter method, Gordon pointed out, was the manner prescribed in the *Directory for Election of Ministers* enacted by the General Assembly on 4 August 1649, although that gave the eldership the first moves in the exercise of the right of election.[9] The general principles of this position were endorsed by the Popular leader John Adams of Falkirk in 1754.[10]

The constitutional nature of the basic Popular position, however, was compromised as early as 1732 by Gordon who, after committing himself to it, at the same time modified it in two ways. First, he introduced the notion of a 'Presbyterial call', and secondly, he limited the divine right to nominate or elect their own pastor to 'the intelligent religious people of God that reside in that parish'. He postulated two types of Presbyterial call, the first when a presbytery *concurred* with the election or call of a parish within its bounds, and the second when a presbytery made a choice of a minister for a parish which would not or could not make a choice for themselves. A Presbyterial call was necessary for every lawful

---

6 Sher and Murdoch fail to identify a single supporter of this position, apart from Ebenezer Erskine and his followers and subsequent Seceders, during the century. It is curious, therefore, to identify as significant a school of thought within the Church, whose only members were those who had left the Church, and who therefore held little direct influence in it, and presumably also, the isolated individuals who did so later but who did not publish their views before they seceded: R. B. Sher and A. Murdoch, 'Patronage and Party in the Church of Scotland, 1750–1800', in N. Macdougall (ed.), *Church, Politics and Society: Scotland, 1408–1929* (Edinburgh, 1983), pp. 205–6.

7 Willison, *Fair and Impartial Testimony*, p. 46.

8 Sher and Murdoch, 'Patronage and Party', p. 206, argue that this was the policy of the *First Book of Discipline*.

9 Gordon, *State and Duty of the Church of Scotland*, p. 32.

10 John Adams, *An Inquiry into the Powers committed to the General Assemblies of this Church, and the Nature of Deposition from the Holy Ministry, occasioned by the Character and Procedure of the Assembly 1752* (Glasgow, 1754), p. 20.

settlement, but 'the shape in which it comes out does not alter the nature of the thing'.[11] Although it was not Gordon's intention, the concept of a Presbyterial call was taken up and extended by a section of the Popular party which was less committed to the preservation of congregational rights. Gordon's limitation of the right of election to the 'intelligent religious people of God' in a parish was linked to an attempt to exclude those who were not members of the Established Church, and he elsewhere qualified the limitation by adding the rider 'whether they be elders, heritors or heads of families'. It was, nevertheless, a significant departure from the *Second Book of Discipline* which he otherwise endorsed.[12] It is perhaps fair to point out that Gordon's work was a response to what he saw as attempts to undermine the Established Church in the 'Northern Counties' by Jacobites, Episcopalians, or Roman Catholics amongst the gentry.[13] Nevertheless, it marked a significant development from the basic constitutional position of the Popular party, especially as it came from the hand of a leading opponent of patronage.

Espousal of such ideas, and their extension, were not long in appearing. John Lawson, in his *Speech concerning the Settling of Parishes* of 1752, after stating that it was a presbyterian principle that no man should be intruded into a parish, went on to assert that this was not 'pleading the cause merely of the populace, of the weak and ignorant part of mankind', but was also

> pleading the cause of the best, of the most judicious and intelligent in every congregation ... the cause of elders, of heritors, of gentlemen as respected as any in the nation ... of some of the peers of this realm, who, by the rigorous exercise of patronage, are divested not only of a natural right, but a right secured to them by the rules of the Church, and by the laws of the land.[14]

This no doubt was part of an attempt to enlist support for the anti-patronage cause, but it can be seen as embodying a move from the strict constitutional position. Certainly, only two years later in 1754, Adams of Falkirk denounced those who had 'contrived for themselves a sort of construction of the meaning of the word "congregation"' which enabled them to operate a system, based on what they claimed to be the practice of the Church, which 'substitutes the heritors and elders, and sometimes the heritors alone, and sometimes the rich and noble of them ... in place

---

[11] Gordon, *State and Duty of the Church of Scotland*, pp. 27–33.

[12] Ibid., pp. 33–5.

[13] Gordon claimed that it was quite a common practice in the north and north-east of Scotland for Episcopalian or non-juring patrons and heritors to attempt to influence presentations and elections by transferring rights to trustees qualified in law: Gordon, *State and Duty of the Church of Scotland*, pp. 2–4.

[14] Lawson, *Speech concerning the Settling of Parishes*, p. 21.

of the congregation'.[15] To some extent he was supported by the author of the *Loud Cry for Help to the Struggling Church of Scotland* of 1753, probably John Maclaurin (later to be Lord Dreghorn of the Court of Session). He asserted that 'We do not pretend that all men have an equal right in calling a minister upon an Establishment', and that that right remained with those to whom the law gave it, but struck a more 'Popular' note by asserting that as men, Christians, Protestants and Presbyterians, members of the Church of Scotland had 'a right to judge for ourselves in matters concerning religion'. For example, dissatisfaction with the doctrine or ministry of an established minister could be relieved by going to another either in or out of the Establishment.[16] Departure from unacceptable ministers could only be prevented by the settlement of ministers who could retain the love and affection of their people.[17] Then followed a defence of the prejudices of the common people as being based on valid grounds throughout history from Classical times.[18] But the pattern of rejection of unlimited congregational rights was quickly established, however, and within a few years John Witherspoon himself disclaimed any belief in the unlimited exercise of a congregational vote in the moderation of a call.[19]

For much of the second half of the eighteenth century, however, the Popular position wished to deny the right of heritors to separate consideration in the moderation of the call. Gordon, for example, maintained that heritors had no divine or ecclesiastical right to vote in the election of a minister in a parish in which they did not reside or 'hold communion in Gospel-ordinances', except as 'religious parishioners' in which case they were included in the Session or eldership, or amongst the people of the congregation.[20] Willison, likewise, would have prohibited the settlement of a parish 'contrary to the mind of the eldership and Christian people', though he was careful to stress that all judicatories and ministers should have

> a due regard to all members of Christ's flock, and to all serious praying Christians, and not to despise those who are poor and

---

15 Adams, *Inquiry into the Powers committed to the General Assemblies*, p. 24.

16 [John Maclaurin, later Lord Dreghorn], *A Loud Cry for Help to the Struggling Church of Scotland. Being a Letter from an Elder in Glasgow, to the Several Members of Kirk Sessions thro' the Land. Proper to be read and seriously considered before the Election of Members to the Next General Assembly* (Glasgow, 1753), p. 7. The blatant political position it espoused (p. 9) would seem to rule out Rev. John Maclaurin as its author. Throughout the second half of the 18th century, Popular ministers studiously avoided the making of overtly political comment.

17 Ibid., pp. 7–8. This point was supported by an elaborate and apparently authentic analogy drawn from experience of pleading before the Court of Session. It strongly supports the idea of a legal hand in the authorship of the work.

18 Ibid., pp. 8–9.

19 See below, pp. 128–9; and John Witherspoon, 'Speech in the General Assembly on the Transportation of Dr. C', in *Works*, p. 287.

20 Gordon, *State and Duty of the Church of Scotland*, p. 35.

mean in the world, but to esteem and put honour upon them, and seek an interest in their prayers, and have a regard to their inclinations in planting parishes. And in all decisions about settlements ... to guard against the fear of man which brings a snare.[21]

In other words, Willison, too, while anxious to defend the rights of all the congregation, ascribed an important role to the eldership as a separate body.

Apart from this division of opinion within the Popular party on the nature of a call, there was unanimity that the Church was a unique institution and that secular assumptions about the nature of society and authority in a society were inapplicable. The Church was not just a human society, it was a society which was concerned with religious acts and it derived its authority from God alone. This raised the issue of freedom of conscience. In the words of John Adams of Falkirk, who was Moderator of the General Assembly of 1744:

> The essence of religious acts, as such, consists in their being done out of regard to the authority of God alone, and in whatever degree the mind is influenced by other motives and considerations, particularly by the commandments of men, its acts in so far cease to be religious – It cannot therefore be supposed that God has given to any man, or society of men, an authority which shall bind the consciences of others, that is, that shall oblige them to do *religious* acts, because they are prescribed by that authority – For an authority, purely human, which should by itself bind the conscience, and be the immediate reason of obedience in matters of religion, would be inconsistent with the very essence of true religion, and tend to its destruction.[22]

This doctrine is crucial to an understanding of the Popular position and was, of course, the main feature of the Popular response to the Moderate 'Reasons of Dissent in the Case of Inverkeithing'. No minister, argued Adams, could be deprived of his benefice except by 'a departing from the laws of Christ, and the great ends of his institution' since the whole purpose of an establishment bestowing benefices 'seems plainly to have been to encourage, and support able, active, and faithful ministers in the discharge of their ministerial functions'. Church courts, furthermore, could have no liberty to pardon some and punish others who were equally guilty. That was the prerogative of the Crown in civil government. In ecclesiastical government the judicatories were limited in exercising the penal laws of Christ's government by a fixed and invariable standard – his own authority.[23] Sometimes, 'regard to the laws

---

[21] Willison, *Fair and Impartial Testimony*, p. 120.
[22] Adams, *Inquiry into the Powers committed to the General Assemblies*, p. 19.
[23] Ibid., pp. 25, 28.

of God, the success of the Gospel, and the edification of the body of Christ' called for severe government, but there was a distinction to be drawn between civil and religious societies and their laws:

> civil society calls for a strict and rigorous observation of those laws, upon which the order and security of it depends, because the very essence of civil society, as such, consists in outward order. – And therefore, every plea is imperfect and unreasonable by which disobedience is attempted to be justified, if it once appears that the laws requiring such obedience, are the laws of the society ... with regard to religious societies, there is something very different, in which are two things totally distinct, the œconomical or constitutional part ... and the radical: the first, wherein the particular outward order, form, or discipline – The last – wherein the very life of religion, as such, consists. – With regard to the last, there is, perhaps, less indulgence to be expected – But with regard to the first, there is great latitude; and a Christian meekness of spirit will lead to great forbearance towards scrupulous minds, when opposition to the outward form and oeconomy, arises from a tender and honest, though mistaken, regard to the more substantial part. – A contrary conduct and spirit wears too much the appearance of political and dangerous designs in religion – It looks like enlarging, and laying a wider foundation on, for enslaving conscience, and introducing spiritual tyranny. – In the infancy of such designs, men have always attempted to confound two things that ought ever to be carefully distinguished – The nature of religion itself – and the outward form under which it subsists.[24]

Adams's definition of the Popular position on the nature of church government and church discipline, then, embodied a complete rejection of the Enlightenment-inspired conceptions put forward by the Moderate authors of the 'Reasons of Dissent in the Case of Inverkeithing' of 1752. It was also a much more succinct and tightly argued definition than that put forward in the Popular 'Answers to the Reasons of Dissent'.[25]

II

As has been noticed, the patronage cases of the years after 1740 were in the main legal disputes. The case of Torphichen, however, which came before the Assembly of 1751 after a brief debate in 1749, was more significant and marks the start of the first phase of the eighteenth-century patronage dispute: the phase which stressed liberty of conscience. In spite of the instructions of the 1749 and 1750 Assemblies to proceed to settle the presentee to Torphichen, the Presbytery of

[24] Ibid., pp. 29–30.
[25] See below, pp. 104–7.

Linlithgow had declined to do so. The 1751 Assembly censured the Presbytery, again instructed it to settle the presentee, and appointed a 'riding committee' to carry out the settlement should the Presbytery still decline, as in fact it did. The original objections to the presentee were that he could not be heard in the church, and that his opponents 'never could submit to his ministry, in that he had accepted of a presentation without the consent and concurrence of almost the whole parish'. The Presbytery of Linlithgow justified its refusal to settle the presentee on three grounds: the strong opposition in the parish to the settlement; the threat of the scattering of their own parishes if they should have a hand in it, and the consequent rendering useless of their own ministries; and the argument that it was agreeable to presbyterian government, and the constitution of the Church, that 'the authority of its judicatures should always be exercised in a subordination to the authority of Christ, and with a tender regard to the conscience'. The Presbytery argued that the injunctions of higher courts should never be arbitrary or binding in all cases whatsoever. Nevertheless, they accepted that the sentences of the Assembly had to be executed, although they insisted that this should and could be done by using men whose ministries would not suffer by executing them, and who would not violate their consciences by doing so.[26] This was, of course, a plea for the continuance of the use of the much-maligned so-called 'riding committees'.

In other words, the congregation objected to the physical incapabilities of the presentee, and in effect claimed the congregation's right of veto. Strictly, they would seem to have required congregational approval before acceptance of the presentation. The Presbytery, on the other hand, was most concerned with the effectiveness of the ministry within the Church and the Church's unity for that purpose in the face of the risk of secession, and with the constitutional primacy of liberty of conscience. At the same time, the Presbytery accepted the authority of the higher courts of the Church and that their decisions should be implemented providing that the other principles were respected. As early as 1751, therefore, the complex and potentially paradoxical principles inherent in the Popular position were clear. There was a definite tension between the doctrine of the Church as the Body of Christ, and the concept of the Church of Scotland as a body committed to the principle of Establishment and operating the law of patronage as a result.

The Presbytery's line of argument, however, was extended and made more explicit in a speech made at the bar of the Assembly by a member of the Presbytery, almost certainly John Adams of Falkirk.[27] The speech pointed out that the Seceders had been unable to justify their breaking

---

26 Morren, *Annals of the General Assembly*, i, pp. 181, 199–200.
27 Ibid., pp. 200–8. The tentative identification is made on p. 206, note. See also *Scots Magazine*, xiv (Mar. 1752), pp. 137ff.

off from the Church as a result of being forced to act contrary to their own consciences, but had been forced to base it merely on their disagreement with certain actions of the Church. Adams went on to raise the spectre that the Secession had now established an alternative for parishes feeling themselves oppressed. He attempted to grapple with what was to become the Moderate position the following year. In doing so, he revealed how the Popular party was coming to view its opponents. Assemblies subsequent to that of 1749, it was asserted, were acting only with consideration of their own authority and without regard to the circumstances of the case: 'All was to be sacrificed at once to this single principle, submission to authority ...'[28] The argument that 'conscience has no concern in the orders of superiors, but in obliging to obey them' was rejected, as were the claim that the rights of private judgement could have no place in such matters, and the contention that it was a breach of faith to decline any command since the ministers of the Church vowed obedience on entering the Church. The first and most essential right of private judgement in the Scottish Establishment, it was claimed, was the right to decide what was a matter of conscience in relation to one's personal conduct.[29] Such, of course, followed directly from the doctrine of the Church.[30] In view of this speech, and in view of the fact that an attempt led by John Home and William Robertson to have the Presbytery of Linlithgow suspended rather than censured was defeated, there are some grounds for regarding the 'Reasons of Dissent in the Case of Inverkeithing' the following year, as being the response to a Popular polemic arising from the Torphichen case rather than as an *ad hoc* response to the Inverkeithing case which has come to be regarded as the manifesto of the Moderate party.

The speech from the bar at the 1751 Assembly, however, developed two further lines of defence which were to become increasingly common in the next few years: if the usefulness of ministers was destroyed not only would the people suffer spiritually, but they would also, as events had proved, fall under the influence of one or other of the dissenting parties, 'some of whom are well known to teach wild and pernicious principles of government, as they do of religion'.[31] The Popular apologetic at the Assembly was therefore ready, as early as 1751, to adopt secular arguments when opportune. The argument concluded with the assertion that no body would maintain that absolute and unlimited obedience was required or promised in a Protestant Church, and a distinction was drawn between absolute obedience and absolute submission, the latter of which required peaceable and respectful retiral in the face of the Church's judgement.

---

[28] Morren, *Annals of the General Assembly*, i, p. 203.
[29] Ibid., p. 204.
[30] See above, pp. 33–5.
[31] Morren, *Annals of the General Assembly*, i, p. 206.

In spite of such arguments, however, the Assembly decided to censure the Presbytery of Linlithgow. Their decision provoked a dissent by Principal William Wishart to which twenty-one ministers and one elder adhered. The reasons for the dissent, which embodied the views of a member of the party who cannot be regarded as sharing the theological views of the majority, took the Popular response to patronage a step further.[32] Three reasons for the dissent were given. First, Church censures should be inflicted only on open transgressors of the laws of Christ, and not for failure to obey the commands of an assembly of fallible men when the disobedience arose from a conscientious regard for the laws of Christ according to a man's best understanding of them. The Assembly's decision, therefore, was derogatory to the laws of conscience of which God alone was Lord, and to the sole absolute authority of Christ in his Church. Secondly, Presbyterian church government as described in the Church's standards and in the laws of the Establishment did not imply that the supreme judicature was vested with absolute authority or infallibility. Every man had an inalienable right to judge for himself what was 'in the Lord', as the subscription to the Westminster Confession put it. And thirdly, the sentence was unnecessary to support the constitution and authority of the Church.[33] What was clearly implicit in these reasons was the defence of the primacy of conscience in determining response to ecclesiastical decisions, and a conception of the Church as a unique type of body whose constitution ultimately rested on grounds, the interpretation of which had to remain subjective in many ways.

If the Popular case was stated exhaustively and with considerable clarity, the response of Popular commissioners to the Assembly was much less clear. It highlighted the uncertainty which must exist about who exactly should be classified as members of the party, about the nature of relationships between the 'leadership' and the 'rank-and-file', and about whether a distinction should be drawn between hard-line and more accommodating factions within the party. The 1751 Assembly would seem to have had a Popular majority in that it agreed without a vote to a letter instructing its commissioners in London not merely to seek redress of the grievance of patronage, but also to guard against extension or stricter enforcement of it.[34] Furthermore, although the election of the Moderator was seen as a trial of strength between supporters and opponents of the stipend augmentation scheme, both nominees were of Popular sympathies.[35] If, in fact, the Popular party did have the majority, the complex nature of its response was clear in the voting on the Torphichen case, and there was more than a hint of an ambivalent response on the part of many of its adherents. The

---

32 See also below, pp. 110–12.
33 Morren, *Annals of the General Assembly*, pp. 209–11.
34 Ibid., pp. 194–5.
35 Ibid., p. 190.

Presbytery of Linlithgow's defence of its actions was partially effective, in that, while the Assembly voted 200 to 11 against suspension of the Presbytery, there was a majority in favour of censure. Nevertheless, the Assembly decided only to enforce the previous two Assemblies' appointment to ordain and admit the presentee, and set up a riding committee to act if the Presbytery did not comply.[36] To a considerable extent, this ambivalent response was seen the following year at the Assembly in the voting on the Inverkeithing Case.

III

The Inverkeithing Case, which saw the dominance of the Moderates clearly established in the General Assembly, first appeared at the November 1751 and April 1752 meetings of the Commission of Assembly. At the 1752 Assembly, the Moderates were in control, and their candidate, Patrick Cuming, was chosen Moderator by a very great majority.[37] The case, as is well known, related to an allegedly unpopular presentee whom the Presbytery of Dunfermline had refused to settle. The case had been carried on appeal to the Commission of Assembly and thence to the Assembly itself. After a lengthy debate, the Presbytery was ordered, by a vote of 102 to 56, to admit the presentee and report back. There were eleven dissents, mainly on the grounds that the appointment of five ministers as a quorum instead of the usual three was 'a very material alteration in our constitution', but also because it was argued that this was in fact contrary to the interests of the presentee who could have been settled long ago by the methods formerly used, that is, by a riding committee. The Presbytery of Dunfermline still declined to admit the presentee and the Assembly voted to depose one of the ministers of the Presbytery by a vote of 93 to 65. Thereafter, 52 voted for the deposition of Thomas Gillespie, minister of Carnock, and 102 declined to give their votes.[38] There has been some speculation concerning the reasons why Gillespie was singled out,[39] but it is of greater importance to analyse the debate which was carried on over the issue, and in particular to look at what were regarded as the manifestos of the Moderate and Popular parties. Recently, the former, the 'Reasons of Dissent in the Case of Inverkeithing', has received considerable attention,[40] but the answer to it has received scant notice rather than the analysis it deserves.[41]

---

[36] Amongst the 11 members were the future Moderate leaders William Robertson, John Home, and Hugh Blair. See Drummond and Bulloch, *Scottish Church*, p. 58.

[37] Morren, *Annals of the General Assembly*, i, p. 260.

[38] Ibid., p. 269.

[39] Ibid.

[40] E.g., Drummond and Bulloch, *Scottish Church*, p. 65; Chitnis, *Scottish Enlightenment*, pp. 62–4; and Sher, *Church and University in the Scottish Enlightenment*, pp. 52–4.

[41] Its contemptuous dismissal by Drummond and Bulloch is inexcusable: Drummond and Bulloch, *Scottish Church*, p. 66.

It is not proposed to enter upon a detailed discussion of the arguments of the 'Reasons of Dissent in the Case of Inverkeithing' since this may be found elsewhere.[42] They may be summarised as dissenting from the decision of the Popular-dominated Commission, which had voted against censuring the Presbytery, on the grounds that its decision was inconsistent with the nature and first principles of society in general, with the nature and preservation of ecclesiastical society, with Presbyterian church government, and with the practice and procedure of the Church of Scotland. Laxity with regard to censure of ecclesiastical disobedience would lead to laxity in the area of doctrinal declension. The action of the Commission, it was argued, exceeded its powers and undermined the constitution of the Church, its Establishment and the authority of the Assembly.

The Popular reply was contained in the much lengthier 'Answers to the Reasons of Dissent from the Sentence of the Commission in the case of Inverkeithing, March 11, 1752; drawn up by the Committee appointed for that purpose, and dated May 16'.[43] Some of the lines of argument had appeared already, others were newer and pointed more towards the future. The 'Answers to the Reasons of Dissent' commenced by seizing on the very foundation of the Moderate case, which was held to require absolute obedience to the judgements of a society, and so was contrary to the principles of the Confession of Faith by destroying liberty of conscience as well as reason. To assert such unlimited authority in the supreme powers in every society, and to apply it to ecclesiastical government, would be as much as was claimed by any Pope. Even civil powers allowed the choice of active obedience or passive submission to their wills and punished only active disobedience. It was suggested that the dissenters' case militated against the obligation of men, as rational creatures, to answer for their deeds on the Day of Judgement, when it would be no defence to plead that they were willingly obeying the commands of earthly superiors.[44]

The reasoning contained in this section was, it must be admitted, much less coherent, and in some ways much less convincing, than the corresponding section of the Moderate 'Reasons of Dissent'. Apart from the fact that the Popular document was the work of a committee of eight men,[45] whereas the Moderate document was probably the work of

---

42 Most conveniently in Chitnis, *Scottish Enlightenment*, and Sher, *Church and University in the Scottish Enlightenment*. See above, note 40.

43 Morren, *Annals of the General Assembly*, i, pp. 243–60. The *Scots Magazine* published 'An Abstract of the Answers to the Reasons of Dissent ... ', xiv (May 1752), pp. 229–38. This version is, however, identical to that given by Morren.

44 Morren, *Annals of the General Assembly*, i, p. 248 and note. Extensive quotations were given from the anonymous *Occasional Writer* which Morren ascribes to the Lord Advocate of the time who earlier, as William Grant, had been Solicitor-General and Procurator of the Church. Morren describes him as 'a supporter of the Moderate Party (though he had formerly written a tract against Patronage)' (p. 248).

45 Ibid., i, p. 230. The 7 ministers were the Moderator (James Mackie), Principal Wishart,

William Robertson, there were several reasons why this was so. The Moderate case embodied a profoundly secular vision. The Popular apologetes, with their biblical view, were of necessity operating in unfamiliar territory. The assumptions on which they based their view were simplistic by philosophical standards, although not by theological ones. Apart from stating their theocentric view of society, the Popular case at this point tended to limit itself to an attempt to discern inconsistencies and invalidities in the Moderate argument.

The Popular response to the second reason of dissent was much more coherent, and convincing. The Moderate dissent had stated that 'this sentence of the Commission is absolutely inconsistent with the nature and preservation of ecclesiastical society in particular'.[46] Here the Popular apologists were stung by the assertion that their contention that church censures should only be applied to open transgressors of the laws of Christ himself, and that not obeying the commands of an Assembly of fallible men if one's conscience led one to disobedience, was 'calculated to establish the most extravagant maxims of Independency', and to overthrow the Church's constitution. To counter this allegation, the 'Answers to the Reasons of Dissent' produced a clear distinction between the functions of the Church and the ecclesiastical functions of an Establishment. Christ's commission to his Apostles, and hence to the Church in general, comprised the whole purpose of their work and was to 'teach all men to observe all things whatsoever he had commanded them'. Church censures were one part of the methods by which they were to teach men these things, and were therefore to be confined to those who neglected or refused to observe what Christ had commanded. When the civil government and the laws of the land gave the Church another power to do with granting or withholding civil emoluments to the ministers of the Church, the courts were not acting as ministers of Christ inflicting Church censures, but as trustees of the public executing those laws which had been given to them to execute, unless, of course, transgressions of those laws of the land also involved transgression of the law of Christ. The power given by Christ to his ministers had nothing to do with giving or taking away civil privileges or emoluments. Furthermore, the reason legal emoluments were bestowed on ministers was with a view of service done by them to religion and the public. To turn men out of their benefices for not acting contrary to principles in which they were supported by the standing rules of the Church, and for endeavouring to be useful to religion and to the public, was absurd.[47]

In other words, contrary to the Moderate thesis that all members of the Church were bound to obey the orders of the courts or, if they were

---

John Adams, Lawrence Hill, George Lindsay, Robert Walker, and Alexander Steadman. The elder was Albert Munro.

[46] Ibid., i, p. 249.

[47] Ibid., i, pp. 249–51.

to become aware that the decisions being consistently made by the supreme judicatures could not be reconciled with their consciences, to withdraw from the Church, the Popular party produced a theory of the Church which removed the legal aspects of the Establishment from entanglement with the essentially spiritual nature of the Church. It was a solution of considerable shrewdness, for it was strongest where the Moderates were probably at their weakest, in their inability to produce coherent biblical support for their position on the nature of the Church.

The remaining 'Answers' rejected Moderate notions of the 'absolute' authority of the Assembly, and the 'obedience' they required to it, stressed the principle of the Church that no minister should be intruded on a congregation without its consent, and rejected the Moderate assertion that acceptance by the Commission of Assembly of the Presbytery's refusal to settle was inconsistent with the practice of the Church.[48]

The 'Answers to the Reasons of Dissent' concluded with a lengthy assertion that leniency in such matters, instead of encouraging disobedience and displaying the weakness of the Church, would in fact encourage simplicity and godly sincerity, and would preserve and improve the strength of the Church by refraining from giving arbitrary and unnecessary commands. Such reasoning cannot be regarded as more than the expression of conventional platitudes with reference to the issues under scrutiny. It is also true that in the course of the last section of the 'Answers', the comparison between ecclesiastical and civil government, so essential to the Moderate case, was explicitly rejected. The 'Answers' contended that the purpose of civil government was the preservation of the outward peace of society, and that its object was only the outward actions of men. It was the outward actions of men which civil government punished without regard to the inward principles from which they proceeded. In contrast, in ecclesiastical discipline and censures the object was the actions of professed Christians when they transgressed the law of Christ, and the objective of discipline was the reformation of the mind and the maintenance of the Church as a pure religious society. Great scope had therefore to be allowed to the exercise of the conscience in such matters.[49]

What is inescapable in a comparison of the positions in the Moderate 'Reasons of Dissent' and the Popular 'Answers' is the gulf between their preoccupations and their conceptions of the nature of the Church. For the Moderates, as Chitnis puts it, 'the prime issues ... were integration, authority, and freedom from political interference'.[50] For the Popular party, however, the starting-point was their theological stress on the doctrine of the Church. The Church had been commissioned by Christ

[48] Ibid., i, pp. 256–7.
[49] See above, pp. 104–5.
[50] Chitnis, *Scottish Enlightenment*, p. 64.

to preach the Gospel and to teach the people to do what he had commanded them. It could be aided in its tasks by an Establishment such as was possessed by the Church of Scotland, but such an Establishment was essentially a civil matter. Its purpose was to aid the Church in fulfilling its mission, and any aspect of it or result from it which hindered the Church should be rejected.

The implications of this for patronage are clear. The spectre of Erastianism was raised and the effectual carrying out of Christ's commission to his Church was threatened. The problem for the Popular party was that their Moderate opponents were more influenced by secular ideas of order and authority than they were by theological ones relating to the purpose of the Church or liberty of conscience. The one area, however, where for the time being the Popular case could not be answered by the Moderates to their own satisfaction was the Popular delineation of the detrimental effects of the enforcement of patronage on the loyalty of the people. This could be seen as leading to the resort of the Moderator of 1752, Patrick Cuming, to the threat of the withdrawal of the civil support guaranteed to the Establishment by the Treaty of Union of 1707 if discipline in the Church was not maintained.[51] The dilemma of the Popular party was perhaps shrewdly identified by Cuming, who may well have perceived the strength of Popular commitment to the Establishment in view of its 'usefulness'. The doctrinal offensive of the Popular party against patronage had failed and its polemic became based more on the consequences of its excessive or arbitrary enforcement. In other words, the Popular party began to stress that the operation of patronage was defeating the whole purpose of Establishment and could lead to inevitable schism. This marks the start of the second phase of opposition to patronage. In comparison with the stress of the published works, however, at the Assembly the Popular party failed to deploy the full range of 'constitutional' arguments which were to become such a prominent feature of the main Popular publications on patronage. This was presumably because their appearance was a response to the debate in 1752 rather than the elaboration of ideas which were used in the Assembly itself.

IV

It should not be assumed, however, that defeat in the Assembly saw the demise, even temporarily, of Popular agitation against patronage. In 1753, the Synod of Glasgow and Ayr sent an overture to the Assembly against forcing ministers, under pain of deposition, actively to execute such settlements as appeared to them to be contrary to the Word of God, the standing rules of the Church, and her constantly avowed

[51] Morren, *Annals of the General Assembly*, i, pp. 289–90.

principles. The Synod accepted by implication the use of riding committees, and, by means of several references to overtures being regularly transmitted to presbyteries, indicated its belief that the majority of presbyteries were against enforced settlements.[52] By this new emphasis on procedure the Popular attack on patronage entered its second phase in which an attempt was to be made to ameliorate its effects, and to argue for its end by emphasising its inconsistency with the purpose of establishment and with the constitutional principles of the Church. Such a strategy would have been in keeping with the constitutional emphases of Adams's *Inquiry into the Powers committed to the General Assemblies of this Church*, and Maclaurin's *Nature of Ecclesiastic Government*.[53]

The commencement of this second phase was indicated when four Popular ministers of the Synod of Lothian and Tweeddale, in a dissent from an overture of the Synod, claimed that the actions of the preceding Assembly in effect deprived ministers of the privileges of the civil establishment in a summary and arbitrary way without a regular process.[54] The most obvious case, however, which can be identified as marking the emergence of this second phase in the patronage struggle, was the case of Biggar which reached the Assembly of 1753. Here, the Popular party attempted to defeat the supporters of patronage by proving the latters' actions illegal or unconstitutional. They chose to do so by basing their arguments on the Moderates' own case for consistency and legality in Church government as was to be found in the 'Reasons for Dissent in the Case of Inverkeithing'. This device was to remain a standard feature of Popular polemic for the remainder of the century. The Popular position is to be found in the 'Reasons of Complaint against the sentence of the Commission, unanimously offered, to the next General Assembly by the Presbytery of Biggar'. These contained most of the legal, theological, and ecclesiastical arguments used by the Popular

---

52 Ibid., ii, pp. 1–2. It is worthy of note that later Popular opinion did not share the acceptance of riding committees apparently current at this time. In the Appendix to his *Life of Erskine* published some 50 years later, the Popular leader Sir Harry Moncrieff Wellwood attacked their use as neither sanctioned by constitutional law nor justified by expediency, failing to remove the prejudices of the people, and lowering the respect for the ministry. See Sir Henry Moncrieff Wellwood, *Account of the Life and Writings of John Erskine, D.D.* (Edinburgh, 1818), p. 457.

53 See below, pp. 113–14, and note 66.

54 Morren, *Annals of the General Assembly*, ii, pp. 4–9. Associations had been formed and public meetings held by ministers in the Synod of Glasgow and Ayr to stir up opposition to the deposition of Gillespie, and criticisms of the deposition had been made in the course of public worship. A paper had been submitted to the western Synod objecting to the use of public worship for such purposes, but the debate had resulted in the passing of a much watered-down version urging tolerance, abstention from mutual reproach, and suchlike expressions. The Moderate eastern Synod was provoked by this into passing an overture condemning the Glasgow Synod and supporting the General Assembly. As a result, Moderates in the Synods of Glasgow and Ayr, and Lothian and Tweeddale were seen by the Popular party as limiting or trying to limit freedom of speech and as restricting ecclesiastical liberty.

party to try to persuade the Moderate-controlled General Assembly to ameliorate the worst features of the patronage system. The Popular argument attempted to establish that the decision enjoining the Presbytery to proceed to settle an unsuitable presentee was legally and constitutionally unsound. The first part of the 'Reasons of Dissent in the Case of Inverkeithing' centred on various legal technicalities relating to the respective powers of presbyteries, the Commission of Assembly, and the Assembly itself, along with the right of one court to alter the decisions of the previous one after a year.[55] The second part of the Dissent made two further points in relation to the nature of calls which pointed the way to the subsequent strategy of the Popular party. It was claimed, in the first place, that the Commission's judgement was an attempt to abrogate the invariable practice and procedure of the Church in that it disregarded the non-concurrence of virtually all parishioners and heritors. Secondly, it was alleged that the decision introduced a new law and form of procedure that patrons could not relieve the Church by making a second presentation, and that the Church could do nothing but settle, even when there was no concurrence, and that it was doing so in an irregular manner, without it being referred to all the presbyteries for majority consent. Neither the civil nor the ecclesiastical law justified the decision since the law of patronage did not lay the Church under any compulsion to ordain even the most unexceptionable presentee, nor did it give him any right to the benefice without ordination. To justify the decision, the law would have had to state that it did. The Complaint concluded by suggesting that the Commission had been 'packed' by a 'designing few' for the particular diet appointed to judge the case.[56]

The grounds for dissent in the Biggar case are important for four reasons. In the first place, it marked the emergence in the Assembly of a legal rather than a theological opposition to patronage at the time secular considerations were being dealt with in the published works of the party. Secondly, it raised the issue of the nature of the 'concurrence' required to justify settling a presentee. Thirdly, it indicated Popular confidence in their control of the majority of the presbyteries. Fourthly, it implied the Popular belief that a section of the Moderate party was determined to enforce patronage irrespective of whether or not the law actually required it. The following six years were a period of numerous presentation disputes, but they were all conducted in terms of the principles and arguments which were used in the case of Biggar, and in

---

55 The 'Reasons of Complaint' do not, however, appear to have been influenced by either Adams's or Maclaurin's ideas on the subject. See above, pp. 96, 98–9; and below, pp. 110–17.

56 Ibid., pp. 35–41. It is interesting to note the unanimity of the Presbytery in its complaint against the Commission's sentence. It is possible to identify at least 2 Moderate members of the Presbytery at this period from the *Fasti*: H. Scott, *Fasti Ecclesiae Scoticanae: The Succession of Ministers in the Church of Scotland from the Reformation* (Edinburgh, 1915–28).

terms of the interpretation of the 1690 Act which abolished patronage and gave the elders and heritors the right to nominate a minister subject to the approval of the congregation and presbytery.[57]

V

How, then, was all this related to the powers of the General Assembly and its relationship to the constitution of the Church as expounded in the published works of members of the Popular party? The most detailed exposition of the Popular position relating to the powers of the General Assembly was given by John Adams of Falkirk, who had, of course, been involved at the centre of the Torphichen case. He dealt with the issue in his *Inquiry into the Powers committed to the General Assemblies of this Church* of 1754. In view of this, an extended analysis of Adams's position is called for. In this work, which was prompted by the Inverkeithing Case and the deposition of Gillespie in 1752, the first issue which he sought to elucidate was the relationship between the ordination vows of ministers (and elders) and the authority of the judicatories. He rejected the argument that the ordination vows made every act of disobedience a formal transgression of the vows or a breach of the conditions on which membership of the society and its privileges were forfeited. The ordination vow was to support and maintain the constitution 'with regard to doctrine, worship, discipline, and government, as laid down in our acts and standards; and to submit to our superiors exercising an authority *agreeable to and consistent with these*'. To defend absolute obedience to the judicatories was to fail to distinguish two things which the vows inseparably linked: the obedience insisted on; and the doctrine, worship, and discipline established in the Church. When the orders of the superiors were founded on the latter, they were indisputable; if not, they were 'despotic and arbitrary'. If they were inconsistent, it was worse, and one or the other must be neglected. The honest man had to choose between 'his faith and the constitution' on the one hand, and the capricious acts of men, 'who can have no manner of right to demand obedience which would have that effect' on the other.[58] The proper authority of the Church, and proper regard for the decisions of its courts, therefore, could only be effectually supported by steady adherence to its 'established principles, and constitutional laws'.[59] The argument that, since the Church had powers from Christ himself of doing everything for edification and order, it must consequently have

---

57 Sher and Murdoch, 'Patronage and Party', pp. 200–2. Sher and Murdoch interpret the 1690 Act as giving the landed interest the upper hand in the selection of ministers for vacant churches outside the burghs and consequently argue for the predominance of a 'Whig commonwealthman' theory as being the most important hallmark of the Popular party's opposition to patronage.

58 Adams, *Inquiry into the Powers committed to the General Assemblies*, pp. 19–20.

59 Ibid., p. 31.

the power of enforcing that order by excluding from her society those who refused to submit to such regulations as she might judge appropriate, was rejected as specious on the grounds that 'the order and oeconomy of the Church of Christ, as the Church of Christ' was not 'left to the indefinite determination of any one, or any number of fallible men'. The order established by such men was not so essential to the Christian Church that refusal to comply with it would be deemed by Christ himself a violation of his laws, 'and subject the offender, in his name and authority, to the censures that are peculiar to the open transgressors of his laws'.[60]

Adams was perfectly prepared to allow that church courts could make illegal decisions, which were usually justified, he claimed, under the term 'the practice of the Church'.[61] Indeed, he came quite close to arguing that the Church of Scotland could act illegally and be a false Church when he asserted that the difference between a true and a false Church lay, not in the fact that 'the one can authorise iniquity, and the other cannot; but in this, that the one is directed in all her determinations by the laws of Christ, and the other by false and pernicious principles'. If the true Church deviated from the laws of Christ, in that case she acted the part of the false Church, and such instances were to be condemned 'and cannot be in any ways binding on the consciences of men, whether of minister or private Christian, without sacrificing the regard due to the authority of God, and to his ministers enforcing his laws'.[62]

Adams then turned to delineate the nature of the change which had occurred in the relationship between the Assembly and the inferior courts of the Church. Originally, the authority of Assemblies and the subordination of judicatories were designed as a fence around the constitution. Recently, however, important parts of constitutional laws and church-order were being disregarded, and the authority of presbyteries was being destroyed by licentious appeals and the encouragement given to them by arbitrary decisions. Presbyteries and synods were now regarded as the officers of the General Assembly and its Commission 'to execute their will and pleasure without asking questions', instead of as possessing the legislative powers which had been usurped by the General Assembly. Parishes were little more than tracts of land and congregations 'must not pretend to either conscience and sentiments of their own, much less to rights or privileges'. As well as these objections to the existing state of affairs based on doctrinal or constitutional considerations, Adams also drew attention to a practical factor relating to the need for adherence to the constitution. He argued that it was essential to prevent confusion and inconsistency arising from

[60] Ibid., p. 18.
[61] Ibid., pp. 32–3.
[62] Ibid., p. 18.

the annual change in the membership of the General Assembly, or the unscrupulous use of artifice or the operation of interest.[63]

More important, however, Adams argued for the radical power of the presbytery against that of the General Assembly. General Assemblies were 'not the church, but her delegates, vested with a limited power, and which she may limit further, as shall be found useful'. The subordination of judicatories was not the constitution but a defence around the doctrine, worship, and discipline which, as laid down in the public authorised standards and Acts of Assembly, made up the constitution. The constitution and the established principles of the Church 'lodge a discretionary power in presbyteries, to judge of all acts and orders given out by men, even General Councils', and presbyteries were committed in the strongest possible way to watch over the doctrine and discipline of the Church, to the utmost of their power.[64]

Adams's exposition remained the Popular party's conception of the Church of Scotland and its organs of government. As such, it was a consistent and potentially effective doctrine on which to base its opposition to the Moderate party with its conception of the Church derived from philosophical ideas about the nature of society, and its policy of the enforcement of patronage. Unfortunately for the Popular party, even though the Moderates were unable effectively to counter its arguments, it was unable to persuade them to change their policy.

Slightly earlier than Adams's work, the anonymous *Loud Cry for Help to the Struggling Church of Scotland* covered similar ground. Like Adams's *Inquiry*, it arose from the deposition of Thomas Gillespie in 1752, and the main drift of its argument was a dissection of the legality of the Assembly's action. It concluded by denouncing the decision as denying fundamental principles of the doctrine of the Church. After referring to his reading of the Puritan divines who drew up the Westminster Confession of Faith, the author affirmed his belief that Christ, in his capacity as supreme Head and King of the visible Church, had laid down the terms of admission into it, and the qualifications of its members and ministers. Any Church which added to or subtracted from its terms of communion sinned grievously and would be subjected to severe trial. The section dealing with the deposition of Gillespie concluded with an attack on the lawyers in the General Assembly, the vast majority of whom had supported the deposition, for their assertion that men could not have a scruple of conscience at obeying the sentences of their superiors whatever the decision.[65]

Whoever was the author of the *Loud Cry for Help*, there seems to be little doubt that John Maclaurin of Glasgow was the author of the impressive *Nature of Ecclesiastic Government, and of the Constitution of the*

[63] Ibid., pp. 30–2.
[64] Ibid., pp. 32–5.
[65] *Loud Cry for Help*, pp. 15–23.

Church of Scotland Illustrated. Being a Second Conference on the Terms of Communion attempted to be imposed on the Church of Scotland by a prevailing Party in the General Assembly. Also arising from the Gillespie affair, this work was an attempt to construct a coherent constitutional defence of the Popular position. It is, by the standards of the day, an impressively learned work, showing familiarity with and quoting freely from a wide range of Continental authorities ranging from Pufendorf, Turretine, and Pictet to Montesquieu, Bossuet, and Rollin, and referring to English Deists on the way.[66] While the starting-point of the work was in some ways the fear that Moderate policies would lead to Popery, Deism, or even Atheism, the emphasis was not overwhelmingly directed towards the specific case which provoked it. The objective, in fact, would appear to have been the creation of a theory of church government with which to counter the arguments of the Moderate 'Reasons of Dissent in the Case of Inverkeithing'.

The essential difference between civil and ecclesiastical government, Maclaurin argued, was that the former had as its object only temporal property, and things belonging to this present life, whereas the latter had as its object the eternal salvation of souls. The first might be yielded to others to dispose of without sin or indeed any significant loss, but the care of our eternal interests, contrary to the position of the 'Reasons of Dissent in the Case of Inverkeithing', was inalienable in its nature, the duties it inferred were immutable, and the potential loss absolute.[67] A further difference between the nature of civil and ecclesiastical government was that the former had a 'legislative' power whereas the latter had only a 'ministerial' power. By this, Maclaurin meant that civil government bound the conscience by reason of the nature of law in things not forbidden by God, whereas the 'ministerial' power of church government consisted of enforcing the laws of Christ who was the only legislator in the Church. If ecclesiastical rulers ordered anything in a manner disagreeable to Christ's word, they exceeded their commission, and had no right to be obeyed because Christians were Christ's subjects, not theirs. The authors of the 'Reasons of Dissent' mistook this

---

[66] John Maclaurin, *The Nature of Ecclesiastic Government, and of the Constitution of the Church of Scotland Illustrated. Being a Second Conference on the Terms of Communion attempted to be imposed on the Church of Scotland by a prevailing Party in the General Assembly* (Glasgow, 1754), pp. vi–vii, 13–16, 120. See also Macleod, *Scottish Theology*, pp. 189–97. There is some uncertainty about the authorship of this work and of the *Loud Cry for Help*. The British Library Catalogue identifies them as the works of two separate authors. The Catalogue of New College Library, Edinburgh, ascribes them to Rev. John Maclaurin of the Ramshorn Church. The National Library of Scotland possesses only Maclaurin, *Nature of Ecclesiastic Government* which it identifies in the same way as the other two libraries. Maclaurin also issued *The Terms of Ministerial and Christian Communion imposed on the Church of Scotland by a prevailing Party in the General Assembly, in opposition to the great Bulk of both Office-bearers and private Christians* (Glasgow, 1753), but it differed little from the nature of the subsequent work which contains a more detailed presentation of the arguments of the earlier one.

[67] Maclaurin, *Nature of Ecclesiastic Government*, p. 11.

Protestant doctrine, Maclaurin alleged, for an Independent doctrine and thus felt justified in attacking those who condoned the actions of the Presbytery of Dunfermline. Christ himself expressly differentiated the government of our civil rulers, and that of the officers of his Church. As a result of this, even the Apostles disclaimed any dominion over the Church.[68] The question had been debated since the Reformation, he asserted, and the Moderates had no justification for confusing an issue which divided Protestants and Papists with the doctrines which divided Presbyterians and Independents.[69]

The *Nature of Ecclesiastic Government* further differentiated between the natures of ecclesiastical and civil law by arguing that since Christ's kingdom was not a temporal one its laws were directed towards men's hearts and consciences, and were not therefore to be enforced by means of temporal punishments. Civil magistrates, in contrast, had a power not only to enforce the laws of God but also to make laws of their own which concerned matters of indifference, so that it was a sin for subjects to refuse obedience to them. The Church, even in matters of disobedience to the laws of Christ, if the proper means of reproof and instruction failed, had to proceed to cut off the guilty from participation in the spiritual benefits pertaining to Christ's subjects and from the society of the members of his Church. In matters left undetermined by Christ, the Church, or any part of it, had no power to bind the conscience. It was invalid to argue from civil government to church government for a further reason: the nature of censure or punishment was different. A censure inflicted by a church judicatory could not be lifted without a confession of guilt and a profession of repentance, whereas in civil law the inflicting of the requisite punishment was regarded as a sufficient expiation of the offence.[70] By implication, the whole strategy of the Moderate 'Reasons of Dissent in the Case of Inverkeithing' in arguing from the nature of society and civil government to the nature of the Church and ecclesiastical government was invalid. Even more, it was irrelevant.

There was a further important distinction to be drawn between civil and ecclesiastical authority. In contrast to the former, in a Christian society there was no visible power that had a right to determine authoritatively for those within it what the supreme power, namely Christ, had left undecided. There was no power in Christian society that was 'strictly and properly supreme'. The governors of Christian society indeed had full power to enforce Christ's laws in a 'ministerial, subordinate, and executive' sense, but they had no power to make any

---

68 Ibid., pp. 11–12. Maclaurin refers to Luke 22, 25; 2 Corinthians 1, 24; 2 Corinthians 4, 5; 1 Peter 5, 3; and Matthew 23, 8–10.
69 Ibid., p. 13.
70 Ibid., pp. 17–19. See also pp. 30–1, in which the responsibilities of civil and ecclesiastical rulers in relation to the same crime are similarly differentiated.

laws of their own which bound the consciences of Christ's subjects. The Assembly, therefore, had only this 'executive' power.[71] In addition, while the judgement of the Assembly was final in the constitutional sense that it was the last 'public judgement' which could be made, it was obligatory for the Christian always to exercise his private judgement in the matter, since even an ecclesiastical synod could do wrong. The Church was not to be treated as being in principle the same as a civil society in the way embodied in the 'Reasons of Dissent'. It followed from this, furthermore, that the theory of 'absolute and unlimited active obedience to superior judicatories', regarded by Maclaurin as stated in the 'Reasons of Dissent', was denied by the doctrine of the Church of Scotland.[72]

Maclaurin then proceeded to make a distinction between a free and a despotic government, and to contrast legal government with arbitrary government.[73] He maintained that the difference between a free and a despotic government was that the former was 'a legal government or a government *by laws*', whereas the latter was 'an *arbitrary* government where the *mere will* and pleasure of those who have the administration in their hands prevails over the laws'. True liberty consisted in living in a society where laws prevailed, where the supreme administrators of the government, that is the executive powers, were so bound by them that individuals were protected and punished according to them. The advantage that British subjects had over most of the rest of the world consisted in being under 'the government of *laws*, and not of *men*'.[74] The final three pages of the *Nature of Ecclesiastic Government* were taken up with an attempt to establish that the actions and arguments of the Moderate party in the Gillespie Case proved that the Church of Scotland no longer had a *legal* constitution. The first reason in the Moderate 'Reasons of Dissent in the Case of Inverkeithing' confused the rights of the General Assembly in its *legislative* capacity with those when it acted in its *executive* or *judicative* capacity. Maclaurin quoted Montesquieu's *L'Esprit des Lois* in his support. In its legislative authority, the Assembly's decisions were binding; when its executive decisions did not conform to the constitution of the Church, there could be no obligations on members of presbyteries to obey them. Secondly, if it was argued that the Assembly was 'unlimited in her executive power', it had the effect of

---

71 Ibid., p. 46.
72 Ibid., pp. 95–101.
73 See below, p. 117.
74 Maclaurin, *Nature of Ecclesiastic Government*, p. 119. There would seem to be an interesting connection here between these ideas and the political ideas of the 16th-century Scottish Reformers and the 17th-century Puritans deriving from the 'nature-grace' model of federal theology. The possibility of this line of thought was suggested by a lecture given by Professor J. B. Torrance of Aberdeen on 'The Calvinism of the sixteenth century' at the Universities and Colleges Christian Fellowship Associates [UCCFA] Historians Study Group for Scotland, held at the University of Stirling, 4 Oct. 1986. Key works are George Buchanan, *On the Right of Scots*; the *Vindiciae contra Tyrannos* (1579); and especially Samuel Rutherford's *Lex Rex* (1644).

rendering the whole body of the laws of the Church useless. Thirdly, to argue that the Assembly had the whole legislative power, and therefore must be obeyed, was to disregard the *legislative* power of the presbyteries who had at least a *nominal* share in it.[75] As he argued in his proposed 'Humble Remonstrance of the —————— of ——————' to the General Assembly, attached to the *Nature of Ecclesiastic Government*, 'there cannot be a *more effectual* usurpation of the legislative power, than the enforcing of a thing so contrary to our standing constitutions by the actual infliction of this censure [on Gillespie] in a mere executive capacity amounts to'.

The Moderate line of reasoning, therefore, had led to the disregard of the 'Form of Process' in the case of Gillespie; and the influence of 'secular men of high rank in the world' appointed by negligent presbyteries as commissioners to the Assembly which, when combined with the doctrine of the unlimited executive power of the Assembly, would enable them 'to overturn every article of our *doctrine, worship, discipline, or government*, that might happen to incur their displeasure'. If obedience to the arbitrary commands of the Assembly in its executive capacity was to be substituted for the laws of the Church, and insisted upon as a term of ministerial communion, it would be holding the ministry on a basis which was uncertain and liable to change in a way that might prove destructive to the interests of Christ's kingdom. It would be unconstitutional and it might render it impossible for ministers to adhere inviolably to their ordination vows, 'notwithstanding of whatever trouble or persecution may arise', if they should be ordered by any superior on earth. In other words the Moderate position opened the door to an Erastian Establishment. The great part of the ministers of the Church of Scotland and by far the greater part of the elders and members, Maclaurin asserted, adhered to the position he had delineated. The proceedings of the 1752 Assembly in deposing Gillespie should be reversed, and failing that, the question should be transmitted to presbyteries. Failing both these alternatives, the majority in the Assembly should at least justify their actions in terms of the constitution of the Church.[76] The strain of defeatism evident in many Popular perceptions of the situation is again obvious.

The significance of Maclaurin's *Nature of Ecclesiastic Government* lies in the way it complemented Adams's *Inquiry into the Powers committed to the General Assemblies*. The latter work was perhaps at its strongest in its rejection of the ideas of ecclesiastical government espoused by the Moderates in the 'Reasons of Dissent in the Case of Inverkeithing', and in its advocacy of the concept of the Church as a unique institution deriving its structure and constitution from its nature as the Body of Christ on earth. When it came to the analysis of the relationship between

75 Maclaurin, *Nature of Ecclesiastic Government*, pp. 121–3.
76 Ibid., pp. 143–52.

the General Assembly and the constitution of the Church, Adams's reasoning was much looser. Maclaurin, while in no way moving away from traditional Scottish conceptions of the doctrine of the Church, produced a much more developed theory of the constitution of the Church of Scotland, derived largely from Montesquieu, which based the Popular position on a clearly defined differentiation between the legislative and executive powers of the General Assembly.[77] Both Maclaurin's work and the contemporaneous *Loud Cry for Help*, however, by removing the debate from a predominantly theological context into political and legal areas, may be seen as paving the way for the secularisation that was to dominate Popular thought on patronage in the 1760s.

VI

Before turning to the development of the new, secularised approach to the nature of the Church and its implications, however, it is desirable to assess the impact of the theories that had been propounded on the issue of patronage up until the 1750s. The evidence suggests that the Popular reaction to patronage was aroused not by objections to the institution in principle, but by concern about its effect on the ministry. Consideration of the wider questions of the constitution of the Church and its government raised questions of the nature and necessity of a call to a parish. As a result of the debate over patronage, much that was written on these subjects related to the powers and membership of the General Assembly and its Commission. The essence of the Popular position appeared in John Witherspoon's 'Reasons for Dissent from a Vote of the General Assembly of the Church of Scotland, the 21st of May 1757, Receiving the Commissions of several elders not attested in terms of the Act 9. Assembly 1722'. This document shows signs of having been influenced by the arguments of Maclaurin's *Nature of Ecclesiastic Government*. Commissions from 'constituents', argued Witherspoon, bound members of the Assembly to determine all cases according to the constitution of the Church of Scotland 'but vest us with no power of determining contrary to that constitution'. The underlying justification for this was that

> It is the very essence and security of a free constitution, that then, not men, not judges, but laws bear rule. When laws are suspended, dispensed with or set aside, by the decisions of any executive court, that security ceases, and despotism prevails.[78]

---

[77] See below, pp. 113, 115.

[78] Witherspoon,'Reasons for Dissent from a Vote of the General Assembly of the Church of Scotland, the 21st of May 1757, Receiving the Commissions of several elders not attested in terms of the Act 9. Assembly 1722' (n.p., n.d.), pp. 1–2.

Appreciation of the implications of this are crucial for an understanding of the approach of the Popular party at the Assembly to the problem of patronage. The party was convinced that the constitution of the Church of Scotland was, to use Witherspoon's terms, a free constitution, and that patronage was contrary to it and incompatible with the spiritual purpose of the Church. Their perception, therefore, was that the way to counter it was by rational argument both in publications and at the Assembly. In view of this, what proposals did the party apologists put forward to secure their objectives?

James Gordon was the first to enunciate the policy which was to become the Popular strategy, at least until the Moderate 'Reasons of Dissent in the Case of Inverkeithing', and, in a somewhat different form, for fifteen or twenty years after that. He argued that the Church had the power to end the grievance of patronage, because the Act of 1719 was intended to make the Church 'easy' under the system of patronage, since it allowed its collapse if ministers and probationers declined to accept presentations.[79] John Willison's *Fair and Impartial Testimony* opened its detailed analysis of patronage with this very point. The 'Door of Patronage' was the means by which a corrupt ministry entered the Church. Those who were 'erroneous, immoral, intruders, supporters of patronage, and spoilers of Christian congregations of the rights which Christ hath purchased for them', if they did not repent, should be 'purged out of the Church'.[80] The 1719 Act was the equivalent of a plain repeal of patronage, because no Presbyterian would accept a presentation.[81] In addition to such legal arguments, however, Willison produced six 'Reasons against Patronages'. First, according to the authority derived from Christ, the head and founder of the Church, only the Church herself, with her officers, should exercise the power of nominating and electing ministers and officers to the Church. Secondly, it was contrary to the practice of the primitive and purest ages of the Church, and the Church Fathers declared in favour of the liberty and power of the Church to choose her own pastors without any extrinsic influence whatever. Thirdly, it was contrary to Scripture, to Antiquity and Reason, and to the interest and safety of the Church that the power of choosing pastors should be in the hands of heretics and profane men, both because of the possibility of the power falling into the hands of declared enemies of the Church, and because of the possibility of simony. Fourthly, patronage was a plain encroachment on 'the natural rights of mankind, and upon the laws of free societies'; and the Churches of Christ were as free societies as any anywhere in the world, because their liberties to choose their own pastors came from Christ and

---

79 See Gordon, *State and Duty of the Church of Scotland*, pp. 18–19.
80 Willison, *Fair and Impartial Testimony*, pp. vii–xii.
81 Ibid., p. 45. See also Adams, *Inquiry into the Powers committed to the General Assemblies*, pp. 22–3, where the same argument is advanced.

should not be in bondage to any in the matter. Fifthly, it was a cruel oppression to societies of men who valued their immortal souls and desired proper spiritual guides for their edification, comfort, and eternal concerns to place them under the care of patrons who were liable to be 'indifferent about the concerns of their own souls, being negligent, erroneous or profane', and as a result unlikely to be 'much concerned to choose proper pastors to take inspection of the souls of others'. And, sixthly, as aforementioned, patronage was to be seen as an open door for 'a corrupt ministry' to enter the Church as had been established in those churches which were dominated by patronage.[82]

Those who accepted presentations, however, were especially condemned by Willison. They were partners in sin with the patrons 'by homo-logating [their] usurped power, and strengthening [them] in it'. Those who accepted presentations were 'properly the oppressors of the Church of Christ'. They encouraged and hardened patrons in their guilt and sinful usurpation, and obstructed their conviction, repentance, and reformation. The acceptance of presentations, indeed, was presented as the root cause of much that was to be deplored in the Church. It led to

> simoniacal pactions and intrigues, unchristian contentions and divisions in judicatories, oppressive concussions in parishes, vexatious prosecutions and appeals, and many scandalous intrusions in churches, to the great discredit of religion, and reproach of the ministerial character.

Ultimately, it led to schism. On the basis of the *Second Book of Discipline*, those who accepted presentations were chargeable with defection and breach of faith. Willison touched on the doctrine of the Church when he argued that the system of presentation and acceptance of presentation inverted Christ's appointed order in the Church in that a minister's right to maintenance should be consequential to his ordination to the ministry. It was an 'inversion contrary to Christ's stated order, and the nature of things', and it led ministers to limit the success of the Gospel and their own ministries by offending the parishes concerned, as well as others, by their conduct. This offence was worsened when it was seen that there was no need to accept presentations.[83] The idea that acceptance of presentation before ordination was an inversion of the proper order of things was logically developed to include the suggestion that ministers could be seen as seeking their livelihoods rather than the success of the Gospel,[84] or, as Adams put it, as turning Christ's 'sacred institution' of ordination 'into a mere passport, to a temporal benefice'.[85]

---

[82] Ibid., pp. 46–8.
[83] Ibid., pp. 48–51.
[84] Lawson, *Speech concerning the Settling of Parishes*, p. 18.
[85] Adams, *Inquiry into the Powers committed to the General Assemblies*, p. 23.

Adams, in fact, took the argument a stage further when he integrated it into his case against the deposition of Gillespie in 1754. The purpose of granting a benefice was 'to encourage, and support able, active and faithful ministers in discharge of their ministerial functions'. This being the case, it could be forfeited only if the minister departed from the laws of Christ and failed to fulfil the purposes of his ministry. The office of the minister and the benefice, therefore, stood or fell together. As well as accepting the general direction and implications of Willison's analysis of the reasons against patronage, Adams's work extended the range of the argument by maintaining that those who accepted presentations, together with members of Assemblies which appointed their ordination to a parochial charge, were chargeable with a breach of their ordination vows.[86] This last point, however, perhaps owed more to the Assembly's treatment of the Presbytery of Dunfermline, which refused to comply with its instructions to ordain the presentee to Inverkeithing, than to a concept which emerged from the overall Popular analysis of the reasons against patronage.

In short, then, Popular ideology concerning patronage stressed two concepts: the unique nature of the Church as deriving its purpose and authority from the commands of Christ himself and, as a result, not being susceptible to analysis by means of secular social or philosophical theories; and the existence of the Church of Scotland's constitution which both precluded patronage and provided the means for the removal of its effects. Persuading the Moderate-controlled Assembly to accept either of these concepts or to modify its enforcement of patronage was another matter, and failure to do so led to the development of a more secular polemic against patronage and of the associated secularised strategy from the early 1750s. The case for this strategy is the third issue emerging from Popular publications on patronage.

VII

The Popular assessment of the reasons for its failure to persuade the Assembly were uniform throughout the second half of the century. It criticised those who were elected as ruling elders to be commissioners to the Assembly, and the way in which the Assembly and, especially, the Commission of Assembly were open to influence by factions and by the Government; but the failure was also the result of the absence of a coherent Popular strategy.

As early as 1732, James Gordon had been arguing in favour of denying the right of separate representation at the General Assembly to universities, royal burghs, and non-residing commissioners, including heritors, from presbyteries. Furthermore, he maintained that the method of

<hr>

[86] Ibid., pp. 23–5.

nominating the Commission of Assembly and defining its functions were not founded on the Word of God, and that it was not, by Scriptural definition and example, 'an ecclesiastick Synod'.[87] Willison, when referring to the Assembly of 1734 and its efforts to appease the Seceders, referred to the opposition 'of great men, ruling elders, who had a strong party in the House to support them', and in general ascribed a political motivation to opposition to Popular efforts to tackle the patronage problem.[88] The Assembly's failure over the years to do anything was ascribed to 'pusillanimity, or sinful fearfulness of offending the Government', regard for patrons and heritors, and the influence of the Crown which was alleged to have the patronage 'of most of the Churches of Scotland', strong influence from the Court, and 'the activity of several leading ministers, who had their dependence upon or expectations from that airth'.[89] Adams of Falkirk, on the other hand, ascribed the deposition of Gillespie to the cowardice of those who did not vote, and particularly to the lay eldership whose judgement in such matters should be of less weight since they had no part in the execution of such sentences, and would therefore be less interested in their nature and more indifferent about their consequences.[90] By the 1760s, however, Popular suspicions about the role of the ruling eldership had become less pronounced.[91]

More revealing than analysis of why the Popular party thought they had been unsuccessful in attempts to persuade the Assembly to oppose patronage, however, is analysis of what they proposed to do about it. The apparent inability of the Popular party to produce concrete proposals for gaining control of the General Assembly in the short term is striking. Willison, for example, certainly saw the patronage issue as being part of the much larger problem of spiritual declension in the Church as a whole.[92] He advocated that greater concern should be shown by members of the judicatories for the support of the truths that they had sworn to uphold in their subscriptions to the Westminster Confession of Faith. His proposals for dealing with patronage were a mixture of exhortation of the Assembly to enforce the existing legislation limiting the rights of patronage and acceptance of presentations, and a set of administrative proposals. The latter commenced with the suggestion that acceptance of, or adherence to, a presentation should be treated as contravention of the ordination formula if it stood in the way of a presbytery's right of free moderation of a call or a parish's right to

---

[87] Gordon, *State and Duty of the Church of Scotland*, pp. 157–66.
[88] Willison, *Fair and Impartial Testimony*, p. 76.
[89] Ibid., pp. 51–2. Recent research on the extent of Crown influence in the patronage system, however, indicates that it was not as considerable as was believed by the Popular party at the time. See Sher and Murdoch, 'Patronage and Party', pp. 198–203.
[90] Adams, *Inquiry into the Powers committed to the General Assemblies*, p. 31.
[91] See below, pp. 128–42, 147–50.
[92] See above, pp. 58–68.

free election. The Assembly should endeavour to ensure the absence of 'any compulsion or undue influence' in the calling of ministers, and should adopt measures to transport and remove ministers to whom parishes could not be brought to submit. Appeals from synods should only be to the General Assembly or to the meeting of the Commission immediately after the Assembly when their members were numerous, 'it not being agreeable to Presbyterian principles and parity, that the greater number of ministers should be subjected to the authority and judgement of a lesser'. Presbyteries should be most careful and conscientious in licensing men to preach the Gospel, and should enquire into their 'true godliness' and Scriptural doctrine, and also into 'their sentiments concerning patronage and other grievances of the Church'. The Assembly should declare that it was the duty of ministers to testify against the corruptions of the times, 'and even against what is wrong in the Acts and Proceedings of the Church judicatories'. Presbyteries should also be strictly conscientious in attesting that ruling elders who were to sit in Assemblies or Commissions were qualified according to the Act of 1722. And finally, Willison urged that the Assembly should investigate the rights of Colleges and royal burghs to choose ministers or elders to sit in the General Assembly.[93] In other words, Willison was proposing to defeat patronage by the rigorous selection of ministers and elders in order to reduce the presence at the Assembly of those who supported patronage. The other proposal of substance was to reduce the influence of the Commission of Assembly. Everything that Willison proposed, however, ultimately depended on a majority of presbyteries being prepared to adopt a systematic and sustained policy of excluding from the Assembly all who would not take a consistent anti-patronage stand. Analysis of dissents from the decisions of the General Assembly suggests that such a policy would have had no chance of implementation even if presbyteries were to have been prepared to adopt such a divisive course of action.[94]

The inability of the Popular strategists to produce an alternative policy with any real chance of success was revealed clearly enough in Adams's *Inquiry into the Powers committed to the General Assemblies* as well as in the *Loud Cry for Help*. After considerable analysis, Adams produced four proposals: undue solicitation and jobbing at Assemblies should be dealt with by enacting that such practices would lose the cause of those adopting them; no sentences or orders issued found to be inconsistent with the standing rules of the Church should have any effect, irrespective of whatever precedents or former practices might be pretended; all presbyteries should be enjoined to call their Assembly commissioners to a strict account and those found faulty in terms of their commission should be censured; and no sentence should be

93 Willison, *Fair and Impartial Testimony*, pp. 118–21.
94 See below, p. 124.

insisted upon if presbyteries concerned in its execution deemed it to be illegal or unconstitutional until the case was considered by the next General Assembly and dealt with according to the laws and rules of the Church.[95] The lameness of the proposals, with the exception of the last, which was aimed at the Commission, is obvious. The proposals of the *Loud Cry for Help* were equally unrealistic, as were Maclaurin's proposals for obtaining the reversal of the deposition of Gillespie in the *Nature of Ecclesiastic Government*.

The factors behind the attraction of a political or secular strategy are seen clearly when the *Loud Cry for Help*'s proposals for immediate implementation in the courts of the Church are compared with those of Willison's *Fair and Impartial Testimony*.[96] The *Loud Cry* urged Sessions who concurred in its views to wait upon their minister if he is inclined to support 'the tyrannical measures now in vogue', to expostulate with him to consider the divided state of the Church, and to represent the absurdity of treating with contempt those he had in his care 'while he almost worships the gentry who trample upon his character, and despise his ministrations'. Secondly, it urged elders not to consider secession, because 'the high-flying clergy' said that no opponent could do them as much harm out of the Church as in it. Thirdly, kirk sessions should choose elders who would promise to attend the presbytery and synod. This point the author saw as critical since there were seldom half as many elders as ministers present, though by right the numbers should have been equal. The author had 'always looked upon the elders as representatives of the people, and therefore expect[ed], when the elders are all or mostly absent, to find the interest of the people in a great measure neglected'. Fourthly, Presbytery elders should also remember that they should vote for 'proper' commissioners to the General Assembly, 'not regarding whose turn it is'; that they should ensure that those chosen were duly qualified according to the relevant Acts of Assembly; and that evidence of qualification should be obtained. Evidence of conduct of family worship and attendance at public worship should especially be sought. Fifthly, kirk sessions throughout the nation should send representations or remonstrances to the General Assembly. This device had proved useful in the past. If it was a privilege of inferiors in the civil state to petition their superiors against grievances, the same privilege must also exist in an 'Ecclesiastick Society', and surely as much 'mildness and tenderness' could be expected in the Church as in the State. And, finally, kirk sessions should seek and follow 'the advice of such ministers as you esteem to be the most prudent and faithful'.[97]

Such proposals embodied a retreat from the specific type of administrative proposals made, for example, by Willison in 1744 and in

---

[95] Adams, *Inquiry into the Powers committed to the General Assemblies*, p. 34.

[96] See also above, pp. 97, 118–19, 121–2.

[97] *Loud Cry for Help*, pp. 30–2.

1754 by Adams of Falkirk in his *Inquiry into the Powers committed to the General Assemblies*.[98] Several of the *Loud Cry*'s proposals were little more than the expression of pious hopes. The ecclesiastical strategy was beginning to crumble. Apart from this, the *Loud Cry for Help* is notable for its almost 'populist' emphasis on the rights and role of 'the people'. In general, however, there can be little doubt that the closely argued, legalistic reasoning of the work opened the minds of many supporters of the campaign against patronage to the possibility of a political and secular strategy to replace the ecclesiastical initiatives which were so signally failing.

It is not unreasonable to suggest, therefore, that the secularisation of the Popular analysis of and response to patronage, and the development of a new strategy based on the role of the heritors, were the result of growing awareness of two matters. First, the attempt to fight patronage by appealing to what the Popular party understood to be the constitution of the Church was doomed to failure because of inflexible Moderate domination of the Assembly. Secondly, the attempt to persuade the presbyteries to preclude any supporter of patronage from appearing as a commissioner to the General Assembly was seen to be futile.

There are three possible implications of this perception of the unwillingness or inability of the presbyteries to co-operate in Popular proposals for combating the Moderate majority in the Assembly. All have implications for the interpretation of the Popular party and its role in the eighteenth-century Church. First, there is the possibility that the party had limited *reliable* support at the Assembly. It is notable, for example, that there was a wide disparity between the numbers of those who were prepared to vote against the Moderate view of disputed settlements and the numbers of those who were prepared to adhere to dissents concerning them. Furthermore, there were considerable fluctuations in the numbers voting for Popular motions at the same Assembly. This was pronounced at and after the deposition of Gillespie. As a result the second possibility arises, that the rank-and-file of the party had lost heart before those in the leadership.[99] Most important, however, is the third possibility: that at presbytery, and even at the General Assembly, the common assumption of a wide division between Popular and Moderate ministers is not valid and that, apart from the issue of patronage, there was little evident party division at all.[100]

---

98 On Willison's proposals, see above, pp. 121–2; on Adams's proposals, see above, pp. 122–3.
99 See above, pp. 102–3; and below, pp. 150–1.
100 McIntosh, 'Popular Party in the Church of Scotland', esp. pp. 41–51, 53–64, 77, 87. See also above, pp. 26, 87–9; and below, pp. 237–8.

CHAPTER FOUR

Liberalism and the Secularisation of the Popular Party, 1760–1785

In 1753, new elements were introduced to the patronage dispute by the reasons of dissent from the General Assembly's decision in the case of the disputed presentation to Biggar. These elements related to the appearance of a legal rather than a theological focus to the opposition to patronage. For most of the next thirty years also, there appears to have been a decline of interest in theological matters in general. There were few publications from members of the Popular party on doctrinal issues, there seems to have been little interest in pursuing allegations of heresy against ministers of the Church, and while issues of the day did produce analysis by Popular writers, the theological content was more in the nature of pre-suppositions regarding the nature and objectives of society than to do with subjecting contemporary issues to a theologically informed scrutiny.

At the same time, however, there was a clear willingness on the part of the Popular party to become involved in specific political issues and even to espouse political causes to an extent not previously evident. Perusal of the evidence suggests that from around 1760 the emergence of a more secular strategy of opposition to patronage made members of the Popular party more open to participation in more straightforwardly political areas. There came to be a perceived parallel between what was seen as the denial of Christian liberty in ecclesiastical matters by the Moderates, and the denial of civil liberty in secular society by the political allies of the Moderates, that is, by the Tory government of the period. The Popular party as a result came to be increasingly aligned with liberal forces in the State.

I

It should not be thought, however, that the appearance of a secular or political emphasis in the evolution of the Popular strategy for combating patronage was merely the result of Popular impotence at the General Assembly. There was, in fact, an ideological foundation for the move away from a more narrowly theological approach to the problem. As early as 1754, John Adams concluded his *Inquiry into the Powers committed to the General Assemblies* by attempting to enlist lay and even Governmental support for the Popular position by linking the threat of alienating the people from the civil constitution to their hostility to violent settlements and encroachments on the ecclesiastical constitution. This in turn was tied to the growth of Dissent and its implications for the landed interest. Tenants would use their incomes to set up and endow dissenting congregations with their buildings and stipends, and finance which would otherwise have been available for land improvement and payment of rents would not be put to such use.[1]

As has been noticed, John Maclaurin's *Nature of Ecclesiastic Government*, published in the same year, also introduced a note of political theory to the debate; while, in particular, the *Loud Cry for Help* of 1753, although it had evangelical stresses, was very much a political document. This work displayed a Whig tone, by identifying patronage as having been introduced by a Tory ministry hostile to Presbyterianism.[2] The idea of 'concurrence' being introduced to replace the doctrine of the call was condemned,[3] and the argument was taken up that the Church had the power to make the law of patronage what it thought it fit to make it.[4] From here on, however, the *Loud Cry for Help* took on a more profound significance in the development of the Popular response to patronage. The author regarded the most common argument in favour of settling ministers with little or no concurrence as being the fear that refusal to settle a presentee without a good reason would provoke the patrons, who were 'mostly great men', to bind patronage more closely on the Church by an Act of Parliament. Then, in a passage which may well have been the origin of the later strategy of attempting to enlist the support of the landed gentry for the Popular cause, he argued that it could safely be said that all the heritors, elders, and heads of families would prefer patronage to be forced on them by an Act of Parliament than by an Act of Assembly for two reasons: first, it was more honourable to submit to the stronger rather than weaker master, and Parliament was stronger than the Assembly 'as consisting of two Houses to one, besides the King, not to mention smaller differences'; and, secondly, it was preferable to be wounded by a distant source, rather than by one with which one was closely connected and related.[5] Apart from the Erastianism implied in this position, this assessment opened the way for a political offensive against patronage.

---

[1] Adams, *Inquiry into the Powers committed to the General Assemblies*, pp. 36–7.

[2] *Loud Cry for Help*, pp. 5–7. The *Loud Cry for Help* struck an evangelical note early on when it commented unfavourably on the alleged tendencies to levity of the 'younger clergy' and their abhorrence of 'a religious Professor of the grave kind'. It held that the end of ordination was the salvation of souls by the successful preaching of the Gospel, and that settlements made under the existing system of patronage did not have the glory of God in view (pp. 5–7).

[3] Ibid., p. 10.

[4] See above, pp. 62, 118.

[5] *Loud Cry for Help*, p. 11.

The *Loud Cry* continued that the rights of the Church of Scotland, if they were not asserted before Parliament, would lose their force because of disuse, in the same way as many ministers throughout the country had lost the power of discipline over the nobility and gentry.[6] If brought before Parliament, the case against patronage would not be lost, first of all because the King, 'whose candour and goodness are universally acknowledged, as well as his abilities to discern his own interest well known', could easily see that violent settlements were contrary to the interest of the Crown, since alienation of the Presbyterians would lead the Ministry to seek the political friendship of the Jacobites. The old spectre of Jacobitism was then raised by identifying the strongest supporters of patronage as those who in the 1747 Assembly were most in favour of allowing 'disaffected nonjurant Episcopalian heritors' a share in the election of a Presbyterian minister. The argument further alleged that those ministers who were settled contrary to the will of their people were forsaken by their people, had least to do at home, always wandered most abroad, spent the most money, and were therefore the strongest supporters of stipend augmentation, which was contrary to the interest of the heritors, several of whom were Members of Parliament! The 'keenest, fiercest and most indiscreet' prosecutors of the stipend augmentation scheme were known to be 'the Abettors of presentations', whereas those ministers who 'used in settlements to have some small consideration of US the vulgar, and consequently, to show comparatively less regard to the gentry ... discovered the greatest modesty and deference' in the matter.[7]

As has been noted,[8] the case of the disputed presentation to Biggar in 1753 introduced new elements to the patronage dispute which were contained in the reasons for dissent from the Assembly's decision on the case relating to the appearance of a legal rather than a theological focus to the opposition to patronage.

The six years after the eighteen months or so which saw the Assembly deal with the case of Biggar and the publication of the *Loud Cry for Help*, Maclaurin's *Nature of Ecclesiastic Government*, and Adams's *Inquiry into the Powers committed to the General Assemblies*, was a period of numerous presentation disputes, but they were all conducted in terms of the principles and arguments which were used in the case of Biggar, and in terms of the interpretation of the 1690 Act which abolished patronage and gave the elders and heritors the right to nominate a minister subject

---

[6] The point being made here was that the infidelity of the nobility and gentry had necessitated an appeal to the heritors. The subsequent 'Crosbie' initiative of the 1760s could therefore be seen as brought about by spiritual decline in society, especially among its upper ranks. As such, it would provide an interesting application of 'commonwealthman' theory as applied by Sher and Murdoch, 'Patronage and Party', pp. 208–14.

[7] *Loud Cry for Help*, pp. 13–14.

[8] See above, pp. 108–10.

to the approval of the congregation and presbytery.[9] Possibly the most important of these disputes was the Kilconquhar Case of 1760 in which a settlement was opposed by the normally Moderate-dominated Presbytery of St Andrews on the grounds that the Commission of Assembly had exceeded its powers. In the Assembly debate, John Witherspoon made a key speech in which he took up the Popular argument for a conceptual differentiation between calling a minister to a pastoral charge and calling a minister on an establishment, that is, to a congregation in a church where either the State or some other body contributes to the upkeep of the ministry, and has legal rights relating to who should be called. Witherspoon (who subsequently dissented along with five other ministers from the Assembly's decision to enforce the settlement), accepted that the ordination of a pastor without the support of his congregation was sometimes felt by conscientious ministers to be necessary, though it was not the situation in the Kilconquhar case, but went on to make an assertion open to misinterpretation:

> I do not believe, and I know nobody so foolish as to believe what is commonly imputed to us, that any Christian, as such, has a right to call a minister on an establishment. We know that nobody has a right to call a minister on an establishment except those to whom the law has given it; neither would I contend that every man ought to have a right, though we had it in our power to make laws on that subject, since this seeming equality would be a vile inequality.[10]

Superficially, this would seem to have been paving the way for the view that after 1760, under men like Andrew Crosbie and Sir Harry Moncrieff Wellwood, the Popular party had an elitist Whig view of Church government based on the ideology of 1688–90 and the 'commonwealthman' tradition, rather than being a fundamentally 'Popular' grouping at all.[11] To include Witherspoon and his supporters in this thesis, however, is to fail to see the significance of much of the rest of the speech. Witherspoon went on to argue that, since any man in the country had the right to adhere to the minister of his choice, and since a legal pastor could be of little or no service to his people if he was on bad terms with them, it was the indisputable duty of a church court never to make unpopular settlements without a real necessity. He rejected the argument that the people could easily be led in a direction other than

---

[9] Sher and Murdoch, 'Patronage and Party', pp. 200–2. As noted earlier, Sher and Murdoch interpret the 1690 Act as giving the landed interest the upper hand in the selection of ministers for vacant churches outside the burghs and consequently argue for the predominance of a 'Whig commonwealthman' theory as being the most important hallmark of the Popular party's opposition to patronage. Presumably, although they do not analyse individual presentation disputes, they would see the Kilconquhar case of 1760 as evidence for their position: see above, p. 110, note 57.

[10] Morren, *Annals of the General Assembly*, ii, p. 204.

[11] Sher and Murdoch, 'Patronage and Party', p. 211.

that in which they wished to go, and held that such settlements could only lead the people to believe that ministers who accepted such settlements had no more than a desire for a comfortable benefice and stipend for life.[12]

Witherspoon's position was not, therefore, that the people should have no say in the appointment of a minister, but that the actual method of selection was not crucial, so long as the minister settled was acceptable to them. Witherspoon's case stressed the idea of providing ministers acceptable to their congregations as essential to the concept of establishment. If, however, the system allowed unacceptable ministers to be appointed, the whole purpose of establishment and the provision of a legal stipend was nullified, the purpose of establishment being 'to provide a sufficient and useful pastor to the people within the bounds of a certain parish'.[13] In other words, although the Presbytery of St Andrews, which was usually Moderate in complexion, did not use the argument, Witherspoon, its most articulate advocate on the floor of the Assembly, defended it by maintaining that the grounds for opposition to the patronage system lay in the nature of the role of the ministry in relation to the members of the Body of Christ. To see the Popular position as the ideology of an elitist socio-political grouping within the Church is to misapprehend the significance of the evangelical religious impetus behind it. It is to mistake tactics for objective.[14]

---

12 Morren, *Annals of the General Assembly*, ii, pp. 201–7. Cf. the *Loud Cry for Help*'s assertion that liberty of conscience could lead to leaving one minister for another if dissatisfied. See above, p. 97.

13 Cf. Gordon, *State and Duty of the Church of Scotland*, pp. 27–35.

14 Morren, *Annals of the General Assembly*, ii, p. 204. In the patronage debate in the early 1760s there occurred an interlude in the second phase of the controversy. It centred on the respective rights of Church courts and municipal corporations in the presentation of ministers to burgh charges. This was the so-called 'Drysdale Bustle' of 1762–4 in Edinburgh which has received detailed analysis elsewhere, and which need not be repeated here (e.g., J. Cater, 'The making of Principal Robertson in 1762: politics and the University of Edinburgh in the second half of the eighteenth century', *Scot. Hist. Rev.*, xlix [1970], pp. 60–84; and R. B. Sher, 'Moderates, managers, and Popular politics in mid-eighteenth-century Edinburgh: the "Drysdale Bustle" of the 1760s', in J. Dwyer, R. A. Mason and A. Murdoch (eds.), *New Perspectives on the Politics and Culture of Early Modern Scotland* (Edinburgh, 1982), pp. 179–209). The case of Lady Yester's Church, for such was the 'Drysdale Bustle', was an attempt by the Moderate leadership in conjunction with the Edinburgh Town Council to place a Moderate minister, Rev. John Drysdale, in a vacant Edinburgh charge. As such, therefore, it was an integral part of the Moderate–Popular struggle. The whole debate, however, with one small exception, was carried on in legal terms as to whether the Town Council had the sole right of presentation. This was contested by the Popular ministers and their supporters in the General Sessions of the city. The only area of the debate where non-legal issues acquired prominence was when an objection to the Council's action was made on the grounds that such presentations would alienate the minds of the people from attending the regular ministry, would lead to the erection of separate places of worship to the detriment of the morals of the people, and would be destructive to the revenue of the poor's house which was largely maintained by the collections at the church services. The Moderate response to this line of argument was the expression of pious hopes that no well-disposed persons would neglect their duty, that the Town Council would always choose ministers

II

The Assembly of 1766 that debated the overture of the Committee on Schism marks both the end of the second phase of the patronage debate, which emphasised the negation of the purposes of establishment by patronage and its unconstitutional nature, and the beginning of the short third phase, in which an attempt was made to gain the support of the 'landed interest'. The committee had been set up by the previous Assembly, which had been unexpectedly under Popular control, and its report is usually regarded as marking the peak of Popular opposition to patronage. The committee's overture identified patronage as the cause of the growth of the Secession, and proposed that the Assembly should set up a committee to discuss with presbyteries and the 'landed interest' the matter of how to reform the abuse. The overture, which was rejected by 99 votes to 85, marked the beginnings of the emergence of a coherent ecclesiastical and secular polemic at the Assembly. By the mid-1760s, the Popular party, or at least its leaders, had decided that the benefits of patronage in the context of the Scottish Establishment were too considerable to be rejected out of hand, but they were still committed to the maintenance of an acceptable ministry for each congregation. Amelioration had to be the goal. The problem was how to attain it. In 1766, the answer was an attempt to enlist the support of men of property by a crude appeal to their economic interests, but this should not be misread and interpreted as paving the way for an attempt by a socio-political group to extend their influence in and their ideas to the Church.[15] What, then, was the real nature of the Popular position in the Schism debate?

most conducive to the interests of true religion and sound morals, and an assertion of faith in the loyalty of the people to the ordinances of the Gospel and in their charity to the poor: Morren, *Annals of the General Assembly*, ii, p. 275. It should be noted, however, that the General Sessions, which included both Moderate and Popular ministers and their supporters, disapproved unanimously of the exercise of the right of patronage; and that, on the other side, no exception was ever made to the presentee by Popular members. The significance of this has so far gone unregarded. It was one of several instances of substantial agreement between members of the two parties which seem to have occurred regularly away from the higher echelons of party leadership: ibid., ii, p. 285. There was an even more striking instance of this type of cross-party agreement in the famous St Ninian's case of 1766–73, in which Moderate members of the Presbytery of Stirling voted unanimously for the hard-line anti-patronage policy of the Popular majority for 7 years. See McIntosh, 'Popular Party in the Church of Scotland', pp. 42–9, 54. See also below, pp. 142–3, 242.

15 There would seem to be two reasons why Sher and Murdoch develop their theory in the way they do. First, there is a failure to comprehend the religious or spiritual impulse in the issue of settlements, i.e. the necessity of an acceptable minister to provide for the spiritual needs of a congregation. And secondly, there is a reliance on a limited range of pamphlet literature which obscures the nature of the overall balance of views as revealed in the Assembly debates: Sher and Murdoch, 'Patronage and Party', p. 211.

The Popular case rejected arguments that schism was a necessary evil and that supporters of the overture were persecutors of the Seceders.[16] Indeed the overture aimed at remedying the grievances of which the Seceders complained. It then distinguished two senses in which the term 'the rights of the people' in calling their pastors could be used:

> it might seem to relate to the natural right which every man has to choose or judge for himself in religion, and everything belonging to it; and therefore, in particular – to choose his own pastor, to whom he was to commit the care of his soul, and on whom he was to depend for daily instruction and comfort: Or, 2, It might relate to the question, Who had a right in fact, or who ought in justice to have the right, of calling a parochial minister upon an Establishment?[17]

The first sense, it was argued, belonged to every individual and could not be denied by any consistent Protestant. The second, it was contended, was not asserted by anyone. This developed Witherspoon's argument put forward six years earlier in the case of Kilconquhar,[18] and it went on to maintain that 'probably nobody would plead for every adult inhabitant having an equal share since a seeming equality would be a real inequality'.[19] Where any power of judgement was left to the Church, the general principle and end to be regarded was the settlement of a 'Gospel ministry' which was for the edification of the people within a certain district. If this end was not met, it was just so much of the public money thrown away.

At this point, the Popular argument moved away from the more theological and spiritual in the direction of ecclesiastical considerations, and here the seeds of subsequent misinterpretation begin to appear. Four consequences of settling churches by presentations were identified: patrons were led to see the right of presentation as a piece of private property to be disposed of in their own private interests; the wishes of men of rank and influence in the parishes were disregarded; a student's or probationer's character and behaviour were made virtually irrelevant; and whole parishes were disrupted and ministers were rendered useless in both civil and religious capacities. There would appear to be two possible reasons for the insertion of the reference to men of rank and influence in this section of the overture. There was the implication that there were many in the parish as good as one patron, and there was an

---

16 *Scots Magazine*, xxviii (Jul. 1766), pp. 337–41; xxviii (Aug. 1766), pp. 393–9. The account of the debate in Morren, *Annals of the General Assembly*, ii, pp. 329–47 is a verbatim reprint of the report by the correspondent of the *Scots Magazine*.

17 *Scots Magazine*, xxviii (Aug. 1766), p. 395; Morren, *Annals of the General Assembly*, ii, p. 339.

18 See above, pp. 128–9. The first appearance of this distinction, of course, occurred in the *Loud Cry for Help*. See above, p. 97.

19 *Scots Magazine*, xxviii (Aug. 1766), p. 395; Morren, *Annals of the General Assembly*, ii, p. 339. The exact meaning of this last statement is unclear. The similarity to the almost identical statement in Witherspoon's earlier speech prompts the speculation that this idea may also have been part of his contribution on this occasion. See above, p. 128.

attempt to detach heritors from patrons. There is no evidence that its insertion at this stage of the overture was made as part of a socio-political philosophy. The point was that men with as good claims as many patrons to a say in the choice of ministers were being excluded. The issues were still purely ecclesiastical.[20]

After that, the Popular case became more secular. The overture espoused secular arguments so forcefully that much more significance has been read into them than can be justified when their context is taken into consideration. It was argued that the existing system was contrary to the interests of religion and to the civil interest of the country, and also to the revenue of men of property, since the erection of new churches outside the Establishment would render the lower classes less able to pay their rents or to increase them. Every new establishment of that kind was, in effect, a tax on land. The possibility of greater indifference about religion would increase ignorance and vice, which would be immediately destructive to industry, whether agriculture or manufacturing. A distinctly unspiritual analysis of the social function of religion followed. It was argued that men of higher rank could supply the want of religion by a sense of honour or other worldly principles so as to serve their country and themselves; the common people without religion were almost constantly idle and poor at the same time. If they retained their religion and were obliged to set up separating meetings, the country would be saddled with an immense charge, while the Established ministers would receive their stipends without work and would seem excrescences on the body politic. Furthermore, violent settlements were greatly detrimental to the poor's fund. If the evil of secession were to spread and the greatest part of the congregations were to be driven away from the Established Church, either the poor would starve or the heritors would have to maintain them by a voluntary taxation which would soon be so badly executed that parliament would institute a poor rate similar to the much-complained of one in England.[21] The substance of this section of the 1766 overture was so alien to all that had gone before, and, virtually to all that came after, that to seize upon it and to argue that the Popular party's position on patronage was dominated by it and that the party was the vehicle of an elitist socio-political group is superficial.

20 The argument took on a more political emphasis by the refutation of the Moderate contention that patronage led to peace and good order on the grounds that such peace and order as was produced was that found under tyrannical and arbitrary governments. Liberty produced greater apparent disorder in public proceedings but more comfort and happiness, and only occasional and temporary dissent. The example of the system of patronage operating in the Church of England was dismissed as invalid and useless since it led to the neglect of parishes and a church membership 'perhaps more ignorant and profane than the members of any Protestant church in the world': Morren, *Annals of the General Assembly*, ii, pp. 341–2.

21 Ibid., pp. 340–3.

Following this secular digression, the Popular apologists returned to ecclesiastical concerns and stressed that they were complaining that the law, as it stood, had been made much harsher by ecclesiastical decisions than the statute necessitated. It was claimed that the Court of Session had in fact confirmed the power of the church courts to appoint the legal pastor of the parish, though they had allowed the patron to retain the stipend. And the Popular case concluded by rejecting as invalid the argument that it was for the presbyteries to take care in the licensing of probationers, since presbyteries could be deceived or unfaithful.[22] Finally, the proposal to consult with gentlemen of influence and property was justified as flowing from the persuasion that no effectual relief could be obtained but by their concurrence.[23] In other words, the proposal to enlist the support of men of property was a purely pragmatic move.

There were, then, some curious inconsistencies in the latter part of the debate on the overture of the Committee on Schism submitted to the 1766 Assembly. It is clear that the Popular case had three central points: first, the distinction between the religious or spiritual nature of the call of a congregation to a man to be their minister, and the question of who should call a minister to be appointed to a charge on a legal establishment; secondly, the unfortunate consequences, both religious and civil, of settling presentees irrespective of the wishes of the people; and, thirdly, the conviction that the Church had the legal power to ameliorate the situation which was leading to secession if only it were prepared to adopt the obvious alternative to settling every presentee almost automatically, namely, by foregoing the stipend and settling a man acceptable to the congregation. This interpretation, however, poses a problem: why was there such a strong attempt to involve 'men of rank and property' on the Popular side and to justify the attempt on such uncharacteristically non-religious grounds? There were two possible reasons. First, it may have been a concession to an articulate and aggressive section of the party, which was possibly providing the most effective debate on the floor of the Assembly; Andrew Crosbie was probably its most important member. Secondly, and more likely, there was an increasing awareness in the Popular party that the control of the Assembly was a matter of management of the lay eldership. If they could be brought to support the Popular cause, then the exercise of patronage could be reduced to spiritually acceptable proportions.[24] What was not present was the suggestion that the landed interest should be recruited for a parliamentary role in the abolition of patronage, nor any suggestion

---

22 This argument was made at its most explicit in the period before the Schism debate by Dr George Kay in his closing address as Moderator of the 1759 Assembly. See Morren, *Annals of the General Assembly*, ii, p. 397.

23 See above, note 16.

24 See above, pp. 120–3; and below, p. 135.

for a permanent role for the landed interest in patronage or in the Establishment.[25]

In the aftermath of the Schism overture, many of these ideas reappeared in an anonymous pamphlet of 1766 entitled *A Short History of the Late General Assembly of the Church of Scotland, shewing the Rise and Progress of the Schism Overture, the Reasonableness or Necessity that some Restriction be put on the Exercise of the Patronage Act, and the Means which the Church hath in its own Power to mitigate or remove that Grievance.*[26] In this hitherto overlooked publication is to be found the exposition of most of the ideas which were later popularised by the lay leader, Andrew Crosbie, in his *Thoughts of a Layman concerning Patronage and Presentations.*[27] The work was characterised by a pronounced political awareness or preoccupation in its analysis.[28] It stressed that the propounders of the Overture did not mean that popular elections should take the place of presentations 'whatever might be meant by some warm ministers and elders', but that what was sought was some mitigation of the law, 'or that some regard should be had to the elders and residing heritors in settling a vacant parish'. Election by the majority of heads of families would seldom result in the candidate of greatest merit being preferred and would soon 'introduce a weaker set of clergy than have hitherto filled the pulpits of Scotland'.[29]

Two main reasons were advanced why the author of *A Short History* believed that the heritors could be counted upon to oppose unpopular presentations. First, patronage was prone to produce ministers who might be disagreeable companions to the gentlemen-heritors, and therefore the heritors would endeavour to obtain some relief against the rigid exercise of patronage. Secondly, dissent promoted by unpopular presentations would adversely affect the heritors economically.[30] In other words, the second reason was virtually the same as was advanced by Adams a decade earlier. While the *Short History* expressed uncertainty as to what the promoters of the Schism overture meant to do if the motion had been successful, it unequivocally rejected as improper the idea that the General Assembly should enforce the principles of the 1719 Act concerning acceptance of presentations. Instead, it advocated that

[25] Such a case was, of course, made 3 years later in the 1769 Assembly. See below, p. 136.

[26] *A Short History of the Late General Assembly of the Church of Scotland ...* (Glasgow, 1766).

[27] Crosbie may have had a hand in the earlier work, though there is no indication that such was the case. The Glasgow publication would tend to suggest that the author could have been a member of the solidly Popular Presbytery of Glasgow, and, judging from the sentiments contained in it, probably a ruling elder. See, e.g., Andrew Crosbie, *Thoughts of a Layman concerning Patronage and Presentations* (Edinburgh, 1769), pp. 35–7.

[28] It is worth pointing out that the work ascribed the origin of support for the Schism Overture to dissatisfaction with the acquittal by the 1765 Assembly of Carson of Anwoth on an immorality charge, and the desire of some at least in the Assembly of discomfiting Principal Robertson, 'the chief Ecclesiastic Conductor of the Assembly': *Short History*, pp. 8–9.

[29] Ibid., pp. 30–1.

[30] Ibid., pp. 33–4.

presbyteries should not transport a minister already in a charge unless there was a sufficient call; that the 1732 Act lodging the power of election in the conjunct body of the heritors and elders should be re-enacted; and that there should be a return to popular doctrines, sentiments, and language in preaching since the absence of these latter features were the key to the growth of schism.[31] The first of these three alternatives did not embody any significant advance on the strategy of the earlier supporters of the Popular position, while the last was not likely to have been any more successful if it was patronage which was placing non-Popular ministers in pulpits. The second alternative was, then, the key one. The *Short History*, however, is of interest in a further way in that, for the first time, it gave a detailed analysis of the Assembly membership and attempted to establish the nature of the Moderate majority. After drawing attention to the in-built ministerial majority in presbytery representation arising from the two-to-one representation of ministers to ruling elders, it was argued that this advantage was negated by lay representation from the royal burghs and the universities, the ability of Edinburgh lawyers and gentlemen to represent distant parishes or royal burghs, the inability of ministers to represent another presbytery, and the inability of increasing numbers of ministers to attend the Assembly for financial reasons.[32] This produced a situation where the Moderate interest found it easier to prevail.

Apart from its introduction of a secular and political perspective to the debate in a more fundamental way than hitherto, and its analysis of the reasons for Moderate domination of the Assembly, the *Short History* also dealt with the possibility of a Governmental policy of weakening the democratic power in the Church in order to promote monarchical power in the State. To do so, it was argued, the Government promoted patronage in order to disjoin the people from their ministers, it had a deliberate policy of pauperising the clergy, it welcomed the absence of the nobility and gentry from worship in order to discredit the clergy, and it encouraged the divisions between the Moderate and Popular parties in order to divide the clergy and overcome their potential influence. The use of pensions, rich benefices, chaplaincies and other such devices succeeded wonderfully well in ensuring that matters in the Assembly went 'entirely to the satisfaction of the ministry'. Certain of the clergy, in turn, entertained the judges 'copiously and cheerfully' and this led to further biased voting.[33]

In brief, then, the *Short History of the Late General Assembly* introduced, for the first time, a completely secular basis into what had hitherto been a religious or ecclesiastical debate. The context in which it put forward its views was political rather than ecclesiastical. It took the debate firmly

---

[31] Ibid., pp. 37–9. See also above, pp. 65–8, 97, 128.
[32] *Short History*, pp. 40–2.
[33] Ibid., pp. 48–53, 56–7, 60–5.

into the political arena. There was certainly no mention of the spiritual function of the ministry, and little of the constitution of the Church. When referring to the religious state of the Highlands and Islands, the purpose of the erection of parishes was that of 'instructing and civilising them', and the function of a minister was seen somewhat ambiguously as 'teaching the people their duty to God and man'.[34] Both of these concepts embodied a process of secularisation of the patronage debate which was to become even more pronounced until the early 1770s.

III

Although the Popular party had been defeated on the Schism Overture in 1766, it was successful in the 1768 Assembly in securing the appointment of a committee to correspond with the landed interest, the royal burghs, and the presbyteries on the grievance of patronage with a view to seeking redress from Parliament. But this strategy, which implies increased influence within the party of Andrew Crosbie and similar advocates of the lay interest, engendered no response.[35] In the ensuing Assembly, the Moderates defeated an attempt to reappoint the committee by 115 votes to 87. The 'Reasons of Dissent' of Crosbie and others of the Popular party added little to what had already been said during the Schism debate, except to raise the spectre of civil disloyalty arising from separation from the ecclesiastical Establishment; it linked the arguments used against the reappointment of the committee to arguments destructive of civil and religious liberty and in favour of arbitrary power of any kind. Patronage was also linked with Jacobitism, disloyalty and disaffection to the present constitution. In addition the dissent also spoke of patronage as depriving the landed interest and the elders of 'their just right in the election of ministers of the gospel'.[36] This was the first time that this argument had been advanced at the Assembly although it had appeared in the publications on the subject.

In the aftermath of the defeat of 1768 there appeared the key contribution of Andrew Crosbie, his *Thoughts of a Layman concerning Patronage and Presentations* of 1769. Crosbie, an advocate, was possibly

---

[34] Ibid., pp. 51–3.

[35] See Sher and Murdoch, 'Patronage and Party', p. 210.

[36] *Scots Magazine*, xxxi (May 1769), pp. 227–8. Sher and Murdoch stress this line of argument in their thesis that the Popular party was dominated by men seeking to restore the primacy of the landed interest in the filling of vacant churches: Sher and Murdoch, 'Patronage and Party', pp. 207–11. While there were doubtless significant numbers of men within the Popular party who were concerned to do so, it would not seem to have been a dominant group at the time. This is substantiated by an examination of developments in the patronage debate over the next 16 years. Sher's and Murdoch's position neglects the overall drift of the anti-patronage case until around 1784; it gives undue emphasis to a small number of pamphlets from a very narrow period; and it disregards the fundamental Popular conception of the separation of congregational and civil rights in the settlement of ministers. On this last aspect, see above, pp. 97, 128–9.

the original of Sir Walter Scott's Councillor Pleydell in *Guy Mannering*. He was to be the leading lay figure on the ranks of the Popular party until he was involved in a bank failure, as a result of which he died in 1785 in great poverty. It is obvious from the first page of Crosbie's work that he argued from different premises from all the previous works on the subject except the *Short History*. Indeed, the tenor of the opening paragraphs was closer to that of the Moderate 'Reasons of Dissent in the Case of Inverkeithing' than it was, for example, to Willison's *Fair and Impartial Testimony*. After an introductory paragraph which blandly informed the reader that 'religion is of the utmost importance to mankind', and that those 'who feel sentiments of religion' would exert themselves to their utmost in its interest and extension, there followed a section which, while derived quite closely from Popular social and political thought, gave an unequivocal secular vision of the purpose of religion:

> Even those who have never felt its force, will own, that it is a matter of attention to human society. Experience will tell them, that in proportion as religion is unknown, the social ties are weak. Order and good government must assume it for their chief support: for it is religion alone that can form the principles of by far the greater part of the human race; who, if ignorant of it, will hardly be sensible of moral obligations at all.
>
> Hence, even those who are insensible to the impressions of religion, will from self-concern, and from a desire of the security and tranquillity of society, wish to forward its interest among men. They may differ perhaps in their ideas of what the real interest of religion is; but they will nevertheless endeavour to prevent its annihilation.[37]

Further indication of the nature of Crosbie's conception of the nature of society was revealed immediately thereafter. The majority of all societies consisted of men 'who are unable to form proper opinions of things themselves, far less to argue upon abstract ideas'. The common people of all countries had no time to make such enquiries and had not the education to do so in any case.[38] Few were so stupid or insensible as to be unconscious of 'the existence of a Supreme Being', and of the due reverence and duty they owed to him, but without instruction this sense only produced ' a gross and absurd superstition' or a careless reliance on the Deity's protection without knowledge of or implementation of his laws.[39]

[37] Crosbie, *Thoughts of a Layman*, pp. 1–2. It is, of course, true that these sentiments are perfectly in accord with Popular thought on the nature and purpose of government. See above, pp. 81–4; and below, pp. 219–28.

[38] Cf. Gordon, *State and Duty of the Church of Scotland*, p. 33; and Lawson, *Speech concerning the Settling of Parishes*, p. 21. See above, p. 96.

[39] Crosbie, *Thoughts of a Layman*, pp. 2–3.

The function of an established ministry, therefore, was to instruct such people of the 'true nature and end of religion', and 'to form their ideas with respect to religion'. This had to be done frequently if it was to be effectual. The most important services to society were to be expected from an established clergy; through their efforts, all the inhabitants of a country, but especially 'the lower class of people', were 'imbued with the principles of religion, and their manners are formed according to its dictates, which include every important duty incident to human life'.[40] In proportion to the conscientiousness of the ministry, 'the manners of a people are more or less perfect; and that country may be said to be in the highest state of civilisation, where the purest doctrines of religion are most universally taught, and where the clergy are most assiduous in discharging their duty of teaching them'.[41]

To achieve these ends, Crosbie produced as criteria for entrance to the ministry a list of qualifications which were markedly unspiritual when compared with those of earlier Popular writers. The responsibilities of the ministry were not only to conduct public worship but also to discharge pastoral duties such as catechising, visiting the sick, friendship and companionship with the parishioners, and the clarification of their religious doubts. As qualifications for these duties,

> polite literature, and elegant erudition, will be of no use. Plain sense, a sincere heart, and a sufficient knowledge of practical divinity, are the chief requisites in a pastor; together with a competent knowledge of controversial divinity, in case a parish falls to his charge where Popery or schisms prevail.

Learning was not a disadvantage, however, and might in fact enable a minister to rise in popular esteem and be more useful to the public, though it should not be seen as an essential part of the qualifications for the ministry.[42] The contrast between this kind of definition and the predominantly spiritual requirements of, for example, Willison, is striking.[43]

It followed from Crosbie's views on the qualifications for entrance to the ministry that qualifications for admission to a particular parish

---

40 Ibid., p. 3. Later in the work, Crosbie asserted that it was the office of the minister 'to instruct all his parishioners, without distinction, in the principles of religion', and went on to maintain that these should be urged on their minds 'as the rule of their life and conduct': ibid., p. 32. It would appear that Crosbie's theology was not dissimilar to that of the Moderates.

41 Ibid., pp. 3–4.

42 Ibid., p. 33. Crosbie was, in fact, taken up on this very point by the main answer to his pamphlet: Henry Grieve, *Observations on the Overture concerning Patronage* (Edinburgh, 1769), p. 14, quoted by Sher and Murdoch, 'Patronage and Party', p. 213. Failure to comprehend Crosbie's position on the special responsibilities of the ministry to the lower classes led to Alexander Carlyle's missing the point Crosbie was making here in his *Usefulness and Necessity of a Liberal Education for Clergymen* (Edinburgh, 1793), pp. 1–2, referred to in Sher, *Church and University in the Scottish Enlightenment*, p. 159.

43 See above, pp. 64–8.

should be based on similar considerations. If the parish was viewed in a theoretical way, 'the man to whom the people are willing to listen for instruction' was the most proper person to instruct them if he was capable of doing so. If such a man could not be found, 'he to whom the people shew the least aversion to listen is, *ceteris paribus*, preferable to any other'. A pastor should know the doctrines he was to teach and be able to teach them, and the people should be willing to have him instruct them. If either or both were absent, his labours would be futile, the people would degenerate in manners and knowledge, he would become a burden on the Establishment, and he would prevent others from performing the functions which he could not. It followed that the simplest and most obvious method of settling a minister was by the election of the people, combined with 'a proper scrutiny into the abilities of the man chosen by the people'. If he was ignorant or incapable of instructing, he should be rejected.[44] In this, Crosbie was following a conventional Popular line of thought relating to the obligation of the Church to provide an effectual ministry, though his conception of its purpose was not notably spiritual. Few Popular ministers, too, would have accepted that the divinity courses at the universities and the system of presbyterial examination of the attainments of candidates for licence would have allowed an ignorant or incapable man to be ordained.

Crosbie then turned his attention to the system of patronage. He argued that presentations were not agreeable to the original constitution of the Church of Scotland (by reference to the *First* and *Second Books of Discipline*), and that patronage had its origins in the medieval Church of Rome; and he refuted alleged legal and historical arguments in support of patronage.[45] Arguments in its support on the grounds that endowment of a benefice carried with it the right to presentation were refuted, on the grounds that patrons at present possessed the teinds in lieu of the right of patronage, as were arguments on the basis of administrative expediency. He then raised the spectre of the link between violent settlements and ideas of political liberty felt by 'the lower class of mankind in Scotland'. As a result of the existing laws governing qualifications for voting in parliamentary elections in both county and burgh, electors were reduced to a very small number and the lower classes were totally excluded. Instead of spreading the spirit of liberty among the people, or making them aware of their political role, the existing system tended rather to introduce 'aristocratic ideas', and as a result deprived the lower classes of 'every feeling of liberty'. In the election of ministers, the people felt their own political strength and such occasions tended to arouse some sense of liberty, which in any case

---

[44] Crosbie, *Thoughts of a Layman*, pp. 4–6.
[45] Ibid., pp. 7–20. It is interesting to note, however, that Crosbie made only a passing reference to the Act of 1690 which vested the right to call with the congregation, with trial and admission by the presbytery. See ibid., p. 16.

was aroused by the whole system of Presbyterian church government. The political drift of such ideas was revealed when Crosbie attempted to identify support for and opposition to 'genuine ideas of Presbytery' with administrations 'favourable to liberty' and 'governments of an opposite stamp' respectively.[46]

The association of patronage with illiberal government paved the way for an analysis of the evils arising from patronage. Crosbie claimed that out of a total of 944 benefices in the Church of Scotland, the patronage of 334 was in the hands of the Crown, that of 309 in the hands of the nobility, and that of 233 in those of the landed gentry. This caused presentation to be open to political evils of a very serious nature. The right of presentation could be used for corruption in elections, both by local individuals and by the Crown, it could lead to the possibility of simony, and it led to the possibility of enemies of the Church such as Papists or Non-jurants finding the means of undermining the Establishment. It allowed non-religious patrons the chance of presenting immoral presentees, and irresponsible patrons the chance of presenting an unpopular man merely in order to assert their rights over the community for ostentatious reasons. All such abuses opened the way to schism.[47]

Crosbie offered several alternatives. He rejected the idea that patrons and principal heritors were sufficient judges of ministerial qualifications, since their style of life was too different from that of the majority of the people. In his opinion, those of 'the middle rank' were best qualified, because they had some knowledge of their own, and were also able to sense those powers of instruction which would produce the best effects on the lower class. They would know what style of preaching was likely to be most useful in country parishes and which was relevant for large towns in being 'instructive to the people, and better answering the ends of public worship'. It was also unreasonable to exclude the middle rank of people from a voice in the choosing of pastors.[48] This idea fitted well with another suggestion of Crosbie's, that the concept of a 'qualified' person for a settlement was misunderstood. It was usually assumed, he maintained, that a man who 'has sufficient literature, and who can acquit himself upon his trials, is qualified'. Instead, the qualification of a person should depend much more on the circumstances of the presentee and the parish taken in conjunction.[49] The implications of this, though Crosbie did not make them explicit, were that his 'middle rank of people' should have much greater influence in the process of appointing a minister at both parish and presbytery level than they had at the time, since they were in the best position to judge.[50]

[46] Ibid., pp. 23–8.
[47] Ibid., pp. 36–40.
[48] Ibid., pp. 34–5.
[49] Ibid., pp. 21–2.
[50] Just how Crosbie rated the capacity of the ministerial body in a presbytery was not made clear.

To overcome the problem of patronage, Crosbie advanced three propositions: first, that a careful judgement of the qualifications of presentees should be made in the light of the particular circumstances of the parish; secondly, this required precision by the courts of the Church in fixing the requisites of each settlement; and thirdly, the judicatories should be especially precise in defining what call or concurrence was necessary in each case. These suggestions were not radical and did not represent a dramatic variance from conventional Popular thought, but Crosbie did make a break from the traditional viewpoint with his next assertion. The question might be raised, he claimed, 'founded on matter of pure faith and theology, *viz.*, Whether the people have a divine right to call their own pastor or not?' Although Crosbie accepted that it was difficult to determine if there was a question of theology or not, he went on to claim that 'in the present state of the Church of Scotland, it is not so much an article of faith, as a question of political arrangement, when applied to the settlement of a parochial pastor.'[51] He rejected the argument in favour of a congregational call based on the practice of the early or apostolic Church by means of a cursory examination of the election of Matthias to the apostleship, and argued that 'it will appear impracticable, that the whole members of the Church of Scotland should vote in the call of a minister to every particular parish'. Voting should obviously be limited to the members of the particular parish in question. He left out any discussion of the claims of heads of families to have voting rights, and confined his analysis to the relative claims of heritors and elders. After analysis of the difficulties of the various schemes which had been proposed, he put forward a new one whereby the call would be decided by the votes of delegates or commissioners, some of whom would be chosen by the heritors, some by the elders 'considered in their ecclesiastical capacity only', and some by the parishioners. If the patron did not exercise his right of presentation, he would have the right to nominate delegates. This system, claimed Crosbie, would bid fair to remove all the grievances complained of, and was within the power of the Church of Scotland to implement. It could also be applied to burghs without difficulty.[52]

The significance of these proposals was threefold. In the first place, it was assumed that the heritors were entitled to separate representation in the election of a minister. No justification was produced for the assumption other than that they, as the 'middle rank of the people' were best able to judge the qualifications of a minister for a particular parish. The common people were incapable of the conceptual thought necessary to assess the relevant requirements. Secondly, it was assumed that it was necessary and justifiable to balance the interests and representation of the heritors and elders in the process of election. Once again, no justification

[51] Crosbie, *Thoughts of a Layman*, pp. 42–4.
[52] Ibid., pp. 49–51.

for this assumption was produced except the vague expectation that 'all different denominations of people would be represented in such a call', and that such a system would prevent tumults and disturbances. Both these assumptions represented a significant departure from the ideas to be found in earlier Popular publications dealing with patronage. Thirdly, the proposals embodied a change of strategy on the question of patronage. Until Crosbie, the Popular party aimed at the abolition of the practice, or at least at rendering it ineffectual or irrelevant. Crosbie, however, proposed its modification in order to remove the civil consequences of its operation through the agency of the middle-ranking heritors, and to some extent at least in their interests. As such, he neglected the theological and constitutional issues which had been the basis of earlier Popular opposition, and adopted a secular outlook on the problem in the interests of producing a broader-based opposition. Such a strategy did not prove unattractive to a party which had met with lack of success in its efforts thus far. Indeed, it was adopted wholeheartedly for a time.[53]

What has to be determined, however, in view of its lack of success, in view of the transitory nature of the strategy, and in view of its secular orientation, is the question of whether the Crosbie approach represented a genuine strand in Popular opinion, or whether it should be seen as something in the nature of a temporary aberration. The answer to that question is to be sought, not in further publications, for none of real significance was forthcoming until the next century, but rather in the subsequent history of the patronage dispute at the General Assembly.

IV

The defeat of the Crosbie initiative, which aimed at mobilising the landed interest on the Popular side, ended the third phase of opposition and resulted in the fourth phase, which led to a reversion to the constitutional emphasis of the second phase and so to the practice of opposing unpopular presentations by means of drawing attention to the physical limitations of the presentees and by efforts to point out the inconsistency or illegality of Assembly decisions to enforce presentations. Central to this fourth phase was the Popular attempt to defeat patronage by the insistence on the existence of a legal call from the congregation to the presentee, though clear identification of the call as being central to the issue did not emerge until the early 1780s. The new phase, however, began as early as the case of St Ninian's, which came before the Assembly of 1769 in the form of a dissent from a decision of the Presbytery of Stirling, and the case of Glendevon which appeared in 1770.[54]

53 See above, pp. 130–4; and below, pp. 147–50.
54 *Scots Magazine*, xxxi (May 1769), p. 226; xxxii (May 1770), p. 305. Both the *Scots Magazine* and Morren refer to this charge as that of Glendovan: Morren, *Annals of the General Assembly*, ii, p. 308.

The St Ninian's dissent in 1769 hinged on the role of non-jurant heritors and the infirmity of the presentee. In the Glendevon case the question of the definition of a call, and of its moderation, was explicitly raised for the first time. It was maintained by the dissenters from the Assembly's decision to sustain a call to an unpopular presentee to Glendevon, that it was impossible to found 'a pastoral relationship' on a call of three or four persons, and that such a decision tended towards the abolition of the practice of moderating calls at all. The following year, 1771, saw the Popular case at St Ninian's centre around the right of a presbytery to decide if resettlement of a minister already in a charge was for the greater good of the Church, even after a decision of the Assembly to order a settlement on other grounds.[55] This case was argued in detail in the subsequent year, with reference to the various Acts of Parliament, by Dr John Macqueen of Edinburgh, the author of the *Letters on Mr. Hume's History of Great Britain*, who concluded his speech by detailing the grounds for deeming the presentee unsuitable. Andrew Crosbie himself affirmed Macqueen's assertion of the categorical right of the Church courts to decide such matters and its guarantee in terms of the Treaty of Union, and went on to assert that the people, while they did not have an elective voice, did have a negative one to which the Church was bound to listen. Both Macqueen and Crosbie were at pains in this context to reject the claim made by several Moderate speakers that they were opposing the civil constitution of the land with the religious one. Patrick Freebairn, the Popular minister of Dumbarton, took this a step further and gave some credence to theories of a rift in the Popular party. It is, however, much more likely that he was referring to lay Moderates, when he defended 'the rights and judgement of the common people' by attacking the bullying of 'professed lawyers, or men of high office who have seats among us'.[56] What emerged clearly in all the major Popular speeches in this debate was the determination to establish that the Popular position was the constitutional position of the Church, and that it was not contrary to the civil constitution in any way. Indeed, the Popular position in this fourth phase of the patronage dispute could aptly be described as one of 'constitutionalism' in much the same way as the second phase.

The same type of constitutional argument appeared again in 1774 in the reasons for dissent in the Cambuslang case,[57] and in a more detailed dissent in the case of Biggar in 1780.[58] In Biggar, there were originally no subscribers to a call to a probationer, but afterwards four-fifths of the heritors apparently 'concurred', as did several heads of families. The Presbytery declined to proceed and the case was taken to the Assembly.

---

[55] *Scots Magazine*, xxxiii (May 1771), pp. 274–5.
[56] Ibid., xxxiv (May 1772), pp. 226–31.
[57] Ibid., xxxvi (Jun. 1774), p. 297.
[58] Ibid., xlii (May 1780), pp. 274–5.

By a vote of 85 to 77, the Assembly voted to sustain the concurrence and order the Presbytery to proceed, rather than moderate the call anew. Twenty-eight Popular commissioners dissented. They argued that nothing in the case had the form or nature of a call; that the Assembly had ordered the settlement to proceed according to the rules of the Church while the call was still nothing but a blank sheet; that the concurrence came eleven months after the moderation; that the alleged subscriptions were unauthenticated and therefore inadmissible; and that where the consent of the people had not been obtained in accordance with the practice of the Church, an ordination was an absurdity or worse.[59] A similar case, that of Fenwick, saw a settlement enforced by the Assembly, in which the opposition centred around the validity of a call concurred in by only four non-residing heritors out of the whole parish.[60] It is significant, however, in the case of Biggar, that the Popular opposition was unable to produce a clear-cut definition of a call, or at least of what the practice of the Church regarded as a call.[61] Much thought was to be devoted by the Popular party in the next few years to reach a workable definition of the call and the moderation of one.

The case of Fenwick returned to the 1781 Assembly and provoked a dissent which tied the new phase of 'constitutionalism' firmly to the theological and ecclesiastical bases of Popular opposition to patronage. A new settlement had been attempted by the Presbytery of Irvine in accordance with the instructions of the 1780 Assembly, but with almost equal lack of success. The Synod of Glasgow and Ayr suspended procedure and asked the patron to present anew, but twelve members of Synod dissented and the case went to the Assembly. Without a vote, the Assembly agreed to reverse the Synod's decision and appointed the Presbytery to proceed to a settlement. Twenty-five ministers and four elders dissented from the decision as being contrary to the practice of the Church, in that there was not one subscription to the call, and that the four concurrences of non-residing heritors were of dubious legality and disregarded the non-concurrence of forty residing heritors, all the elders, and the great body of the people. The Assembly's decision was therefore unconstitutional and inexpedient. The only results could be the uselessness of the presentee, the alienation of the people of Scotland from the established Church, and the erosion of confidence in the Assembly and the weakening of its authority and the effect of its decisions.[62] In other words, at the foundation of opposition to patronage there was still the conception of a ministry acceptable to the congregation and 'useful' in the spiritual sense.

[59] Ibid.
[60] Ibid., pp. 276–8.
[61] Ibid., p. 275.
[62] Ibid., xliii (May 1781), pp. 272–3.

Immediately after this decision, the 1781 Assembly proceeded to discuss overtures from the Synods of Glasgow and Ayr, Dumfries, and Perth and Stirling concerning the method of settling vacant parishes. The overture from the Synod of Glasgow and Ayr was the most ambitious of the three; it argued that a call should not be sustained or a settlement made in any way

> unless where a majority of the heritors and elders, and other members of the congregation, shall subscribe the call or assent thereto; and that all settlements made without the consent of the congregation, as above, are hereby declared to be null and void ... that no minister, by the constitution of this church, is to be intruded into any parish contrary to the will of the congregation.[63]

This overture was dismissed as incompetent and 'of a dangerous tendency' on a technicality since no member of the Synod appeared to support it. The overture from the Synod of Dumfries sought that the Assembly should gather together in a body all the relevant Acts of the Church relating to the settlement of ministers until 1712 when patronage was restored, and

> that they will declare what is the sense of the church on these laws, and particularly define what concurrence is necessary by these laws to form such a call as the church ought to proceed upon to the settlement of a minister in any vacant congregation ...[64]

This overture, and a part of that from the Synod of Perth and Stirling requesting the Assembly to enjoin 'that the moderation of a call to a presentee shall in no case be dispensed with by any of the presbyteries of this church' were dismissed without a vote.[65] Popular uncertainty about the exact requirements of a call were borne out also in this Assembly by a sentence in the dissent from the decision to dismiss the overture from the Synod of Glasgow and Ayr which referred to 'those happier days of the church, when her ministers were settled by the call, or at least with the consent of the congregations among whom they were to labour'.[66] The central part of the Perth and Stirling overture, however, was an attempt to restrict the ability of superior courts to receive new evidence when hearing appeals or complaints, and to ensure that no letters or writs of concurrence be taken into consideration unless they were regularly authenticated by the relevant presbytery. This overture was dismissed on the grounds that its proposals were already secured by the standing rules of the Church.

[63] Ibid., p. 273.
[64] Ibid., pp. 273–4.
[65] Ibid., p. 274.
[66] Ibid., p. 273.

What is clear from these overtures is that synods under Popular control were responding to specific actions by the Assembly in its handling of the cases of Biggar and Fenwick. These two cases brought to a head the need for a legal definition of a call and the necessity of some means of forcing a Moderate-controlled Assembly to pay due heed to the wishes of congregations.[67] It is clear, also, that the Moderates were either unable or unwilling to allow the Assembly to produce a definition of a call, at least, not in 1781.

That this was so was borne out by the case of Carsphairn considered at the same Assembly. This case was also notable for the dissent which espoused sentiments of an exceedingly 'popular' or 'democratic' kind. The Presbytery of Kirkcudbright had refused to settle a presentee because of sustained opposition by the overwhelming majority of heritors, elders, and heads of families. By a narrow vote of 74 to 72, the Assembly agreed to reverse the Presbytery's decision. The dissent signed by forty ministers and ten elders argued that the Assembly was replacing sustaining a *call* with sustaining *concurrence* with the presentee; and that in the settlement of ministers

> no regard is to be paid to any class or order of men but to the patron; and in particular that the sentiments of gentlemen of landed property will be more regarded than those of the meanest of the people.[68]

Apart from its expression of 'radical' sentiments which could not have been condoned by members of a faction espousing the 'ideology of "commonwealthman" civic virtue',[69] the dissent in the Carsphairn case

---

67 Sher and Murdoch identify an anti-patronage offensive of 1782–5, and link it to the Rockingham–Fox–Shelburne ministry of the period which was considered friendly to 'popular' causes. There would seem to be little reason to dispute that the Popular party was encouraged by the change of ministry, but it is equally clear that in 1781 the Popular party was goaded into action by 2 Assembly decisions which blatantly disregarded the need for a call or even concurrence in a presentation. See Sher and Murdoch, 'Patronage and Party', pp. 202–3.

68 *Scots Magazine*, xliii (May 1781), pp. 276–7. It is interesting to note that the following year, 1782, the Assembly sustained the relevancy of a libel against the presentee accusing him of immorality, possession of unlawful and false deeds, and simony: ibid., xliv (Jun. 1782), p. 329. The Assembly of 1783 affirmed the Presbytery's decision finding the libels proved and revoking the presentee's license. This case, which came 3 times before the Assembly, indicates the reservations which should be applied when considering the validity of Sher and Murdoch's analysis of the number of presentation disputes, 1751–1800. See Sher and Murdoch, 'Patronage and Party', pp. 199–201. Another case, presumably included by Sher and Murdoch, that of Cathcart in 1784, was not a typical presentation case at all, since it was caused by a sympathetic patron's inability for reasons of legal procedure to accommodate a change of mind by the parishioners whom he had already consulted. The Presbytery of Glasgow, however, refused to sustain the call and the patron appealed: *Scots Magazine*, xlvi (May 1784), p. 279.

69 See C. Robbins, *The Eighteenth-Century Commonwealthman: Studies in the Transmission, Development and Circumstance of English Liberal Thought from the Restoration of Charles II until the War with the Thirteen Colonies* (Cambridge, Mass., 1961), pp. 185–95; and Sher and Murdoch, 'Patronage and Party', pp. 207–11.

was subscribed by a greater number of ministers than subscribed any other dissent but one in the period from 1740 to the end of the century, and adherences by ten ruling elders was above the average number of elders involved in dissents on patronage cases.[70] The Carsphairn case deserves considerably more weight being given it than has been the case hitherto.

V

In the following year, 1782, the need for a legal call continued to occupy the Assembly, as an overture from the Synod of Perth and Stirling was presented, with the support of the Synods of Fife, Glasgow and Ayr, Galloway, Lothian and Tweeddale, and Angus and Mearns, which asserted that several presbyteries had ordained ministers without the moderation of a call, and prayed the Assembly to enjoin that no presbytery should in any case dispense with the moderation of a call. This time, the Moderates felt obliged to respond. Professor George Hill, the Moderate leader in the Assembly, while believing that the overture could have been justifiably dismissed, feared the misinterpretation of such a simple resolution and moved that the Assembly 'declare that the moderation of a call is agreeable to the immemorial practice of this Church', but that the overture be dismissed for the present because of inadequate evidence. Another leading Moderate, Dr Macknight of Edinburgh, felt that the situation obviously required more than this and, 'with a view to unite the House', moved that 'The Assembly having considered overtures, declare, that the moderation of a call in settling ministers, is agreeable to the immemorial and constitutional practice of this church, and that it ought to continue.' Although the Assembly had just rejected a request from the Presbytery of Irvine to appoint a riding committee for the settlement of Fenwick by 72 votes to 49, Dr Macknight's motion was approved by 90 votes to 76 and converted into a declaratory act.[71] The reasons for the fluctuation in the Popular vote are difficult to assess. In this instance they were almost certainly complex, since the debate produced a larger vote than usual and probably a larger than usual attendance of commissioners at the diet during which the issue was under consideration.

The Popular party were encouraged by this and by the existence of a sympathetic government at Westminster.[72] The 1783 Assembly saw overtures from the Synods of Perth and Stirling, and Fife requesting it to procure the repeal of the Act of 1712 which restored patronage and the revival of the Act of 1690. The Popular interest's new-found strength was reflected in the voting, which saw the overtures dismissed by only 87 votes to 78. Forty-eight members of the Assembly dissented; among the

70 See below.
71 *Scots Magazine*, xliv (Jun. 1782), pp. 329–30.
72 See below, p. 148.

conventional reasons was the portentous assertion that the question of patronage had been a subject of debate for too long and should be brought to an issue. The refusal of the Moderates even to countenance a debate showed that the majority feared a defeat and were determined to pay no heed to 'the voice of their countrymen'.[73] The existence of the Rockingham–Fox–Shelburne administration coincided with two key Popular conclusions in 1783. The first was that the Moderates were prepared to countenance no change whatsoever in the administration of the patronage system. The second was that action was required to end the patronage wrangle which a significant number of the Popular party felt had been going on for an unacceptable length of time. These two decisions had one logical outcome: a further appeal to Parliament, which might be successful owing to the sympathetic administration in London. This, of course, meant another attempt to enlist the support of the landed interest.

Confidence in the possibility of a Popular majority at the Assembly was short-lived, however, as was confidence in the longevity of the Rockingham–Fox–Shelburne government. The 1784 Assembly rejected overtures urging the repeal of patronage from the Synods of Glasgow and Ayr, and Perth and Stirling, by a huge majority of 90 votes.[74] This points to successful efforts by the Moderate leadership to secure a Moderate 1784 Assembly after the strong Popular representation in 1783. During the course of the debate, little new argument was produced on either side. Moderate overtures from the Synods of Aberdeen, and Angus and Mearns were deflected by Professor Hill's motion that the Assembly did not believe 'that there is any reason for an innovation being made in the mode of settling vacant parishes'. This motion was carried, against the Popular motion for rejection without assigning any reason, by 108 votes to 77.[75] The Moderate-controlled Assembly then proceeded to delete the long-standing instruction to the Commission to seek 'deliverance from the grievance of patronage' without a vote.

In August of the same year the Popular party's position on patronage was affected when the General Sessions of Edinburgh passed an anti-patronage resolution by a majority of four votes. This body, consisting of the representatives of the different kirk sessions of Edinburgh, usually limited itself to discussing matters such as poor relief, civic order, and such like, but on this occasion it supported an application to Parliament on the subject of patronage, and was apparently reacting to an attempt by the Edinburgh town council to return to the exercise of their power of patronage in much the same way as they had in the 'Drysdale Bustle' of 1762. The nine resolutions on the matter were restrained in tone and were largely a restatement of the Popular constitutional position, but

---

73 *Scots Magazine*, xlv (Jun. 1783), pp. 329–31.
74 Ibid., xlvi (May 1784), p. 277.
75 Ibid., pp. 277–8.

they also included an unequivocal statement on the role of the landed interest in the settlement of parishes. The revival of the Act of 1690 would, it was asserted, 'give the landed gentlemen that influence in the settlement of their respective parishes, which they formerly possessed, and which ought always to belong to them'. The resolution went on to assert that it would 'give much satisfaction to the eldership, and to the great body of the people'. It was also claimed that the loyalty of the people to the Crown and government would be increased and that they would be made more ardent in the service of their country.[76] What was absent from these resolutions, however, was the theological basis on which earlier statements had been founded. It was purely legal and constitutional in tone, and reflected once again the second phase in the patronage struggle in the Assembly, during which the Popular party had attempted to adhere to what they believed was the constitution of the Church and its traditional practices. The theology had gone, and with it the attempt to force a religious and ecclesiastical solution to the problem. For the foreseeable future, relief from patronage would depend on political influence.

The demise of the theological impetus in the Popular position on patronage was evident in the debate in the General Assembly of 1785 on overtures from the Presbyteries of Dumfries and Kirkcudbright, and from the Synods of Dumfries, and Perth and Stirling. They proposed consultation of the landed interest and the royal burghs on a repeal or alteration of the relevant laws. The tone of the debate was set by Dr Andrew Hunter of Edinburgh. In moving to grant the overtures, he asserted the propriety of consulting the landed interest, since 'if it should be found, that so responsible a body were averse to any alteration in the mode of settling ministers, then the matter was at an end'.[77] The ensuing debate was almost wholly taken up with the question of the 'propriety' of this consultation; the principles of the issue being debated were scarcely mentioned.[78] The debate was notable, however, for the appearance of Whig 'commonwealthman' ideas. The Honourable Henry Erskine himself, the Popular lay leader and Lord Advocate for a few months in the Fox–North coalition ministry of 1783, stressed that the friends of the motion had pledged themselves to give up the contest for

---

[76] Ibid., xlvi (Aug. 1784), pp. 444–5. The move by the General Sessions was successful for the town council withdrew its appeals from the Presbytery of Edinburgh's sentences in the case and agreed to return to the former practice for settlement of vacancies in the city. It is worthy of note, though, that in its initial response to the General Sessions' resolutions, it turned the Popular 'democratic' argument on its head by arguing that it was in a better position to do the will of the people because its members were elected annually and not, like the kirk sessions, for life. Furthermore, kirk sessions were open to influence by ministers. In any case, the town council needed 'popular' ministers to keep up contributions to the poor's fund: *Scots Magazine*, xlvi (Sep. 1784), p. 501; (Oct. 1784), p. 554.

[77] Ibid., xlvii (May 1785), p. 240.

[78] Ibid., pp. 240–2.

ever if the landed interest should declare against any change in the existing law, but went on to politicise the debate, by identifying patronage as a Tory device to prevent the Hanoverian succession and by asking: 'Can men, pretending to be Whigs, be so fond of a Tory brat?' He concluded his speech by applying Whig 'commonwealthman' ideals. The Assembly, he urged, should consult the landed interest

> 1st, Because they constitute the *country*; the island belongs to them, and they are the most competent judges of the point in debate; 2nd, Because this is properly their own cause, in which their interest is most materially concerned, to which, therefore, when laid before them, they will pay attention, and come to a decision; and that their decision, be it what it may, will lay this long litigated business to sleep for ever.[79]

The attempt to involve the landed interest was, of course, defeated. So ended the fourth and last phase of Popular opposition to patronage, which was marked by emphasis on the constitutional requirement of a valid call from a congregation to a minister acceptable to them. Although the Popular leadership had guaranteed that they would let the issue fall into abeyance, however, it is clear that the rank and file of the party at presbytery and synod level were not prepared to conform.[80] The frequency of patronage disputes declined after 1785, but six cases reached the Assembly between 1786 and 1794.[81] They were not, however, the source of a sustained Popular onslaught on patronage in the manner of earlier cases.

At Assembly level, therefore, the religious dimension of the patronage debate had disappeared. It was almost a secular issue which did affect the Church, but it was an issue which even the Popular party were prepared to settle outside the Church. Why this was so is not clear. It has been suggested that the tensions between different sections of the party which favoured different alternatives to patronage so fragmented it that an effective anti-patronage initiative was difficult, and that

---

[79] Ibid., p. 244.

[80] At least not in the way that Sher and Murdoch seem to suggest: Sher and Murdoch, 'Patronage and Party', p. 202.

[81] The Presbytery of Jedburgh in 1786 requested extracts relating to overtures on contested settlements from the Synods of Fife and Moray in the previous year which the Assembly had dismissed, but the request was refused: *Scots Magazine*, xlviii (Jun. 1786), p. 310; xlvii (Jun. 1785), p. 269. In 1787 there were overtures from the Synods of Perth and Stirling, and Dumfries concerning the sale of patronages: ibid., xlix (May 1787), p. 256; and from the Synods of Glasgow and Ayr, and Galloway the following year: ibid., l (Jun. 1788), p. 305. In 1789, the Presbytery of Irvine and the Synod of Glasgow and Ayr were involved in a heated presentation dispute which came before the Commission: ibid., li (Jun. 1789), pp. 359–60; and the Synod was again before the Assembly in the case of Renfrew in 1790: ibid., lii (Jun. 1790), p. 308. The latter case involved disputed legality of concurrences. In both cases the Assembly ordered settlement of the presentee. The 1794 Assembly rejected as irrelevant a libel against the presentee to Larbert and Dunipace which the Presbytery of Stirling had accepted, and ordered a settlement: ibid., lvi (May 1794), p. 305; McIntosh, 'Popular Party in the Church of Scotland', pp. 51–3.

inability to mobilise the landed interest in their support precluded the formation of an adequate socio-economic power base.[82] Such an interpretation does have relevance for the subsequent century and the struggle which led to the Disruption of 1843, and it no doubt has some relevance for the position in the eighteenth century. It does, however, fail to take into account the fact that the Popular party was at its most convincing and at its most confident when it was arguing on the theological basis of the nature and function of the Church, on the basis of the spiritual purpose of the ministry, and on the constitutional necessity of duly moderated and sustained calls. The Moderates clearly had no answer to these contentions. That they had not was most obvious in debates on the definition of a call. In the late 1760s and again in the mid-1780s, however, the Popular party was diverted, mainly by a group of influential lay leaders, into allowing its case to become secularised and the final decision to be taken out of the hands of the Church. For the Popular party this was catastrophic. The unsolved problem of how to force the Moderate majority in the Assembly to abandon the patronage system led to attempts to persuade it to modify its enforcement of patronage, since such enforcement was constitutionally and legally unnecessary. The unpreparedness of the Moderates to do even that led the Popular party to seek a pragmatic solution to a problem which was essentially one of principle, as was recognised in their publications and in much of their contribution to the debates at the General Assembly.

The reason for the virtual disappearance of the Popular–Moderate struggle over patronage at the Assembly after 1785 is that the Popular party had abandoned the ultimate theological and ecclesiastical grounds of their attack on, and resistance to, patronage. Such a position was possibly inherent in its commitment to the Establishment principle as it was implemented in Scotland, and as such could have been foreseen. Nonetheless, it is difficult to see an ecclesiastical party, committed to an evangelical doctrine of the Church, recovering quickly from such a blunder.

VI

The demise of the spiritual analysis of and response to patronage characteristic of the Popular party during most of the late 1750s and the early 1760s is paralleled by a relative absence of sustained theological endeavour. With one notable and seminal exception, John Erskine's work on the nature of faith, there was no significant publication of a theological nature. To some extent, indeed, the outcomes of the two heresy cases of the period suggest that there was a decided lack of interest in doctrinal matters altogether. None the less, the fact that the majority of the Popular party adopted what was by-and-large a surprisingly tolerant approach to non-orthodox thought and to dissent does

[82] Sher and Murdoch, 'Patronage and Party', pp. 197–215.

not mean that the Church of Scotland saw itself as a voluntary body.[83] The mainstream Popular response to the writings of Hume and other 'infidel writers', remained one of counteracting their ideas by publication and preaching. It veered away from direct attempts at suppression. Deviations from orthodox thought within the Church, however, led to demands for the withdrawal or modification of offending ideas, and to the condemnation of offending doctrines. Ecclesiastical censures, though, were usually avoided.[84]

This interpretation is confirmed by the two best known – indeed the only other significant – heresy cases in the latter half of the eighteenth century, those of Alexander Ferguson of Kilwinning in 1767 and William McGill of Ayr in 1789. The first arose over the allegation that in an article in the *Scots Magazine* Ferguson had expressed suspicious sentiments in point of doctrine, especially justifying dishonesty in subscription by ministers to the Confession of Faith.[85] When his case came before the overwhelmingly Popular Synod of Glasgow and Ayr it was thrown out partly on technical grounds and partly on the grounds of the 'odium, trouble, and expence' to which the Synod would be exposed if it was decided to proceed. Instead, on the casting vote of the Moderator, there was passed a declaration of the Synod's 'disapprobation and detestation of all disingenuity or equivocation in subscribing the Confession of Faith', and an exhortation of all the members to oppose and discountenance such principles. The next day, a complaint named Ferguson and the case dragged on for a further year. In the end, the two parties in the Synod, realising that they were evenly balanced, accepted an overture which expressed the Synod's 'detestation and abhorrence of every doctrine and opinion that is contrary to or inconsistent with that great and capital doctrine of our holy religion, the satisfaction of Christ, and his substitution in our room', as contained in the Confession of Faith. Ferguson's presbytery was instructed to take such measures as would be 'for edification' in view of his age and infirmities. In other words, a compromise was reached, in which the doctrines were explicitly condemned but their proponent allowed to go unpunished.[86] This was very much the typical response of the Popular party during the period under consideration.

83 Drummond and Bulloch, *Scottish Church*, p. 98.
84 See above, pp. 69–74; and below, pp. 155–60, 221–3, 231.
85 *Scots Magazine*, xxix (Apr. 1767), pp. 171ff.
86 Ibid., xxix (Oct. 1767), pp. 553–4; xxx (Oct. 1768), pp. 557–8; xxx (Nov. 1768), pp. 610–12; xxx (Dec. 1768), p. 670; xxxi (Jan. 1769), pp. 51–3; xxxi (Apr. 1769), pp. 220–2. In the March 1769 issue of the *Scots Magazine* there was published a pamphlet entitled 'The Grounds of Process set on foot by the Synod Glasgow and Air against Mr. Alexander Ferguson, minister at Kilwinning', which suggests that those who appealed to the General Assembly over the matter did so in the confidence that they would find a majority there in their favour who would protect the maintainers of Pelagian and Socinian errors: ibid., xxxi (Mar. 1769), pp. 151–3. To talk of 'the casual dismissal' of the case, as do Drummond and Bulloch, *Scottish Church*, p. 107, is clearly mistaken.

The case of Dr William McGill, minister of the second charge of Ayr, reached the Assembly when several members of the Synod of Glasgow and Ayr complained against a decision of the Synod to investigate an alleged *fama clamosa* arising from the publication of McGill's *Practical Essay on the Death of Christ*, which was commonly regarded as being Socinian. The Assembly reversed the Synod's decision and referred the matter back to the Presbytery of Ayr. The offending work was in the end withdrawn, and the case ended in compromise with the acceptance of McGill's explanations and apologies. Shortly afterwards, the Synod of Glasgow and Ayr issued a 'Declaration of Doctrine' which lamented the spirit of the age in giving so much favour to dubious theological publications and stressed the conventional doctrines of the Trinity, the Atonement, and the obligations of divine law as a rule of life, and warned against replacing 'perfect' obedience with 'sincere' obedience as the aim of the Christian. McGill's position was almost certainly a Socinian one, and the failure to censure him was especially criticised by the Seceders; but, although one of the leading advocates of the case against him was John Russel of Stirling, it seems to have aroused little comment from the Popular party as a whole.[87]

While, therefore, there are some indications that doctrinal disagreement from the 1760s to the 1780s was resolved by a somewhat bland restatement of traditional orthodoxies, there was a development and application of those ideas on the nature of society and government which had been enunciated in the years before 1760 and, associated with it, a decided politicisation of the preoccupations of members of the Popular party.

The most striking feature of Popular analysis of secular society in the years after 1760 continued to be its postulation of a crucial link between religious faith and social stability. James Paton of Craig asserted that both justice and morality required scriptural bases;[88] John Snodgrass, the minister of Dundee South from 1774 to 1781 and of the Middle Charge of Paisley from 1781 to 1797, contrasted decline in respect for the Sabbath, and of participation in public, family, and private worship with the dissipation, luxury, and impiety so present in contemporary society, in a similar way to Patrick Bannerman thirty years earlier.[89] Snodgrass also made detailed comment on the remarkable distinction in large cities between the righteous and the wicked; and warned against Christians keeping the society of those 'who are outwardly regular and decent in their deportment, but, at the same time, are strangers to the influence of real religion upon the heart'. Frequent repetition of

---

87 *Scots Magazine*, li (Jul. 1789), p. 359; liii (Dec. 1791), pp. 592–3. On Russel, see below, pp. 184–5.

88 [Paton], *Knowledge of God*, pp. 117 (note), 127–9.

89 John Snodgrass, *The Means of Preserving the Life and Power of Religion in a Time of general Corruption. A Valedictory Sermon to the Inhabitants of Dundee* (Dundee, 1781), pp. 36–7; Bannerman, *Sermon upon Reformation and Revolution Principles*, pp. 18–20.

wickedness reduced our sense of its evil, made us less fearful of its approach, and less anxious to guard ourselves against it. The conversation of the wicked resulted either in the Christian being driven from their society or in his conforming to their behaviour in some measure.[90] Such detailed analysis, however, was rare.

The second identifiable concern among Popular writers in the period continued to be their stress on the social implications of morality. This was based on the belief that, as Alexander Webster asserted in his 1754 Moderatorial Address republished in 1775, 'private happiness is not to be enjoyed on any sure and lasting foundation, but in subordination to the public good'. Failure to appreciate this could only lead to the war of all men against each other. The giving up of personal ease and advantage, furthermore, was blessed by God in a similar way to that in which the spiritual interests of members of the Body of Christ necessarily depended on suffering or rejoicing with one another.[91] A large political body was only really healthy, argued John Erskine more succinctly at the time of the American War of Independence, when the whole relieved the distress of every part.[92]

Beyond such assertions, however, Popular perceptions of the nature of society were not especially theological. Preoccupation with issues which had clear religious or theological implications meant that there was no distinctive Popular response to secular developments except for the questions of relief from civil disabilities of Roman Catholics and the American War of Independence. Moderate *causes célèbres* such as the Militia campaigns between the 1750s and the early 1780s and the Ossian controversy of the same period aroused no Popular interest at all.

As already noted, almost all Popular writers saw government as necessary and as instituted by God as a result of the Fall and the natural depravity of man.[93] Consequently, a conservative conception of government appeared. The struggle over patronage, however, led to a stress on theories of religious liberty of conscience which had parallels with liberal political ideas. Discussion of the implications of God's love for man highlighted aspects of the unity of mankind. The interplay of these ideas led to a dichotomy in the political ideology of the Popular party. Liberal inclinations led some members of the party to gravitate into intellectual alliance with the Foxite Whigs and opposition to the Tory governments of the time, which continued to characterise the party until the outbreak of the French Revolution. The French Revolution's espousal and propagation of anti-Christian ideas, however, combined with its hostility to Great Britain, led to stress on the obligations of Christians to support

---

90 Snodgrass, *Means of Preserving the Life and Power of Religion*, pp. 9, 11–12.
91 Webster, *Zeal for the Civil and Religious Interests of Mankind*, pp. 41–3; see also Snodgrass, *Prospects of Providence*, pp. 26–7.
92 John Erskine, *Shall I go to War with my American Brethren? A Discourse Addressed to All concerned in determining that Important Question* (first publ. 1769, Edinburgh, 1776), p. 15.
93 See above, p. 74.

the existing political establishment. So great was the priority of religious principles in determining attitudes to secular developments that support for the political *status quo* was usually unquestioned.

VII

Apart from occasional requests from presbyteries and synods for some action to stop the desecration of the Lord's Day or general immorality,[94] the only secular subjects which impinged distinctively on the Popular mind were the questions of relief from the civil disabilities of Roman Catholics and the American War of Independence. In other areas it is much more difficult to identify any distinctively Popular response as opposed to a common response from the Church as a whole, though there is some evidence that the Popular party did become more responsive to secular developments as the century progressed. There were several instances towards the end of the century of subjects on which both the Popular party and their Moderate opponents were largely agreed: taxation of ministers,[95] the issue of abolition of the slave trade (as opposed to the question of how to achieve it) in the late 1780s,[96] and in 1790 the operation of the Test Act (which forced Scots public officials in England and Wales to take the sacraments according to the usage of the Church of England) were examples of this.[97] At the end of the day, even over the question of Roman Catholic Relief the two parties often found themselves in agreement about the political realities relating to the Church.[98]

The American War of Independence, however, elicited a clear Popular response. Initially, however, this response was shrouded by a desire on the part of a majority of the party to avoid the appearance of disloyalty. For example, although it was well known in 1776 that significant numbers of the clergy were opposed to the government's management of the crisis which led to the rebellion, and were in favour of addressing the King to recall the troops from America and to put an end to 'so unnatural a war', the Assembly's actual address to the King on the existing situation of affairs showed no signs of such sentiments; it spoke instead of 'the present dangerous and unnatural rebellion', and praised 'the humane means employed by your Majesty to recall our fellow subjects to a sense of their duty'. The committee which drew up

[94] *Scots Magazine*, lv (Jun. 1793), p. 302; lvi (Oct. 1794), pp. 652–3; lix (Feb. 1797), pp. 141–2.

[95] Ibid., l (Jun. 1788), p. 307; li (Jun. 1789), p. 359; liv (Jun. 1792), p. 306; lv (Jun. 1793), p. 303; lxiii (Jun. 1801), p. 445.

[96] Ibid., l (Feb. 1788), pp. 99–100; l (Jun. 1788), pp. 305–6; liii (Jun. 1791), p. 303; liv (Jun. 1792), p. 305.

[97] Ibid., lii (Jul. 1790), pp. 351–2. It is perhaps of significance that the report of the committee to the following Assembly was recorded without debate as Professor Hill moved, and it was unanimously agreed, to proceed to another case. The *Scots Magazine* gave no details of the report and its nature awaits investigation.

[98] See below, pp. 165–6.

the address included at least one Popular minister, Daniel Macqueen of the Edinburgh Tolbooth, and was accepted unanimously by the Assembly.[99] Later the same year, the careful, middle path steered by the mainly Popular opponents of the war was shown in the response of the Edinburgh ministers to the day of general fast called in connection with it. The 'friends to government' were at pains to show 'the absurd and unnatural conduct of the colonists', whereas

> those of an opposite way of thinking were equally assiduous to avoid everything, which, on the one hand, could show the most distant reflection on the Americans, or, on the other hand, give offence to the friends of government.[100]

In spite of this line of response, the following year the draft of the address to the King, drawn up this time by a committee including no known Popular men, and talking of 'the continuance of the unnatural and unjust revolt of his Majesty's subjects', was nevertheless passed unanimously.[101] The same thing happened in 1778, and each year until 1782.[102]

A clear indication of why the Popular party had acted in this way appeared in February 1778 when James Muirhead of Logan, minister of Urr, introduced an overture in the Synod of Dumfries against 'the present ruinous and unnatural war in America'. He withdrew it because of the small attendance, declining such an advantage for 'the friends of liberty', though possibly also because of divided opinions within the Synod. In April, however, the Moderator of the normally Popular Synod wrote to the *Scots Magazine* 'to vindicate themselves, and the people within their bounds, from the false and most injurious aspersions of their principles, with regard to government ...' The letter went on to stress their affection to government, attachment to the existing constitution, loyalty to the King, and their abhorrence of the unnatural rebellion. The letter implied that the overture was not presented at a subsequent meeting of the full Synod, though there was some doubt about this.[103] It is clear, then, that a Popular synod was almost desperate not to be seen as disloyal. In view of Popular belief in the satisfactory nature of the existing constitution and government in general, as detailed in their published works,[104] this reaction was not surprising.

The way out of the corner into which they had put themselves was either not perceived by the Popular party or not believed to be possible until 1782 when unanimity at the Assembly was broken by William

---

99 *Scots Magazine*, xxxviii (May 1776), pp. 271–3.
100 *Caledonian Mercury*, quoted in *Scots Magazine*, xxxviii (Dec. 1776), p. 677.
101 *Scots Magazine*, xxxix (May 1777), p. 271.
102 Ibid., xl (May 1778), p. 267; xli (May 1779), p. 277; xlii (May 1780), p. 273; xliii (May 1781), pp. 270–1.
103 Ibid., xl (Apr. 1778), pp. 220–1.
104 See below, pp. 221–8.

Porteous of Glasgow. He proposed, to the committee drawing up the reply to the King's address to the Assembly, another reply which applauded the appointment of a new ministry 'of the highest abilities, and possessing the confidence of the people'. It went on to hope for the speedy restoration of peace. This letter was remitted to the Assembly *simpliciter*, where it led to 'very long debate'. The Moderates attacked it mainly on the grounds that it was not the business of the Assembly to meddle with politics or to become the vehicle of faction; and that, if carried, it would establish a precedent, and with every change of ministry the whole Church would be split into divisions and political factions. The Popular response was based on one of the same principles which was prominent in its response to patronage at this time – the principle of constitutional consistency. The Assembly had been in the practice of addressing the King upon the state of the nation, and in the past it had addressed him in favour of war against its American brethren, and on other political matters. There was, therefore, nothing novel about the spirit of the proposed address. The new government listened to the voice of the people and acted on constitutional principles. The English bishops had a right to judge matters of politics in the House of Peers, and the Assembly had the right to give its opinion on public affairs, as it had done for the previous two hundred years.[105]

Nevertheless, Porteous's proposal to express support for the new administration was rejected by 86 votes to 49. A dissent was then entered which took the political reasoning of the Popular party a stage further. Amongst other assertions, the Popular party contended that the nature of the link between religion and society gave the Church a right to intervene in government, and especially, in this case, to censure maladministration which affected the welfare of the people.[106]

As well as identifying the Popular party with the political opposition to the Tory government, the debate on the American Revolution indicated that the party had identified itself with relatively democratic political ideas. Admittedly, this identification contrasted with Popular satisfaction with the existing constitution and government of Britain, and was not to survive the outbreak of the French Revolution. There are parallels to be made, however, with the position of the party in the patronage controversy where it made constant references to the right to ecclesiastical liberty.[107]

It is now clear that extensive and highly organised letter-writing took place between evangelicals in Scotland, England and America in the 1740s and 1750s with the aim of providing information about and encouraging revival of religion and missions. Prominent in Scotland in

---

[105] Ibid., xliv (Jun. 1782), pp. 325–8.
[106] Ibid., pp. 327–8.
[107] See, e.g., above, pp. 98–9.

the network were James Robe, John Maclaurin, and John Erskine.[108] As a result of this interest and contact with the American colonies, it is possible that the fundamental reason for Popular sympathy for the American position may well have lain in religious unity and sentiment rather than in political ideology. In 1777, John Witherspoon's fast-day sermon in America had been published by the *Scots Magazine*, together with his *Address to the Natives of Scotland residing in America*.[109] It is true that John Erskine's pro-American pamphlet *Shall I go to War with my American Brethren?* had appeared in 1769, but the publication of Witherspoon's sermon and address with its detailed arguments possibly had a more direct impact on the situation in Scotland. Erskine's work, though popular with the public as its frequent editions indicate, was relatively slight, arguing its case for the Americans from historical and contemporary political considerations.[110]

Witherspoon's contribution to the Scottish debate is to be found in his welding of the religious and political themes into a coherent account of Popular ideology as it affected the issue of the American war. The fast-day sermon was predominantly devotional in intent, and, although he referred to the temporal alternatives of wealth or poverty, liberty or bondage, and national prosperity as a result of the active industry and possession of land by independent freemen as opposed to low production being eaten up by 'hungry publicans while timid proprietors dread the tax-gatherers approach', he was concerned to point to the greater spiritual issues of whether his listeners and readers were to be 'the heirs of glory or the heirs of hell'. Nevertheless, he did produce a picture of the American situation in which spiritual and temporal considerations were closely linked. Providence had singularly interposed to bring success to the 'new and maiden courage of freemen, in defence of their property and right'. He quoted approvingly an observation that 'True Religion' brought the consequences of 'Dominion, Riches, Literature, and Arts'. The American cause was

> the cause of justice, of liberty, and of human nature ... the confederacy of the colonies has not been the effect of pride, resentment, or sedition; but of a deep and general conviction, that our civil and religious liberties, and consequently in a great measure the temporal and eternal happiness of us and our posterity, depended on the issue.

He went on to argue that 'the knowledge of God and his truths have been chiefly, if not entirely, confined to those parts of the earth where some degree of liberty and political justice were to be seen', and that

---

[108] S. O'Brien, 'A transatlantic community of saints: the Great Awakening and the First Evangelical Network, 1735–1755', in *American Hist. Rev.*, xci (4) (1986), p. 819. See also L. H. Butterfield, *John Witherspoon Comes to America* (Princeton, 1953), referred to in Sher, *Church and University in the Scottish Enlightenment*, p. 268, note 28.

[109] *Scots Magazine*, xxxix (Feb. 1777), pp. 93–6; xxxix (Mar. 1777), pp. 113–20.

[110] Erskine, *Shall I go to War with my American Brethren?*, *passim*.

there was not a single instance in history where civil liberty was lost, and religious liberty preserved entire.[111] When Witherspoon referred to the difficulties arising from 'the imperfection of human society, and the unjust decisions of usurped authority', and argued that 'if we yield up our temporal property, we at the same time deliver the conscience into bondage',[112] it is not unreasonable to assume that Popular readers in Scotland found it difficult to resist identification of the Americans' struggle with their own stand against patronage and the Moderates.

As well as providing the Popular party with an ideological basis for sympathy for the American colonists, Witherspoon also provided them with the germ of the idea of opposition, not to the King personally, but to his ministers and their supporters in Parliament. He did not refuse submission to their claims 'because they were corrupt or profligate, although probably many of them are so; but because they are men, and therefore liable to all the selfish bias inseparable from human nature'.[113] Although his line of argument was virtually incompatible with the overall tendency of Popular political thought, its connection with the strategy of Porteous's motion in the 1782 Assembly is obvious. Witherspoon's *Address to the Natives of Scotland residing in America* further developed his political position. This involved assertion of the necessity of American independence, and the denial of its real disadvantage to Britain.[114]

Therefore, although Witherspoon was writing in America, and was doubtless more than a little influenced by American democratic ideals, nevertheless he identified traditional Popular ideas about religious freedom and welfare, and about freedom of conscience, with radical political ideas about liberty, democratic government, and opposition to the existing political system in Britain and the people who stood to gain by it. His views received wide publicity through the pages of the *Scots Magazine* a few years before the first Popular attempt to involve the General Assembly in support for opposition to the dominant political grouping in later eighteenth-century British government. The move was

---

111 *Scots Magazine*, xxxix (Feb. 1777), pp. 94–5.

112 Ibid., p. 95.

113 Ibid. Witherspoon also argued here that 'There are few surer marks of the reality of religion, than when a man feels himself more joined in spirit to a truly holy person of another denomination, than to an irregular liver of his own.' There is a connection in this with Willison's earlier attitude to both the Secession and to the English Methodists, and a noticeable contrast with the Moderate attitude to ministers who had been ordained outwith Scotland. On these matters, see above, pp. 67–8; and below, pp. 205–9.

114 *Scots Magazine*, xxxix (Mar. 1777), pp. 114–17. In the course of his analysis, Witherspoon referred to Hume's 'Three Essays: I. On the Balance of Trade; II. On the Jealousy of Trade; III. On the Balance of Power'. In *Essays Moral and Political* (1741), Witherspoon also made a reference to taxes raised in America only serving 'to feed the insatiable desire of wealth in placemen and pensioners, to increase the influence of the crown, and the corruption of the people'. The reference to the influence of the Crown foreshadowed one of the key arguments used by the writers of the *Edinburgh Review* in their case for parliamentary reform in the next century. See, e.g., *Edinburgh Rev.*, 1808–32.

urged for reasons which bore strong resemblance to those advanced by Witherspoon to defend the Americans in their quest for independence.[115] Witherspoon's publications crystallised the increasing Popular reservations about the existing political situation and gave them the basis of an ideology of opposition. The fall of the Fox–North coalition ministry in 1784, however, stifled the further development of such a political ideology.

VIII

Although aspects of the debate over the American War of Independence were informed by considerations of the nature of society and the relationship of religion to it, the major debate was conducted over a narrowly political field. The implementation of Popular perceptions of the relationship of religion and society is, therefore, to be seen most clearly in their response to the question of relief for Roman Catholics. It is an issue over which the party has suffered much vilification, but on which the evidence has received little real analysis.[116] The issue was first raised at the Assembly of 1778 where the Moderates, led by Principal Robertson and John Home of *The Tragedy of Douglas* fame, were successful in defeating a Popular move to instruct the Commission of Assembly to watch over the interests of Protestantism and, if necessary, to call an extraordinary meeting of Assembly concerning the Bill. A Popular dissent ensued which, while detesting 'anything which appears persecution for conscience sake', argued that it was necessary to defend the Reformed interest against 'the arts and violence of those whose intolerant principles oblige them to persecute all who differ from them'. Refusal to do anything would only increase the fears of the people. Most importantly, however, greater vigour was necessary to support and preserve the Protestant interest

> as there is good reason to believe, that the Popish emissaries have of late been unusually active and successful. And it is notorious, that in several places in Scotland, and even in the metropolis, Popery has been on the increase for several years past.[117]

---

[115] It should be noted that Witherspoon's *Sermon* and *Address* were also printed in London, probably around the same time that they appeared in Scotland.

[116] The honourable exception to this pattern is Sher in his *Church and University in the Scottish Enlightenment* where he provides a very fair account of the Popular position based on an examination of the main anti-relief literature. His interpretation, though, is flawed as a result of his failure to comprehend the essentially religious and theological motivation of the Popular response to the issue, and by his misinterpretation of the motivation of Assembly members when the crucial vote was taken. This latter misinterpretation appears to have arisen as a result of his assumption that there was a greater degree of support for the Moderate position in the Church as a whole than the evidence justifies. See Sher, *Church and University in the Scottish Enlightenment*, pp. 290–4.

[117] *Scots Magazine*, xl (Feb. 1778), pp. 267, 269–71.

The initial response to the idea of Roman Catholic relief, then, was prompted by concern over inroads made by Roman Catholicism in areas hitherto regarded as firmly Protestant. During the course of the year, the General Session of Glasgow and the Synods of Glenelg, Glasgow and Ayr, Dumfries, Angus and Mearns, Galloway, and Perth and Stirling publicised their concern with the spread of Popery and exhorted their members to take measures against it.[118] Meanwhile the Synod of Lothian and Tweeddale showed a considerable measure of political circumspection. It declared

> their firm adherence to the principles of liberty, and the rights of private judgement; that while they have no intention to interfere with the legislature in matters of civil right, and do by no means wish that any person should be deprived of his inheritance, or subjected to civil penalties for conscience sake; they, at the same time express their hopes, that if such repeal be extended to this part of the united kingdom, the wisdom and attention of the legislature will make effective provision, under proper sanctions, to prevent all the dangers that are apprehended from that repeal.[119]

During the course of the next year or so, several works were published by protagonists on the Popular side. The three most important were the work of leading ministers: William Porteous of Glasgow, John Erskine, and John McFarlan. These three authors established the framework for the debate which continued until the end of the 1779 Assembly: Roman Catholicism was to be seen as a religious, political, and moral system. As a religious system it was entitled to toleration; as a political system it was a matter for the secular authorities; as a moral system, if it encouraged immorality, it should be restricted. Toleration, however, should not imply freedom to propagate publicly its beliefs, and under no circumstances should Roman Catholics be entrusted with the education of the young.

At the end of 1778, Porteous's sermon, which he had preached at the fast-day appointed by the Synod of Glasgow and Ayr in connection with the matter, was published as *The Doctrine of Toleration. Applied to the Present Times.*[120] After a short history of toleration in which Protestant intolerance in the past was castigated, it argued that the Christian position should be that all religions should be tolerated, 'provided that they preach no doctrines which are destructive to the state, or dangerous to the particular members of it'. The existing *legal* toleration in Britain fell short of this principle. Popery could, however, be considered in

---

[118] Ibid., xl (Jun. 1778), p. 331; xl (Oct. 1778), pp. 565–6.

[119] Ibid., xl (Oct. 1778), p. 566.

[120] William Porteous, *The Doctrine of Toleration. Applied to the Present Times: in a Sermon, Preached in the Wynd Church of Glasgow, 10th December 1778. Being a Public Fast, appointed by the Provincial Synod of Glasgow and Ayr* (Glasgow, 1778).

three ways: as a false religion, as a faction in the state, and as a system of immorality. Porteous then established the guidelines which it has already been stated were accepted by other writers. As a religion it should be tolerated; as a faction of the state, the question of toleration should be determined by politicians; but if it was a system of immorality, self-defence forbad toleration. The key issue was the last. Popery, argued Porteous, was an immoral system on three grounds: it taught that no faith was to be kept with heretics in matters where the interest of Popery was concerned; it taught that heretics ought to be destroyed and put to death; and as a result of its doctrines of pardons and indulgences, French monarchs had been given a perpetual right by Pope Clement VI not to keep treaties. Nevertheless, Roman Catholics should retain their present rights. It was likely, though, that few Protestants would wish to allow them to hold public processions, to establish schools and seminaries, or to receive similar extensions to their rights. Furthermore, Porteous, like all the other Popular writers, made quite explicit his complete condemnation of all acts of violence against Roman Catholics or their property.[121]

John Erskine's contribution to the debate was much more apocalyptic, and was in a somewhat more traditional mould. He published his *Considerations on the Spirit of Popery, and the intended bill for the relief of Papists in Scotland* in 1778. Starting from a theological position in which he referred to contemporary Protestant views on the identification of Popery with prophecies in the Book of Revelation, he argued that the world-wide dominion of Popery before its final destruction, while inevitable, should not be hastened by 'fool-hardy experiments'. Still, since it was expedient that one man should die for the people, it was legitimate to impose sanctions on a few to preserve the safety of thousands. He argued at some length that extensions on the rights of Roman Catholics to purchase land could end with Protestant tenants being evicted from many corners of the land. Once again, opponents of relief were enjoined not to weaken their cause by attacks on the persons, property or intended places of worship of Papists, and were encouraged to seek the legitimate means of influencing the legislature in the certainty that Parliament would not disregard the addresses of men of known loyalty.[122] Erskine's work was fairly representative of the views of the more respectable 'hard-line' opponents of repeal.[123]

---

[121] Extracts quoted in *Scots Magazine*, xl (Dec. 1778), pp. 673–5.

[122] Extracts quoted in ibid., pp. 678–9.

[123] Sher's attempt to argue that Erskine was guilty of contributing to the outbreaks of anti-Catholic violence by the use of 'several loose remarks' (Sher, *Church and University in the Scottish Enlightenment*, p. 285) depends on the assumption that the word 'zeal' would be interpreted as indicating approval of the violence. In fact, the concept was a standard one in Popular works and its use in a wide range of contexts did not imply anything more than a sincere commitment to the support of one's principles. See, e.g., Webster, *Zeal for the Civil and Religious Interest of Mankind*.

A more constructive approach to the problem was presented by John McFarlan, who published *A Defence of the Clergy of the Church of Scotland who have appeared in opposition to the intention of an unlimited repeal of the penal laws against Roman Catholics*. He was in favour of the repeal of those statutes then in force so far as they respected succession to property, civil liberty, or the private exercise of religion, but not repeal which gave liberty of public teaching or the education of the young. Voltaire's *Traité de Tolérance* was quoted as proving the failure of Roman Catholics to extend similar toleration to Protestants in Catholic countries, and reference was made to a pamphlet published shortly earlier by a priest in Edinburgh, which endorsed the principles of persecution. McFarlan went on to reject the charge that the opponents of relief fomented disturbances and were the enemies of the administration or disloyal: 'No insinuation can be more unjust, he asserted, 'than to suppose, that we are averse to the present government, or inclined to democratical or republican principles.'[124] This reaction to the suggestion of disloyalty raises the possibility of a fear of similar accusations to those made as a result of the espousal of the American cause among Popular leaders a few years earlier.[125] In view of McFarlan's subsequent leading role in the 1779 Assembly debate, however, it may be assumed that this response to the question of repeal was acceptable to the majority of the commissioners, and was not unrepresentative of views in the Church as a whole.[126]

In the course of the 1779 Assembly, it became clear that the majority of commissioners were against relief, and in the end its Moderate supporters agreed without a vote to McFarlan's motion, which proposed an overture to Parliament urging opposition to the idea of extending the English proposals to Scotland.[127] The Assembly debate, in contrast to the pamphlet debate the previous year, showed some interesting developments in the Popular position. In the first place, opponents of relief were obviously concerned to counter Moderate arguments that the Assembly had no right of interference in what was essentially a political matter.[128] It was asserted that it was invalid to argue that the Assembly should not interfere with the decree of the legislature since the commissioners were members of society as well as guardians of the religious interest of those committed to their care.[129] The minister of Renfrew, Colin Campbell, adopted a more legalistic approach to the dispute on this point by maintaining that relief was directly opposite and

124 *Scots Magazine*, xl (Dec. 1778), pp. 679–80.
125 See, e.g., Sher, *Church and University in the Scottish Enlightenment*, p. 267.
126 Cf. ibid., pp. 290–4.
127 *Scots Magazine*, xli (Jun. 1779), pp. 310–11; xli (Aug. 1779), pp. 409–15; xli (Sep. 1779), p. 474. Robertson's motion to refer the matter to the Commission, with instructions 'to employ every legal and proper endeavour to prevent repeal being passed into law', was thus passed from. The motion as agreed to had an additional but not important last paragraph from Robertson's motion concerning new erections.
128 Ibid., xli (Jun. 1779), pp. 312–15.
129 Ibid., xli (May 1779), p. 226.

repugnant to the laws of the country and especially to the Claim of Right. Furthermore, it was proper for the members of the Assembly to act as the guardians of the people's religious rights and privileges.[130] This argument was given an even more unequivocal airing by McFarlan himself when he moved the motion which was to be adopted:

> there is no other public meeting where the sentiments of this part of the kingdom can be so fully given. We are not to consider this assembly as a general meeting only of the clergy; but by the admission of lay elders from every part of the country, from royal burghs and universities, it is a complete delegation from the whole body of the people. If we agree in our opinions ... such a declaration may be justly considered as expressing the sense of this part of the kingdom. This, publicly and explicitly given, cannot fail to have the greatest influence in preventing such a repeal as has been proposed.[131]

Another striking aspect of the debate was the way in which opponents of relief attempted to predict the way in which it would have significant political consequences. The source of anxiety about this was the conviction that if Roman Catholics were granted the right to educate the young, it would be only consistent to admit them to every office and place of trust in the government, such as those of judge and member of parliament.[132] This conviction led to two consequences: on the one hand, to the attempt to prove that Roman Catholics believed socially and politically unacceptable doctrines, such as those relating to keeping faith with heretics;[133] and on the other, to an attempt to predict the likely social, and especially political, consequences should repeal be granted. The former followed the lines already set out in the published works on the subject, but the latter was especially significant for the way in which it revealed the extent of anti-Catholic feeling in the Church at the time. The central feature of the argument was that relief would lead to sustained attempts to wield and manipulate political power by the Papists. If they were to have the right to purchase estates, it would enable them to finance the extension of Popery and to use their influence at elections for Parliament.[134] This was claimed to be especially dangerous, for it was alleged that there was an unusual quantity of landed property on the market at the time and 'power and influence always follow property'.[135]

---

[130] Ibid., p. 229.

[131] Ibid., xli (Jun. 1779), p. 311.

[132] E.g., ibid., xli (May 1779), pp. 229–31.

[133] E.g., ibid., xli (Jul. 1779), pp. 362–8; xli (Sep. 1779), p. 472.

[134] Ibid., xli (May 1779), pp. 228–9.

[135] E.g., ibid., xli (Jul. 1779), p. 368. An attempt was also made to link Roman Catholicism with infidelity. Campbell of Renfrew, e.g., argued that Popery was the kind of religion most convenient for an infidel in that it exhibited religion in such an absurd light, that virtually anyone would think himself justified in rejecting it. In an entirely different way, the impious man would lay hold on it as a way of being saved after a

For all the determination of the attempt to ensure that relief was not extended to Scotland, and for all the light which the debate throws on Popular attitudes to a key public issue of the day, it should be noted that one of the more significant features which was revealed in the episode, was that the difference between Popular and Moderate was not very wide. In proposing the motion which became the finding of the Assembly, McFarlan went out of his way to defuse the threat of party rivalry clouding the issue:

I therefore hope, that we can hear one another with candour, and not impute that to party spirit, or meaner influence, which arises, it is to be supposed, from the full conviction of our own minds.

Even more striking was McFarlan's eulogy of Principal Robertson which he gave after denouncing the rioting which had occurred and the attacks on Robertson himself:

I think it is my duty at this time to declare, that since I have had the honour to know him, he has acted with a degree of candour and moderation seldom to be found in the head of a party; yea, further, I may venture to say, that I do not believe this country to contain a sounder Protestant, nor is there in the church one more zealous to promote what he believes it to be its interest.[136]

For his part, Robertson, although proposing that the overtures on relief be dropped, revealed that since he believed the opponents of relief were most worried by the idea of Popish ecclesiastics opening schools, he had applied to the Lord Advocate and to the Solicitor-General, and had then proposed to Dr John Erskine and a Popular elder, John Walker, that provisos on this should be inserted. Their response was that, if such a proposition had been made earlier, it might have produced good effects. Nothing would now satisfy the people, they argued, but a resolution to drop the Bill altogether, and Robertson accepted the truth of their representations.[137] At the very least, such exchanges indicate that the differences between the two parties did not preclude amicable and productive consultation.

The significance of the Popular position over Roman Catholic relief was twofold. It demonstrated that Popular opposition to the measure was not merely the manifestation of a narrow religious prejudice existing only within the party, but a complex belief, shared across both parties in the eighteenth-century Church of Scotland, that Roman Catholicism was both religiously and politically too dangerous to be granted further liberty within the country at the time. Care should be taken, in this

lifetime of iniquity, and as the most ready means of silencing his half-stifled conscience: ibid., xli (May 1779), pp. 228–9.
[136] Ibid., xli (Jun. 1779), p. 309.
[137] Ibid., xli (Aug. 1779), pp. 411–12.

connection, not to cloud the picture of Popular commitment to civil liberty by preoccupation with one issue. Like most Protestants at the time, they found it difficult to come to terms with their fears about the nature of the Roman Catholic Church and its intentions towards Britain. Secondly, it provided a practical demonstration of the perception of the nature of the link between religion and society as postulated in Popular social and political thought. The connection in the Popular mind between right religious views, and social and political stability was clearly demonstrated, as was the threat posed to secular society by infidelity.

One further point to be noted concerns the identity of two of the most significant protagonists in the debate over the American War of Independence: John Witherspoon and John Erskine. Witherspoon was probably the ablest opponent of patronage and Moderatism in the eighteenth-century Church of Scotland, as a result of his role as anti-patronage orator and party manager at the General Assembly, and through his authorship of the devastating and unanswered satire on Moderatism, the *Ecclesiastical Characteristics: or the Arcana of Church Policy, being a humble attempt to open up the Mystery of Moderation, wherein is shown a plain and easy way to attaining to the Character of a Moderate Man, as at present in repute in the Church of Scotland.*[138] As for Erskine, he was arguably the greatest theologian produced by the late eighteenth-century Church. It is to his contribution to Scottish theology that we must now turn.

IX

It was consideration of the nature of faith in Christ that led Erskine to produce the work which is the most significant theological treatise by any member of the Popular party in the latter half of the eighteenth century, his *Dissertation on the Nature of Christian Faith*, which appeared in 1765. Drawing significantly, though not slavishly, on the ideas of his American correspondent, Jonathan Edwards, Erskine's analysis remained the classic delineation of Scottish theology on the subject until the Evangelical Revival in the nineteenth century. Such was the esteem in which this treatise seems to have been held that little else was published on the subject by Popular writers after its appearance.

From the beginning of Erskine's *Dissertation on the Nature of Christian Faith* it is obvious that this is different from anything produced in the century by other members of the Popular party. Apart from its narrowly defined subject matter and its theological rather than devotional intent, it marks its author as a theologian of acumen and some independence of mind. For example, Erskine eschewed the lists of truths relating to faith which were a feature of some earlier writers such as Boston and

---

[138] John Witherspoon, *Ecclesiastical Characteristics* ... (1753), in *Works*, vi.

Gillies,[139] took issue with Jonathan Edwards's sermons on justification,[140] and quoted the suspect John Glas sometimes but not always with approval.[141] He was prepared to recruit support from Principal Leechman of Glasgow, probably regarded by most of Erskine's Popular compatriots as being heretical;[142] and he was even prepared to stand apart from 'the generality of Calvinists' in the matter of the place of the consent of the will in the receiving of Christ.[143]

Erskine, like Maclaurin, was in the mainstream of eighteenth-century Popular thought in regarding faith as signifying persuasion or assent. It is, he maintained, the only notion of faith applicable to every passage of Scripture where any kind of faith is mentioned. It is an assent to something revealed and that was true prior to our believing it.[144] It is true, too, that he saw faith as embodying belief in the gospel account of Christ as Messiah,[145] as Son of God,[146] as Saviour of the world,[147] and as Redeemer.[148] As with most other Popular writers on the subject, he understood faith as leading to increased knowledge of God.[149] Like them also, he saw it as leading to the sanctification of the Christian,[150] and ascribed the efficacy of all these beliefs to the operation of the Holy Spirit.[151] There is, therefore, convincing evidence that Erskine stood in the midst of the Popular tradition of thought on the nature of faith; but the matter is considerably more complex. Erskine's whole approach to the question was much more 'doctrinal' than the 'practical' concerns of, for example, Maclaurin, and his preoccupations reflected that approach. He realised that the Popular perception of faith as involving fundamentally intellectual assent to the truths of the gospel allowed a faith which might not be 'saving faith'. The significance of his work, therefore, is that he provided an analysis of faith which made it possible to retain the mainstream, orthodox Calvinist perception of faith as 'saving knowledge' and yet assimilate contemporary insights relating to the operation of the understanding, the will, and the senses. His was, therefore, a modification of the analysis of Maclaurin in response to the intellectual environment of the Scottish Enlightenment.

The first stage in this process was to give the understanding an even greater role in faith than had hitherto been the case. The English

139 Erskine, *Nature of Christian Faith*, p. 167. See above, pp. 45–6.
140 Ibid., p. 178.
141 E.g., ibid., pp. 151, 178.
142 Ibid., pp. 187–8.
143 Ibid., p. 170.
144 Ibid., pp. 139–45.
145 Ibid., pp. 151, 158.
146 Ibid., pp. 151–2, 158–9, 161.
147 Ibid., pp. 161–3, 168–9, 173, 177–8, 180, 183, 190.
148 Ibid., pp. 165–6.
149 Ibid., pp. 181, 183, 185–6, 188–9. On this aspect, Erskine draws significantly on the works of the 17th-century Puritan, John Owen. See, e.g., pp. 181, 187.
150 Ibid., pp. 187–8, 195.
151 Ibid., p. 145.

Puritan, John Owen, was quoted approvingly as asserting that 'Faith is in the understanding, in respect of its being and subsistence: in the will and heart, in respect of its effectual workings.' But in the Scriptures, asserted Erskine, the heart refers to intellectual powers.[152] Faith could not influence temper and conduct 'if it did not include some degree of knowledge and apprehension of what is believed'. Truths, however interesting in their own nature, could not engage the will and affections unless they were understood. Although no man understood the whole of the Christian revelation, and no man assented to it but with 'a general implicit assent', faith was not just a general implicit assent to Christianity or to what was contained in the Scriptures. Such a consent to divine revelation, without understanding what it contained, would not produce conviction of sin in the thoughtless or unconcerned, it would not produce peace of conscience in the convicted, and it would not encourage holiness of heart or life.[153] It was evident, too, that 'faith is not to be found in the generality of those who call themselves Christians'.[154] The reason for this was that a distinction must be drawn between faith and 'saving faith'.

'Saving faith', for Erskine, was knowing what and in whom the Christian believes:

> there is one radical comprehensive truth, assent to which is represented as saving faith, and which supposes, includes, or necessarily infers every other truth thus fundamental. That truth is expressed in a variety of language, in different passages of Scripture ... [that] the only begotten of the Father was sent by him to this wretched world, to be the propitiation and advocate of sinners: and that a fullness of grace dwells in him, and power is given him over all flesh, that he might give eternal life to those given him of the Father. This doctrine is with peculiar propriety termed the truth.[155]

Locke's *Reasonableness of Christianity* was referred to as 'largely and unanswerably' proving that the proposition that '*Jesus is the Christ, the Son of the living God*' was the only proposition in which belief was necessary to be a Christian.[156] Locke, furthermore, pointed out that a man could not give his assent to any affirmation or negation unless he understood the terms conjoined in the proposition, and the thing affirmed or denied. Therefore, said Erskine, to believe that Jesus is the Christ, the Son of the living God, is of no purpose if we understand nothing by it or something

---

152 Ibid., p. 143. The reference is to Owen's *Catechism* but it is not further identified.
153 Ibid., pp. 145–7.
154 Ibid., p. 198. It could be argued that this position is logically implied in John Erskine, *Character and Privileges of the Christian Church*, Dissertation II in *Theological Dissertations*, pp. 84–9, in which he discusses the state of those who make false professions of Christianity.
155 Erskine, *Nature of Christian Faith*, pp. 145, 150.
156 Ibid., p. 152.

different from what the Scriptures reveal.[157] We must believe the proposition 'in the fullest and most emphatical sense of the word'. Saving faith sees Christ as a person of infinite dignity, and consequently as able to bear the Father's anger, to satisfy his justice, to achieve the recovery of fallen souls, and to enable his people to conquer all his enemies. This knowledge lays the foundation for an unlimited trust in him. Without it we would have 'infinitely unsuitable apprehensions of the Son's love in coming to save us, of the Father's love in sending his Son, and of the assurance that with the Son, the Father will freely give us all things'. The necessity of the shedding of blood, at the same time, proves the infinite evil of sin, and the spotless purity and justice of God.[158]

Faith, therefore, is believing what the gospel says about the Father sending the Son to be the Saviour of the world. The way in which Erskine reached this conclusion, however, was different from that of Maclaurin,[159] though he saw its results in similar terms. Salvation purchased and applied by Christ includes deliverance from the guilt and punishment of sin, and restoration to the favour of God; deliverance in this life from the power of sin and the beginning of conformity to God's image; and a deliverance in the end from all the remains of sin and sorrow, and the possession of the fullness of joy and pleasures for evermore. All this leads men to seek 'that better country', renounce the pleasures of sin, and suffer affliction with God's people. Faith is, therefore, 'a lively realizing persuasion of the glories of an unseen world'.[160]

Faith, however, is also concerned with believing in Christ's name, which denotes believing in the doctrine of justification through his merits, and in the doctrine of the glory which is his as Mediator in order to apply the purchased redemption. Faith, therefore, means being persuaded that sinners may be pardoned and accepted through Christ's blood and merits, that he rose from the dead, and that God justifies sinners through his blood and righteousness. It is also the case that since men are unable themselves to satisfy divine justice, they are wholly dependent on God's mercy for salvation.[161] It is increasingly obvious, then, that for Erskine, faith has a strongly 'doctrinal' emphasis.

While, however, faith is concerned with believing in Christ's name, Erskine was also concerned to delineate what faith is not. Where faith is expressed as hearing Christ or hearing his words, or receiving Christ, it may be that this signifies the heart choosing and the affections embracing Christ as prophet, priest, and king, and the whole soul as

---

157 John Locke, *Second Vindication of the Reasonableness of Christianity*, quoted in Erskine, *Nature of Christian Faith*, pp. 152–3.
158 Ibid., pp. 159–61, 166–7.
159 See above, pp. 47, 51–3.
160 Erskine, *Nature of Christian Faith*, pp. 162–3.
161 Ibid., pp. 163–7.

consenting to, approving of, and delighting in the Saviour and in the gospel scheme of salvation. But this is not saving faith although it is connected with it, is always present with it or necessarily flows from it, and therefore is essential to the Christian character. Every believer experiences these actions of the soul, but they are not faith. Coming to Christ or receiving Christ is the 'immediate fruit of faith', rather than faith itself. It is the seeking of all spiritual blessings only in the way of union and communion with Christ from a persuasion that in this and in no other way may the blessings be obtained. So, too, 'drawing near to God', 'coming to the throne of Grace', or 'coming to God through Christ' are not descriptions of faith, but of the believer's application to God through the Redeemer for every blessing.[162]

But Erskine still had to tackle the problem of differentiating clearly between faith and saving faith. The faith of God's elect not only differs from that of others in the thing assented to. The nature and foundation of assent in saving faith is also specifically different from the nature and foundation of assent in self-deceivers. Self-deceivers may have 'orthodox sentiments of religion'. They may understand religious mysteries and knowledge, and yet lack charity. They may even believe by means of miracles and other external evidences that these mysteries constitute a divine revelation. But saving faith, too, is founded on evidence and does not assent to truth without understanding the reasons why. The answer which Erskine produced, in the first place, was that what distinguishes saving faith is the operation of the Holy Spirit:

> The spirit takes from the scripture, the grand evidence of faith which he has lodged there, and carries it to the hearts of the elect, and then the light and power of divine truth so apprehends and overcomes the soul, that it can no longer resist.
>
> That triumphant evidence, is no other than the glory and excellency of the gospel scheme of revelation [marg. salvation] manifested by the holy spirit in such a manner, as produces full conviction, that a scheme so glorious could have none but God for its author.[163]

In the Scriptures, furthermore, the nature of God's wisdom, grace, authority, and other attributes 'are as legible to the faith of the meanest, as of the most learned believers'.[164] When men's minds are enlightened by the Spirit, they can see the divine origin of the Scriptures and their words of grace fall with such power and evidence on the soul of the enlightened sinner that he cannot withhold his assent. The soul, therefore, is 'merely passive' when faced with the operations of divine power. Saving faith may therefore be defined as

162 Ibid., pp. 168–75.
163 Ibid., pp. 176–8.
164 Ibid., p. 181.

a persuasion that Jesus is the Christ the Son of God, flowing from spiritual views of such a glory in the gospel, as satisfies and convinces the mind, that a scheme so glorious could have none but God for its author ...

Such an assent, founded on discovery of the glory of the gospel, is impossible without 'the special saving operations of the Spirit'.[165]

This led Erskine to a brief examination of the doctrine of assurance. A further ground of certainty of their faith for Christians is their experiencing that Jesus is the Christ in his 'enlightening their understandings as a prophet, speaking peace to their consciences as a priest, and renewing their wills as a king'. There is, therefore, not only a knowledge of God and faith in him which precedes our 'espousal' to God, but a subsequent one which involves the knowledge that God is faithful to his promises. This subsequent knowledge involves the feeling of the promises accomplished in the believer. This evidence of faithfulness, however, is not the primary foundation of faith because it comes after belief. It is a certainty from our own feelings rather than 'a crediting of the divine testimony'. It is 'an assurance of sense, not of faith'; it is an assurance of our own particular interest in God's favour and in the operations of his Spirit.[166]

Saving faith, however, is further distinguished from counterfeits by its 'attendants and genuine fruits'. True faith affects the affections and conduct. The truths of divine revelation contribute to the improvement of the believer's spiritual life. God works on men 'in a way suited to their rational natures, and to the established connection between the understanding and will'. He enlightens the understanding so that the will may be attracted to a right choice. As a result, the believer thinks and judges in some measure as does God, and God's mind and will as revealed in Scripture become his. And, as Leechman had said, it is the doctrines of revelation and not its precepts that are the chief means of sanctification. We are prompted to love God, for example, not because of the commandment, 'Thou shalt love the Lord thy God', but by our discoveries of God's beauty and love. The doctrines of Christianity relating to the plan of man's redemption are well calculated to promote holiness of heart and life, and are indeed the origin of both.[167]

Erskine then formulated his final distinction between saving faith and its counterfeits. No one rightly believes that Christ is a Saviour who does not have 'suitable conceptions' of that from which he saves. And no one can have such conceptions without perceiving the goodness and excellence of the gospel salvation and acting upon it so as to desire it, choose it, and rely upon it. The Scriptures often depict faith as a

---

[165] Ibid., pp. 182–5. Cf. Somerville, *Sermons*, pp. 148, 151; see below, pp. 187–8.

[166] Erskine, *Nature of Christian Faith*, p. 186.

[167] Ibid., pp. 186–8. The reference is to Leechman's sermon at the opening of the General Assembly of 1758.

preservative against sinning, and this is accurate since, if we know a thing to be greatly desirable and yet do not desire it, or know it to be dreadful and fail to do our utmost to avoid it, we act contrary to human nature. Belief in the Father sending the Son to be the Saviour of the world implies that the world needed such a salvation, and consequently a belief in the infinite evil of sin, and the infinite obligations to duty. This last supposes a knowledge of and belief in the infinite glory and perfection of God from which those obligations arise. Saving faith always produces a personal application of these truths. A true knowledge of God cannot but influence our dispositions and actions. It is this crucial point which led Erskine to reject the profession of 'the generality of those who call themselves Christians'. 'If men really understood and believed the truth they profess', he says, 'they could not go on thus frowardly in the ways of their own heart.'[168]

Erskine's contribution to Popular thought on the nature of faith would seem to be fourfold: first, he emphasised the all-embracing significance of the role of the understanding in faith; secondly, he delineated the differences between mere intellectual assent or understanding and saving faith, the essence of which difference he saw as epitomised in the central role of the Holy Spirit in applying to believers the evidences for faith in the Scriptures and as producing the conviction that God is the author of the scheme of salvation; thirdly, he analysed the doctrine of assurance in terms of the assurance of faith which satisfies and convinces the mind of the truth of the gospel doctrines of the offer of salvation through Christ, and of the assurance of the senses which concern personal experience of God's promises being applied to the individual; and, fourthly, he ascribed to the operation of the will the development of the spiritual life of the believer which leads to the believer's conformity to the mind and will of God. This last he explained in terms of the connection between the understanding and the will. His analysis led Erskine to conclude that a significant number, if not the majority, of those who profess Christianity do not in fact profess true faith. As a result, the stage was set for a renewed evangelical onslaught on infidelity and lack of belief.[169]

Is there any evidence, however, that Erskine's work made any more impact than Maclaurin's? In the first place it must be emphasised that Erskine, and indeed Maclaurin, did not share the vagueness, imprecision, and conventional expression involved in most Popular writing on the nature of faith. On the other hand, he reflected, as did Maclaurin, the Popular perception of faith as rooted in the understanding of key Scriptural doctrines regarding the person and work of Christ, the importance of the role of the Holy Spirit in making faith possible, and faith as leading to knowledge of God, union with him, or conformity to

168 Ibid., pp. 188–93, 198.
169 See, e.g., ibid., pp. 198–9.

his image. In particular, there is evidence that he was influenced by Gillies's analysis of the faculties of the soul.[170] Erskine shared with earlier writers, too, a certain lack of interest in Christian experience such as in the process of conversion, though he developed such thoughts as they did have about the doctrine of assurance. There are indications, however, that Erskine influenced the two, or perhaps the three, other Popular writers in the latter part of the century who had most to say about the nature of faith. John Dun accepted Erskine's view on the knowledge of God leading to approval of the plan of redemption;[171] Robert Walker adopted his analysis of sanctification being an effect of faith, as well as his assertions about the truths of Scripture being accessible to those of little learning.[172] John Russel, too, possibly derived his ideas on the operation of the Holy Spirit from those of Erskine.[173]

X

Erskine's analysis of the nature of faith, then, embodied contemporary ideas about the nature of knowledge and the operation of the will, and was concerned to resolve the problems posed by earlier writers who defined faith in terms which looked suspiciously like a mere intellectual assent. In doing so he reached the inexorable conclusion that most who professed Christianity in mid-eighteenth-century Scotland were not in fact true Christians at all, since they did not possess saving faith. Failure to appreciate the reasons for the consensus among earlier Popular writers regarding the use of conventional and imprecise terms by most of the few who did touch on the subject, especially preoccupation with the practical results of faith rather than interest in the doctrine or the process itself, and failure to understand the reasons for the rejection of the faith of most Scots by later Popular writers have, as much as anything else, led the historians of Moderatism to dismiss its Popular opponents as being backward-looking in their faith and doctrine, and as having nothing to say of relevance to the eighteenth-century world.[174]

The conventional approach to the nature of faith, that it was concerned with knowledge of or belief in God and the mediatorial role of Christ, came to be regarded as unsatisfactory by some elements within the party, not because they saw it as unscriptural or inconsistent with the doctrinal standards of the Church, but because it was perceived as opening the way to two defective tendencies. The first was its dissociation of the work of sanctification from the act of faith, which

---

170 See above, p. 48; Gillies, *Exhortation*, p. 197.
171 Erskine, *Nature of Christian Faith*, pp. 198–9; see below, pp. 191–2; and Dun, *Sermons*, i. p. 25.
172 Walker, *Sermons on Practical Subjects*, i, p. 282; see below, p. 204–5; and also Snodgrass, *Leading Doctrines of the Gospel*, p. 291, discussed above, p. 79, note 185.
173 Russel, *Reasons of our Lord's Agony in the Garden*, pp. 73, 79.
174 E.g., Voges, 'Moderate and Evangelical thinking', pp. 146–7, 156–7.

could lead to the Moderate treatment of sanctification as arising from the contemplation of the example of Christ, and more generally to a reduction in the levels of holiness and spirituality in the community. This response is clearest in the thought of John Maclaurin, but there is insufficient evidence to indicate that his devotional emphasis was adopted or shared by significant numbers of the party. The second defective tendency was the likelihood that faith would be reduced to the level of mere intellectual assent to the truths of Christianity. The classic response to this position, Erskine's *Nature of Christian Faith* defined much more clearly and precisely the role of the intellect, the senses, and the will in faith than had been done hitherto, and, for the first time in the period, differentiated between a faith requiring an intellectual assent and one which was a 'saving faith'. This distinction is of crucial significance in eighteenth-century Scottish theology, for it revealed the essential invalidity of the assumption of all sections of the Church of Scotland – and did so probably to all sections of the Church in Scotland – that they were preaching the gospel in a Christian society in which the most difficult problem they faced was that of infidelity and the backslider. After Erskine, it had to be accepted – and it seems to have been relatively quickly accepted by most Popular writers and preachers – that the Church was faced with numbers of people who believed themselves to be Christians but who in reality were not. This perception was perhaps the most essential prerequisite for the development of the fully fledged evangelicalism which was to be the hallmark of the nineteenth-century Evangelical Revival. Its absence, or at least its relative absence, before Erskine, calls into question whether the term 'evangelical' should be applied to the members of the Popular party in the earlier part of the period.[175] It certainly cannot be applied in the same sense as it can in the nineteenth century. Appreciation of the problem does more than considerations of doctrinal orthodoxy or ecclesiastical organisation to explain the ambivalent response of erstwhile 'evangelicals' in the Scottish churches to Whitefield in the 1740s and the Haldanes in the 1790s.[176]

The attempts of Maclaurin, Erskine, and the later writers who were influenced by them, to define more clearly the nature of faith, saw a preparedness to be influenced by contemporary secular thought. Maclaurin and especially Erskine were willing to use and to adapt Enlightenment perceptions concerning the human mind and the nature of knowledge and of the will, in explaining basically orthodox theological positions. That they did so more discriminatingly and to

---

[175] For a stimulating definition of 'Evangelicalism' and an analysis of the British Evangelical movement from the 1730s, see Bebbington, *Evangelicalism in Modern Britain*, esp. chaps 1, 2. The work, though, is somewhat generalised in its treatment of the 18th-century period in Scotland.

[176] See below, pp. 205–10.

better success than the Moderates is partly confirmed by their growing intellectual confidence. The demise of Moderatism as an intellectual force could also be adduced in support of such a thesis.

The dominant trends in the Popular party in the period from 1760 to around 1785 embody the two forces of politicisation and liberalism. The ideological basis of opposition to patronage was almost completely secularised by the middle of the 1780s, and as a result the struggle was abandoned at Assembly level at least. Analysis of and comment upon social and political matters by members of the party display a decided espousal of secular liberal ideas, though these were informed by theological and doctrinal presuppositions. If it is allowed that one of the features of a liberal value system is a preparedness to examine traditional assumptions and modes of expression, and to allow perceptions from other disciplines to throw light on accepted truth, then the Popular party also displayed features of what could be described as a liberal approach to its Calvinist doctrines. One should be cautious, however, in adopting such a description of 'Popular theology' in the 1760s to 1780s, for there are no signs of abandonment of classic Calvinism. Rather, what is evident is a determination on the part of the most important theologians in the party to express their doctrine in a way which utilised the relevant perceptions and usages of the day to explain and apply their faith. Having said that, however, the qualification must be made that, compared to the years before 1760 and to those after the mid-1780s, there was a remarkable dearth of important publication by members of the party; the reasons for this can only remain matters of supposition.

CHAPTER FIVE

The Rise of Scottish Evangelicalism: The Last Two Decades of the Eighteenth Century

The closing two decades of the eighteenth century were marked by three profound developments: the continued absence of patronage as a vital issue in the life and mind of the Popular party; the appearance of a 'practical' theology which encompassed both evangelical doctrine and a more analytical approach to social problems; and a retreat from social and political liberalism to an ethos of conservatism in response to the French Revolution. The first of these developments has already been chronicled and analysed.[1] It is the other two which are of concern here.

I

The evidence of publications by members of the Popular party in this period indicates a revival of evangelical preaching and the appearance of a more dogmatic approach to theology. There are reasons to believe that these developments were a response to the near-apocalyptic insight of John Erskine that the majority of those who professed Christianity in Scotland were not really Christians at all since, while they had faith, they did not possess 'saving faith'.

In some respects, however, there was in several areas a marked degree of continuity with earlier thought. For example, in 1794 John Snodgrass of Paisley, in spite of deeming natural religion to be 'a thing which has never yet been defined', felt confident enough to attack those who were bringing Christianity down to that level by denying the existence of such essential doctrines as original sin, the Atonement, the Holy Spirit, and others.[2] John Russel of Stirling stressed the limitations of natural religion,[3] and John Love of Glasgow Anderston stressed the inadequacy of ideas of God derived from it.[4]

Later but more direct use of Wishart's terminology and application of ideas of God as Governor of the universe is to be found in the works of Thomas Somerville, Robert Walker, and James Dun. Somerville argued

---

[1] See above, pp. 150–1.
[2] Snodgrass, *Leading Doctrines of the Gospel*, p. 294.
[3] Russel, *Nature of the Gospel Delineated*, p. 8.
[4] Love, *Majesty of the King of Kings*, p. 2.

that 'the righteous Governor of the universe' could not have intended nations to rise on the depression of others since all his children are the objects of his love, and with him there is no respect of persons. For Somerville, the glory of the Supreme Being, his 'brightest attribute', is his 'goodness'.[5] Walker maintained that all except atheists would accept from the teachings of Reason that God was 'the Creator, the Preserver, the Governor, and the Judge of all the world'.[6] In the course of one of his sermons, Boswell's tutor, James Dun of Auchinleck, responded to the question of how the divine government operates by producing a developed theory of causation.[7] He subsequently used the theory to defend the doctrine of free will against 'Socinian' claims that divine foreknowledge of events and actions prejudiced free will and asserted that foreknowledge was not the same as causation.[8] Emphasis on the attributes of God as Creator and universal Governor, therefore, led to what was a rare discussion of free will written by a member of the Popular party in the latter half of the eighteenth century.

A return to a greater use of Scripture in the development and enunciation of theological reasoning was also evident. This was coupled with a preparedness to declare with much greater rigour doctrines of sin, faith, divine justice, and so on. John Russel of Stirling considered the sinner to be most effectually alarmed by a sense of danger and roused out of a state of fatal security by being assured of his birth under guilt and under sin, from which the only escape is belief in the Saviour, who died that we might live through him.[9] For Russel, the sense of guilt preceded repentance. Likewise for John Love, the sinner's conscience trembled under the load of guilt as he surveyed the inward 'abyss of impurity and desperate wickedness', and looked up to see the 'frowning fiery aspect of that Judge, with whom dwells power, majesty, holiness, terribleness, unbounded, unknown'.[10] Robert Walker of the High Kirk of Edinburgh, however, emphatically denied that God should be seen as an object of terror or as the enemy of human happiness. 'Is it not the obvious tendency, as well as the declared purpose of everything contained in the Scriptures of truth', he argued, 'to prove what the Apostle twice repeats [in 1 John 4] ... GOD IS LOVE?' The ultimate proof

---

5 Thomas Somerville, *A Discourse on our Obligation to Thanksgiving for the Prospect of the Abolition of the African Slave Trade with a Prayer* (Kelso, 1792), pp. 7–8; Thomas Somerville, *A Sermon preached in the Tron Church of Edinburgh, May 7th, 1811, before the Society incorporated by Royal Charter for the Benefit of the Sons of Clergy of the Established Church of Scotland* (Edinburgh, 1811), pp. 10, 20, 27.

6 Walker, *Sermons on Practical Subjects*, i, p. 51.

7 Dun, *Sermons*, i, pp. 73–8.

8 Ibid., pp. 181–2.

9 Russel, *Reasons of our Lord's Agony in the Garden*, pp. 72–3. See also, Snodgrass, *Means of Preserving the Life and Power of Religion*, p. 18.

10 Love, *Benevolence inspired and exalted*, p. 11. See also, Webster, *Supernatural Revelation*, pp. 13, 17.

of this lay in God's reconciling the world to himself in Christ.[11] Since God is infinitely good and independently happy, he shows mercy to the miserable who derived their existence from him, and who in their fallen state are guilty and therefore fearful, suspicious, and difficult to be persuaded that there is so much goodness in God as to pardon their offences freely.[12] The redemption of mankind was an act of the freest and most unmerited grace, and 'a full demonstration of the unbounded love and goodness of God'.[13]

John Russel of Stirling – the 'Black Russel' of Robert Burns's 'Twa Herds' and 'The Holy Fair' – analysed the attributes of God, in his reply to the allegedly Socinian position advocated by William McGill of Ayr in his *Practical Essay on the Death of Christ*, published in 1786. McGill had espoused the view that Christ was afflicted by weakness at the prospect of his coming death when he prayed in the Garden of Gethsemane, and Russel believed that McGill's explanation of this implied a denial of Christ's divinity. In the course of his response, *The Reasons of our Lord's Agony in the Garden, and the Influence of Just Views of them on Universal Holiness*, Russel asserted that the character of God is described as 'inflexibly just, and unspottedly holy', and, acting as the 'moral governor of the universe', upon the supposition of salvation, he required Christ to suffer his wrath for the unjust, that he might bring them to God. The 'infinite wrath of God' is the just desert of sin. God is eternally just, holy, and faithful, and 'the great Judge of all'. All God's ways are unsearchable, but his chosen way of punishing our iniquities by laying them on his own Son shows the extent of his hatred of sin. Sin is the object of his divine indignation and wrath. We cannot conceive how God the Father might love his Son as mediator in the tenderest manner, and yet hate the sin imputed to him, but that is part of God's unsearchability. The doctrine of Christ enduring divine wrath is 'the highest and most illustrious display of the justice and holiness of God'. The inflexible nature of his justice is also manifested at its clearest in this. His delivering up of Christ to suffering demonstrates God's 'infinite love to [*sic*] holiness', and the 'glory of God's holiness'. These views of justice and holiness, says Russel, are 'views of the divine perfections'.[14]

Justice as a key element in the divine attributes was present in the thought of James Dun, and it was also present in areas of John Erskine's

---

11 Walker, *Sermons on Practical Subjects*, i, pp. 181, 207.
12 Ibid., ii, p. 186.
13 Ibid., iv, pp. 279–80. It should be noted that Walker is somewhat complex as a theological figure having been assigned to both Popular and Moderate parties on the basis of his writings. On balance, it would seem that both in terms of his doctrinal positions and his voting record in the General Assembly, he should be regarded as firmly in the Popular camp. See also, H. Watt, 'Robert Walker of the High Church (Hugh Blair's Colleague)', in *Recs. Scot. Church Hist. Soc.*, xii (1958), pp. 82–96; Clark, 'Moderatism and the Moderate Party', p. 231, note 21; Macleod, *Scottish Theology*, pp. 207–8, 213.
14 Russel, *Reasons of our Lord's Agony in the Garden*, pp. 25, 29, 34, 36–44.

work.[15] But some seem to have felt that this new stress may have led to some distortion of the traditional balance between the love and justice of God. Robert Walker, for example, attacked those who tended to see the Son as the generous friend of fallen man and the Father as severe and unrelenting, eager to punish, and reluctant to receive the offered ransom from Christ the Mediator. He acknowledged that these views arose from 'indistinct, and even erroneous, conceptions, of the great scheme of salvation, as revealed in the Gospel', rather than from defective views of the divine attributes themselves.[16] Although Walker seemed to suggest that preoccupation with the justice of God led to erroneous views of the Atonement, there is no evidence in the mainstream Popular works that this was the case. In a sermon of 1801, though, John Russel adopted a substantially different approach in his identification of three elements in 'just views of the divine perfections' from which all true religion derives: the *original* and *essential* greatness of God; the spotless holiness of God, appreciation of which leads to contemplation of his unsearchable wisdom displayed in the plan of salvation by Christ; and the mercy of God which 'streams forth to the sinner, thro' the blood of the great Emmanuel'.[17]

There was another approach, however, which is usually regarded as being typical of the Popular party as a whole. It defined the attributes of God in terms of his power, wisdom, holiness, and especially his justice. The starting-point for these writers was usually the Atonement: if God so hated sin that he was prepared to cause his Son to suffer his divine wrath to remove its consequences, then it followed that justice was crucial to the character of God. He was fundamentally holy. His love was to be seen rather as mercy than as benevolence. This emphasis produced a devotional emphasis centred on Christ as enduring divine wrath for men. It also merged with a much older devotional tradition exemplified in John Maclaurin's famous sermon, *Glorying in the Cross of Christ*.[18]

Thomas Somerville, writing around half a century later, was prepared to call benevolence 'that most noble principle of our nature' or 'the most exalted pleasure of which the human nature is susceptible'.[19] He was even prepared to maintain that since Christ was perfectly man and clothed in our nature he was therefore benevolent, tender, and compassionate,[20] but he still felt that benevolence was the feeblest and most indolent of the public affections.[21] Every affection of human nature

---

15 Erskine, *Fatal Consequences and General Sources of Anarchy*, pp. 8, 40.
16 Walker, *Sermons on Practical Subjects*, ii, pp. 139–40.
17 John Russel, *True Religion the Foundation of True Patriotism. A Sermon preached in the High Church of Stirling to the Loyal Stirling Volunteers, Yeomanry, etc., on the Fast Day, February, 1801* (Stirling, 1801), pp. 7–13.
18 Maclaurin, *Glorying in the Cross of Christ*, in *Works*, i, pp. 61–102.
19 Somerville, *Discourse on ... the Abolition of the African Slave Trade*, p. 9; Somerville, *Sermon preached in the Tron Church*, p. 20.
20 Thomas Somerville, *Sermons* (Edinburgh, 1813), p. 155.
21 Somerville, *Discourse on ... the Abolition of the African Slave Trade*, p. 9.

applied to its proper object led to the promotion of private and public good; but lusts, the depraved affections or the inordinate indulgence of legitimate appetites, which were originally intended to promote the accommodation and conveniences of life, had perverted and slighted the doctrines of the gospel and were a propensity of human nature. In short, man was debased by the domination of sin.[22] Somerville identified, though possibly unwittingly, the difficulty faced by any theologian who tried to combine doctrinal orthodoxy with Enlightenment ideas as they were transmitted by Wishart.

The more rigorous implementation of a more dogmatic approach to theology is to be seen in the analysis of the Fall and its consequences. Robert Walker, for example, found human nature 'wholly diseased and corrupted' by it, 'our understanding was darkened, filled with prejudices against the truth, and incapable of discerning spiritual objects'.[23] Man's temper was naturally depraved and his natural powers impaired though not destroyed, for he used them successfully in his worldly concerns. But when it came to loving God, he could not, and in fact loved the things which were contrary to his nature.[24] In fact, the corporeal appetites of man led to the Fall in the first place.[25] The essence of this diagnosis was accepted, usually implicitly, by virtually every Popular writer. What, then, were the results of the Fall so far as they affected human nature?

In the first place, there was a broad band of agreement about a range of character defects and religious failings. Man was given over to evil passions such as anger and cruelty. His nature was fickle and changeable, and in need of reformation. He manifested a delusive and detestable intellectual pride, or pride in human wisdom. He was inclined to love the world, and he was prone to indulge his lusts and love of pleasure.[26] There were more serious religious consequences. Even Wishart had been prepared to concede, if somewhat vaguely, that man's passions rebelled 'against Love and Light'.[27] Thomas Somerville of Jedburgh, a Moderate theologian who voted with the Popular party at the General Assembly on matters of patronage, was more explicit: man

---

22 Somerville, *Sermons*, pp. 162, 81, 481, 448–9.
23 Walker, *Sermons on Practical Subjects*, i, p. 192. See also Snodgrass, *Means of Preserving the Life and Power of Religion*, p. 10: The Christian religion is 'by no means congenial to the natural tendencies of the human mind'; p. 36: 'the deep depravity of the human heart'. Snodgrass was also prepared to assert without qualification that 'truth' is 'the great object which the human mind pursues in all its investigations': ibid., p. 14.
24 Walker, *Sermons on Practical Subjects*, iv, p. 283. See also John Love, 'On the Corruption of Man's Whole Nature', in *Memorials*, ii, pp. 118–22.
25 Walker, *Sermons on Practical Subjects*, iii, p. 358.
26 Dun, *Sermons*, i, p. 96; Dick, *Simplicity and Popularity of the Divine Revelations*, p. 33; Love, *Benevolence inspired and exalted*, p. 20; Snodgrass, *Leading Doctrines of the Gospel*, p. 325; Walker, *Sermons on Practical Subjects*, iv, pp. 354–63; iii, pp. 356–8. A less condemnatory but similar line was taken by Sir Harry Moncrieff Wellwood, *A Sermon preached in St. Andrew's Church, Edinburgh, April 9. 1801, before the Directors of the Asylum for the Blind* (Edinburgh, 1801), pp. 15–16.
27 Wishart, *Charity the End of the Commandment*, pp. 28–9.

'formed after the image of God, made capable of enjoying him', fell from his original dignity, forsook 'every noble purpose and pursuit', perverted his faculties, and forfeited 'life'.[28] Most Popular writers were even more precise: a depraved nature led to a denial of Providence;[29] men's minds became clogged with sense and unbelief;[30] the idea of a crucified Saviour was repugnant and incredible in the judgement of the world;[31] fallen man was fearful of the consequences of sin but suspicious and unwilling to be persuaded of the goodness of God and of his willingness to grant free pardon of offences, and all this led to 'enmity against God';[32] the innate corruption of the human mind prevented perception of the 'comeliness of Christ', and of the deceitfulness of sin.[33] The overall conclusion, then, is clear: the Fall was responsible for man's inability to see the real nature of sin or the offer of salvation through Christ.

In the last years of the century, there were also some signs of doubt about the place that was generally allocated to Reason. For example, John Paton spoke categorically against over-reliance on Reason in matters of religious truth and wished to limit its role to that of a mental process, and John Love drew attention to the 'feebleness of our disabled reason in matters relating to the spiritual government of God and to his attributes'.[34] In general, however, in the whole area of the reliability of Reason there was great pressure to limit the effects of the Fall because of belief in Reason's usefulness in arguing for the truth and validity of Christianity.[35]

On the other hand, in spite of all these doubts, Popular thought was concerned to stress the rationality of the Christian religion. Reason and religion combined to produce assent to religious truth.[36] By the 1790s this line of argument was becoming commonplace. Reason argued for belief in a future life, maintained John Dun, and atheism and reason were incompatible.[37] The use of reason and religion was urged to press home the need for holiness and moral duties.[38] No part of our rationality was lost by acceptance of sacred truths that were not fully comprehensible by the human mind, but only a delusive pride in human understanding.[39] It was unreasonable, argued John Snodgrass, to reject

28 Somerville, *Sermons*, pp. 448–9.
29 Dun, *Sermons*, i, p. 68. Dun, in fact, gives David Hume as an example of this, though he gives no specific reference to the latter's works.
30 Love, *Benevolence inspired and exalted*, p. 21.
31 Snodgrass, *Leading Doctrines of the Gospel*, pp. 289–90.
32 Walker, *Sermons on Practical Subjects*, ii, p. 186.
33 Muckersy, 'Excellence of the Gospel', pp. 291–2.
34 [Paton], *Knowledge of God, passim*; Love, *Benevolence inspired and exalted*, p. 1.
35 E.g., John Erskine, *The Riches of the Poor. A Sermon. Preached before the Governors of Heriot's Hospital* (Edinburgh, 1804), p. 13.
36 Macqueen, *Letters on Mr. Hume's History*, p. 312; Webster, *Supernatural Revelation*, p. 18; Erskine, *Prayer for those in Civil and Military Offices*, p. 28.
37 Dun, *Sermons*, i, pp. 10–11, 69; ii, p. 141.
38 Russel, *Nature of the Gospel Delineated*, pp. 38–9.
39 Love, *Benevolence inspired and exalted*, p. 20.

the plain and obvious meaning of revelation because we could not comprehend it or reconcile it with other principles which we held to be necessary. It was, in fact, a 'dictate of the highest reason' to accept divinely revealed truth.[40] Approaching the issue from a different direction, Robert Walker argued that the doctrines of truth should be tested by Scripture and Reason. Reason would lead to the acknow-ledgement of God as Creator, Preserver, Governor, and Judge. The omniscience of God, for example, could be rationally deduced from the dictates of natural religion, as did Scripture itself.[41] It is not unreason-able to argue, therefore, that the Popular assessment of the nature of man was a response to contemporary intellectual pressure which, in the late eighteenth century, was perceived to be seeking the assurance that conventional Christian doctrine was capable of rational belief. By the 1790s the Popular party was confident that it was, a confidence which may have helped to foster the growing assurance of evangelicalism in the next twenty or thirty years.

The same trends are evident in writing on the nature of sin. John Snodgrass was exceptionally explicit: 'The Scripture doctrine ... of original sin, is so far from being absurd or unreasonable, that it goes a greater length in accounting for appearances than any other principle that has yet been discovered'.[42] Sometimes specific types of sin were examined. Thomas Somerville referred to the sins of intemperance, especially those relating to drinking and swearing; and John Love gave a list of 'Evils of the Present Day'.[43] Whereas earlier discussions of the evil of sin tended to be somewhat generalised, towards the end of the century the strictures of Popular writers became much stronger, though their frequency did not especially increase. Sin was infinitely evil and incurred God's infinite abhorrence. It was of 'inconceivable malignity'.[44] Even Robert Walker declaimed on the 'frightful aspect' of sin, which was so deep and black that only the blood of Christ could wash it away, and catalogued the different types of sin and their malignity.[45] For John Russel of Stirling, it was the contemplation of Christ on the cross which led to the soul being filled with 'the keenest indignation at sin'. We

[40] Snodgrass, *Leading Doctrines of the Gospel*, p. 297; Snodgrass, *Means of Preserving the Life and Power of Religion*, p. 38.
[41] Walker, *Sermons on Practical Subjects*, i, pp. 46–59. Walker, in fact, heads in the direction of identifying Reason with the soul when he subsequently says: 'I might tell you, how mean it is to let sense give law to reason, and to prefer the earthly taberna-cle to its immortal inhabitant': ibid., iii, p. 374.
[42] Snodgrass, *Leading Doctrines of the Gospel*, p. 299.
[43] Somerville, *Sermons*, p. 290; Love, *Memorials*, i, p. 370.
[44] Russel, *Reasons of our Lord's Agony in the Garden*, pp. 45–6; David Johnston, *The Heinousness and Aggravation of Theft, illustrated in a Sermon preached in the Old Church of Edinburgh, on the 29th of Nov. 1787* (Edinburgh, 1788), p. 15; John Love 'On the Nature of Sin', 'On the Evil of Sin', in *Memorials*, ii, pp. 112–15; Somerville, *Fatal Con-sequences of Irreligion*, p. 29.
[45] Walker, *Sermons on Practical Subjects*, ii, p. 283; v, p. 356. On Walker, see above, p. 178, note 13; and below, p. 186.

should be exceedingly sorrowful when we think of how our sins led to his sufferings. The heinousness of sin could only be completely seen in those sufferings and not in the effects of sin. Our view of Christ's suffering, especially in his soul, should lead to the creation of the utmost abhorrence in believers of all manner of iniquity. Every rational creature ought to avoid sin with the utmost care as a result of its appearing as an infinite evil in the sufferings of the Son of God.[46]

The conclusions which can be drawn from writings on sin, however, are limited and tentative through lack of evidence. Two Popular writers who wrote at length about it were John Russel and Robert Walker, but the sermons or theological writings of the more prominent members of the party show no particular evidence that they saw the 'preaching up' of the evil and consequences of sin as central to the preaching of the gospel. They saw contemplation of the nature and work of Christ in the Atonement as essential. There was the beginning of a change of emphasis in the last years of the century, when a more narrowly theological and Christocentric conception of sin began to emerge to replace the earlier tendency to see sin in terms of its manifestations in society and in the church as infidelity in general, declining observance of public and family worship, and excessive luxury in particular.[47] John Russel's *Reasons of our Lord's Agony in the Garden*, as has been noted, was written specifically to counter what he regarded as the Socinian views of William McGill of Ayr, since they divested God of his character as 'infinitely righteous and holy' and made sin seem less malignant and God's wrath no part of the just desert and demerit of sin.[48]

II

The varied nature of Popular theological thought on the issue of sin is seen particularly clearly in writings on the nature of the Atonement. The three authors who contributed most to the discussion of the subject each came from different theological traditions within the party.[49] They were Thomas Somerville, John Russel, and Robert Walker. In God's giving his Son to be a priest to die for his rebellious subjects, we see 'the highest possible effort of the infinite love of God', said John Russel. God the Father was not solicited by any creature, not even by Christ, he maintained, to form the plan of redeeming love. The plan of redemption originated in his own free, sovereign, good pleasure.[50] Robert Walker, around the same time as Russel, was to argue that the

---

46 Gillies, *Exhortation*, p. 38; Russel, *Reasons of our Lord's Agony in the Garden*, pp. 80–1, 45–7.

47 Again, there is a connection to be made here with the 19th-century Evangelical Revival.

48 Russel, *Reasons of our Lord's Agony in the Garden*, pp. 47–8. See above, pp. 153, 177–8.

49 See, e.g., above, pp. 46–8; and below, pp. 235–7.

50 Russel, *Reasons of our Lord's Agony in the Garden*, pp. 64–5; Russel, *Nature of the Gospel Delineated*, p. 15.

entire view of God in Christ reconciling the world to himself led to the reaffirmation of the Apostle John's conclusion that 'God is love'.[51] Maclaurin had earlier underlined this point most effectively of all when, in contradistinction to the generality of Moderate authors, he argued that Christ's intercession was not the cause of God's love or goodwill to sinners, but rather the effect of it. Christ's intercession and sacrifice were intermediate and subordinate causes by which the love of God produces its effects on transgressors, suitably to the glory of his justice and holiness. Both Christ's sacrifice and his intercession are manifestations of God's perfections.[52]

Of much greater significance than perceptions of the Atonement as originating in and embodying the love of God towards sinners, however, was that strand of Popular thought which, following the line enunciated in its analysis of the divine attributes, interpreted the essence of the Atonement as the satisfaction of divine justice. It became the central feature in the analysis of the two most important contributors to the debate, Russel and Walker. Before their time, John Maclaurin had asserted: 'By the propitiation of Christ's blood God declares his righteousness in the remission of sins, so that he may be just, and the justifier of the sinner who believeth in Jesus.'[53] Or, as John Gillies had put it slightly earlier than that, Christ 'satisfied Justice and obeyed the Law'.[54] Probably the central analysis of the issue, however, was provided by Russel in *Reasons of our Lord's Agony in the Garden* of 1787.[55]

For Russel, the glory of God's justice requires the infliction of eternal punishment. In the economy of our redemption, the Father is to be considered as sustaining the character of the great Judge of all. The inflexible justice which he embodies is evidenced in the exaction of the last farthing of the debt incurred by the elect from the hands of his Son. The Socinian doctrine is to be rejected as failing to give accurate and affecting ideas of the justice and holiness of God.[56] From the justice and holiness of God, Russel also argued for the necessity of the Son's bearing divine wrath. Man, being a rational creature, is infinitely bound to love God, and it follows that it was infinitely culpable of him to withdraw that love even for a single moment and to transfer it to any other object. Where there is a crime of infinite evil, surely that crime deserves infinite punishment. Since infinite evil cannot be punished in the finite body of man in this life, eternal punishment in Hell is a necessary consequence

51 Walker, *Sermons on Practical Subjects*, ii, p. 207.
52 Maclaurin, 'Essay on Christian Piety', in *Works*, ii, p. 99.
53 Ibid., pp. 80–1.
54 Gillies, *Exhortation*, p. 39.
55 There is, in fact, some evidence to suggest that study of the Atonement increased in the latter part of the century possibly as a result of the publicity surrounding the affair. E.g., 8 of the 13 works so far identified as containing significant discussion of the Atonement were published after McGill's work appeared in 1786. Of course, some of the sermons contained in them were possibly preached earlier.
56 Russel, *Reasons of our Lord's Agony in the Garden*, pp. 34, 37, 41, 43, 47.

of sin, and for man to escape that consequence, it requires that someone else suffers God's wrath for sin. Christ, motivated by 'sovereign and self-moving love', substituted himself in the stead of sinners, and consented to suffer the whole punishment due for the sins of the elect. He could not deliver his people from God's wrath in any other way than by bearing the divine wrath in his own soul.[57] To say that Christ delivers us from eternal wrath by affording us the means and motives of repentance is to trifle with the holiness, justice, and faithfulness of God, and to show no regard for his character as 'the moral governor of the world'. Christ is, in fact, to be seen as suffering *justly* from the hands of God. If he did not bear divine wrath in the character of our Surety, then our sins do not deserve that wrath, and as a result the sinner need not be much alarmed about his present situation, for the eternal punishment for sin is not much more than a dream.[58] Acceptance of these doctrines does not require comprehension in finite human minds. The reasons for Christ's agony in the Garden are revealed to our faith but not explained to our reason. The fact that they are 'incomprehensible mysteries', along with the divinity of the Son and of the Holy Ghost, the all-atoning sacrifice of Christ, justification through faith in his sacrifice, and sanctification by the Holy Ghost, is not grounds for their ridicule by Socinians.[59]

This form of analysis of the Atonement enabled Russel, and all the other writers who used the terms, to see Christ's work as substitution,[60] as imputation,[61] as sacrifice,[62] as punishment,[63] as surety,[64] as propitiation,[65] and as intercession.[66] Russel came to three conclusions regarding the significance of seeing the doctrine of the Atonement essentially as Christ's bearing the divine wrath. The doctrine, first of all, lies at the very foundation of Christianity. Those who deny it are not really Christians, and its denial threatens their souls. Secondly, without the doctrine of Christ's Atonement Christianity cannot exist. And finally, it denies the idea that the religious ideas of a man are of no consequence providing that he leads a good life. This is 'the pestilential principle which infidels wish to inculcate and disseminate', and, if it were true, preaching the gospel would be in vain. Appreciation of the importance of these perceptions is a starting-point for an understanding of the

[57] Ibid., pp. 29–33.
[58] Ibid., pp. 33, 73.
[59] Ibid., pp. 13, 71.
[60] Ibid., p. 28; Maclaurin, 'On Prejudices against the Gospel', in *Works*, ii, p. 21.
[61] Dick, *Simplicity and Popularity of the Divine Revelations*, p. 27.
[62] Ibid.; Snodgrass, *Leading Doctrines of the Gospel*, p. 304; Walker, *Sermons on Practical Subjects*, i, p. 142; ii, p. 173; Russel, *Reasons of our Lord's Agony in the Garden*, pp. 28, 56, 71; Muckersy, 'Excellence of the Gospel', p. 294.
[63] Russel, *Reasons of our Lord's Agony in the Garden*, pp. 23–4.
[64] Ibid., pp. 33, 51, 73.
[65] Ibid., pp. 35, 45; Maclaurin, 'Essay on Christian Piety', in *Works*, ii, p. 80; Somerville, *Sermons*, p. 428; Savile, *Dissertations*, p. 76.
[66] Dun, *Sermons*, ii, p. 112.

nature and causes of Popular opposition to the operation of Patronage throughout the century.[67]

The thought of Robert Walker concerning the Atonement, however, is notable for some important divergences from what most Popular authors seem to have regarded as the essential features of the doctrine. These divergences involved stress on the concept of Christ as mediator, and on his role in the reconciliation of God and man. Walker was not the first nor the only Popular thinker to have done so, for Maclaurin, Macqueen, and Love had all used these terms,[68] but these ideas dominated his thought. To some extent, Walker embodied the mainstream assertions: that the denial of Christ's divinity (the prime point of Socinianism), of his satisfaction for sin, and of the necessity, virtue and efficacy of his grace all vilified the great Redeemer and detracted from his true honour and dignity; that men despise Christ when they do not receive him as 'their alone Saviour, as the true, the living, nay the only way to the Father';[69] that Christ's blood is the price which redeems the soul, expiates the guilt of sin, and gives full satisfaction to divine justice.[70] On the other hand, Walker placed a much more pronounced emphasis on the recovery of the relationship between God and man in Christ's atoning work. Christ, he said, is the sole mediator between God and man, who, by his atoning sacrifice, has satisfied divine justice, 'and purchased the Holy Spirit to heal our diseased natures, and thereby render us meet for the perfection of our happiness, in the enjoyment of that God who cannot behold iniquity'. Christ is 'our relief'. The purpose of his coming into the world was to bring us to God. God is, in Christ, reconciling the world to himself by the ministry of his Spirit. The entire view of God in Christ reconciling the world to himself leads to the confirmation of the truth that 'God is love'.[71] There is certainly to be seen in Walker's work, therefore, a stress on human happiness and the love of God which is completely different from what is found in, for example, the work of Russel.

In so far as Walker has been identified as embodying a more 'liberal evangelical' approach to theology, it is not unreasonable to find his views encapsulating those of other members of the Popular party. For example, John Snodgrass, by no means normally as flexible on such theological matters, wrote of the believer being bound 'to his benevolent and divine Redeemer' by 'a sense of his unmerited and stupendous love

---

67 Russel, *Reasons of our Lord's Agony in the Garden*, pp. 74–6.
68 See above, p. 46. Macqueen, *Letters on Mr. Hume's History*, p. 311; Love, *Benevolence inspired and exalted*, p. 13; Maclaurin, 'Essay in Christian Piety', in *Works*, ii, pp. 98–9.
69 Walker, *Sermons on Practical Subjects*, i, pp. 141–2.
70 Ibid., ii, p. 283. The legal vocabulary is interesting in this connection and is one of the hallmarks of Scottish covenant theology. See M. C. Bell, *Calvin and Scottish Theology: The Doctrine of Assurance* (Edinburgh, 1985), *passim*. See also Walker, *Sermons on Practical Subjects*, i, p. 279.
71 Ibid., i, pp. 142, 279; ii, pp. 140–1, 207.

shed abroad upon his heart by the Holy Ghost' and displaying 'a growing perception of the excellency and glory of God, as he has revealed himself to us in the face of Jesus Christ ... [which] makes us to delight in communion with him, and desire above all things to be transformed into his image'.[72] Apart from Snodgrass, the only evidence of this being the case, however, seems to be contained in the work of John Muckersy. After talking of the 'strenuous and successful endeavours' of Christ for our salvation, Muckersy went on to assert that the believer in Christ 'sees in his character his teacher, his example, his sacrifice, and his portion'. All our situations and our sentiments bear 'some relation to the Son of God in our nature', and bring 'his important mission' to view. Christ is the only relief from the 'malady' of sin. This, in fact, is very similar to Walker. More significant, however, is Muckersy's assertion that, even in the corrupted state of man's nature, there is a principle which leads him to admire generosity, courage, and solicitude when exerted on behalf of others, and this principle is especially found when we contemplate 'the instructions, the example, and the sufferings of Christ'.[73] The importance of Muckersy in the discussion of the Atonement is that while on the one hand he faithfully repeated Walker's earlier position, on the other he drew on the Moderate tendency to stress the exemplary aspects of the Atonement. This balance in his thought places him much closer to the Moderate position than Walker, whose doctrine of salvation derives much more from the traditional one.

In the later years of the century, some men who were clearly Moderate in their theology were to be found in the ranks of the Popular party. Notable among them was Thomas Somerville. He saw the Atonement almost exclusively in terms of Christ's mediation. It is pleasant, he wrote, to contemplate our deliverer as 'the man Christ Jesus', clothed in our own nature and therefore not only benevolent, but tender and compassionate to human kind. The doctrine of mediation excludes vanity or boasting on our part because all is dispensed through a mediator, as the reward for his obedience.[74] It is important, he maintained, to accept Christ not only as the propitiation for our sins, but as the pattern for our conduct.[75] His discussion of the reason why Christ was appointed by God for the work of redemption, however, bears no similarity to that of other Popular writers. Even Wishart, for example, had confined himself to a relatively conventional view in maintaining that Christ came into the world 'to recover and reclaim men from vice, and bring them back to that conformity to God in holiness and

---

72 Snodgrass, *Means of Preserving the Life and Power of Religion*, p. 19.

73 Muckersy, 'Excellence of the Gospel', pp. 293–5. On Walker, see above, p. 186.

74 Somerville, *Sermons*, p. 155.

75 Ibid., pp. 426–8; Somerville, *Sermon preached in the Tron Church*, pp. 2–8, 13, 17–19, 21, 27; Wishart, *Indispensible Necessity of a Holy and Good Life*, p. 18.

goodness, in which (and in his favour) their only true happiness lies ... to deliver men from this degenerate and miserable condition'.[76] Somerville, in contrast, held that Christ was invested by God with 'a special and appropriate interest in this world' since he made it and has presided over it, and that this is the foundation of his subsequent mediatorial office. Since he created the world, 'there was a fitness in his being involved to restore it', to enlighten, redeem and judge it, and finally to become 'the author of eternal salvation to all them that obey him'.[77] For Somerville, furthermore, the Atonement was an area of controversy: there was need to beware of making the doctrine of mediation the occasion of 'improper and unbecoming notions' concerning the good-ness of God, in which obsession with the love of the Redeemer led to seeing him as the primary cause of salvation. He made exactly the same point as Russel had done earlier.[78] It is a dangerous misconception, he went on to argue, to consider the doctrine of the mediation 'merely as an article of speculative faith', and to see it as an affair carried out from start to finish without any concurrence or effort on our part.[79] Although the charges were made in no way specific, this was presumably aimed at the more conventional, orthodox positions.

The charge of lack of human involvement in the act of Atonement, however, as implied in Somerville's assessment, arose in part from his disregard, or at least his blurring, of the Westminster standards' distinction between justification and sanctification, which was accepted implicitly by virtually all Popular writers, and in part from a lack of sympathy with more conventional views about the nature of the believer's response to the analysis or contemplation of the Atonement. For Somerville, the doctrine of mediation promoted 'an unassuming and lowly temper of mind', and led to goodwill and charity to all mankind, and to the abolition of national and other antipathies between men.[80] For our spiritual lives the example of Christ on the cross related to our cultivation of the virtues of well-doing, gratitude, patience in suffering, and humility, and in our preparedness to be taught, guided, and saved by him. This, maintained Somerville, is how we should look at Christ on the cross.[81] Muckersy adopted a similar position when he maintained that Christ's example is given for the imitation, instruction, and precept of believers. 'Do not satisfy yourselves', he wrote

> with abstract enquiries into the nature of your faith, and the
> sincerity of your love, but bring the question to the sure test of

[76] Ibid., pp. 20–1.
[77] Somerville, *Sermons*, pp. 147–8. See also Somerville, *Sermon preached in the Tron Church*, p. 11.
[78] Russel, *Reasons of our Lord's Agony in the Garden*, pp. 64–5; Russel, *Nature of the Gospel Delineated*, p. 15.
[79] Somerville, *Sermons*, pp. 148, 151; cf. Walker, *Sermons on Practical Subjects*, i, pp. 139–40.
[80] Somerville, *Sermons*, pp. 155–8.
[81] Ibid., pp. 426–8.

conduct, in preferring him to the dearest objects of affection, and his law and service to the most amiable pursuits ... in the daily walks of life we are called on to give him a single and undivided attention.[82]

Muckersy's overall position, though, was much more eclectic than Somerville's.

Attempts to delineate further a characteristic viewpoint incorporating attention to the example of Christ, attributable to a 'liberal-evangelical' tradition in Popular thought, founder, however, on a lack of evidence. The most significant potential representative of it, Robert Walker, had little to say of the consequences of the Atonement in the lives of believers. Christ had 'purchased the Holy Spirit to heal our diseased natures, and thereby render us meet for the perfection of our happiness in the enjoyment of that God who cannot behold iniquity', is about as explicit a statement concerning this aspect of the Atonement as can be found in his work.[83] It would seem, in fact, that for Walker the Atonement was primarily a theological matter and not really a devotional one at all. For John Russel, however, the doctrine of the Atonement had much practical, devotional significance for the lives of believers. The viewing of Christ's sufferings should create in the minds of believing men the utmost abhorrence of all iniquity. On a more positive level, Christ's bearing the wrath of God lays the deepest foundations for spiritual joy, and the sense of the sinner's dependence on God in Christ for deliverance should lead to true humility. It leads to 'godly sorrow' for sin without which real religion cannot exist. Awareness of the infinite love of God manifested in the Atonement results in the redeemed consecrating their bodies and souls in the service of their redeeming Lord and in spreading 'the sweet savour of the knowledge of Christ'. The whole of evangelical holiness, according to Russel, consists in conformity to the will of God's precepts and submission to the will of his providence, and the doctrine of Christ's bearing divine wrath promotes this.[84] While much of what Russel stressed was not dissimilar to some of Somerville's emphases, the latter derived them from the contemplation of the sufferings of Christ on the cross, whereas Russel drew his from the more theological implications of Christ suffering divine wrath.

The doctrinal importance of the Atonement in this connection, therefore, was its purpose of promoting holiness. 'Socinian' denial of Christ's divinity, implied in McGill's questioning of the orthodox position on Christ's agony in the Garden of Gethsemane, struck at the

82 Muckersy, 'Excellence of the Gospel', pp. 292–3.
83 Walker, *Sermons on Practical Subjects*, i, p. 142. See above, p. 186.
84 Russel, *Reasons of our Lord's Agony in the Garden*, pp. 49, 52–4, 58, 61, 64, 67. For Erskine, too, the sufferings and obedience of Christ on the cross bestow on believers 'all things pertaining to life and godliness, to time and to eternity': Erskine, *Riches of the Poor*, p. 11. See also, Savile, *Dissertations*, p. 76.

very heart of Scriptural teaching on the nature of holiness. It did so initially because it failed to give 'just and affecting ideas of the justice and holiness of God'. If accurate views of the divine perfections are a foundation for 'genuine Christianity in the soul', inaccurate ones must lead to false religion. The contemplation of the 'soul sufferings' of Christ, however, not just the physical ones, led to just views of God and thence to universal holiness.[85] 'Socinian' principles prevented discernment of the intrinsic evil of sin, and thereby divested God of his character as infinitely righteous and holy. In doing so, they veiled the sinner's sight from seeing the necessity of a Saviour and encouraged continuance in impenitence and unbelief. 'Socinian' doctrine divested the Lord of the glory of being a complete surety. By presenting Christ as a mere man, suffering only in his body, it could not produce a godly sorrow in the sinner and therefore could have no influence at all on his repentance, and certainly could produce no foundation for it. It furthermore denied the freeness of the gift of salvation in Christ. The Socinian's submission to Christ was not 'a rational, holy submission', but a blind submission to a system of irrational and absurd principles.[86]

Apart from the questions of whether it was a justified attack on McGill's position and whether it was seen by some as an attack on the implications of Moderate thought in general,[87] this conclusion can be seen as an attack on the principles of some who are to be regarded as members of the Popular party. Thomas Somerville's interpretation of the Atonement, for example, would have been seen by someone of Russel's viewpoint as being on the high road to a fully-fledged Socinian position. It is possible to suggest, therefore, that a feature endemic in the Popular party was tension caused by the theological differences of its members, which earlier may well have hindered the formation and organisation of a coherent and effective ecclesiastical opposition to the Moderates in the General Assembly. In fact, the cross-currents of theological thought in the Church of Scotland in the latter half of the eighteenth century made such a task probably well-nigh impossible. It was the common theological base provided by the Evangelical Revival of the nineteenth century which made possible the emergence of the much more cohesive and effective anti-intrusion movement of those years.

Popular thought on the nature of the Atonement in the last two decades of the eighteenth century, then, displayed both the diversity of emphases and the cross-currents of influence which typified the party throughout the second half of the eighteenth century. There is displayed the threefold division of orthodox, near-Moderate, and what might be termed 'progressive orthodox', and there was present a preparedness

[85] Ibid., pp. 43–4.
[86] Ibid., pp. 47, 51, 61–2, 67, 70–1.
[87] See, e.g., the Synod of Glasgow and Ayr's 'Declaration on Doctrine', *Scots Magazine*, liii (Dec. 1791), pp. 592–3.

either to adopt or to modify, or to respond to insights derived from other positions. It is clear, too, that even in discussions of the doctrine of the Atonement, there was an underlying 'practical' purpose.

III

Another trend which manifested itself in the later years of the century was a return to a greater devotional emphasis even in discussing more doctrinal issues. For example, John Love – who had been the minister of a Presbyterian church in London, where he was one of the founders and first secretary of the London Missionary Society, before returning to Scotland to be the minister of Glasgow Anderston in 1800 – wrote of the sinner breaking forth under divine influence from the gloom of condemnation into the kingdom of God's Son, and spoke in general terms of Christ's being manifested to bear the sins of many, to reconcile them to God, and to raise them to infinite blessedness.[88] John Snodgrass wrote at the same time as Love of the atoning sacrifice and meritorious obedience of Christ as being the only grounds on which pardon of sin and acceptance with God into eternal life could be obtained.[89] Robert Walker, in a passage whose devotional emphasis in many ways is reminiscent of John Gillies, also epitomised the point being made about the imprecision of Popular thought concerning conversion:

> Doth the guilt of sin terrify you? Do you fear that a just and holy God can never accept such offenders as you have been? Here Christ is our relief; who was wounded for our transgressions, and bruised for our iniquities; who paid our debt, and hath purchased and sealed our pardon with his blood. The curse and condemning sentence of the law are indeed terrible; but if we have truly fled to Christ for refuge, he hath nailed them to his cross, and will give us a full and free discharge.[90]

Here is to be seen the essential emphasis on Christ as the comfort and Saviour of sinners and the previously noted tendency of Popular writers to express the nature and process of conversion in conventional terms.[91]

For John Dun faith was a matter of accepting God's covenant. It meant cleaving to Christ as our righteousness, strength, and Redeemer; submission to his laws, resembling him in temper and conduct, striving for the highest degree possible of perfection in holiness in this life; and seeking him as the healer of spiritual diseases, as comforter and supporter in death and in judgement. This near-Moderate emphasis was balanced by the devotional concept of total surrender to the Lord: faith also meant

---

[88] Love, *Benevolence inspired and exalted*, p. 13.
[89] Snodgrass, *Leading Doctrines of the Gospel*, p. 304.
[90] Walker, *Sermons on Practical Subjects*, i, p. 279.
[91] See above, p. 48.

dedication, devotion and hearty surrender to God, and that surrender must be entire and involve the submission of all to the will of his providence as well as to his laws. We are, concluded Dun, most truly and nobly our own when we are most entirely God's.[92] Robert Walker, too, accepted this concept of faith as union with God since he stressed that the duties of morality and works of righteousness were to be seen as the effects and evidences of faith in Christ and love to God, and that they could not be manifested without being 'ingrafted into Christ'.[93] Sir Harry Moncrieff Wellwood, the minister of Edinburgh St Cuthbert's for fifty-two years from 1775, also saw the virtues of Christianity deriving their obligation from the authority, the doctrines, the precepts and the example of the Son of God as 'the test of our relation to him'.[94] For John Snodgrass, the relevant terms were 'communion' with God, and 'conformity' to his image.[95] John Love, though, defined true faith in terms of three predominantly devotional criteria: when the soul leans confidently on Christ for justification and acceptance; when the soul is drawn to love him in whom it trusts; and when the soul is drawn to yield itself to Christ as Lord.[96] Love, however, was very much an exception to the pattern of Popular perceptions of the nature of faith.

The main features of late eighteenth-century Popular thought on the nature of faith, then, demonstrate a somewhat different emphasis from what had been the case earlier. Not only was there general agreement that faith was a matter of knowledge of or belief in God and the mediatorial role of Christ, there was also a perception that it was concerned with the nature of the Christian's relationship with God. The perceptions of John Erskine had indeed been built upon.

Concomitant with the rigour and dogmatic emphasis of much late eighteenth-century Popular theology, there was a renewed interest in

---

[92] Dun, *Sermons*, i, pp. 25–7.

[93] Walker, *Sermons on Practical Subjects*, ii, p. 74, 79–80.

[94] Sir Henry Moncrieff Wellwood, *A Sermon on 2 Corinthians ii, 17. Preached February 14, 1799, at the Ordination of Mr. Walter-Fogo Ireland, appointed Assistant and Successor to Dr. David Johnston, as Minister of North Leith. To what are subjoined, The Charge to the Minister, and the Exhortation to the People* (Edinburgh, 1799), p. 28. Moncrieff Wellwood succeeded to the baronetcy of Tippermalloch on the death of his father in 1771.

[95] Snodgrass, *Means of Preserving the Life and Power of Religion*, p. 19. The only variation on this line of analysis seems to have appeared later in a sermon of John Muckersy's, 'The Excellence of the Gospel'. Muckersy saw faith as the means or the ground of union with God: Christians, he held, are 'distinct from the world by their conduct, and united to Christ by their faith ...'; that faith 'must be the ground of our union with the Saviour'; belief in the gospel carries along with it 'the experience of the favour of God': Muckersy, 'Excellence of the Gospel', pp. 287–8. Dun put the same point when he maintained that the knowledge of God and ourselves leads to approval of the plan of redemption by Christ as worthy of God and well-suited to man. Faith, for Dun, was belief in Christ as Messiah, Teacher, atoner, and interceder, and acceptance of him in all his offices: Dun, *Sermons*, i, p. 25; ii, p. 112. Walker made the same point, too, when he asserted that the comfort of a Christian results from the knowledge and belief of 'interesting facts, attested by God, and faithfully recorded in the Scriptures of truth ...': Walker, *Sermons on Practical Subjects*, i, pp. 282–3.

[96] Love, *Memorials*, i, p. 368.

the origins and nature of the on-going work of sanctification in the life of the Christian, that is, in the way in which the Christian's life is changed as a result of faith. Not only that, Popular theologians at opposite ends of the theological spectrum are often to be found sharing the same emphases. For example, on the one hand John Russel wrote of the Christian contemplating with delight God's wisdom in the institution of salvation through Christ in a way which is not dissimilar to that figure of orthodox suspicion, William Wishart, who, while failing to give a clear-cut definition of piety, had spoken of the 'devout mind' feeling delight and joy in contemplation and adoration of the 'amiable Perfections of God'. The source of the delight, of course, was more specific in Russel's case.[97] On the other hand, Thomas Somerville, along with other Moderate theologians, stressed the obligation on the Christian to look to Christ as a pattern for our lives, and the evangelical John Dun asserted that submission to Christ's laws, constantly striving to obey them, to resemble Christ in temper as well as in conduct, is 'the highest degree of perfection in holiness that we are capable of in this life'.[98] All, however, were concerned to define or delineate the essential features which were the hallmark of the Christian life.

For Russel, piety included contemplation of Christ bearing God's wrath, indignation at sin, a sense of Christ's love, sorrow for one's own sin, and a desire to live for the glory of God. He analysed at some length the means of promoting holiness, and produced a list which had much in common with Macqueen's of thirty years earlier. Holiness is promoted by godly sorrow for sin, which arises from the sense of God's infinite love as demonstrated in the work of redemption, by gratitude to God resulting from it, and especially by submission to the various appointments of God in the course of his providence. 'The whole of evangelical holiness', maintained Russel, 'consists in conformity to the will of God's *precepts*, and submission to the will of his *providence*.'[99]

Fourteen years after the appearance of his *Reasons of our Lord's Agony in the Garden*, Russel returned to the emphasis on this type of description of holiness. The 'divinely illuminated man' contemplated 'with peculiar delight, the unsearchable wisdom of God, displayed in the formation and execution of the plan of salvation by Jesus Christ'. The features of true religion are 'the lively traces of the holy image of God, delineated on the soul'. The sense of God's greatness produces just sentiments of our meanness and unimportance, and awareness of divine purity leads to abhorrence of sin; all lead to a holy and humble confidence in God's boundless mercy in Christ and 'forms the character of him who truly

---

[97] Wishart, *Difference betwixt Moral Good and Evil*, p. 19; Russel, *True Religion the Foundation of True Patriotism*, p. 9.

[98] Somerville, *Sermons*, pp. 426–8; Dun, *Sermons*, i, p. 26.

[99] Russel, *Reasons of our Lord's Agony in the Garden*, pp. 58–60, 62–3, 67, 72, 79–84; cf. Macqueen, *Letters on Mr. Hume's History*, pp. 298, 307, 312–13, 321, 325–7.

fears the Lord'. The resultant deep impressions on the heart have a transforming influence on the Christian's life and conversation, and he 'departs from sin' or renounces 'the love of all sin in the heart, and the practice of all sin in life'.[100] In his later works, Russel became more insistent on a close link between sound doctrine and true holiness, and at the same time underlined the importance of holiness. Second only to the extension of his own glory, it was 'the great object in the view of God ... to promote holiness in his own people'.[101]

While this definition of the nature of holiness found its most detailed expression in the works of Russel, who continued in the tradition of Macqueen, Blair, and Bonar of earlier years, it was the dominant line taken by members of the Popular party.[102] There was a steady stream of Popular works which treated holiness in this way. John Snodgrass, writing in 1781, saw the Christian's obligation as one of keeping himself in the love of God, which meant 'the lively and vigorous exercise of all the religious and devout affections in the soul'. The principles of real holiness in the soul depended on the discovery of the Lord's infinite amiableness which aroused and drew forth our affections to him. Prayer was the means of deriving these spiritual blessings from God; and frequent contemplation of God led to the development of a divine character, 'like unto God'. These were the effects of a devout and pious disposition and led to their presence in life and conversation.[103] John Muckersy, likewise, urged Christians to glory in nothing save the cross of Jesus and count all things 'valueless and insipid' compared with the excellence of the knowledge of Christ. Furthermore, sincerity of love to Christ should be tried by the test of preferring Christ above all else.[104] This, of course, postulated a spiritual rather than a practical test. The characteristic of the first group, then, was that the defining features of the life of a Christian lay in the nature of his relationship to God, and in the cultivation of personal devotion.

The second line of interpretation of Christian piety or holiness, the blend of devotion and practice, saw its most masterful exposition in Robert Walker's *Sermons on Practical Subjects*, published in 1796. 'Godliness, in general', said Walker, is the subjection or devotedness of the soul to God himself. It is the practical acknowledgement of his unlimited sovereignty, and the unreserved dedication of the whole man to his service. It is not assent to religious truth, nor natural sweetness of temper or disposition, nor abstention from gross sins, nor giving a portion of our hearts or time to God.

---

100 Russel, *True Religion the Foundation of True Patriotism*, pp. 9, 13–14.
101 Russel, *Nature of the Gospel Delineated*, pp. 26–7; Snodgrass, *Means of Preserving the Life and Power of Religion*, p. 20.
102 E. g., Bonar, 'Nature and Tendency of the Ecclesiastic Constitution', p. 15.
103 Snodgrass, *Means of Preserving the Life and Power of Religion*, pp. 7–8, 19, 27–9.
104 Muckersy, 'Excellence of the Gospel', pp. 289, 291–2.

We are not *godly*, whatever we profess or seem, if, in our most deliberate and affectionate choice, we do not prefer the one true God, and the enjoyment of his favour, to all that can be found throughout the wide extent of his works; if we make not his will the measure of ours, his law the sovereign guide of our conduct, and his glory the ultimate end of our obedience.

Having stated these general points of principle, Walker proceeded to give a further list of practices which are the hallmarks of godliness. Godliness includes a supreme love to God himself and a desire to please him; it consists in the conquest of our corrupt and rebellious passions; it ennobles the soul with a holy indifference to earthly things; it embodies a vehement thirst after the enjoyment of God himself; and it is manifested by a steadfast course of holy living and by a uniform and unreserved obedience to all God's commandments.[105]

John Erskine made the same point,[106] and at the end of the century, Moncrieff Wellwood asserted it even more forcefully: it was his chief purpose in publishing a collection of his sermons

to represent the doctrines and the duties of Christianity as insepa-rably united, in the faith and practice of those who embrace it. Practical religion is of much more importance than the solution of difficult questions; and the sanctification and salvation of those who profess to believe the gospel, than the soundest opinions.[107]

Stress on the example of Christ, which is the hallmark of the third stream of interpretation, is to be seen at its clearest in the writings of Somerville.[108] He was at one with the Moderates in disputing the type of devotion shown by all the Popular writers mentioned so far. He denounced the idea that the love owed to Christ was fulfilled by meditating on him, by feeling our hearts overflowing with joy and praise, and by attending public and family worship. It could be fulfilled only by dwelling on his love, his doctrine, his character, and his humility and benevolence, and by looking forward to the time when we will 'be made like him, and see him as he is'.[109] Examination of the example of Christ, rather than meditation on the nature of the Atonement or the believer's relationship to God, as was the case with the first and second approaches, led to the understanding of the powerful sanctifying influence of the scriptural injunction to 'Look at Jesus'.[110] Somerville

---

105 Walker, *Sermons on Practical Subjects*, i, pp. 112–20.
106 Erskine, 'Qualifications necessary for Teachers of Christianity', pp. 13–22, 25–7; Bannerman, *Sermon upon Reformation and Revolution Principles*, p. 33.
107 Sir Henry Moncrieff Wellwood, *Sermons* (Edinburgh, 1805), p. xiii.
108 See above, pp. 187–9.
109 Somerville, *Sermons*, pp. 254–5.
110 Somerville, *Sermon preached in the Tron Church of Edinburgh*, p. 16.

elsewhere posed the question: 'Who then is the best Christian?' and answered it by the assertion

> Not the man who is the most learned and orthodox, and most zealous in the outward professions of love to Christ; but the man who is the most humble and self-denied, the most charitable and useful. Such is the man who continues in the love of Christ.[111]

This type of idea is more than a little reminiscent of Wishart's assertion that the Creator did not form us to be idle and merely contemplative, but to be active and useful, virtues which can only be fulfilled by following the example of Christ.[112] The laws of Christ, Somerville continued, 'contain a complete system', and his example 'exhibits a perfect pattern of every moral duty'. One's love of Christ is demonstrated by 'studying to excel in love to mankind', by avoidance of systems of faith which restrict charity, or lead to intolerance, and bitterness towards fellow Christians.[113] The connection between these ideas and those of Wishart concerning universal benevolence is striking.[114]

Somerville's contemplation of Christ on the cross produced a profoundly different response from that of most other Popular writers. It 'awakens the ingenuousness of the mind, and inculcates perseverance in well-doing, by the pleasing influence of gratitude, as much as by a sense of duty'. When Somerville contemplated Christ on the cross, he burst out (unwittingly, perhaps, implying a doctrine of justification by works),

> I feel my courage and magnanimity revived. I discern a conformity, in my lot and circumstances, to those to which he submitted. I glory in this resemblance. O that I may be conformed to him in patience and humility, then shall I also hope to partake of the glory to which he is exalted![115]

Somerville proceeded to a polemical definition of 'the true Christian'. He castigated study of the life and doctrine of Christ from curiosity, knowledge of the speculative truths of religion, contention with zeal for the faith while strangers to its 'practical influence', and confiding in the merits of Christ without possessing or desiring to possess likeness to his dispositions which 'constituted his meritorious righteousness'. Rather, the Christian is exhorted

> To accept Jesus, not only as the propitiation for our sins, but as the pattern of our conduct; to contemplate the virtues of his life, as well as the fruits of his death; to have it for the paramount desire of our

111 Ibid., p. 321; see also Somerville, *Sermons*, pp. 148–9.
112 Wishart, *Indispensible Necessity of a Holy and Good Life*, pp. 16–17.
113 Somerville, *Sermons*, p. 322.
114 See above, pp. 39–41.
115 Somerville, *Sermons*, p. 426.

hearts, to be taught, and guided, and saved by him; – this indeed is looking at Jesus.[116]

There would appear, then, to be a direct connection between the thought of Somerville and that of Wishart when the latter maintained that contemplation of the divine perfections led the devout mind 'to form his own mind and conduct more and more after the Model of that exalted pattern of moral excellence'.[117] There were, then, at least one or two Popular writers who shared the Moderate view that the essence of Christian living lay in following the example of Christ's life on earth, rather than in the cultivation or implementation of inward piety or devotion.

It should not be assumed, however, that the perspectives revealed in the thought of those who saw the essence of piety as lying in spiritual experience were not apprehended by others who did not share their overall position on the subject, and vice versa. For example, John Dun echoed Macqueen when he spoke of 'grateful, rational piety towards God', and is not far removed even from Russel when he advocated submitting all to the will of God's providence as well as to his laws, and the dedication, devotion and surrender to God of all we have, and are, and can do; when he spoke of hearts having felt 'the power of religion' by which he meant communion with God by meditation, prayer, reading, speaking, and hearing God's word; when he stressed that language flowing from a devout heart in turn produced devotion in the hearts of others who heard us; and when he urged frequent communicating, watchfulness, and self-examination.[118] Yet Dun stood virtually in the Moderate tradition when he asserted that resembling Christ in temper and conduct was the highest degree of perfection in holiness of which man was capable in this life; that 'living in the Lord' involved submission to Christ's laws, delighting in his ordinances, breathing the same spirit, and treading the same paths with the divine Leader – being, like him, 'without guile'; and of righteousness as implying, as the source of everything, 'that faith which purifieth the heart, and produces benevolence – charity – love'.[119] Somerville, on the other hand, was not very far removed from Russel when he argued that meditation, praise, and attendance at ordinances were inadequate to acquit ourselves of the love we owe to Christ, and urged heartfelt contemplation of Christ's doctrine, character, humility and benevolence, and eager anticipation of seeing and dwelling with Christ in glory as touchstones of our love to him.[120] Even members of the Popular party closest in theological sympathies

---

116 Ibid., pp. 426–8.
117 Wishart, *Difference betwixt Moral Good and Evil*, p. 19.
118 Dun, *Sermons*, i, p. 26; ii, pp. 133, 141.
119 Ibid., i, pp. 26, 35–6; ii, p. 112.
120 Somerville, *Sermons*, pp. 254–5. It is interesting to note, however, that Somerville followed Macqueen rather than Russel in seeing attendance at public worship as a declaration of our love to Christ rather than as a means to holiness.

to what is generally taken to be Moderatism, therefore, manifested surprising similarities to the positions of some of the most orthodox.

Popular thought on the nature of piety as reflected in *practical* Christian virtue gives a hazy picture, although that is not surprising in view of the concentration on spiritual virtue. Generally speaking, it is possible to suggest that Popular thought warned against involvement in the world, stressed the way in which its pleasures or interests were transitory and therefore not worthy of serious concern, or directed the Christian to spiritual improvement or evangelistic effort. Snodgrass urged prayer to maintain a constant intercourse with heaven and frequent 'godly conference' with fellow Christians 'to minister to each other's spiritual benefit, and to be helpers in each other's joy'. A mind occupied with worldly cares could not be in a suitable frame for spiritual activity. A sense of sin, for Snodgrass, should lead to the renunciation of all temporal enjoyments as vain and unsatisfying, and to the cleaving to God as one's only portion.[121]

The renewed doctrinal rigour and the devotional emphasis of Popular writing in the last two decades of the century seems also to have been associated with a renewed confidence in the unassailability of the Christian faith. As late as 1790, John Dun maintained that every 'unbarbarian' and every unbiased man admitted, or could easily be made to admit, that God made the world. There were many practical atheists, he said, but no rational man who was an atheist in theory.[122] Such conviction of the essential rationality of the Christian position remained secure until the end of the century and beyond. James Steven, preaching in 1802, confidently spoke of the foundations of Christianity being too deeply laid to be threatened by 'human sophistry' and argued that in fact such attacks only gained Christianity greater credit and esteem. Likewise, David Savile asserted that Reason was forced to admit that God exists though it had to concede ignorance as to the manner of his existence.[123]

Little attempt was made to link this conviction of the rationality of the Christian faith to specific doctrines. Apart from Savile's assertion of the rationality of the doctrines of the eternal existence of God, of his unchangeability, of his unlimited and perfect attributes, and of the existence of only one such Being,[124] the only serious application of this line of thought is in Snodgrass's *Leading Doctrines of the Gospel*. Snodgrass

---

121 Snodgrass, *Means of Preserving the Life and Power of Religion*, pp. 41–3; see also Snodgrass, *Prospects of Providence*, pp. 26–7. David Johnston of North Leith was something of a solitary voice when he gave an explicit list of steps to enable people to refrain from dishonesty: Johnston, *Heinousness and Aggravation of Theft*, pp. 17–27.

122 Dun, *Sermons*, i, p. 69.

123 James Steven, *The Unrivalled Felicity of the British Empire. A Sermon preached at the Salters' Hall, November 7th, 1802, at the Commemoration of Our Great National Deliverance* (London, 1802), pp. 8, 21–2; Savile, *Dissertations*, p. 8.

124 Savile, *Dissertations*, pp. 4–20.

denied that it is reasonable to reject revelation because we are unable to comprehend it or to reconcile it with other principles which must be held, and he also is noteworthy for his direct and explicit assertion of its truths. He maintained that the doctrine of original sin, for example, is not absurd or unreasonable because it answers more of men's questions than any other principle yet uncovered, and noted that 'men of sensibility' fail to supply any substitute for the doctrines of the gospel which they reject so vehemently.[125] Popular apologists were not necessarily content to leave their analysis at this general level but sought to offer specific examples of the consequences of natural depravity. Love referred to the 'big and fallacious words of prejudiced bigots' or of infidel scoffers at the majesty of the Son of God which influenced many 'in the present dissipated age';[126] and James Somerville of Stirling maintained that the most readily identifiable cause of folly and irreligion was the neglect of masters and heads of families to instruct their children and servants in the principles of religion and morality.[127]

More common still was the argument concerning the deleterious effects of luxury on the lives of the upper ranks in society. A striking example was in a sermon of Robert Walker's. He stressed the consequences for faith of human depravity together with analysis of the effects of national affluence on spirituality:

> Luxury is the common attendant upon affluence: This unfits the mind for serious thinking, and breeds a coldness and indifference towards spiritual things; in consequence of which, a secret disaffection to those laws which would restrain him, soon takes root in the heart of the sensualist, till, wearied with the struggle betwixt Reason and Appetite, he at length sets himself in opposition to God and his ways; reproaches with the names of ostentation or hypocrisy, all serious religion and godliness in others; turns away his eyes from the light which reproves him, and even doth what he can to extinguish it altogether.[128]

John Snodgrass contrasted decline in respect for the Sabbath, and in participation in public, family, and private worship, with the dissipation, luxury, and impiety so present in contemporary society, in a similar way to Patrick Bannerman thirty years earlier.[129] John Erskine himself identified the formal, superficial, lukewarm religion of many and

---

125 Snodgrass, *Leading Doctrines of the Gospel*, pp. 297, 299, 319. It is interesting to note that Russel argued that the acceptance of Adam's role as federal head or representative of all his posterity is the fundamental principle on which divine revelation proceeded. A secret or open denial of it was the first step to infidelity: Russel, *Reasons of our Lord's Agony in the Garden*, p. 5.

126 Love, *Majesty of the King of Kings*, p. 17.

127 Somerville, *Fatal Consequences of Irreligion*, pp. 2–9.

128 Walker, *Sermons on Practical Subjects*, i, pp. 466–7.

129 Snodgrass, *Means of Preserving the Life and Power of Religion*, pp. 36–7; Bannerman, *Sermon upon Reformation and Revolution Principles*, pp. 18–20.

contrasted it with the way in which riches, honours and pleasures were esteemed more than the favour of God. The upper ranks' contempt for religion, he warned, would have fatal consequences for them, for it would communicate itself to the lowest orders in society and lead to revolution and tyrannical and cruel rule.[130] Infidelity was thus essentially a spiritual as opposed to an apologetical problem. It was to be fought not by attacks on the various writers who were assaulting the faith, but by encouraging godliness, piety, and spirituality.

IV

Such considerations reveal that the old problem of the causes and remedies of 'infidelity' was still very much with the Church in the closing years of the century. There had always been a strand in Popular thought which traced infidelity to such origins as the growth of Deism and its influence, and to the activities of those who sought to use arguments for religious liberty as an occasion for propagating atheism and infidelity.[131] This response was evident as late as 1799 when Moncrieff Wellwood maintained that the progress of the gospel had been reduced and obstructed by 'the variety of human inventions which men of worldly passions have attempted to graft on it'.[132] John Snodgrass in 1794 had attacked the watering down of the gospel to the level of natural religion as making Christianity pointless. Singled out for especial condemnation was the denial of the doctrines of original sin, the Atonement, and the Holy Spirit. Stress in preaching on the morality of the gospel was attacked on the grounds that it obscured the importance of Christian piety, sobriety, humility, self-denial, contempt for the world, and heavenly-mindedness. It led men to believe that these holy virtues were no more than unattainable ideals. The Christian churches in general had fallen from their former purity and zeal as shown by the languishing of religion, and the spread of infidelity and licentiousness. In Scotland, this was due to the Church's departure from 'those great and cardinal doctrines which had once been its glory'.[133]

Robert Walker advanced a similar but much more qualified diagnosis. Those who professed a general regard for Christ but entertained or published opinions inconsistent with real esteem for him were attacked, as were those who denied his divinity and satisfaction for sin and those who denied the necessity, virtue, and efficacy of his grace. All, in effect, vilified the Redeemer and detracted from his true honour and dignity.[134]

---

130 Erskine, *Fatal Consequences and General Sources of Anarchy*, pp. 43–4.
131 Webster, *Supernatural Revelation*, p. iii; Webster, *Zeal for the Civil and Religious Interest of Mankind*, pp. 347–8; [Paton], *Knowledge of God*, pp. 121–2.
132 Moncrieff Wellwood, *Sermon on 2 Corinthians*, p. 16.
133 Snodgrass, *Leading Doctrines of the Gospel*, pp. 294, 299, 319, 326–7, 333.
134 This is little more than a restatement of Willison's case made 40 years earlier. See above, pp. 61–8.

Walker went on to castigate those who did not receive Christ as their only Saviour and as the only way to the Father. Such decline in spiritual perceptions among hearers of the gospel, he suggested, were caused by a secret unbelief of which they were unaware: they were not thoroughly persuaded of the truth of the Scriptures; their position was that the Scriptures *may* be true and so, while they were not downright infidels, neither were they true believers.[135] In spite of his near-Moderatism, Thomas Somerville subscribed to this view, though for somewhat different reasons: errors and misconceptions of the gospel, he maintained, 'interwoven with essential tenets during the ages of ignorance and superstition', had given sceptics in the present time the most specious arguments for calling into question its sacred origin.[136] The progress of this scepticism was to be noted by remissness in attendance on the ordinances of worship and public duties of the Christian religion by many who professed reverence to Christ. Ministers were at least partly to blame, he believed, because they often tended to encumber the gospel with 'foreign and eccentric difficulties' which the ill-disposed used to disparage the Christian faith. An even greater danger, according to Somerville, was the resulting lukewarmness of pretended friends to religion. There was, in other words, a decline of piety. Not only was there a desertion of ordinances by 'a great proportion of people in the higher ranks of life', the ordinances were not even attended by 'the generality of professing Christians' as had been the case. This led to laxity in family worship and private devotion. All these manifestations of infidelity or lukewarmness could be laid at the Church's door.[137]

Those who shared this response would have agreed with the two Edinburgh ministers Robert Dick and Sir Harry Moncrieff Wellwood, when they asserted that some branches of human learning were highly useful for vindicating the honour of divine revelation, and for guarding men against both 'Enthusiasm' and infidelity.[138] As earlier, the analysis of infidelity as irrational and therefore as not embodying a fundamental threat to either Christianity or the Church led to a relatively muted and conventional response. It involved the defence of revelation and natural religion as being rational, and defence of the truth of Christian doctrine especially that regarding the nature and existence of God. It was fundamentally educative and above all confident.

The second analysis of the cause of infidelity, its identification as a spiritual problem, led to the formulation of a cohesive programme for recovery. Snodgrass, and Walker in particular, offered a spiritual answer

---

135 Walker, *Sermons on Practical Subjects*, i, pp. 141–2, 147.
136 There is something of a hint here of response to some of Hume's arguments in his *History of Great Britain*.
137 Somerville, *Sermons*, pp. 462–8. For the striking similarity of this to Willison's views on the matter, see above, pp. 61–8.
138 Dick, *Simplicity and Popularity of the Divine Revelations*, p. 26. See also, Moncrieff Wellwood, *Sermon on 2 Corinthians*, p. 31.

to deal with the encouragement given by human depravity to infidelity. Both of them started by accepting the primacy of the Holy Spirit. As Snodgrass wrote:

> the suggestion of human ingenuity must be excluded; the means which unerring wisdom has appointed must be adopted; the word of salvation must be clearly and faithfully declared; and, like the first teachers of Christianity, those to whom it is committed must, 'by manifestation of the truth, commend themselves to every man's conscience as in the sight of God'... But let it not be forgotten, that after all that can be done in this important work, the whole is in the hand of God, and therefore success is to be expected only from his favour and blessing.[139]

The converse of stress on the decline of evangelical preaching, which has been noticed as a cause of infidelity in the earlier works of Webster, Warden, and Paton, was obviously a desire for its revival.[140] Perhaps most notable of all the suggestions made for the improvement of current preaching was the list of defects which John Love gave in 1778. This was unusual in the specificity of its reference to what he believed to be too common: failure to distinguish between grace and counterfeits of grace (by which he meant the need to insist that there was no intermediate position between openly avowed profanity or hypocrisy and true grace or regeneration); failure to distinguish between the different exercises of faith, repentance, love, and new obedience; the offering of only general directions in the work of self-examination without details of how to discover what it is to believe; the absence of preaching on particular 'heart plagues' (such as hardness of heart, blindness of soul, and so on); and the lack of any solution to problems of perplexity and distress; preaching as if there were only a few unbelievers in the congregation; and the want of trembling at the divine visitation on the Jews.[141] If Love's diagnosis was accurate, there would appear to have been a neglect of evangelical preaching even within the evangelical wing of the Popular party around the late 1770s.

Thomas Somerville, one of those in the Popular party furthest removed in his theological sympathies from the likes of Snodgrass and Love, also subscribed to the same need for revived evangelical preaching. He argued that when ministers set about reading the Scriptures they should forget, at least temporarily, the interpretations and opinions they had previously adopted, and rather

> indulge no wish or purpose, but that of discovering the genuine doctrine of the gospel, and of embracing it; fervently praying to

---

139 Snodgrass, *Leading Doctrines of the Gospel*, p. 334.
140 See above, pp. 60–3; and Paton, *Knowledge of God*, pp. 128–9.
141 Love, *Memorials*, i, p. 370; cf. John Erskine's position on the distinction between an intellectual faith and 'saving faith' as discussed above, pp. 167–72.

God to free our minds from every prejudice and party attachment, and to inspire our hearts with a supreme love of the truth ... From the Scriptures alone, we can derive pure, rational notions of all the doctrines and duties of the Christian religion, their relative importance and subordination, and the views and motives, most pertinent and powerful for inculcating them on the people under our care.[142]

There was, he maintained, no point in using sermons to attack infidelity, since the sceptics were not likely to be at public worship to hear them, and in any case the proper answers to objections were too complicated for treatment in any single discourse. If ministers were alarmed at the growth of scepticism, they should adhere conscientiously to the simplicity and purity of the gospel and avoid encumbering it with unnecessary difficulties which could be seized upon by the opponents of the faith.[143] There was little in this which would have been unacceptable even to John Willison. Somerville agreed, too, with Willison in noting the decline of piety, the desertion of public worship by 'a great proportion of persons in the higher ranks of life', and the increasing laxity in the practice of family and private devotions.[144] A parting of the ways would have occurred, however, when Somerville went on to declare

It is therefore more than ever incumbent upon preachers of the gospel, to inculcate the importance of social worship, and the necessity of piety towards God, in order to lay the foundation of every social and moral duty.[145]

Probably more indicative of the extent to which Willison's analysis had permeated the thought of the Popular party as a whole was the stress to be found in one of Robert Walker's sermons on 'preaching Christ'. Preaching Christ Jesus the Lord was, asserted Walker, the great means appointed by God for the conversion and salvation of sinners, and therefore it was 'not only highly reasonable, but absolutely necessary'. Lectures on morality might restrain men from scandalous sin, but it was the gospel alone which could make a sinner a saint. It alone could change men into the divine image, so renewing their nature that they might be suited for the enjoyment of God. Preaching Christ, or 'the peculiar doctrines of the Gospel', had in every age been the means of

---

[142] Somerville, *Sermons*, pp. 461–2.

[143] Ibid., p. 466. See also above, p. 201.

[144] See Willison, *Fair and Impartial Testimony*, in *Practical Works*, p. 900, where he linked the Act of Union with the decline of family religion among the nobility and gentry, and identified the multiplication of public oaths with the progress of atheism, deism, and infidelity. He elsewhere argued that the Seceders, although unjustified in their secession, were maintaining an honest and scriptural witness against the same things which he was attacking: ibid., p. 930.

[145] Somerville, *Sermons*, p. 468.

'convincing and converting sinners, and of building them up in holiness and comfort, through faith unto salvation'. To the extent that this had been neglected, 'the power of godliness hath declined and languished, till a cold formality hath at length given way to the open profession of infidelity itself'. Where revivals of religion had occurred, they had been introduced and sustained by the blessing of God on the preaching of the doctrines of Christianity. What was meant, though, by the preaching of Christ? Walker adduced three criteria. Ministers should make Christ the principal subject of their sermons; they should handle every other subject in such a way as to keep Christ constantly in the minds of their hearers; and they should make the advancement of Christ's kingdom, and the salvation of men, the sole aim of their preaching.[146] While Willison, Walker, and other members of the Popular party would appear, therefore, to have insisted on a more Christocentric emphasis in preaching which laid much less stress on the *example* of Christ than those closer to the Moderate position, it is important for the analysis of the Popular response to infidelity and scepticism to notice the place which members of both wings of the party ascribed to the efficacy of the preaching of the gospel in a pure and simple form as the main antidote to defection.

Although apparently no other member of the Popular party explicitly espoused Willison's critique of Moderate preaching, four decades later Robert Walker followed his support for stress on the preaching of Christ as an antidote to infidelity,[147] by taking up his analysis of moral preaching indirectly. It was not sufficient, Walker argued, to publish the laws of Christ unless they were published as his laws, and unless the arguments advanced for obeying them were those 'peculiar to his gospel'. The 'great duties of morality' should be depicted as 'the genuine effects and proper evidences of faith in Christ and love to God'. In particular, ministers should remind their hearers that they should not rely on any actions of their own for their justification, but that they should renounce all confidence in them and 'seek to be found in Christ alone'. The apostles themselves introduced, on all occasions, 'the peculiar doctrines of Christianity' and always urged the duties they were commending 'by those regards which are due to Christ himself'.[148] The similarities to what Willison had maintained earlier are striking. By implication, then, Walker thought many ministers of the Church of Scotland were failing to urge morality as a duty arising from our obligations to Christ. He went on, though once again by implication, to level a much more fundamental charge, that of failure to preach about

---

146 Walker, *Sermons on Practical Subjects*, ii, pp. 78–81, 70–6.

147 This probably explains Clark's assertion that the distinction between 'moral' and 'gospel' preaching was something of a cliché. Willison was one of the four Popular authors to whom he makes reference: Clark, 'Moderates and the Moderate Party', p. 373. For Willison's views on Moderate preaching, see above, pp. 65–8.

148 Walker, *Sermons on Practical Subjects*, ii, pp. 73–5.

the necessity of faith in Christ. Understanding of the nature of faith was essential because

> Morality grows out of faith in Christ, as the branches grow from the stock. This, and this only, is the principle of that holiness, without which no man can see God. Whosoever, therefore, would preach morality with any hope of success, must begin here, and lay the foundation of it in that faith which purifieth the heart, and worketh by love; otherwise his sermons may supply fuel to pride and vainglory, but shall never be the means of saving one soul. In vain do we attempt to improve the fruit till the tree be made good. Let sinners first be ingrafted into Christ, and then works of righteousness will follow in course.[149]

Walker's emphasis, however, was not the same as that of Willison. While both agreed that morality was the fruit of faith, Willison's emphasis was on the Christocentric response of the Christian, while Walker's analysis was rooted in the nature of faith and its doctrinal foundations. It was a more intellectual response, and probably reflected the influence of Walker's contemporary, John Erskine, and his analysis of the nature of faith.[150]

V

Confidence in the viability of the Christian faith against the threat posed by infidelity and heresy has already been noted, and it is clear that the Popular party increasingly saw the problem of heresy and unorthodox belief as a phenomenon to be prevented before it occurred, rather than as something to be repressed after it had manifested itself. The consensus that had been reached, however, that deviations from orthodoxy were best countered by care in the licensing of probationers, came to be seen as inadequate or inappropriate in the closing two decades of the century. In 1780 there was a Popular dissent from an Assembly decision on the grounds that it encouraged non-attendance of students on the regular divinity classes, 'whereas private study is apt to lead to singular notions, and is consequently productive of schism and heretical opinions'.[151] In the 1780s a series of Popular overtures to the Assembly requested the enforcement of the regulations relating to the courses of divinity students.[152]

The Popular position on the matter had ramifications in two areas: in the admission to the ministry of the Church of Scotland of men who had received their theological education, or had been ordained in other churches, outside Scotland; and in the response to the missionary and

---

[149] Ibid., pp. 79–80.
[150] See above, pp. 166–73.
[151] *Scots Magazine*, xlii (May 1780), p. 273.
[152] Ibid., xliii (May 1781), p. 273; xlvii (May 1785), p. 270; xlviii (Jun. 1786), pp. 306–7.

church planting activities of the Haldane brothers in the 1790s. In the first place, there is some evidence that the Moderate party used the regulations regarding the theological training of divinity students as a means of excluding potential supporters of the Popular position concerning patronage. In 1790, a licentiate of the Scots Presbytery in London was unanimously refused permission to preach as a probationer in Scotland, since his petition was inconsistent with the Act of Assembly of 1779 respecting persons going to be licensed and ordained outwith the bounds of the Church.[153] In May 1798, however, a more complex case came before the Assembly. A presentation had been made to the parish of Brechin of a man who had received his theological education in England and had been ordained there. He had had a charge in Dublin, had been the minister of the 'Presbyterian chapel' in Perth, had been refused admission by the Assembly, but had acted as a Sunday evening lecturer in Perth and had been admitted as a minister of the Church by the Presbytery of Chanonry. The Presbytery of Brechin had referred the matter to the Assembly. Here it was moved by the Moderate leader, Dr George Hill, that the presentee had not received a proper university education in philosophy and theology, that there was not satisfactory evidence of his ordination in England, that the Presbytery of Chanonry's action was rash and unwarrantable, and that therefore the presentation should not be proceeded with. A counter motion was moved by Moncrieff Wellwood, which found the presentee ordained a minister in England and qualified to accept a presentation, and urged that the Assembly should therefore sustain it and order the presbytery to proceed to a settlement. The Moderate motion was carried by 'a very great majority', but several of the supporters of the Popular motion dissented.[154] Although the evidence is perhaps slight, there is the possibility that the Popular party found difficulty in maintaining an effective opposition to the Moderate policy, since the legislation they supported as a means of preventing the spread of heresy was deemed applicable at least by some of its members to applicants from England. What had originally been a Popular policy of insisting on sound theological training to counter heresy may well have become embroiled in wider controversies.

The second area, that is, the situation which arose over the Haldane brothers' missionary activities in Scotland, suggests confirmation of this. The response of the great majority of the Church of Scotland was contained in several overtures from different synods to the Assembly of 1799 with regard to the employment of persons to preach in the parishes of the Church who were not duly licensed by some presbytery, and who had not received a regular education in one of the Scottish universities. The Assembly unanimously agreed to the overtures,

153 Ibid., lii (Jun. 1790), p. 309.
154 Ibid., lx (May 1798), pp. 358–9.

prohibited the preaching of such persons, and unanimously passed a declaratory act arguing that the requirement of prudence and strictness in the trial and judgement of those who were to be pronounced faithful and apt to teach was laid down by the Apostles, and that the laws regarding the education of candidates for the ministry were based on the rules of Scripture. It went on to argue that it was crucial for the interests of true religion, the sound instruction of the people, the quiet of their minds, and the peace of the Church and State, that unqualified ministers should not be countenanced by ministers of the Established Church. Ministers were forbidden to employ or to hold ministerial communion with such persons. This was justified, without comment by the Popular party, on the grounds

> that it is essential to the unity and good order of the church, and implied in the principles of Presbyterian Government, that no minister shall presume to set up his individual judgement in opposition to the judgement of those to whom at his ordination he promised subjection in the Lord.[155]

It is difficult to argue that there was much difference between this assertion and the main argument of the Moderate 'Reasons for Dissent in the Case of Inverkeithing' nearly fifty years earlier.[156] This time, however, the Popular party was responding to an attack on presbyterian polity from outside the Church. Before proceeding further, however, a qualification needs to be made. It should not be assumed that all parts of the Church, or of the Popular party, were especially worried about the activities of the Haldanes. The 1799 Assembly had also seen overtures concerning the setting up of Sunday Schools by the Haldanes and their followers. At the next Assembly it was reported that less than a quarter of the presbyteries had made any report on the matter, though requested to do so. Even when the matter was deferred to the following year less than half had complied.[157] This low priority given to the whole matter by many in the Church of Scotland is reflected in an absence of detailed discussion of the subject by Popular writers or commissioners to the Assembly.

There remains, however, the question of why the Popular party adopted a hostile attitude to the Haldanes in view of their doctrinal sympathies with them; it is, after all, in marked contrast to the attitude of the Popular party to the Secession, at least in its early days. There were several reasons for the hostility. In the first place, there were various features of the Haldanes' movement which were particularly alien to the Scottish ecclesiastical environment at the time.[158] Apart from the question of

---

[155] Ibid., lxi (Jun. 1799), pp. 419–20.
[156] See above, pp. 104–7.
[157] *Scots Magazine*, lxi (Jun. 1799), p. 422; lxii (Jun. 1800), p. 429; lxiii (Jun. 1801), p. 446.
[158] For much of this discussion I am indebted to a paper given by Dr Deryck Lovegrove

church government, the Haldanes were probably seen as embodying several English influences to which the Scottish ecclesiastical tradition was profoundly hostile. There was large-scale itinerant preaching and ministry south of the Border which was, of course, incompatible with the whole settled system of presbyterial church organisation. There also seems to have been a movement in the late 1790s in England aiming at the reduction of denominational differences and rivalries which could be connected, at least in the minds of Scottish observers, with the Haldanes. Secession and its subsequent growth and rivalry with the Established Church was linked in the minds of Popular churchmen with the departure of Greville Ewing from Lady Glenorchy's Chapel in Edinburgh in 1798, and with the demission of his Stirling charge in 1799 by William Innes, who had accompanied the Haldanes on their preaching tour to the north in 1798. The Haldanes' practice of withholding their approval from ministers who did not meet their standards, which were based on the simplicity of their preaching as well as doctrinal criteria, also alienated many potential sympathisers in the Popular party. The Haldanes made the situation worse by their opposition to the commutation of public repentance for immorality to a fine. There is no evidence that the relaxing of ecclesiastical strictures in this area did not have the support of most Popular ministers by this time. The Haldanes were seen as threatening the strength of the link between Church and State, and presumably also there was doubt about the new role and importance which they gave to the laity. The absence of direct reference to such matters by members of the Popular party, though, is marked.

It is important to realise, however, that real Popular opposition did not appear until after the Haldanes started to engage in the training of preachers in 1799. Even then the issue was not clear-cut, for it was complicated by the desire of the Popular party to recognise English ministerial credentials.[159] In the Synod of Lothian and Tweeddale in 1798 there was a move, presumably aimed at the Haldanes, to request the Assembly to prohibit the occasional employment of preachers who were not members of the Church of Scotland. It was opposed by Popular members of the Synod on the grounds that there was no law either of Church or State prohibiting it, that the laws and regulations adduced by the supporters of the proposals were concerned with applications for the ministry of the Established Church, and that it had been the practice since the Reformation to invite to preach 'worthy and respectable

of the University of St Andrews to the 1982 Conference of the UCCFA Historians' Study Group for Scotland, entitled 'The Haldane brothers and their context: breaking the mould of Scottish Ecclesiasticism'. This has now been published as: D. Lovegrove, 'Unity and Separation: contrasting elements in the thought and practice of Robert and James Alexander Haldane', in K. Robbins (ed.), *Protestant Evangelicalism: Britain, Ireland, Germany, and America, c.1750–c.1950. Essays in Honour of W. R. Ward* (Oxford, 1990), pp. 153–77.

159 *Scots Magazine*, lxi (Jun. 1799), pp. 419–22. See above, pp. 205–7.

ministers of other churches, who had come here to visit their friends or the country, and that no bad consequences had ever been known to occur as a result'. It was desirable, furthermore, to have communion with men 'who have one faith, one baptism, and one hope of their calling', and 'most consistent with that liberality for which the Church of Scotland has ever been distinguished'. The Churches of England and Scotland differed only in form, it was maintained, and many of the English dissenters were at one with the Scottish Church in doctrine, discipline, and worship, so that it showed a most illiberal and bigoted spirit to shut Scottish pulpits to them.[160] But, in spite of all these arguments, the perceived hostility of the Haldanes to ecclesiastical establishments was a stumbling block for the Popular party, and one which caused them to be classified alongside the enemies of the gospel who were 'labouring to sap the foundations of true religion, and to overturn all religious establishments'. In January 1799 the Haldanes set up the first of nine seminary classes, and the Popular party raised no further protests against the moves aimed by the Assembly at countering their activities. They were passed unanimously.[161]

It was this commitment to the Scottish concept of Establishment which explains the Popular party's acquiescence in some of the steps taken to ostracise Popular ministers who left the Church such as James Bayne of Paisley,[162] Greville Ewing of Lady Glenorchy's,[163] and William Innes of Stirling.[164] In the last case, although a Moderate motion which condemned the Presbytery of Stirling for accepting Innes's resignation *simpliciter* was passed by the Assembly with a majority of more than two to one, even the defeated Popular motion had described Innes's practices as 'schismatical and divisive, and if established by proof would have inferred the highest censures of the Church'.[165]

It is evident that in responding to doctrinal innovation, as indeed to schism or ecclesiastical innovation, the Popular party's ideological positions were influenced by more practical considerations. The first was their perception of the nature and benefits of the Establishment, which was conceived to be based on Scriptural authority and was not to be diluted or compromised. The primacy of strictly controlled and orthodox educational procedures as a means of ensuring support for it explains their hostility not only to the Haldanes' preachers, but also to their introduction of Sunday Schools with what were seen as unqualified

---

160 *Scots Magazine*, lx (Nov. 1798), pp. 789–90. It is of course true that the Haldanes also antagonised Moderate ministers in the Church. James Haldane was especially opposed to Socinian ministers and the first appearance of a 'tabernacle', which occurred in the Elgin area, was probably in response to an Elgin minister who had introduced his own Socinian catechism to schools. See above, note 158.
161 *Scots Magazine*, lxi (Jun. 1799), pp. 419–20.
162 Morren, *Annals of the General Assembly*, ii, pp. 313–29.
163 *Scots Magazine*, lxi (Jun. 1799), p. 421.
164 Ibid.
165 Ibid.

teachers.[166] Secondly, there was a concern that proper procedure should be followed even if that meant less rigorous censure of heresy than some would seem to have wished. It was not surprising that this should have been so, in view of their constant battles with the Moderates over patronage in which they consistently stressed the constitutional nature of their contentions. Thirdly, there is some evidence that the Popular party came to value increasingly highly for the Church 'that security for the Stability of her doctrine, worship, discipline and government, she enjoys from the avowed conformity of all her office-bearers to her standards'.[167] In other words, the Popular party was not inclined to regard the threat of infidelity as best met by a rigorous policy of ecclesiastical censure. It had come to believe that it could best be promoted, within the Church, by a commitment to unity on the basis of allegiance to its doctrinal standards. Both these positions would appear to postulate a considerable degree of doctrinal confidence.

VI

The development of a more 'practical' theology was also reflected in a sustained analysis of social and political issues by Popular writers. The earlier Popular commitment to the idea of religion being the foundation of social stability continued in the 1780s and beyond the end of the century. In 1790, John Erskine held that Christianity promoted diligence, frugality, and the faithful discharge of every trust, and thus contributed to success in the different offices and employments of life.[168] A large political body was only really healthy, he had argued at the time of the American War of Independence, when the whole relieved the distress of every part.[169] John Dun of Auchinleck also drew this causal connection between religion and social stability, but gave it a significantly different emphasis, when he argued that

> when our Princes, Nobles and Commons shall, through infidelity and deism, lose a sense of religion, and, through luxury and vice, lose a sense of honour, then the fair fabric of the British constitution shall moulder, decay, and fall to ruin.[170]

As a result of this analysis, some Popular thought openly castigated the life style of the upper class. John Warden, for example, argued that

166 Ibid., lxi (Jun. 1799), p. 422; lxii (Jun. 1800), p. 429. There is doubtless some connection between the Haldanes' establishment of Sunday Schools and the reawakened interest in the salaries of schoolmasters reflected in overtures to the Assembly at this time. See ibid., lxii (May 1800), p. 361; and lxiv (Jun. 1802), pp. 525–6.
167 From a unanimously passed motion of Principal Hill in the Assembly of 1800 concerning the use of questions at ordination other than those of the Formula of 1691: ibid., lxii (Jun. 1800), pp. 428–9.
168 Erskine, *Riches of the Poor*, p. 9.
169 Erskine, *Shall I go to War with my American Brethren?*, p. 15.
170 Dun, *Sermons*, ii, p. 53. See also Love, *Radical Cause of National Calamity*, p. 33.

infidelity and profanity abounded, and that vice was fashionable and kept in countenance by the example of the great;[171] and John Love declaimed against 'the detestable vices, which the great and wealthy have long exemplified', which were 'now diffused through all the inferior orders of society'.[172]

It was John Erskine, however, who delineated most clearly the nature of the operation of the relationship between religion and society in his *Fatal Consequences and General Sources of Anarchy*, which, published in 1793, was no doubt a response to the political and religious ideas of the French Revolution:

> Anarchy is occasioned by transgressing the great laws of religion. Without justice, integrity, and kindness, in the various intercourses and connexions of life, there is no social happiness. Now religion, alone, inspires that love to mankind, which habitually inclines to those virtues, and guards against the temptations, and supports under the trials and difficulties, with which the exercise of them is often attended. Religion produces the most perfect union: for it inspires, with the same general principle of action, supreme regard to the glory of God, unfeigned affection to our neighbour, and a willingness to sacrifice, whatever its own nature opposes, or, through peculiar circumstances, becomes incompatible with, these. In proportion as the law of love is observed, and God's will done on earth, as it is in heaven; rulers and subjects cheerfully perform their respective duties, and are happy in one another ... The honour, the perfection, the comfort of each individual, rejoices the whole community; and the prosperity of the community, rejoices each individual. Where there is no religion, the firmest support of government is removed, the surest bond of social union is broken, and a wide door is opened for vice to enter, and to usher in disorder and misery.[173]

Shortly after the turn of the century, David Savile of the Canongate Chapel-of-Ease returned to the same theme, although he linked it much more closely to the concept of divine law. 'Irreligion and immorality are as injurious to the peace and order of society as to the best interest of the individual', he declared.[174] Observation of God's law was also the law of society. It preserved the comforts and indeed the existence of society, for without the fear of God, there would be no attention paid to truth, honesty, sobriety, temperance, kindness, and beneficence. The country would be a prey to disease and pain, as it would be to treachery,

---

[171] Warden, *Happiness of Britain illustrated*, p. 56.
[172] Love, *Radical Cause of National Calamity*, p. 20. These points overlap with the earlier discussion of the poor morals of the upper class. See above, pp. 60, 199–203.
[173] Erskine, *Fatal Consequences and General Causes of Anarchy*, pp. 35–6. See also pp. 25–6.
[174] Savile, *Dissertations*, p. viii.

robbery, murder and massacre: 'Man would become a very devil; and earth be really converted into hell.' On the other hand, if all men conscientiously kept God's law, poverty would be unknown, oppression would not exist, war would cease, and men would dwell together as brothers, in love and unity. The world would again be paradise.[175] There was, argued Savile, a correlation between progress in righteousness, in growing regard for divine law, and proportional advances towards the depicted state of happiness. Corresponding decline appeared where people made progress in vice. Whoever lived in violation of divine law was not only a traitor to God, he was also an enemy of his country. Society and faith were thus united:

> If we have any reverence for God, any regard for the good of society, any regard for our present peace and eternal felicity, we must listen to the voice of God, and be all zeal to obey his *law*.[176]

In a move which reveals the theological cross-currents operating within the Popular party, Thomas Somerville went further and specifically linked the good of society with the mediation of Christ. Not only did the latter suggest strong arguments for exercising good will and charity to all mankind, the doctrine of the mediation abolished antagonism and ill-feeling between nations and hostile communities, and would 'reconcile them by the sacred bonds of religious affection'.[177] He repeated his affirmation of the essential link between religion and the existence of society in a sermon 'On Oaths'. Policy and legislation, the protection of the innocent, and the detection and punishment of the guilty all required the underpinning of belief in the existence of God, and the fear of his name:

> Feeble and unregarded the threatenings of the law must often prove, were they not to be ratified by the sanction of future rewards and punishments. Narrow, and easily eluded, the discernment of the most upright and sagacious magistrate, if an appeal to an infallible Judge did not overawe the accuser and the accused.[178]

The Popular party, therefore, continued to be united on the vital role of religion as the basis of society.

The social implications of virtuous behaviour led to the development of a critique of wealth.[179] The trend had first manifested itself in the

---

175 Ibid., pp. 167–8. John Russel was possibly the origin of this idea for, in his *Nature of the Gospel Delineated* of 1796, he attacked 'That pernicious practice of enforcing the obligations of morality, without the sanctions of religion': Russel, *Nature of the Gospel Delineated*, p. 38.

176 Savile, *Dissertations*, p. 173. See also James Somerville, *Practical Sermons*, p. 249.

177 Somerville, *Sermons*, p. 156.

178 Thomas Somerville, 'On Oaths', Sermon III in R. Gillan (ed.), *The Scottish Pulpit: A Collection of Sermons by Eminent Clergymen of the Church of Scotland* (Edinburgh, 1823), pp. 57–8.

179 See above, pp. 79–81.

work of Witherspoon, who believed in a cyclical pattern of growth and decline.[180] John McFarlan of the Canongate, while accepting Witherspoon's assessment of the existing state of British society, took a less pessimistic view of urbanisation. While conceding that cities 'offer so many temptations to extravagance and dissipation, that a young person of warm passions and inexperience in life is in the utmost danger of ruin', on the other hand he doubted whether they were such national evils as were often thought. Such evils were unavoidable in an advanced state of society which was bound to embody luxury and dissipation. McFarlan argued that if the threat of poverty, disease, and contempt did not restrain a young man from extravagance and profligacy, then his virtue or manly resolution could never have been well established.[181]

In eighteenth-century Scotland, most Popular thinkers were more concerned with the social consequences of the possession of wealth than they were with those of poverty. Poverty was a social problem if it was not brought upon oneself, and not a socio-religious or moral problem as was wealth.[182] John McFarlan, though, paid attention to the problem of poverty on a moral level. He identified sloth as one of the most frequent causes of poverty, and declared there to be no habit to which mankind in general was more inclined.[183] Later in the 1780s, David Johnston argued the same case.[184] That poverty as such did not appear to require attention was the result of two factors. First, as David Savile put it, 'the poor, the humble, and the helpless; these (and especially if they be deserving creatures) we feel naturally disposed to compassionate and aid'; furthermore, in the words of Moncrieff Wellwood, 'the RELIEF of the miserable, and the GENERAL INSTRUCTION of the poor', were 'essential and peculiar characters of the Messiah's reign'.[185] Aid for the poor was taken for granted to be a Christian duty. Secondly, the latter half of the eighteenth century was a period of sustained, though slow,

---

[180] Witherspoon, *Serious Enquiry into the Nature and Effects of the Stage*, p. 69. See also above, p. 81.

[181] John McFarlan, *Tracts on Subjects of National Importance* (London, 1786), pp. 33–5, 37–8. See also p. 31.

[182] Snodgrass, *Leading Doctrines of the Gospel*, p. 291.

[183] John McFarlan, *Inquiries concerning the Poor* (Edinburgh, 1782), pp. 23–4. After making this point, however, McFarlan proceeded to divest this assertion of its moral impact by claiming that it really only applied to the 'lower stations of life', and that in the 'higher ranks of life' such factors as ambition, a sense of honour, or fear of contempt, stimulated men to shake off sloth and raise themselves, by 'the exertion of their active powers to a state of affluence and distinction'. McFarlan's equanimity about the ability of the upper classes, though, was not shared by other Popular critics of society. See, e.g., Somerville, *Fatal Consequences of Irreligion*, p. 16; and Erskine, *Fatal Consequences and General Sources of Anarchy*, p. 19.

[184] Johnston, *Heinousness and Aggravation of Theft*, p. 21.

[185] Savile, *Dissertations*, p. 141; Moncrieff Wellwood, *Sermon preached in St. Andrew's Church*, pp. 38–9.

growth in prosperity, which affected many sections of the community.[186] In most areas, it was believed that poverty was being held in check by the traditional system of poor relief at the hands of the kirk sessions.[187] On occasions when the parochial system of poor relief was in difficulty, the response was to seek aid from special collections authorised by presbyteries. More widespread problems were met with the appointment of fast days and calls to communal repentance.[188] Preoccupation with the dangers and obligations of wealth, therefore, reflected the increasing wealth in all sections of the community. Acceptance of the Christian obligation to be charitable and relative complacency about the causes and extent of poverty in Scotland was a constant assumption in Popular thought on the subject.

The clearest delineation of Popular social thought on poverty and wealth was John Erskine's sermon of 1804, *The Riches of the Poor*. It demonstrates the coherence of Popular thought on the matter in the second half of the century, and the extent to which secular developments were not perceived to require new responses. It is not unreasonable to interpret Erskine's analysis as an enjoinder of social quiescence on the deprived in society, and as such it was based on his conservative approach to government.[189] Certainly, the place of poverty and riches was seen as part of God-given order, and the inferiority of material as opposed to spiritual wealth was stressed. While the overall aim of the sermon was to explain why the poor had no real cause to envy the wealth and life of the rich, the analysis started with a discussion of the relationship of the will of God to poverty and wealth. The distinction between rich and poor arose naturally from the right of property. A community of goods was neither appropriate nor possible in man's present depraved state. It would encourage the indolent and dissipated to do nothing, and it would provide them with the comforts of life by depriving the sober and industrious of the fruits of their labours. As a result, diligence would be discouraged, and all the ills deriving from lack of the necessities of life would be common.

> It was therefore the will of God, that every one should have the exclusive right to what he acquired by honest labour, a right to possess and enjoy it himself, and to bestow it upon or bequeath it to others, as he pleased.[190]

---

186 On this see, e.g., Campbell, *Scotland since 1707*; Smout, 'Where had the Scottish economy got to', pp. 45–72; Devine and Mitchison, *People and Society in Scotland*, vol. I; and the various other works on Scottish economic history.

187 On this subject, see Mitchison, 'Making of the Old Scottish Poor Law', pp. 58–93; Cage, 'Debate: the making of the Old Scottish Poor Law'; Mitchison, 'A rejoinder', pp. 113–21; Mitchison, 'Creation of the Disablement Rule', pp. 199–217; and Cage, *Scottish Poor Law*.

188 See, e.g., McIntosh, 'Popular Party in the Church of Scotland', pp. 16–19.

189 See below, note 226.

190 Erskine, *Riches of the Poor*, pp. 4–5.

If the right to property was destroyed, all would be reduced to misery by the uncertainty of retaining tomorrow what they possessed today. This, in fact, was the basis for society, since greater or lesser societies were necessary to secure property by providing for the general protection by giving power to one or more. From these distinctions of fortune and power all ranks derived benefit. The rich needed inferiors to provide the conveniences of life, and the poor needed superiors to encourage and reward their labours. God was not unjust in placing men, who were no worse or no better than their neighbours, in poverty or trying situations, because all that we had was the gift of his Providence, and he could do what he wished with his own. He did not regard the rich more than the poor, and in any case, the greatest calamities of life affected rich and poor equally. Although Erskine's discussion of the role of property indicates that he was acquainted with at least some of the work of Ferguson, John Millar, and Kames, it is important to note that the whole structure of his view of the problem of poverty was theological.[191]

Witherspoon's ideas in this area were taken up by Robert Walker in one of his *Sermons on Practical Subjects* of 1796, where he argued that the rich, in proportion to their abundance, should contribute to the necessities of their fellow creatures, and castigated those who argued that 'by the plenty of their tables, the splendour of their dwellings, the sumptuousness of their equipage, and other articles of their luxury, they find employment for the poor in providing for their consumption'. This certainly benefited society, but it avoided facing up to the moral and religious issues of obligations to society and gratitude to God for his gifts: 'For what mark of gratitude to God is it, that we consume his bounty upon our own pleasures, although, in so doing, we cannot avoid distributing a part of it to our fellow creatures?'[192]

Witherspoon probably also influenced Thomas Somerville, who, in a sermon delivered in 1786, ten years earlier than the publication of Walker's sermon, made the same point that indirect provision for the poor did not meet the requirements of Christian charity. Somerville's work was much more concerned with specific schemes of charitable relief and does not seem to have contributed to Walker's thought on the issue.[193] Worldly prosperity, maintained Somerville, obliged exemplary

[191] Ibid., pp. 1–3. See Adam Ferguson, *Essay on the History of Civil Society* (1767), ed. D. Forbes (Edinburgh, 1966), pp. 11–12, 82, 125; John Millar, *Origin of the Distinction of Ranks* (1771), in W. C. Lehmann, *John Millar of Glasgow, 1735–1801: His Life and Thought and his Contribution to Sociological Analysis* (Cambridge, 1960), pp. 176, 204, 250; John Millar, *Historical View of the English Government from the Settlement of the Saxons in Britain to the Revolution in 1688* (London, 1803, 1st pub. 1786), i, pp. 3, 76–7, 358; Henry Home, Lord Kames, *Sketches of the History of Man* (1774), vol. I (Edinburgh, 1807), p. 97; Henry Home, Lord Kames, *Historical Law Tracts*, p. 57, 88–156. For a discussion of the views on this matter of these writers, see Chitnis, *Scottish Enlightenment*, pp. 100–11.

[192] Walker, *Sermons on Practical Subjects*, iv, p. 362.

[193] Witherspoon, *Serious Enquiry into the Nature and Effects of the Stage*, pp. 22–3.

charity. The poor were God's representatives on earth and alms were a test of gratitude to him. Persons who owed their wealth to ingenuity and labour were too ready to hold poverty in contempt, to ascribe it to 'indolence and demerit', and to be opposed to charity. They argued that it was harmful to industry, that there ought to be no fixed or legal provision for maintaining the poor, and that exceptional measures in times of crisis tended to multiply candidates for charity and to increase the distress. He countered these arguments by stressing that the giving of alms was a precept of the Christian religion, by pointing out that objections could be brought to any scheme of benevolence and that there was therefore no hope of universal approval of any scheme, and by asserting that hard-hearted men were always in the forefront of opposition to charitable proposals. Donations of charity with incitement to industry, however, would be the most successful and the benefits derived the longest lasting. Even the 'idle and undeserving', while they should not take priority to the industrious and virtuous, 'must not be consigned to irretrievable wretchedness'.[194]

Those of the Popular party who wrote on the subject of wealth and poverty were unanimous that there was a moral and religious obligation on the wealthy to contribute part of their wealth to the relief of the poor, and that they could be regarded as seriously accountable to God if they did not. Equally unanimously, however, they held out little hope that the wealthy would honour their obligations. The reason was that the wealthy were less likely to be godly than the multitude of mankind. As already noted, Witherspoon put the point in connection with his argument against the theatre:

> The far greatest number of the world are ungodly ... And as none can attend the stage, but those in higher life, and more affluent circumstances than the bulk of mankind, there is still a greater proportion of them who are enemies to pure and undefiled religion ... This does not at all suppose, that those in high life are originally more corrupt in their nature than others, but it arises from their being exposed to much greater and stronger temptations.[195]

This was because the rich were tempted to luxury and to irreligion because of it. Witherspoon's suspicion of wealth was reinforced by his pessimistic, cyclical interpretation of national development in which wealth led to luxury which was the precursor of a return to poverty.[196] John Erskine, too, accepted such a cyclical theory when he argued that increasing luxury and dissipation derived from the increase of commerce

[194] Somerville, *Sermons*, pp. 485–8.
[195] Witherspoon, *Serious Enquiry into the Nature and Effects of the Stage*, p. 35; see above, pp. 80–1.
[196] Ibid., p. 69. See above, p. 81.

and wealth.[197] Even John McFarlan – who saw wealth and civilisation as the marks of an advanced state of society and therefore as leading to the introduction of pleasures and fashionable amusements, and regarded their attendant problems as being more than counterbalanced by the role of wealth in preserving the distinction of ranks necessary for the maintenance of stability, orderly government and justice – asserted that the increase of luxury introduced selfishness, venality, and corruption of manners. McFarlan politicised the potentiality of wealth by arguing for a more equal distribution of land ownership since

> there are then no temptations to the refinements of luxury, by the overgrown wealth of individuals, nor is the great body of the people bowed to servility by an abject dependence. No man is so much exalted above the multitude as to attempt a tyranny over his country.[198]

Luxury increasingly became the object of attack, and a preoccupation with it is the third theme of Popular thought on social issues. John Dun put the moral dangers of wealth with dramatic starkness: 'Man ... is he rich? [He is tempted to] sensuality.'[199] John Snodgrass went further, and linked dissipation and luxury with impiety.[200] In some respects, though, sensuality induced by luxury led to an even greater charge being levelled against luxury and ultimately against wealth by Robert Walker. In a passage already referred to, he identified it with the growth of infidelity:

> Luxury is the common attendant upon affluence: This unfits the mind for serious thinking, and breeds a coldness and indifference towards spiritual things; in consequence of which, a secret disaffection to those laws which would restrain him, soon takes root in the heart of the sensualist, till, wearied with the struggle betwixt Reason and Appetite, he at length sets himself in opposition to God and his ways; reproaches with the names of ostentation or hypocrisy, all serious religion and godliness in others; turns away his eyes from the light that reproves him, and even doth what he can to extinguish it altogether.[201]

This analysis subsequently led Walker to identify the following as evidence of a worldly mind: discontent with one's present state, whether rich or poor; the consideration of wealth and happiness to be inseparable; and the consideration of industry in endeavouring to obtain a share in this world's goods to be superior to diligence in preparing for the next. Adoption of even moderate goals in wealth and property still implied

197 Erskine, *Shall I go to War with my American Brethren?*, p. 30.
198 McFarlan, *Tracts on Subjects of National Importance*, pp. 5–7.
199 Dun, *Sermons*, i, p. 42.
200 Snodgrass, *Means of Preserving the Life and Power of Religion*, p. 37.
201 Walker, *Sermons on Practical Subjects*, i, pp. 466–7, quoted above, p. 199.

slavery to the world; 'competence' was different for the rich and the poor; bequeathing wealth to charitable purposes was only 'an absurd delusion' since it was only offering one's worldly possessions to God after they had been abused when they could have been properly used.[202] Men indeed should be suspicious of prosperity, for it was difficult to possess much wealth without loving it to excess. There was an added spiritual dimension, too, for the devil 'would give all his servants liberal portions in this world if he could'.[203]

Although there were relatively few writers who contributed to the debate, Popular analysis of wealth and poverty had three themes. First, it was accepted that charity was a fundamental obligation for the Christian. Secondly, wealth could be used in two ways: virtuously, when a significant proportion of it was devoted to aiding the poor or improving the lot of all in the community; or reprehensibly, when it was devoted to luxury and self-indulgence. The latter was more likely. And thirdly, luxury was to be condemned as evil in itself and as having the consequences of sensuality and even infidelity. The general view was that the virtuous use of wealth would be the exception rather than the rule, since there was a profound tendency in the pursuit and possession of wealth for the claims of true religion and godliness to be lost sight of, however good the intentions.

Is it possible, then, to conclude that there was a discernibly evolving Popular view of the nature of society? The answer is a qualified affirmative. There was, in the first place, a clear conviction that there was a significant, even a crucial, connection between faith and social stability. Decline of faith led to the collapse of society. Infidelity was to be feared not just on religious grounds, but also on social ones. Towards the end of the century, furthermore, the approach to morality based on Wishart's ideas of universal benevolence was being replaced by a more directly Scripturally based one which gave greater emphasis to the conception of divine law.

Strikingly absent, however, was any stress on the social implications of Calvinist doctrines of original sin, total depravity, or consideration of the question of free will. The only Popular writer to raise the last issue was John Dun. After stressing the social implications of men's actions, he argued that, when the good or evil of actions extended beyond the persons who performed them and potentially did good or hurt to others, the providence of God intervened to hinder, to order, or to permit it depending on whether other men were likely to be improved by it or not, and on whether they deserved well or ill of God. Man in society was a free agent but he was still governable by God.[204] Dun's

---

202 Ibid., iv, pp. 364–7.
203 Ibid., pp. 378–9.
204 Dun, *Sermons*, i, pp. 99–100.

voice, however, was very much a lone one, and even he tended to attach praise or blame to actions depending on their effect on others.

VII

As was the case from the 1740s, almost all Popular writers saw government as necessary and as instituted by God as a result of the Fall and the natural depravity of man. As a consequence, the emergence of a conservative view of government was a logical development. At the same time, though, Popular political thought embodied an espousal of more liberal ideas supported by parallel theories of religious liberty of conscience, and by ideas of the unity of men through all being the objects of God's love. As a result of these concepts, there developed a dichotomy in the ideology of the party. The liberal impetus led some of its members to oppose the Tory government of the period, and to adopt an intellectual alliance with the Foxite Whigs. The outbreak of the French Revolution, however, with its propagation of anti-Christian ideas together with its hostility to Britain led to a thorough-going stress on the obligations of Christians to support the existing political establishment.

In contrast to their position on the religious basis of society, some Popular writers were prepared to allow a greater leeway to secular explanations of the nature and operation of government. This flexibility, however, became less marked in the aftermath of the French Revolution. Thomas Somerville was the closest adherent of Wishart's position that the origins of government were to be found in human nature. All schemes of government, he held, exhibited the 'necessary connection between vice and misery', and maintained the connection between good and evil. The 'seeds, or elements, of civil government are placed in the frame, and social disposition of human nature'; therefore government should be considered as 'a branch of divine Providence'. Proof of the proposition was that sin was actually punished in this life.[205]

Following from Wishart, several Popular writers accepted the possibility of secular explanations of the origin of government. John Russel applied secular considerations especially in relation to the form of government. He declared that nowhere in the New Testament did God sanction any particular form of government, so that errors inherent in any particular constitution were the result of weaknesses or imperfections in human understanding, of 'pre-possessions', or of 'pre-conceived prejudices'.[206] Christianity had existed and flourished under all types of civil government. The only religious point to be accepted about the origin of civil government was that since the Fall, the state of the world had been such as to necessitate its institution. Civil government, asserted Russel, while it had 'the sanction of divine authority', was introduced before the

---

205 Somerville, *Sermons*, pp. 48–9.
206 Russel, *True Religion the Foundation of True Patriotism*, p. 15.

commencement of the New Testament dispensation. Civil magistrates' powers, therefore, commenced with the existence of civil society and were in no way either increased or reduced by Christianity.[207] Furthermore, as several Popular writers accepted, the exclusion of direct, divine approbation allowed alternative explanations of the basis of government and made possible the use of Enlightenment ideas about the origin of society.

John McFarlan of the Edinburgh Canongate was an example of the use of a secular approach. He arrived at the subject in his *Tracts on Subjects of National Importance* of 1786 (which he dedicated to Henry Dundas), through his discussion of the stages of development experienced by societies. Nations, he argued, progressed from youth to maturity in a process from the commencement of political existence to its final dissolution. These different stages required different rules and regulations for their government. In the earlier stages, manners were pure and simple, and there were few temptations to fraud and violence. A small number of plain laws were all that was necessary. But as a nation increased in wealth, numbers, and 'the refinements of life', there was a loss of primitive virtue, and the rise of selfishness, avarice, and ambition which in turn led to fraud and violence. A variety of new laws were needed, therefore, and 'a strict, executive government' to prevent injuries and oppression.[208] The origin of government, then, lay in the loss of virtue and the increase of vice which went hand in hand with the development of society.

In spite of the way being opened to accept secular theories of the origins of government, few Popular writers did so, and most analysed the subject in theological terms. John Erskine, for example, asserted that it was the purpose of government to restrain men from injuring each other and to defend them from attacks by public enemies.[209] Without it there would be disorder, misery, robbery, murder, and so on. It was therefore necessary, 'from the depravity of mankind', that there should be courts and magistrates with power and authority to prevent these evils and to secure the peace and order of society.[210] God, furthermore, was in complete control of rulers, who had no power to serve the public, or to hurt it, except it was given by God: 'They are ministers of God, and their services are in kind, degree, and continuance, just what God, whose ministers they are, sees meet.'[211] John Love, a decade later, made the same point: no degree of civil power could be attained 'without, at least, permissive ordination from above'.[212] John Russel argued that the very appointment of civil government supposed men to be apostate

207 Ibid., p. 18.
208 McFarlan, *Tracts on Subjects of National Importance*, pp. 6–7.
209 Cf. Wishart. See above, p. 75.
210 Erskine, *Prayer for those in Civil and Military Offices*, p. 5.
211 Ibid., p. 18.
212 Love, *Majesty of the King of Kings*, p. 7.

creatures. When they acknowledged the need for civil government, they should be humbled before God because apostasy had introduced disorder and confusion into God's beautiful, orderly, and harmonious world. Hence, true religion was the foundation of a right view of the nature of government and of true patriotism.[213]

There was, however, little discussion of the positive aspects of the purpose of government. Russel limited himself to the assertion that the end of civil government was the preservation of peace and the promotion of the good of society.[214] The function of the monarch, maintained John Dun, was to govern by fixed and stated laws, and his power was exercised by means of aiding, protecting, and relieving, in distributing justice, and tempering it with mercy. Government ministers, to whom power was delegated, were accountable for maladministration to the representatives of the people, and to the supreme judicature. This process secured 'the dignity of the sovereign' and 'the welfare of the people'. The overall system was sanctioned by its being glorifying to God and in accordance with his laws:

> The prince has the honour of being the minister of God for good to his people; of ruling subjects, not slaves; of governing by law, and not by caprice: and the people, conscious of their own rank, are happy in obeying a legal monarch – in security from oppression under him – in power of doing whatever the laws permit – and of not being compelled to do what the laws do not command – *in which the very essence of true and perfect civil liberty does consist.*[215]

Assumption of the existence of fundamental natural rights led Popular thought in the direction of the political liberalism which was one of the main characteristics of the Popular party for much of the second half of the eighteenth century. In many cases the discussion of matters relating to government arose from issues such as the nature of vice, and religious toleration and liberty.

Acceptance of the need for government, combined with the assumption of the inalienable right to liberty of conscience (based usually on the argument from the right to religious liberty in particular),[216] led Popular writers to a 'contractual' view of the nature of government. For example, John Dun, writing in 1790, at the start of the French Revolution, argued that the British constitution had always been founded on the liberty of the people. Such liberty was an essential part of the type of government which was usual among 'the northern nations'. The people had their acknowledged rights, and the obligations between them and their governors was reciprocal. Their kings were legal kings, not

213 Russel, *True Religion the Foundation of True Patriotism*, pp. 26–8.
214 Ibid., pp. 14–15.
215 Dun, *Sermons*, ii, p. 58.
216 See, e.g., Bannerman, *Sermon upon Reformation and Revolution Principles*, pp. 5–6.

arbitrary tyrants: they were bound by the laws of the community, framed with the people's participation and consent.[217] There was, in fact, a balance of political power. British government lay between the extremes of 'despotic power' and 'popular licentiousness'. The only real threat to this was the potential loss of 'a sense of religion' by 'our Princes, Nobles and Commons' as a result of the espousal of infidelity and deism, and a loss of 'a sense of honour' through luxury and vice.[218] This idea was emphasised shortly afterwards by Love and Erskine, the latter linking the contempt of religion among the upper classes with the possibility of violent revolution: a mob, which, following the example of the great, had no character or honour to lose, could attack the property of their rulers, seize the reins of government, and rule with tyranny and cruelty.[219] The guarantee of freedom, according to Dun, lay in the moderating influence of the balance between the regal, aristocratic, and popular powers or orders. The 'Aristocratical Power' was perhaps crucial as it kept both the others within bounds.[220] The influence of the collective body of the people as a whole was guaranteed by their freedom and frequency in the choice of new representatives. The proof of the true liberty of any people is that they cannot be deprived of any part of that liberty, or of the benefit of it, except by their own fault. Freedom, however, in its very nature was liable to abuse. A connection existed here between national freedom which embodied 'civil dignity', and free will which was the foundation of 'moral worth'. To restrict either more than God had done would be, in effect, to annul and destroy them.[221] Effective government required a balance between consultation of the wishes of all in the legislative power, and immediate action on the part of the legislative power. As a result, republics were 'weak and contemptible', as was exemplified by the Italian Republics and even Holland, which had required assistance from monarchies in the past.[222]

---

[217] Dun, *Sermons*, ii, pp. 51–2. The correlation between such views and the attempt of the Popular party to persuade the General Assembly to adhere to the 'constitutional' position regarding liberty of conscience in the patronage debates is striking. See above, pp. 93–105.

[218] Ibid., p. 53. See above, pp. 210, 220.

[219] Love, *Radical Cause of National Calamity*, p. 20. On this, see above, p. 211. Erskine, *Fatal Consequences and General Sources of Anarchy*, pp. 43–4.

[220] There would seem to be a possible connection between this kind of conception of the role of the aristocracy in government, the effects of luxury, and the need for balance in the constitution, with the attempt made by the Popular party under the leadership of Andrew Crosbie and Henry Erskine to recruit the landed gentry to the anti-patronage cause. It could well be, also, that Whig lay leaders of the party were not unaware of the political possibilities of such an alliance. See below, pp. 133–42, 149–50.

[221] Dun, *Sermons*, ii, pp. 54–5. It is interesting to observe that Dun went on to argue that Scottish liberty had been restricted in three ways: by arbitrary excise laws, by the removal of the legal right of enforcing church discipline by the 1712 Act which prevented compulsion of scandalous persons and witnesses to compear at church courts, and by the reintroduction of patronage. See ibid., pp. 55–7.

[222] Ibid., pp. 57–61.

This type of analysis was applied to the constitution of Great Britain with near unanimity. Indeed, throughout the second half of the century, the only qualifying notes in the litany of satisfaction with the state of Britain were sounded by John McFarlan in his *Tracts on Subjects of National Importance* of 1786, and, in a general way, by John Erskine in the early 1790s. The strength or weakness of a nation, McFarlan asserted, was in proportion to the number of its industrious and virtuous inhabitants, who would find themselves interested in supporting or defending their country. McFarlan tied this thesis to a radical argument for a more equal distribution of land. This, combined with good government, would afford the best prospects for security of liberty and property to individuals, as well as promoting love of one's country.[223] McFarlan, who inherited a landed estate,[224] certainly seemed to flirt with radicalism by arguing that ownership of large tracts of land by a few increased the possibility of 'haughty lords' attempting a tyranny over their country.[225] But while he argued for a *more* equal land distribution, he was not in favour of equality. Strict execution of justice seemed incompatible with an equal distribution of property. The distinction of ranks was necessary to maintain that subordination on which justice depended, for the multitude would not accept the government of equals, and some degree of superior wealth or property was necessary for the preservation of the distinction. This superiority produced respect for those of superior wisdom or social ascendancy.[226] McFarlan's radicalism, therefore, was not political radicalism as such, but rather concern lest socio-economic developments should make it harder for the common man to be virtuous and industrious, and easier for the great landowners to gain more than their due share of the constitutional balance of power.

Erskine, in his *Fatal Consequences and General Sources of Anarchy*, also made the general point, possibly overlooked at the time, that even the best forms of government and law and the wisest administration were not perfect. Anything, therefore, was 'of a malignant tendency, which discourages legal and constitutional measures, for reforming what is wrong, and remedying what is defective'. The threat and fear of anarchy and disorder prevented even the most proper and reasonable alterations

---

[223] McFarlan, *Tracts on Subjects of National Importance*, pp. 2–3.

[224] H. Scott, *Fasti Ecclesiae Scoticanae: The Sucession of Ministers in the Church of Scotland from the Reformation*, 7 vols. (Edinburgh, 1915–28), i, p. 29.

[225] McFarlan, *Tracts on Subjects of National Importance*, pp. 4–5.

[226] Ibid., pp. 6–7. This particular section of McFarlan's work was supported by references to David Hume, *Observations on the Reign of Henry VII*; Adam Smith, *Wealth of Nations*, in *Works* (Edinburgh, 1811–12); Robert Wallace, *Dissertation on the Numbers of Mankind*; Richard Price, *Essays on the Population and Unhealthiness of London*; and to the works of the French theorist Quesnai and his followers: ibid., pp. 10–19. Several years later, John Erskine took up the point about the distinction of ranks, tying it not only to the administration of justice, but also extending it to social happiness in general. It was anarchy to turn the relationships upside down: Erskine, *Fatal Consequences and General Sources of Anarchy*, pp. 4–5.

being attempted. Party spirit had the same effect.[227] There is no evidence, though, that this reservation made any impact on Popular thought at the time.

Inherent in Popular thought, however, was an impulse towards conservatism. Ultimately, this derived from the Scriptural injunctions, of Romans 13 and 1 Peter 2, to obedience to the divinely ordained established powers. In the minds of Popular writers this was more assumed than analysed. More in the forefront of their minds was the connection between religion and society. As Dun asserted, since God has supplied us with all the benefits we enjoy

> It becomes us to cherish in our minds a proper esteem and reverence, a due affection and zeal, for our most holy religion, and our excellent civil polity. We should be careful not to disgrace our profession by vicious practices, or intolerant principles, equally ruinous to a nation.

He went on to reinforce the nature of the duty of Christians as it related to British society at the time:

> The daily remembrance, and the due sense of what we owe to Almighty God, as a highly favoured people, and as citizens and members of the best regulated polity, will, and ought to engage us in a conscientious discharge of every branch of duty arising from that relation: to aid, assist and concur with our governors, according to our several stations and abilities, in pursuing the great ends of government, in procuring the peace – the security – the welfare of the whole community: in promoting order, unanimity, probity and justice among our fellow-citizens: in discouraging and restraining all immorality and profaneness, and every kind of vice, as the bane of society – the sure destruction of states and empires: and always to testify our regard to the laws of our country, by a ready and cheerful obedience to all who are in authority – by reverence to magistrates of every degree – and by distinguished reverence to the highest.[228]

Such an analysis, although it was almost certainly not intended to be, could be construed as a manifesto of political conservatism. It arose from satisfaction with the capacity and willingness of the system of British government to act in accordance with the laws of God to produce an adequately moral society and to preserve religious freedom. It was 'the peculiar Blessing of Britons to enjoy Liberty and Government in Perfection', asserted Patrick Bannerman; and most would have agreed with John Warden who claimed that the national liberty of Britons was

---

227 Ibid., pp. 10, 29.
228 Dun, *Sermons*, ii, pp. 68–9.

'greater than anywhere else in the known world'.[229] In view of this, it was the duty of Christians to accept the British government's legitimate authority, and to give it their consistent support and obedience.[230]

Thomas Somerville, writing in the same period as Dun, accepted the same assessment of the existing state of the government of Britain. He declared that the British constitution was adequate for 'the reformation of every abuse, and the accomplishment of every beneficial institution, suggested by the increasing light of the world in which we live'.[231] Two decades later, in 1813, he subscribed to the idea that 'the social and external felicity' enjoyed by members of the British Empire had never been greater, and he enumerated as evidence for this the mildness and wisdom of the laws, the regular and impartial administration of justice, the increase in manufacturing, the extension of commerce, agricultural improvements, more liberal recompense of labour, legal provision for the poor, the flourishing state of the arts and sciences and their application to provide comfort and utility, and 'the abounding accommodation of life' across the social classes.[232] James Steven of the Crown Court Church, London, and then of Kilwinning, who was one of the founders of the London Missionary Society, had foreshadowed Somerville on this topic when, at the turn of the century, he linked the firm establishment and the wise administration of the civil government, and due honour and cheerful obedience to it, with the flourishing of the political body, the maturing of learning, freedom, the arts and sciences, and trade and commerce. The fruits of honest industry would descend from generation to generation in such a nation; and in this situation rulers and subjects would perform their respective duties without encroachment or oppression on one side, or agitation on the other.[233] Steven went on to argue that while the British constitution was not absolutely perfect (for that would be unreasonable to expect), it had certain guardians, provided by its terms, to provide for the reform of abuses, supply deficiencies, and oversee improvements. Nowhere was rational, genuine, practical freedom more fully present than in Britain.[234]

The relationship between godliness and obedience to the civil authorities was delineated at length by Russel in his *True Religion the Foundation of True Patriotism* of 1801. Its objective was 'to deprecate those

---

229 Bannerman, *Sermon upon Reformation and Revolution Principles*, p. 38; see also pp. 17, 26, 39; and Warden, *Happiness of Britain illustrated*, p. 10.
230 See, e.g., Bannerman, *Sermon upon Reformation and Revolution Principles*, p. 17. This type of appraisal of the government's qualities contributes, too, to an understanding of the Popular party's attempt to seek parliamentary action to remedy the grievance of the patronage system.
231 Somerville, *Discourse on ... the Abolition of the African Slave Trade*, p. 22.
232 Somerville, *Sermons*, pp. 284–5.
233 Steven, *Unrivalled Felicity of the British Empire*, p. 14.
234 Ibid., pp. 14–17.

evils, which evidently arise from the want of fear to God, or from the want of respectful homage due to the Sovereign'.[235] When men enter into civil society, they surrendered some rights in order that the remaining ones could be more effectually secured. In this, Russel would seem to be harking back to the contractual approach of Dun a few years earlier, and to Erskine's analysis of the purpose of government.[236] When authorities, to secure the ends of the preservation of peace and the good of society, executed laws agreeable to reason and to divine revelation, it was the duty of subjects to obey. Only when the commands of a king evidently interfered with those of 'the Supreme Governor of the world' did the obligation to obey the civil powers cease. Such was in accordance with common sense, as well as reason and religion. Those who resisted the exercise of lawful authority, furthermore, would incur deserved punishment from the civil powers. If they did not repent, they would receive higher punishment from God 'whose authority in the institution of civil government, they despise; and, whose order established in the world, they endeavour to reverse'.[237] In other words, Russel was throwing the full panoply of divine justice into the scales against those who would question legitimately established civil government. The king should be honoured, since he had been placed at the head of our government 'by the wisdom of an all-superintending Providence'. Especially should we be thankful that he was not a despot but only the supreme civil magistrate, not elevated above the law, and that he was 'officially authorised, the appointed guardian of the rights and privileges of his subjects'. The true notion of 'equality' in Britain was embodied in the way he was *equally* bound to protect all his subjects in the possession of their 'just rights and immunities'. This, asserted Russel, was the only notion of equality that could exist in civil society.[238]

Russel, furthermore, took his theories down to the everyday areas of society by extending the respect due to the king to all 'inferior rulers and magistrates in their official capacity'. These derived their authority from the king, and, since the monarch possessed his just authority from God, any insult offered to an inferior magistrate, in his public capacity, was really offered to the king and ultimately, therefore, to God. Magistrates might personally be wicked men, but their office was to be highly respected because it derived its origin from divine authority.[239] In all this, however, with the exception of points made in connection with the French Revolution, there was little of significant difference from the analysis given almost sixty years earlier, in the face of the Jacobite threat, by David Blair of Brechin in his sermons on *The Fear that's due unto God*

---

[235] Russel, *True Religion the Foundation of True Patriotism*, p. 5.
[236] See above, pp. 211, 220–2.
[237] Russel, *True Religion the Foundation of True Patriotism*, p. 18.
[238] Ibid., p. 19.
[239] Ibid., pp. 22–3.

and the King, or from John Warden's *Happiness of Britain illustrated*.[240] Popular concepts of monarchy, then, in some ways showed little sign of real development.

The applicability of these ideas to the situation in which Britain found itself on the outbreak of the French Revolution is obvious, so obvious that few Popular writers saw need to comment directly on it. The French Revolution was the proof of the validity of their analysis of the attractions of the British constitution. Steven did refer explicitly to the perniciousness of French Revolutionary principles. That liberty, or rather licentiousness, which allowed freedom to be false, malicious or injurious in writings or actions was not allowed in Britain, but all persons were under the protection of laws which were just in principle and impartial in operation. Men of talent, irrespective of social origin, could rise to preferment. Liberty of the press guaranteed the absence of arbitrary government. So-called liberty in France, on the other hand, perverted its first principles and became nothing more than ambition, venality, and despotism. British society should be contented, and show devout gratitude to God.[241] John Russell was more emphatic on the point. Disunity, discord, and the alienation of men's minds from each other threatened the peace of civil society, and even its very existence. The people must therefore do their utmost, depending on divine grace, 'to counteract the influence of those impious tenets, relating both to church and state, which have, with so much *art* and *industry*, been disseminated among us, by the emissaries of France'. Russel declared that he was more afraid of the spread of French principles than of their military success. The call to opposition to the French revolution was couched in the language of a rousing call to opposition to the spiritual enemy:

> Let every one therefore, who is a determined enemy to these principles, show, that he hates their atheism, their infidelity, and their other licentious doctrines, – by cordially embracing the interesting truths of divine revelation, – by attending statedly the places of public worship, where these truths are preached, – and, by living daily under their happy influence. And let all those, who hate their detestable principles of anarchy, confusion and depredation, exert their combined influence, in support of that excellent system of salutary laws wherewith we are blessed.[242]

The most consistent element, then, in Popular analysis of the nature and purpose of government was the delineation of an integral link between civil polity and religion. Government was seen as having its

---

[240] Blair, *Fear that's due unto God and the King*, pp. 32–6. 45–7; Warden, *Happiness of Britain illustrated*, p. 39.

[241] Steven, *Unrivalled Felicity of the British Empire*, pp. 14–17.

[242] Russel, *True Religion the Foundation of True Patriotism*, pp. 20–2.

origins in the nature of society, but as a result of the loss of virtue and increase of vice which were the result of wealth and luxury or, in the minds of the more orthodox or the more evangelically inclined, the result of the Fall of Man, an increasing amount of government action was necessary. In the opinions of most Popular thinkers, and especially of those whose theological positions were more rigorous, the crucial nature of man's apostasy from God meant that right religious perceptions were essential to an understanding of the nature of government and of the reasons why God had sanctioned it.

Assumption of the essential nature of religious liberty, as the result of the existence of the right to liberty of conscience, led to the espousal of doctrines of political liberty. This in turn led to the emergence in Popular thought of a contractual theory of government. In this theory, a balance of power between king, aristocracy, and people was held to be essential. True liberty, it was believed, consisted of liberty within the law. Such a theory showed more than passing resemblance to traditional doctrines of Christian liberty within the law of God.

These convictions, in an almost paradoxical way, merged into a complacent analysis of the existing political situation in Britain. The manifest blessings which God was apparently bestowing on Britain and her Empire indicated that God was giving his approval to the existing constitutional arrangements. Since magistrates were appointed by the king, whose rule enjoyed God's approval, revolt or even the questioning of their authority was an impious act. Infidelity among the ruling classes was a serious threat to the long-term stability of the system, for infidelity led to the loss of civic virtue. The religious element was thus of key importance. This conservative political philosophy emerged most explicitly in the period of the French Revolution and was strengthened by its outbreak. It is no coincidence that the majority of Popular writing on the subject appeared after 1789. French Revolutionary ideas posed a two-fold threat: first, they endangered political stability and threatened anarchy; but secondly, and more importantly, they threatened the religious principles on which, in Popular minds, the whole governmental structure was based. The ideas espoused by France had to be opposed for religious as well as political reasons. There was, therefore, no alternative to support for the Government, even in its policy of repression, during the period of the Revolution and subsequent war. Such ideas as might have derived from secular thought were articulated within a theological framework and by means of essentially religious and theological concepts. For most Popular thinkers, religion was paramount and thoroughly controlled their political perceptions.[243]

---

[243] Only a few Popular writers were directly influenced by the thought of the Scottish Enlightenment, and that only in the areas of cyclical theories of national development, and social structures. John Millar's *Origin of the Distinction of Ranks* of 1771 informed Erskine and McFarlan. Millar, too, espoused cyclical theories of the rise and

VIII

The subject of the abolition of the slave trade, while apparently raised in the first instance as a Popular initiative, was remarkable for the unanimity which it produced throughout the Church. It also provoked a debate both within the Church as a whole and within the Popular party as to how to proceed in matters concerning the government of the country. The first occasion on which the matter was discussed in the ecclesiastical courts, so far as was recorded in the secular press, occurred early in 1788 when the Presbytery of Edinburgh debated the issue. A motion to petition Parliament for the abolition of the trade was moved and seconded by two Popular ministers, Robert Walker of the Canongate and Thomas Randall of the Tolbooth parishes. John Erskine also suggested that the Moderator of the previous General Assembly should be requested to call a meeting of the Commission in order to procure the sentiments of the whole Church. Both motions were unanimously accepted and a cross-party committee appointed to prepare and transmit the petition.[244]

The same year, overtures relating to the slave trade were sent up to the Assembly from three synods. The Assembly was unanimous on the measure, but debate ensued on the manner in which it should be pursued. The proposal to petition the House of Commons was strongly opposed by the Lord Advocate and others on the grounds that Parliament in general paid little attention to petitions from bodies of men 'not personally or patrimonially' interested in the issues. The Popular Dean of the Faculty of Advocates, Henry Erskine, and other ministers, both Popular and Moderate, considered it equally effective, and more consonant with the dignity and practice of the Church, to confine themselves to a resolution. A Moderate-led group, including Alexander Carlyle and the Lord Advocate, were in favour of mentioning

---

decline of societies. There is little evidence, however, that Popular thinkers were influenced by the thought of Ferguson, Hume, Kames, Smith, or Robertson on the importance of property in relation to government and law, though there is reason to believe that they were indebted to secular thinkers on the nature of wealth. On Millar, see Millar, *Origin of the Distinction of Ranks*, pp. 291–2. See also, p. 204; and Millar, *Historical View of the English Government*, i, p. 127; Ferguson, *Essay on the History of Civil Society*, pp. 81–2; David Hume, *Political Discourses* (London, 1908), pp. 3–4; Home, *Historical Law Tracts*, pp. 88–156; Smith, *Wealth of Nations*, in *Works*, iv, pp. 72–81; William Robertson, *Works* (London, 1812), iv, pp. 265–6; vi, pp. 311–13, 372. For a discussion of the ideas concerning property of these representatives of the Scottish Enlightenment, see Chitnis, *Scottish Enlightenment*, pp. 106–11. For a discussion of the ideas of the Moderate literati of Edinburgh on matters referred to in this chapter, see Sher, *Church and University in the Scottish Enlightenment*, pp. 206–11. Sher refers to: Robertson, *Works*, ii, pp. 155–6 (*History of Scotland*); to Hugh Blair, *Sermons*, ii, pp. 86–7; v, no. 6; and to Alexander Carlyle's sermon, *National Depravity the Cause of National Calamities* (Edinburgh, 1794). It is interesting to note that Moderate thought was more influenced by covenantal theory on the subject, especially in relation to the American War of Independence, than was Popular thought.

244 *Scots Magazine*, l (Feb. 1788), pp. 99–100.

the Assembly's views in the proposed address to the King, but this was opposed by Erskine and others on the grounds that an address to the King on a subject already before Parliament was highly unconstitutional, if not in fact a breach of privilege. In this they were immediately supported by the Lord Advocate. In the event, Erskine proposed a motion approving the spirit of the overtures from the synods, and asserting that

> the General Assembly think themselves called upon, as men, as Christians, and as members of this national church, to declare their abhorrence of a traffic contrary to the rights of mankind, and the feelings of humanity, and their earnest wish, that the wisdom and mercy of the legislature may be speedily exerted for the relief of that unhappy portion of their fellow creatures.

This motion met with general approbation, but another motion was made by several members who were still in favour of a petition to the House of Commons. Supporters of Erskine's motion argued that if this motion were to be passed by a small majority, it could lead outsiders to believe that the Assembly was divided even on the principle of the matter. This argument was succeeded in persuading some of the second motion's supporters to abandon their point, but a number remained who thought it affronting to those synods and presbyteries which had already petitioned Parliament if the Assembly did not follow a similar mode of action, and they insisted on a vote. The move for a petition, however, was defeated by 64 votes to 30.[245]

The debate on the slave trade may appear of little importance in throwing light on the distinctive views of the Popular party, in that there would seem to have been little difference on the issue between its members and those of the Moderate faction. The issue does indicate, however, a developing division within the Popular party over the way in which objectives should be pursued when they involved the secular authorities. Differences emerged between one group, which had its most articulate spokesman in Henry Erskine and which believed in the efficacy, or at least the desirability, of working within a legally constitutional approach in dealings with the state, and another group of Popular men who were less sensitive to such arguments. Around the same time there is evidence of the emergence of a more pragmatic and 'constitutional' approach to the problem of patronage with which Erskine was identified.[246] The 'constitutional' approach to the slave trade, however, although dominant at Assembly level, was not necessarily successful at presbytery level, for petitions to Parliament continued.[247]

---

[245] Ibid., l (Jun. 1788), pp. 305–6.

[246] See above, pp. 128–50.

[247] E.g., The Presbytery of Stirling petitioned Parliament for the abolition of the slave trade in 1792. In this petition, the traffic was specifically linked with the prevention of

A further instance of this new approach of the Popular leadership in the last two decades of the century to issues of secular concern occurred in 1790, when the Presbytery of Jedburgh sent up an overture to the Assembly respecting the operation of the Test Act. It urged the Assembly to take steps to secure relief from the provisions forcing those in public office in England to take the sacrament according to the usage of the Church of England. A considerable number of Popular men supported the overture, including Sir Harry Moncrieff Wellwood and Henry Erskine. They were opposed by a smaller number of Moderates including Professor Hill of St Andrews, Robertson's successor as leader of the Moderates, together with the Lord Advocate and the Lord President. Moncrieff Wellwood then moved four resolutions, the last of which asserted that it was the duty of the General Assembly, as guardian of the Scottish religious establishment, to use the earliest opportunity to obtain effectual relief from the grievances arising from the Test Act. The other resolutions were the same in spirit and effect. In order to ensure unanimity, he and his supporters consented to several alterations by Professor Hill, and the resolution was then passed; the establishment of a committee to pursue the matter was unanimously agreed, and Moncrieff Wellwood was named convenor.[248]

IX

In general terms, then, a survey of the attitudes of the Popular party to political and governmental issues reveals two main trends: the emergence of a liberal, and in some ways even radical, approach to such issues; and an increasing political sensitivity over how to achieve their ends in secular matters, which was seen in Popular tactics in the management of their ecclesiastical cause in the General Assembly. The former trend led them in the direction of the ideology of the Foxite Whigs, and the latter was spearheaded by a group of men who either were or had sympathy with them. Whatever potentialities a liberal political orientation may have had, however, it was to be stifled by the French Revolution and the consequent re-emergence of an ideology of political conservatism.

'the Propagation of the Gospel among unenlightened Nations'. See McIntosh, 'Popular Party in the Church of Scotland', p. 59. Furthermore, the 1791 Assembly saw further petitions from the Synods of Lothian and Tweeddale, and Merse and Teviotdale which were approved in spirit but not proceeded with. Another overture the following year resulted in a further motion, unanimously passed, expressing the Assembly's abhorrence of the trade. See *Scots Magazine*, liii (Jun. 1791), pp. 351–2; and liv (Jun. 1792), p. 305.

248 *Scots Magazine*, lii (Jul. 1790), pp. 351–2. It is possibly significant that the report of the committee to the following Assembly was recorded without debate, as Professor Hill moved, and it was unanimously agreed, to proceed to another case. The *Scots Magazine* gave no details of the report and its nature awaits investigation. See ibid., liii (Jun. 1791), p. 302.

It was only in the case of their response to the issues raised by the American Revolution that the Popular party differed completely from their Moderate opponents. Other issues portray a considerable measure of cross-party agreement. The exception to this generalisation was over the issue of Roman Catholic relief, and even here the Popular position was accepted at the end of the day by the Moderates as being the only realistic policy. Notable also, however, was the way in which in the whole range of secular matters, the initiative in Assembly business was being seized by a group of younger Popular leaders centred around Henry Erskine and Sir Harry Moncrieff Wellwood. Time after time, from the 1780s onwards, the Moderates were to find themselves responding or reacting to Popular proposals. As yet, they still retained their majority on most issues, but their intellectual dominance was being eroded by a Popular party which was gaining in acumen and confidence as a result of their handling of secular issues.

The actions of the Popular party at the General Assembly indicate the operation of the two main features in Popular ideas about government. During the period of the American Revolution, the liberal impetus within the party's ideology moved it in the direction of political liberalism. As a result of belief in the vital nature of the link between religion and society, and of conviction that it was the prerogative of the Assembly to speak on behalf of the Scottish people in matters of general concern – which latter conviction was shared by the Moderates – the party displayed unity in secular matters. In the last two decades of the century, however, the same convictions swung the party in the opposite direction, towards political conservatism. This was in the main a response to the French Revolution, although the seeds of the move were already present in the party's perceptions of the theological obligations of obedience to established authority.

CHAPTER SIX

Conclusion: The Popular Party: Towards a New Understanding of the Eighteenth-Century Scottish Church

While it is difficult to generalise, and while such generalisations as might be made cannot apply with equal validity on all issues, it must be accepted that the Popular party was not a monolithic organisation either in matters of doctrine and ideology or in matters of its responses to the ecclesiastical and secular problems with which it was faced. Not only that, it must also be stressed that members of the party displayed only limited consistency with respect to their position within the Popular spectrum of theological and secular opinion.

The first point revealed by the study of the Popular party's theological and ideological positions is that it was a doctrinally complex party, and even on some issues a diverse one. The diversity is evident in the existence of three groupings in most areas of doctrine. The first group of men saw little or no need to express theological truths in other than conventional terms, or were little interested in the technicalities of theological discussion; the second, significant beyond their numbers as a result of the influence of the ideas of Principal Wishart of Edinburgh, held a theology similar to that of the Moderate leadership; and the third, while orthodoxly Calvinist in its theology, responded to contemporary secular thought and used it to express their doctrinal positions. From this third group came an increasingly evangelical impetus within the Church.

It is also evident that the pattern did not operate with consistency in all areas of doctrine. For example, it appeared when the doctrines relating to sin and salvation were being discussed (though with little regard to the use of key theological terms); it was present to a notable extent in Popular attempts to define the nature of faith and the nature of holiness; and to some extent it was to be found in the question of how best to defend Christian society against infidelity. Individual figures, however, did not remain in the one grouping from subject to subject, and there was considerable cross-fertilisation of ideas. Furthermore, the diversity of theological opinion was sometimes embodied in the absence of any clear-cut division of opinion; while in other cases there was no agreement at all. The question of the role and importance of natural religion as a source of religious knowledge saw substantial disagreement within the party, and a very limited consensus that natural religion gave adequate proofs of the existence and perfections of God, of the immortality of the soul, and of the blameworthiness of man if he chose to disregard the proofs. Likewise there was only limited agreement on the nature of man. Beyond accepting that the Fall led to man's natural inability to comprehend the nature of sin and the offer of salvation through Christ, the members of the party displayed differing views on the extent to which the testimony of the conscience was valid or reliable. In matters relating to practical Christianity, that is to the requirements of Christian living, and to the response to infidelity and atheism, even the more evangelical members of the party were divided. In general terms, the party was hampered in any attempt at doctrinal unity by a commitment to the essential rationality of the Christian religion and the consequent desire of some, but not all, to accommodate what the contemporary secular world took to be in accordance with Reason.

On the other hand, while it is clear that there was a substantial diversity within the theology of the Popular party, it should also be appreciated that there was a considerable degree of unity at the same time. The most notable area of theological unity occurred concerning the nature of faith: there was little disagreement that faith was essentially a matter of knowledge and belief and that it had to do with the nature of a Christian's relationship with God (though the party's two greatest authorities on the subject, John Maclaurin and John Erskine, differed appreciably). Notable, too, was the extent of agreement that the way to counter the spread of infidelity was by a renewed stress on evangelical preaching. In some respects even more striking, perhaps, was the near unanimity on the question of heresy: the way to counter it was through careful supervision of the education of the ministry, the adoption of proper procedure when it had to be censured, and the belief that unity on the basis of the confessional standards of the Church was a better answer to infidelity than a rigorous policy of ecclesiastical censure.

If, however, substantial qualifications need to be made about the extent of the doctrinal unity of the Popular party, the extent of unity of opinion was much greater in secular matters. There was a stress on the essential role of religion as the basis of society and as the guarantor of social stability, and an implicit acceptance of Calvinist conceptions of fallen human nature as necessitating government. This led to an initially conservative view of politics. At the same time, a commitment to religious and civil liberty of conscience led to adoption of doctrines of political liberty. There was, therefore, an inherent tension in Popular attitudes to society and government which was shared by all sections within the party. The conservative impulse explains why there was so little difference from the Moderates on most political issues; the commitment to religious and civil liberty explains why there was a

Popular–Moderate split on the American War of Independence. The only exception to this pattern occurred over Roman Catholic toleration, where the religious fears of the Popular party prevailed over its usual tolerant sympathies. In social and cultural matters, too, the party displayed a very considerable degree of unity. Dominating the social perceptions of the party was a preoccupation with the growth of luxury. Luxury led to inattention to poverty, to sensuality, and to infidelity. The virtuous use of wealth was the exception; possession of wealth led to the loss to sight of true religion and godliness. Although culture was viewed with some suspicion at the start of the period under examination, by the 1760s, if not earlier, cultural activity came to be seen increasingly as a legitimate area for the Christian provided it could be used for the glory of God. The overall pattern on secular issues, therefore, was one of greater unity than that in theological areas. In the secular field there was also often a measure of common ground between the Popular party and the Moderates. Combined with the degree of unity to be found in theology between mainstream Popular theologians and Wishart Moderates within the party, some at least of whom were influenced by 'evangelical' emphases, it must raise the possibility that the division between the two parties was less than appears if the Moderate leadership is regarded as representative of the views of that party as a whole.

It is possible, therefore, to define certain areas of unity and disunity in the theological and ideological positions of members of the Popular party but it is obvious that the picture which emerges is not especially coherent. In other words, the term 'Popular party' has limited use as a concept to denote the doctrinal or ideological positions of those who opposed the patronage system in the later half of the eighteenth century. There clearly were theological tensions within the party, whose members ranged from theological Moderates to arch-traditionalists. The theological position was complex, and in some areas confused. What is clear is that it is impossible to make valid generalisations about the whole party simply from one grouping within it, namely the traditionalist faction, as was done at the time by the Moderate leadership and which has continued to be done by their later sympathisers. Far less is it valid to produce a caricature of the party as a whole on that basis.

On the other hand, this is not to deny that a term such as 'Popular theology' has any validity at all. This is especially true if the major tendencies within the party are analysed. The overall picture is that of a party in which the dominant characteristic was one in which Scriptural revelation was seen to be the starting-point for all theological and religious activity. Whether in writing of the primacy of revelation over natural religion as a source of religious knowledge, or of the attributes of God as ascertainable through analysis of the Atonement, or of the centrality of the Atonement for Christian faith, stress on the authority of Scripture as divine revelation was common to all Popular writing. Human philosophy remained only subsidiary. From time to time inconsistencies arose when secular insights which sometimes had theological implications were accepted in peripheral areas.

It should not be assumed, however, as has often been done, that in view of this the Popular party should be described as 'evangelical' in the modern sense of the term. The main reason for this is that until John Erskine published his *Dissertation on the Nature of the Christian Faith* in 1765, there were few Popular ministers who perceived themselves to be preaching to a majority of men who were not Christians. Furthermore, there were few members of the Popular party who allowed much role to the senses in the process of conversion or in the nature of assurance of salvation. Post-Wesleyan evangelicalism gave a place to feelings and the emotions as tests of the validity of religious experience which, with the exception of John Erskine, was relatively unknown in Popular writings. Even for Erskine, the role of the senses was limited to the assurance of God's promises being applied to the individual in the matter of salvation. For most members of the Popular party, affinity with, and support for, the international evangelical movement was much more orientated around the exaltation of scriptural doctrines and right perceptions of the Atonement and of man's consequent relationship with God, than around concern with the characteristics of religious experience.

It should also not be assumed that the Popular party remained doctrinally or ideologically static throughout the period under consideration. At the doctrinal heart of the Christian religion, namely the question of the nature of faith, the two most important theologians produced by the party, John Maclaurin and John Erskine, displayed a preparedness to be influenced by, and to use, contemporary secular thought concerning the operation of the human mind and of the will, and on epistemology. The process was continued by later writers. These contemporary insights were used to express basically orthodox theological positions. It could be argued that preparedness to be influenced by contemporary thought led to the absence of a Popular consensus in areas such as the relevance of natural religion, the attributes of God, and the nature of man. In the latter case especially, Popular thinkers saw orthodox perceptions being challenged by Enlightenment thought, and they moved to modify traditional positions as a result. In secular matters, too, Popular thinkers were influenced by contemporary thought. There was a move towards liberal positions, until the trend was dramatically halted by the French Revolution. Ideas of universal benevolence, derived from William Wishart, led to the appearance in Popular works of a moral relativity in which all actions were regarded as having social implications which determined their morality. It was largely accepted that civic virtues could be inculcated by educative means irrespective of theological considerations. It was generally assumed that revelation did not contribute significantly to the analysis of human society. The increasingly dominant grouping within the party, however, was able to apply contemporary ideas in a constructive way. That led to the development of an increasingly confident evangelicalism, which led to the appearance of the nineteenth-century Evangelical Revival in Scotland. This dominant section of the party, therefore, had a much more seminal influence than has hitherto been suspected.

Thus, while the Popular party should not be regarded as having any tight theological unity, it came to be dominated intellectually and possibly numerically by a group of influential thinkers who were broadly evangelical in their outlook. Admittedly, care should be exercised over the use of the term 'evangelical', since their perceptions of the nature of saving faith and such central doctrines as the Atonement were orientated towards an intellectual rather than an experiential conception of conversion and faith, and their preaching was not directed to the emotions of their hearers in the way that later nineteenth-century evangelical preaching often was. Nevertheless, this dominant 'evangelical' emphasis within the party is the element which gives the term 'the Popular party' the degree of theological validity which it has.

Analysis of the patronage dispute reveals that the Popular party displayed the same features of diversity, unity, and evolution as were present in its theology and ideology. For the majority of the party, the seeds of the dispute ultimately lay not in differences about Church–State relations or about the rights of congregations to decide who should be their ministers, but rather in perceptions about the nature and purpose of the Christian Church, the nature of faith, and the function of preaching. For most of them, the problem with patronage was that it restricted the likelihood of faithful ministers of the gospel being appointed who would preach for the salvation of their parishioners' souls. Such a priority, of course, can only be understood in the light of its protagonists' theological position. This raises the question of the grounds for opposition to patronage of members of the party who did not share the 'evangelical' perceptions of the majority. The answer is, as was revealed for example in the 'Reasons' attached to Principal Wishart's dissent in the Torphichen Case of 1751, that patronage was seen by some of even Moderate theological persuasion as incompatible with the constitution of the Church. It was at bottom even Erastian. This perception cut across theological divisions.

The response of the Popular party to Moderate control of the General Assembly as it affected the patronage issue was determined by three factors. First, the perception of the majority was that the Christian Church was a unique institution deriving its purpose and its authority from the commands of Christ himself. This meant that anything which interfered with its role and authority had to be fought for spiritual and theological reasons. Patronage, therefore, was a spiritual issue best fought with spiritual weapons. Secondly, there was the perception of almost all the party that the issue had a constitutional dimension, since patronage was contrary to the laws and privileges of the Church of Scotland, and was therefore also to be debated in 'legal' terms. Commitment to the principle of Establishment and a high estimation of the benefits which it was regarded as bringing for the propagation of the gospel introduced a secular, political, and legal dimension to the debate. Thirdly, a pragmatic response developed when faced by Moderate immovability on the issue. This response embodied a preparedness to utilise a secular strategy when it became clear that the Moderate hegemony in the General Assembly would not countenance any change in its policy of adherence to and enforcement of patronage. This last development undercut the fundamentally theological basis of opposition to the patronage system, and in the end led to the virtual disappearance of the issue until the next century.

Rather than being the touchstone for analysis of the Church of Scotland in the latter half of the eighteenth century, therefore, the patronage controversy should be seen as more in the nature of a separate issue, though one of importance which affected the whole Church and which preoccupied the minds of many. Exclusive focus on the issue serves only to obscure a balanced and more comprehensive picture of the life of the Church. Also, concentration on the ideology and role of the Moderate leadership has produced a picture of a divided Church. It has obscured the extent of unity which existed between Popular and Moderate factions on many issues, and it has drawn attention away from the study of the relationship between the Church and people of Scotland. Analysis of the Popular party in the latter half of the eighteenth century, apart from revealing the nature of the party and the limitations of the use of the concept of the 'Popular party' as a historiographical tool, has highlighted these deficiencies. The way forward for the study of the Scottish Church in the period involves a supplementing of the history of ideas and a moving away from preoccupation with the debates and actions of the General Assembly, and from preoccupation with the significance of a small group of possibly unrepresentative Moderate literati.

The attempt of this study to do so suggests that far from the key issue in the Church of Scotland in the latter half of the eighteenth century being the dispute between the Popular and Moderate parties over patronage, of much greater importance was the evolving theological alignment. The division of Popular theological writers into three main groups actually applies to the *whole* Church, suggesting that instead of dividing it into two parties, we should think in terms of three parties in the eighteenth-century Church. First, there were traditionalists: orthodox Calvinists who stressed Church polity and who saw little need or justification for diverging from traditional forms and modes of doctrinal expression. Secondly, there were liberals, formally Calvinistic but influenced in varying degrees by Stoic ethics and in general by what is known as Moderatism. This position, in its purest form, was epitomised by the Moderate literati. There are signs, however, from the existence in the Popular party of Moderates and near-Moderates, that Moderatism was almost certainly not so monolithic as is usually assumed. Thirdly, there was a group which, for want of a better term, may be regarded as 'Evangelicals'. They were orthodox, like the first group, but they were 'Enlightened', like the second. The Popular party, that is, the section of the Church of Scotland who opposed patronage, included all three. In 1740, the first group was possibly the strongest within the party; the second group was always small; the third group grew until by the end of the century it was dominant. If it were to be established that the Moderate party contained the same elements, though obviously in different proportions, present understandings of the history of the eighteenth-century Church of Scotland would require fundamental revision.

Appendix: Biographical Notes on Important Popular Writers

Adams, John: Minister of Dalrymple (1726–44) and Falkirk (1744–57). Moderator of General Assembly of 1744. Strongly defended Presbytery of Linlithgow in the case of Torphichen in 1751.

Anderson, George: Missionary at Abertarff and Chaplain at Fort William (1733–41). Governor of George Heriot's Hospital, 1741. His several publications concerned the theatre and apologetic against deist writers.

Bannerman, Patrick: Minister of St Madoes (1741–6), Kinnoull (1746–60), and Saltoun (1760–90).

Blair, David: Minister of Lochlee (1729–33), and Brechin and Kelimore (1738–69). Believed to have opened the first Sunday evening school in Scotland.

Bonar, John: Minister of Cockpen (1746–56), and Perth (1756–61). Published one of the main apologetical works against Hume and Kames, and one of the major ones on ecclesiastical polity.

Crosbie, Andrew: Advocate and lay leader of the Popular party at the General Assembly. Possibly the original of Scott's Councillor Pleydell in *Guy Mannering*; was involved in a bank failure and died in 1785 in great poverty.

Dun, John: Minister of Auchinleck (1752–92). Tutor to James Boswell the biographer.

Erskine of Carnock, John: Minister of Kirkintilloch (1744–53), Culross (1753–8), New Greyfriars (1758–67), and Old Greyfriars (1767–1803). Colleague of Principal Robertson in Old Greyfriars; remained on amicable terms with him despite their different theological and ecclesiastical positions. One of the most important eighteenth-century Scottish theologians; corresponded with the famous Jonathan Edwards of New England; and actively propagated the cause of foreign and home missions.

Gillies, John: Minister of Glasgow (Blackfriar's) (1742–96). Son-in-law of Rev. John Maclaurin, whose mantle he seems to have assumed as a leader of the Popular party in the West. Most prominent at the Assembly for his opposition to the war with the American colonies and to Roman Catholic emancipation. A key figure in the evangelical propaganda network of the mid-eighteenth century; published on a wide range of subjects.

Gordon, James: Minister of Premnay (1706–9), Bourtie (1709–17), Alford (1717–35), and Alloa and Tullibody (1736–49). Elected but not appointed Professor of Divinity at Kings College, Aberdeen. Moderator of General Assembly of 1734. A leading opponent of patronage during the early years of the Secession.

Logan, George: Minister of Lauder (1707–19), Sprouston 1719–22), Dunbar (1722–32), and Trinity (Edinburgh) (1732–55). Moderator of the General Assembly of 1740 which deposed the Seceders. Numerous publications, almost all concerned with the issue of patronage.

Love, John: Minister of a Presbyterian congregation in London where he was founding secretary of the London Missionary Society. Minister of Glasgow (Anderston) (1800–25). Became secretary of the Glasgow Missionary Society. Highly regarded for the devotional warmth of his preaching and writings.

McFarlan (Warden), John: Minister of the Canongate (1765–88). Published mainly on social and political matters.

Maclaurin, John: Minister of Luss (1719–23), and Glasgow (Ramshorn) (1723–54). One of the ablest preachers and theologians of the eighteenth-century Church of Scotland; his sermon *Glorying in the Cross of Christ* is widely regarded as the epitome of Scottish evangelical preaching of the century. A widely read scholar, also active in poor law reform and promoting improvements in living conditions in Glasgow. A relative of the advocate of the same name, who took the title of Lord Dreghorn on being elevated to the Court of Session, and who supported the Popular party.

Macqueen, Daniel: Minister of Dalziel (1736–40), Stirling (1740–56), and Edinburgh (Old Kirk) (1758–77). Took an active part in the patronage struggles around Edinburgh, and was influential in Popular circles.

Moncrieff Wellwood, Sir Harry: Minister of Blackford (1771–5), and Edinburgh (St Cuthbert's) (1775–1827). Moderator of the General Assembly of 1785. Assumed the leadership of the Popular party at the Assembly from the 1780s onwards, and was one of the most influential churchmen of his day. Probably the ablest ecclesiastical manager produced by the party; it could be argued that his skill led to the beginning of Moderate decline at the Assembly. A prolific author; published numerous sermons as well as works on Church government and patronage. His biography of John Erskine is an important source for the history of the Church of Scotland in the latter half of the eighteenth century. He inherited a baronetcy in 1771 on the death of his father, whom he also succeeded as minister of Blackford.

Muckersy, John: Minister of West Calder (1794–1831). Notable for his literary and linguistic interests, and probably one of the small group of Popular men who had theological affinities with the Moderates.

Porteous, William: Minister of Whitburn (1760–70), and Glasgow (St George's) 1770–1812. One of the more prominent members of the Popular party in the West. Active opponent of Roman Catholic emancipation. Wrote on a range of contemporary issues.

Randall, Thomas: Minister of Inchture (1739–70), and Stirling (1770–80). Compiler of *Tracts concerning Patronage* which attempted to establish a wider-based opposition to patronage. One of the leaders of the Presbytery of Stirling in its seven-year defiance of the Moderate-controlled General Assembly in the St Ninian's case of 1766–74, for which he was rebuked at the bar of the Assembly.

Russel, John: Minister of Kilmarnock (High) (1774–99), and Stirling (1799–1817). The 'Black Russel' of Burns's 'Twa Herds' and 'The Holy Fair'; a preacher of great power and an able polemicist. A leading figure in the attack on 'Socinianism' in the later eighteenth century.

Savile, David: Minister of Dunfermline (St Andrew's) (1799), and Canongate Chapel-of-Ease (1799–1810). Published several works, most with a theological or philosophical emphasis.

Snodgrass, John: Minister of Norrieston Chapel-of-Ease (1772–4), Dundee (South) (1774–81), and Paisley (Middle) (1781–97). Wrote prolifically on a wide range of subjects.

Somerville, James: Minister of Scots Church, Rotterdam (1775–9), Whitburn (1779–93), and Stirling (1793–1817). His sermons were published posthumously. Notable in the Presbytery of Stirling for his strong Popular line, but also for his efforts to maintain amicable relations with Moderate members.

Somerville, Thomas: Minister of Minto (1767–73), and of Jedburgh until the 1830s. Declined the Chair of Church History at Edinburgh in 1798. A prolific author on a considerable range of subjects. A theological Moderate, but voted with the Popular party on the patronage issue. His *My Own Life and Times* is a valuable record of the issues and characters of the late eighteenth-century Church of Scotland.

Steven, James: Minister of Crown Court Church, London (1787–1803), and Kilwinning and Dalgarven (1803–24). One of the founders of the London Missionary Society. The subject of Burns's satirical poem 'The Calf'.

Walker, Robert: Minister of Straiton (1738–46), South Leith (1746–54), and Edinburgh (High Kirk) (1754–83). A leading opponent of patronage, his sermons were published under the editorship of the leading Moderate, Hugh Blair.

Webster, Alexander: Minister of Culross (1733–7), Edinburgh (Tolbooth) (1737–84). One of the main leaders of the Popular party in the mid-eighteenth century; also an eminent statistician who compiled the 1765 *Census of the Population of Scotland* and performed the actuarial calculations for the Ministers' Widows and Orphans Fund set up in 1742. Defended the Cambuslang revival, was a strong Hanoverian, and is reputed to have first suggested the construction of the Edinburgh New Town.

Willison, John: Minister of Brechin (1703–16), and Dundee (South Church) (1716–50). Probably the most commonly read religious writer in eighteenth-century Scotland, a notable evangelical and supporter of the Cambuslang and Kilsyth revivals of the 1740s (the latter of which started after his sermon on the way back from Cambuslang). His earlier ministry was preoccupied with struggles against Episcopalians and Jacobites; actively countered the Glassites; and fought unsuccessfully for the rehabilitation of the Seceders with whom he sympathised. The earliest and possibly the most fundamental opponent of Moderatism.

Wishart, William: Minister of Edinburgh (New Greyfriars) (1739–45), and the Tron (1745–53). Principal of Edinburgh University 1737. Supported the Popular party on patronage, but his theology was regarded as suspect by many within the party. Charged with heresy but acquitted in 1738. His writings, although Moderate in character, were very influential in the Popular party through his role in the teaching of divinity students.

Witherspoon, John: Minister of Beith (1745–57), and Paisley (Laigh Kirk) (1757–68). In 1768 accepted an invitation to become President of Princeton College, New Jersey. Subsequently became the only clergyman to sign the American Declaration of Independence. Possibly the ablest of the Popular leadership in the mid-eighteenth century; played a key role in the attack on patronage until he left for America. Most famous for his devastating satirical attack on the Moderates, the *Ecclesiastical Characteristics, or the Arcana of Church Policy, being an Attempt to open up the Mystery of Moderation*; but was also an able theologian, and responsible for spreading the Scottish 'Common Sense' philosophy across the Atlantic.

Bibliography

PRIMARY SOURCES

Adams, John, *An Inquiry into the Powers committed to the General Assemblies of this Church, and the Nature of Deposition from the Holy Ministry, occasioned by the Character and Procedure of the Assembly 1752* (Glasgow, 1754).

Anderson, George, *The Use and Abuse of Diversions. A Sermon on Luke xix, 13, with an Appendix, shewing that the Stage in particular is an Unchristian Diversion* (Edinburgh, 1733).

——, *An Estimate of the Profit and Loss of Religion, Personally and publicly stated: Illustrated with References to Essays on Morality and Natural Religion* (Edinburgh, 1753).

——, *A Remonstrance against Lord Viscount Bolingbroke's Philosophical Religion* (Edinburgh, 1756).

Bannerman, Patrick, *A Sermon upon Reformation and Revolution Principles. Preached in the Church of Stirling, April 10, 1751: By Appointment of the Very Reverend Synod of Perth and Stirling* (Edinburgh, 1751).

[Bannerman, Patrick], *An Address to the People of Scotland, on Ecclesiastical and Civil Liberty* (Edinburgh, 1782).

Blair, David, *The Fear that's due unto God and the King, consider'd and recommended; in two Sermons preached at Brechin, April 11th, 1744* (Edinburgh, 1744).

Bonar, John, *Observations on the Character and Conduct of Judas Iscariot, in a Letter to the Rev. Mr. J. P.* (Edinburgh, 1750).

——, 'The Nature and Tendency of the Ecclesiastic Constitution in Scotland' (preached before the Synod of Perth and Stirling, 16 April 1760), in *The Scotch Preacher*, vol. I (Edinburgh, 1775).

[Bonar, John], *An Analysis of the Moral and Religious Sentiments contained in the Writings of Sopho, and David Hume, Esq.* (Edinburgh, 1755).

[Bryden, William], *The Cause between Patronage and Popular Election decided by the Presbytery of Friesburgh, at their Meeting on the 3d [sic] of January 1769* (Edinburgh, 1769).

Carlyle, Alexander, *Autobiography*, ed. J. H. Burton (London, 1910).

——, *Anecdotes and Characters of the Times*, ed. J. Kinsley (London, 1973).

Crawford, William, *Works* (Edinburgh, 1748).

Crosbie, Andrew, *Thoughts of a Layman concerning Patronage and Presentations* (Edinburgh, 1769).

Dick, Robert, *The Simplicity and Popularity of the Divine Revelations, and their Suitableness to the Circumstances of Mankind* (Edinburgh, 1758).

——, 'The Counsel of Gamaliel considered', in *The Scotch Preacher*, vol. II (Edinburgh, 1776).

Dun, John, *Sermons* (Kilmarnock, 1790).

Edinburgh Review, 1808–32.

Erskine, John, *The Signs of the Times Consider'd* (Edinburgh, 1742).

——, *Theological Dissertations* (London, 1765).

——, 'Ministers of the Gospel cautioned against giving offence', in *The Scotch Preacher*, vol. I (Edinburgh, 1775).

——, *Shall I go to War with my American Brethren? A Discourse Addressed to All concerned in determining that Important Question* (first publ. 1769, Edinburgh, 1776).

——, *Prayer for those in Civil and Military Offices recommended, from a view of the influence of Providence on their characters, conduct, and success. A Sermon. Preached before the Election of the Magistrates of Edinburgh, Oct. 5 1779* (London, 1779).

——, *The Fatal Consequences and General Sources of Anarchy. A Discourse on Isaiah, xxiv, 1–5* (Edinburgh, 1793).

——, *Discourses preached on Several Occasions* (Edinburgh, 1798–1804).

——, *The Riches of the Poor. A Sermon. Preached before the Governors of Heriot's Hospital* (Edinburgh, 1804).

Ferguson, Adam, *Essay on the History of Civil Society* (1767), ed. D. Forbes (Edinburgh, 1966).

Gillies, John, *An Exhortation to the Inhabitants of the South Parish of Glasgow, and the Hearers in the College Church* (Glasgow, 1750–1).

Gordon, James, *The State and Duty of the Church of Scotland, especially with respect to the Settlement of Ministers set in a just light* (Edinburgh, 1732).

Grieve, Henry, *Observations on the Overture concerning Patronage* (Edinburgh, 1769).

Hutcheson, Francis, *Considerations on Patronages* (1735), in Thomas Randall, *Tracts Concerning Patronage, by some eminent hands* (Edinburgh, 1770).

Johnston, David, *The Heinousness and Aggravation of Theft, illustrated in a Sermon preached in the Old Church of Edinburgh, on the 29th of Nov. 1787* (Edinburgh, 1788).

Lawson, John, *A Speech concerning the Settling of Parishes in general, and more especially relating to the Settlement of the Parish of Terreagles* (Glasgow, 1752).

Logan, George, *A Treatise on Government: shewing, That the Right of Kings of Scotland to the Crown was not Strictly and Absolutely Hereditary* (Edinburgh, 1746).

——, *A Second Treatise on Government: Shewing, That the Right to the Crown of Scotland was not Hereditary, in the Sense of the Jacobites* (Edinburgh, 1747).

Love, John, *The Majesty of the King of Kings: A Sermon, preached on the subject of the Revolution, Nov. 9, 1788* (n.p., n.d.).

——, *The Radical Cause of National Calamity. A Sermon, Preached at the Scotch Church, Crown Court, Russell St., Covent Garden, October 27, 1794* (n.p., n.d.).

Love, John, *Benevolence inspired and exalted by the Presence of Jesus Christ. A Sermon* (London, 1794).

——, *Memorials of the Rev. John Love* (Glasgow, 1857).

McFarlan, John, *Inquiries concerning the Poor* (Edinburgh, 1782).

——, *Tracts on Subjects of National Importance* (London, 1786).

Maclaurin, John, *The Terms of Ministerial and Christian Communion imposed on the Church of Scotland by a prevailing Party in the General Assembly, in opposition to the great Bulk of both Office-bearers and private Christians* (Glasgow, 1753).

——, *The Nature of Ecclesiastic Government, and of the Constitution of the Church of Scotland Illustrated. Being a Second Conference on the Terms of Communion attempted to be imposed on the Church of Scotland by a prevailing Party in the General Assembly* (Glasgow, 1754).

——, *The Works of the Rev. John Maclaurin*, ed. W. H. Goold (Edinburgh, 1860).

Maclaurin, John (Lord Dreghorn), *Apology for the Writers against the Tragedy of Douglas, with some Remarks on that Play* (Edinburgh, 1757).

——, *Considerations on Patronage* (Edinburgh, 1766).

[Maclaurin, John (Lord Dreghorn)], *A Loud Cry for Help to the Struggling Church of Scotland. Being a Letter from an Elder in Glasgow, to the Several Members of Kirk Sessions thro' the Land. Proper to be read and seriously considered before the Election of Members to the Next General Assembly* (Glasgow, 1753).

——, *The Philosopher's Opera* (Edinburgh, 1757).

Macqueen, Daniel, *Letters on Mr. Hume's History of Great Britain* (Edinburgh, 1756).

Moncrieff Wellwood, Sir Henry, *A Sermon on 2 Corinthians ii, 17. Preached February 14, 1799, at the Ordination of Mr. Walter-Fogo Ireland, appointed Assistant and Successor to Dr. David Johnston, as Minister of North Leith. To what are subjoined, The Charge to the Minister, and the Exhortation to the People* (Edinburgh, 1799).

——, *A Sermon preached in St. Andrew's Church, Edinburgh, April 9. 1801, before the Directors of the Asylum for the Blind* (Edinburgh, 1801).

——, *Sermons* (Edinburgh, 1805).

——, *Account of the Life and Writings of John Erskine, D.D.* (Edinburgh, 1818).

Morren, N., *Annals of the General Assembly of the Church of Scotland, 1739–1766* (Edinburgh, 1838–40).

Muckersy, John, 'The Excellence of the Gospel', Sermon XII in R. Gillan (ed.), *The Scottish Pulpit: A Collection of Sermons by Eminent Clergymen of the Church of Scotland* (Edinburgh, 1823).

[Nisbet, Patrick], *A Seasonable Address to the Citizens of Glasgow, Upon the Present Important Question, 'Whether the Churches of that City shall continue free, or be enslaved to Patronage?'* (n.p., 1762).

[Paton, James], *An Attempt to Show that the Knowledge of God, has, in all ages, been derived from Revelation or Tradition, not from Nature* (Glasgow, 1773).

Porteous, William, *The Doctrine of Toleration. Applied to the Present Times: in a Sermon, Preached in the Wynd Church of Glasgow, 10th December 1778. Being a Public Fast, appointed by the Provincial Synod of Glasgow and Ayr* (Glasgow, 1778).

Randall, Thomas, *Tracts Concerning Patronage, by some Eminent Hands. With a Candid Inquiry into the Constitution of the Church of Scotland, in relation to the Settlement of Ministers, and Remarks upon a late Pamphlet, entitled, 'Observations on the Overture concerning Patronage', in answer to the 'Thoughts of a Layman concerning Patronage and Presentations'* (Edinburgh, 1770).

Richardson, Andrew, *A Free and Arbitrary Government Compared, in two sermons* (Edinburgh, 1746).

Robertson, Robert, *Submission to the Present Government Asserted and the Justice of the Revolution Settlement Vindicated* (Edinburgh, 1753).

Robertson, William, *Works* (London, 1812).

Russel, John, *The Reasons of our Lord's Agony in the Garden, and the Influence of Just Views of them on Universal Holiness* (Kilmarnock, 1787).

——, *The Nature of the Gospel Delineated, and its Universal Spread founded upon the Declaration of Jesus Christ: A Sermon* (Ayr, 1796).

——, *True Religion the Foundation of True Patriotism. A Sermon preached in the High Church of Stirling to the Loyal Stirling Volunteers, Yeomanry, etc., on the Fast Day, February, 1801* (Stirling, 1801).

Savile, David, *Dissertations on the Existence, Attributes, Providence, and Moral Government of God: and on the Duty, Character, Security, and Final Happiness of His Righteous Subjects* (Edinburgh, 1807).

Scots Magazine, vols. II–LXVII (1740–1805).

Snodgrass, John, *An Effectual Method of Recovering our Religious Liberties, addressed to the Elders of the Church of Scotland, Showing, That they may easily bring about a total Change of Administration in this Church, and thereby remove the principal Grievances arising from the Law of Patronage; with particular Directions for attaining this desirable End* (Glasgow, 1770).

——, *The Means of Preserving the Life and Power of Religion in a Time of general Corruption. A Valedictory Sermon to the Inhabitants of Dundee* (Dundee, 1781).

——, *Prospects of Providence respecting the Conversion of the World to Christ* (Paisley, 1796).

——, *The Leading Doctrines of the Gospel Stated and Defended* (1794), in J. Brown (ed.), *Theological Tracts, Selected and Original*: vol. III (Edinburgh, 1854).

Somerville, James, *The Fatal Consequences of Irreligion and Negligence in the Heads of Families. A Sermon preached in the Tron Church of Edinburgh on the Twenty-third of May 1790* (Edinburgh, 1790).

——, *Practical Sermons* (Edinburgh, 1827).

Somerville, Thomas, *A Discourse on our Obligation to Thanksgiving for the Prospect of the Abolition of the African Slave Trade with a Prayer* (Kelso, 1792).

Somerville, Thomas, *The Effects of the French Revolution, with respect to the Interests of Humanity, Liberty, Religion, and Morality* (Edinburgh, 1793).

——, *A Sermon preached in the Tron Church of Edinburgh, May 7th, 1811, before the Society incorporated by Royal Charter for the Benefit of the Sons of Clergy of the Established Church of Scotland* (Edinburgh, 1811).

——, *Sermons* (Edinburgh, 1813).

——, 'On Oaths', Sermon III in R. Gillan (ed.), *The Scottish Pulpit: A Collection of Sermons by Eminent Clergymen of the Church of Scotland* (Edinburgh, 1823).

——, *My Own Life and Times* (Edinburgh, 1861).

Steven, James, *The Unrivalled Felicity of the British Empire. A Sermon preached at the Salters' Hall, November 7th, 1802, at the Commemoration of Our Great National Deliverance* (London, 1802).

Walker, Robert, *Sermons on Practical Subjects* (London, 1796).

Warden, John, *The Happiness of Britain illustrated: in a Sermon* (Edinburgh, 1749).

Webster, Alexander, *Supernatural Revelation the only sure Hope of Sinners* (Edinburgh, 1741).

——, *Divine Influence the True Spring of the Extraordinary Work at Cambuslang and Other Places in the West of Scotland* (Edinburgh, 1742).

——, *Zeal for the Civil and Religious Interests of Mankind recommended* (1754), Sermon XVI in *The Scotch Preacher*, vol. I (Edinburgh, 1775).

Willison, John, *The Practical Works of the Rev. John Willison*, ed. W. M. Hetherington (Glasgow, 1844).

Wishart, William, *Charity the End of the Commandment: or, Universal Love the Design of Christianity. A Sermon* (London, 1731).

——, *The Certain and Unchangeable Difference betwixt Moral Good and Evil. A Sermon preached before the Societies for the Reformation of Manners, at Salters' Hall on Monday, 3rd of July, 1732* (London, 1732).

——, *Public Virtue Recommended. A Sermon preached in the High Church of Edinburgh, on Thursday, May 8th, 1746, at the Opening of the General Assembly of the Church of Scotland* (Edinburgh, 1746).

——, *Discourses on Several Subjects* (London, 1753).

Witherspoon, John, *A Serious Enquiry into the Nature and Effects of the Stage. Being an Attempt to show, That contributing to the Support of a Public Theatre, is inconsistent with the Character of a Christian* (Glasgow, 1757).

——, *The Trial of Religious Truth by its Moral Influence. A Sermon, preached at the opening of the Synod of Glasgow and Air* [sic], *October 9th, 1759* (Glasgow, 1759).

——, *The Works of John Witherspoon, D.D.* (Edinburgh, 1804–5).

[——], *An Alarm to the Church of Scotland on the Apparent Prevalence of a Worldly above a Spiritual and Religious Interest in her Supreme Judicatory, Exemplified in the Proceedings of the last General Assembly, in a Letter from a Member thereof to a Reverend Brother* (Edinburgh, 1771).

[——], *A Collection of the Acts of Parliament relating to Patronage, and the Settlement of Vacant Parishes: with Remarks; shewing, That the Law gives no Countenance to the Rigour that has, of late Years, been exercised by the supreme Judicatory of this Church* (Glasgow, 1772).

[——], *The Differences in the Judicatories of the Church of Scotland with Regard to Patronage, Illustrated, by a Member of the Church, Under the Case of the Settlement of the Parish of Lintrathen in Angus, determined on a Remit from the last Assembly to their Commission; and now again sent back to the Assembly by a Majority of the Presbytery of Meigle* (Edinburgh, 1772).

[——], *Patronage Demolished, and the Rights of the Christian People restored; or, Eight Reasons, drawn from Scripture, Common Sense, and Experience, why the ensuing General Assembly should apply to Parliament for the Repeal of the Act restoring Patronages in Scotland* (Edinburgh, 1769).

[——], *The Progress and Present State of the Law of Patronage in Scotland, from which it appears that the People of Scotland Have a Constitutional Right to Demand a Repeal of the Act Restoring Patronages* (Edinburgh, 1783).

[——], *Reasons of Dissent from the Decision of the late General Assembly in the Cause of St. Ninian's. With a Short Narrative of the Proceedings therein* (n.p., n.d.).

[——], *A Short History of the Late General Assembly of the Church of Scotland, shewing the Rise and Progress of the Schism Overture, the Reasonableness or Necessity that some Restriction be put on the Exercise of the Patronage Act, and the Means which the Church hath in its own Power to mitigate or remove that Grievance* (Glasgow, 1766).

SECONDARY SOURCES

Bebbington, D. W., *Evangelicalism in Modern Britain: A History from the 1730s to the 1980s* (London, 1989).

Bell, M. C., *Calvin and Scottish Theology: The Doctrine of Assurance* (Edinburgh, 1985).

Brackett, W. O., 'John Witherspoon: His Scottish Ministry' (Edinburgh University Ph.D. thesis, 1935).

Brown, C. G., *The Social History of Religion in Scotland since 1730* (London, 1987).

Brown, S. J., *Thomas Chalmers and the Godly Commonwealth in Scotland* (Oxford, 1982).

Buchanan, J., *The Doctrine of Justification* (Edinburgh, 1867).

Burleigh, J. H. S., *A Church History of Scotland* (Edinburgh, 1983).

Cage, R. A., 'Debate: the making of the Old Scottish Poor Law', *Past and Present*, lxix (1975).

——, *The Scottish Poor Law* (Edinburgh, 1981).

Cameron, N. M. de S. (organ. ed.), D. F. Wright, D. C. Lachman and D. E. Meek (gen. eds.), *Dictionary of Scottish Church History and Theology* (Edinburgh, 1993).

Campbell, A. J., *Two Centuries of the Church of Scotland, 1707–1929* (Paisley, 1930).

Campbell, R. H., *Scotland since 1707: The Rise of an Industrial Society* (Edinburgh, 1985).

Cater, J., 'The making of Principal Robertson in 1762: politics and the University of Edinburgh in the second half of the eighteenth century', *Scot. Hist. Rev.*, xlix (1970).

Cheyne, A. C., *The Transforming of the Kirk: Victorian Scotland's Religious Revolution* (Edinburgh, 1983).

Chitnis A. C., *The Scottish Enlightenment: A Social History* (London, 1976).

Clark, I. D. L., 'Moderatism and the Moderate Party in the Church of Scotland, 1752–1805' (Cambridge University Ph.D. thesis, 1963).

——, 'From protest to reaction: the Moderate regime in the Church of Scotland, 1752–1805', in N. T. Phillipson and R. Mitchison, *Scotland in the Age of Improvement: Essays in Scottish History in the Eighteenth Century* (Edinburgh, 1970).

Cunningham, J., *The Church History of Scotland, from the Commencement of the Christian Era to the Present Century* (Edinburgh, 1859).

Devine, T. M., and Mitchison, R. (eds.), *People and Society in Scotland*, vol. I (Edinburgh, 1988).

Drummond, A. L., and Bulloch, J., *The Scottish Church, 1688–1843: The Age of the Moderates* (Edinburgh, 1973).

Fawcett, A., *The Cambuslang Revival: The Scottish Evangelical Revival of the Eighteenth Century* (London, 1971).

Ferguson, W., *Scotland: 1689 to the Present* (Edinburgh, 1968).

——, review of R. B. Sher's *Church and University in the Scottish Enlightenment*, in *History*, lxxii (1987).

Hetherington, W. M., *The History of the Church of Scotland* (Edinburgh, 1841).

Hont, I., and Ignatieff, M. (eds.), *Wealth and Virtue: The Shaping of Political Economy in the Scottish Enlightenment* (Cambridge, 1983).

Lachman, D. C., *The Marrow Controversy* (Edinburgh, 1988).

Logue, K. J., *Popular Disturbances in Scotland, 1780–1815* (Edinburgh, 1979).

McCain, C. R., 'Preaching in Eighteenth-Century Scotland: A Comparative Study of the Extant Sermons of Ralph Erskine (1685–1752), John Erskine (1721–1803), and Hugh Blair (1718–1800)' (Edinburgh University Ph.D. thesis, 1949).

MacInnes, J., *The Evangelical Movement in the Highlands of Scotland, 1688–1800* (Aberdeen, 1951).

McIntosh, J. R., 'Evangelicals in Eighteenth-Century Scotland: The Presbytery of Stirling, 1740–1805' (Stirling University M.Litt. thesis, 1981).

——, 'The Popular Party in the Church of Scotland, 1740–1800' (Glasgow University Ph.D. thesis, 1989).

Mackay, J., *The Church in the Highlands, or, the Progress of Evangelical Religion in Gaelic Scotland, 563–1843* (London, 1914).

Macleod, J., *Scottish Theology in Relation to Church History since the Reformation* (Edinburgh, 1946).

Macpherson, J., *A History of the Church in Scotland from the Earliest Times to the Present Day* (Paisley and London, 1901).

——, *The Doctrine of the Church in Scottish Theology* (Edinburgh, 1903).

Mathieson, W. L., *The Awakening of Scotland: A History from 1747 to 1797* (Glasgow, 1910).

Mechie, S., 'The theological climate in early eighteenth-century Scotland', in D. Shaw (ed.), *Reformation and Revolution: Essays presented to the Very Reverend Principal Emeritus Hugh Watt, D.D., D.Litt. on the Sixtieth Anniversary of His Ordination* (Edinburgh, 1967).

Mitchison, R., 'The making of the Old Scottish Poor Law', *Past and Present*, lxix (1975).

——, 'A rejoinder', *Past and Present*, lxix (1975).

——, 'The creation of the Disablement Rule in the Scottish Poor Law', in T. C. Smout (ed.), *The Search for Wealth and Stability: Essays in Economic and Social History presented to M. W. Flinn* (London, 1979).

Mossner, E. C., *The Life of David Hume* (London, 1954).

Murdoch, A., *'The People Above': Politics and Administration in Mid-Eighteenth-Century Scotland* (Edinburgh, 1980).

Nuttall, G. F., *Calendar of the Correspondence of Philip Doddridge, D.D. (1702–1751)* (London, 1979).

O'Brien, S., 'A transatlantic community of saints: the Great Awakening and the First Evangelical Network, 1735–1755', in *American Hist. Rev.*, xci (4) (1986).

Pomeroy, W. D., 'John Willison of Dundee, 1680–1750' (Edinburgh University Ph.D. thesis, 1953).

Rankin, J., *A Handbook of the Church of Scotland* (Edinburgh, 1888).

Reisen, R. A., '"Higher Criticism" in the Free Church Fathers', *Recs. Scot. Church Hist. Soc.*, xx (pt. 2) (1979).

Rendall, J., *The Origins of the Scottish Enlightenment* (London, 1978).

Robbins, C., *The Eighteenth-Century Commonwealthman: Studies in the Transmission, Development and Circumstance of English Liberal Thought from the Restoration of Charles II until the War with the Thirteen Colonies* (Cambridge, Mass., 1961).

Ryley, G. B., and McCandlish, J. M., *Scotland's Free Church* (Edinburgh, 1893).

Scott, D., *Annals and Statistics of the Original Secession Church: till its Disruption and Union with the Free Church of Scotland in 1852* (Edinburgh, 1886).

Scott, H., *Fasti Ecclesiae Scoticanae: The Succession of Ministers in the Church of Scotland from the Reformation* (Edinburgh, 1915–28).

Sefton, H. R., 'The Early Development of Moderatism in the Church of Scotland' (Glasgow University Ph.D. thesis, 1962).

Sefton, H. R., 'Robert Wallace: an early Moderate', *Recs. Scot. Church Hist. Soc.*, xvi (1969).

——, 'Lord Hay and Patrick Cuming: a study in eighteenth-century ecclesiastical management', *Recs. Scot. Church Hist. Soc.*, xix (1977).

Sekora, J., *Luxury: The Concept in Western Thought, Eden to Smollett* (Baltimore and London, 1977).

Shaw, J. S., *The Management of Scottish Society, 1707–1764: Power, Nobles, Lawyers, Edinburgh Agents and English Influences* (Edinburgh, 1983).

Sher, R. B., 'Church, University, Enlightenment: The Moderate Literati of Edinburgh, 1720–1793' (Chicago University Ph.D. thesis, 1979).

——, 'Moderates, managers, and Popular politics in mid-eighteenth-century Edinburgh: the "Drysdale Bustle" of the 1760s', in J. Dwyer, R. A. Mason and A. Murdoch (eds.), *New Perspectives on the Politics and Culture of Early Modern Scotland* (Edinburgh, 1982).

——, *Church and University in the Scottish Enlightenment: The Moderate Literati of Edinburgh* (Edinburgh, 1985).

——, and Murdoch, A., 'Patronage and Party in the Church of Scotland, 1750–1800', in N. Macdougall (ed.), *Church, Politics and Society: Scotland, 1408–1929* (Edinburgh, 1983).

Stanley, A. P., *Lectures on the History of the Church of Scotland* (London, 1872).

Story, R. H., *The Church of Scotland, Past and Present: Its Relation to the Law and the State, its Doctrine, Ritual, Discipline, and Patrimony* (London, n.d.).

Struthers, G., *The History of the Rise, Progress, and Principles of the Relief Church* (Glasgow, 1843).

Tulloch, J., 'The Church of the eighteenth century, 1707 to 1800 AD', *St Giles Lectures (First Series), The Scottish Church from the Earliest Times to 1881* (Edinburgh, 1881).

Vincent, E., 'The responses of Scottish Churchmen to the French Revolution, 1789–1802', *Scot. Hist. Rev.*, lxxiii (1994).

Voges, F., 'Moderate and Evangelical thinking in the later eighteenth century: differences and shared attitudes', *Recs. Scot. Church Hist. Soc.*, xxii (pt. 2) (1985).

Walker, J., *Theology and Theologians of Scotland, 1560–1750* (Edinburgh, 1872).

Watt, H., 'Robert Walker of the High Church (Hugh Blair's Colleague)', *Recs. Scot. Church Hist. Soc.*, xii (1958).

White, G., '"Highly Preposterous": origins of Scottish missions', *Recs. Scot. Church Hist. Soc.*, xix (2) (1976).

Woodruff, S. A., 'The Pastoral Ministry in the Church of Scotland in the Eighteenth Century, with special reference to Thomas Boston, John Willison and John Erskine' (Edinburgh University Ph.D. thesis, 1965).

Index